2008 ELECTIONS

EDITED BY **Stanley D. Brunn**

Gerald R. Webster

Richard L. Morrill

Fred M. Shelley

Stephen J. Lavin

J. Clark Archer

CARTOGRAPHY BY Stephen J. Lavin and J. Clark Archer

ROWMAN & LITTLEFIELD PUBLISHERS, INC.

Lanham • Boulder • New York • Toronto • Plymouth, UK

Published by Rowman & Littlefield Publishers, Inc.
A wholly owned subsidary of The Rowman & Littlefield Publishing Group, Inc.
4501 Forbes Boulevard, Suite 200, Lanham, Maryland 20706
http://www.rowmanlittlefield.com

Estover Road, Plymouth PL6 7PY, United Kingdom

British Library Cataloguing in Publication Information Available

Library of Congress Cataloging-in-Publication Data
   Atlas of the 2008 elections / edited by Stanley D. Brunn ... [et al.] ; cartography by
Stephen J. Lavin and J. Clark Archer.
        p. cm.
   "Edited by Stanley D. Brunn, Gerald R. Webster, Richard L. Morrill, Fred M. Shelley,
Stephen J. Lavin, J. Clark Archer."
   Includes bibliographical references and index.
   ISBN 978-0-7425-6795-5 (cloth : alk. paper) — ISBN 978-0-7425-6796-2 (electronic)
   1. Presidents—United States—Election—2008—Maps. 2. Voting—United States—Maps.
3. Political campaigns—United States—Maps. 4. Elections—United States—Statistics.
5. Elections—United States—Maps. I. Brunn, Stanley D. II. Lavin, Stephen J. (Stephen James)
III. Archer, J. Clark.
   G1201.F9A8 2011
   324.973'09310223—dc22   2011013488

⊗™ The paper used in this publication meets the minimum requirements of American National
Standard for Information Sciences—Permanence of Paper for Printed Library Materials, ANSI/
NISO Z39.48-1992.

Printed in the United States of America

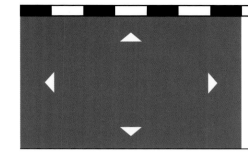

CONTENTS

List of Figures, Graphs, Maps, and Tables   ix

Preface   xiii

Chapter 1
INTRODUCTION   1

Elections   1
The 2008 Presidential Election   2
Insights from a Geographical Perspective   3
Organization of the Atlas   3

Chapter 2
THE 2008 PRIMARIES   9

Presidential Nominees   9
    Fred M. Shelley
New Hampshire Primary   14
    Heather Hollen and Fred M. Shelley
Iowa Caucuses   16
    Heather Hollen and Fred M. Shelley
Pennsylvania Primary   19
    Heather Hollen and Fred M. Shelley

Chapter 3
CAMPAIGNS   27

Estimated Media Advertising Outlays   27
    Gerald R. Webster
Donor-sheds: Individual Contributions
to McCain and Obama   30
    Carl T. Dahlman
Campaign Stops   33
    Gerald R. Webster
Newspaper Endorsements   40
    Gerald R. Webster
The Presidential Placemark Poll   43
    Matthew Zook, Mark Graham,
    and Taylor Shelton
Crowdsourcing Democratic
Transparency: The Twitter
Vote Report   45
    Sean P. Gorman and Andrew J. Turner
Centers of Partisan Voting:
Median Centers of Democratic and
Republican Votes, 2,
2004, and 2008   47
    Richard L. Morrill

Chapter 4
GENERAL ELECTIONS   51

Overview   51
True Believer Country: Areas with the
Highest and Lowest Democratic or
Republican Margins   59
    Richard L. Morrill
Toward a Realignment? The 2008 Election
in Historical Perspective   62
    David Darmofal
Breaking Down the 2008 Vote   65
    Andrew Gelman
What Can We Learn from 2008 Exit Polls?   68
    Heather Hollen and Fred M. Shelley
Early Voting   69
    Daniel Ervin and Nathaniel HadleyDike
Urban-Rural Geography, Voting, and the
2008 Presidential Election   71
    Kimberly Karnes and James G. Gimpel
Comparison with Previous Elections   75
    Fred M. Shelley
The Role of Turnout in Selected States   97
    Richard L. Morrill

The Electoral College and the 2008
Presidential Election 104
  Barney Warf
Metropolitan Areas of Two Million or More 107
  Fred M. Shelley
Micropolitan County Voting 109
  Robert Watrel
Persistence and Change by State
2004 to 2008 112
  Richard L. Morrill
Persistence and Change by County
2004 to 2008 114
  Richard L. Morrill

Chapter 5
REGIONAL PATTERNS AND
SWING STATES: REGIONAL
ANALYSES **121**

Northeast 121
  William Berentsen
Appalachia and the American South 126
  Jonathan I. Leib
The "Bigot Belt" and the 2008 Election 129
  J. Eric Oliver
Triumph of the Carpetbaggers 130
  John McNulty
Midwest 134
  John Heppen
Great Plains 138
  Robert Watrel
Mountain West 142
  Tony Robinson
Pacific Region 146
  John Agnew

The Californization of Colorado 149
  Tony Robinson
Florida 151
  Nick Quinton
Indiana 152
  John Heppen
Missouri 155
  John Heppen
Montana 156
  Fred M. Shelley
North Carolina 159
  Toby Moore
Ohio 161
  John Heppen
Pennsylvania 162
  William Berentsen
Tennessee 165
  Nick Quinton
Virginia 166
  Jonathan I. Leib

Chapter 6
LEADING COUNTIES: 2004 AND
2008 VOTES AND TURNOUTS:
SELECTED ECONOMIC,
DEMOGRAPHIC, AND
RELIGIOUS CORRELATES **171**

Creative Class Occupations 171
  Thomas E. Chapman
Percentage of Workers in Craft
Occupations 174
  Richard L. Morrill
Percentage of Females in the Labor Force 176
  Richard L. Morrill

Farming Employment 178
  Jeffrey R. Crump
Construction Employment 180
  Jeffrey R. Crump
Manufacturing Employment 182
  Jeffrey R. Crump
Unemployment 184
  Jeffrey R. Crump
Population Change by County 186
  Richard L. Morrill
Population by Age 188
  Richard L. Morrill
Leading In- and Out-Migration Counties 192
  Richard L. Morrill
Median Household Income 194
  Richard L. Morrill
Husband-Wife Households 196
  Richard L. Morrill
Poverty Counties 198
  Richard L. Morrill
Persons with a B.A. or Higher Degree 200
  Richard L. Morrill
University and College Counties 202
  Richard L. Morrill
Military Counties 204
  Richard L. Morrill
Obama, Race, and the 2008 Elections:
Dissimilarity Index 206
  Ryan D. Enos
Environmentalists 209
  Richard L. Morrill
Federal Expenditures versus Receipts
by State 211
  Richard L. Morrill
Major Racial/Ethnic Groups 213
  Mark E. Reisinger and John W. Frazier

Latino Voters in the 2008 Elections   225
Melissa R. Michelson
Foreign-Born Population   227
Richard L. Morrill
Religion   229
Barney Warf
Bible Belt   237
Gerald R. Webster

Chapter 7
OTHER KEY 2008 ELECTIONS   **241**

2008 North Carolina Gubernatorial Race   241
Toby Moore
2008 Washington Gubernatorial Election:
Gregoire versus Rossi Reprise   242
Richard L. Morrill
2008 Minnesota Senatorial Election   244
Larry Knopp
2008 North Carolina Senatorial Election   247
Toby Moore
2008 Oregon Senatorial Election   248
Alexander Ginsburg and Matthew Landers
2008 Georgia Senatorial Election   250
Taylor Johnson and Tom Vanderhorst

Chapter 8
NONPARTISAN REFERENDA   **253**

Ballot Measures in the 2008 Election   253
*Joshua R. Meddaugh, Megan A. Gall,
and Joshua J. Dyck*

Arizona: Same-Sex Marriage Referendum   257
Thomas E. Chapman
Florida's Marriage Amendment   258
Thomas E. Chapman
California Propositions 7 and 10:
Alternative Energy Proposals   260
Wesley J. Reisser
California Proposition 2: Prevention of
Farm Animal Cruelty Act   262
Mark Drayse and Jonathan Taylor
California's Same-Sex Marriage Referendum:
Proposition 8   264
Thomas E. Chapman
California's Proposition 8
(Same-Sex Marriage)
and the Race Question   266
*Megan A. Gall, Joshua R. Meddaugh,
and Joshua J. Dyck*
Michigan Proposition 1: A Legislative
Initiative to Permit the Use and
Cultivation of Marijuana for Specified
Medical Conditions   267
*Lisa M. DeChano-Cook
and Mark A. Moody*
Michigan Proposition 2: A Proposal to
Amend the State Constitution to Address
Human Embryo and Human Embryonic
Stem Cell Research in Michigan   270
Lisa M. DeChano-Cook
Assisted Suicide Referenda in Washington   272
Kathleen O'Reilly and Richard L. Morrill

Chapter 9
POST-2008:
CONGRESSIONAL VOTES   **277**

Overview   277
Congressional Vote: Car Voucher Program,
June 2009   280
Kenneth C. Martis
Congressional Vote: Limitation on
Abortion Funding, November 2009   283
Kenneth C. Martis
Congressional Vote: Health Care
Overhaul Passage, November 2009   286
Kenneth C. Martis
Congressional Vote: Greenhouse
Gas Emissions, June 2009   289
Kenneth C. Martis
Congressional Ratings: 111th Congress
(2009–2010)   292
Gerald R. Webster

Chapter 10
TOWARD A MORE PERFECT
UNION: TEN SCENARIOS   **303**

Index   311

About the Contributors   319

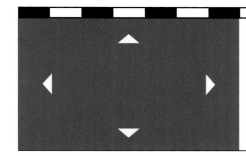

FIGURES, GRAPHS, MAPS, AND TABLES

FIGURES

10.1	Obama and Biden Bumper Stickers	307
10.2	McCain and Palin Bumper Stickers	308
10.3	Obama Stamps from Different Countries: Inauguration and Presidency	309

GRAPHS

4.1	Republican Vote in 2008 by Education, Age, and Ethnic Group	67
4.2	Presidential Election Data, 1920 to 2008	95
4.3	County-Level Vote Correlation with 2008 Election, from 1920 to 2008	96

MAPS

2.1	Candidate Selection Method 2008, Democratic and Republican	11
2.2	Primary Schedules 2008, Democratic and Republican	12
2.3	Primary Leader 2008, Democratic and Republican	13
2.4	New Hampshire Primary 2008, Democratic and Republican	15
2.5	Iowa Caucuses 2008, Democratic and Republican	18
2.6	Pennsylvania Primary 2008, Democratic	20
2.7	Missouri Primary 2008, Democratic and Republican	21
2.8	North Carolina Primary 2008, Democratic	22
2.9	Michigan Primary 2008, Republican	23
2.10	Oklahoma Primary 2008, Democratic and Republican	24
2.11	Tennessee Primary 2008, Republican	25
3.1	Estimated Media Advertising Outlays, Obama and McCain, by State	29
3.2	Donor-sheds: State Reported Campaign Contributions, Totals by State, Democratic and Republican	31
3.3	Donor-sheds: State Reported Campaign Contributions per Capita, by State, Obama and McCain; Combined Total	32
3.4	Presidential Election Campaign Stops, Obama, McCain, Biden, Palin, Number of Stops by State	35
3.5	Obama Visits during the Last Week of the Campaign	36
3.6	Biden Visits during the Last Week of the Campaign	37
3.7	McCain Visits during the Last Week of the Campaign	38
3.8	Palin Visits during the Last Week of the Campaign	39
3.9	Daily Newspaper Endorsements, Obama 2008 Presidential Campaign	41
3.10	Daily Newspaper Endorsements, McCain 2008 Presidential Campaign	42
3.11	Number of Presidential Candidate Mentions in User-Generated Google Placemarks, August 2008	44
3.12	Twitter Vote Report of Polling Conditions, 2008 Presidential Election	46
3.13	Median Centers of Republican and Democratic Votes 2000, 2004, and 2008	48

4.1 Democratic Popular Vote, 2008 Presidential Election 52

4.2 Republican Popular Vote, 2008 Presidential Election 53

4.3 Third Party Popular Vote, 2008 Presidential Election 54

4.4 Bob Barr, Libertarian Popular Vote, 2008 Presidential Election 55

4.5 Ralph Nader, Independent Candidate Popular Vote, 2008 Presidential Election 56

4.6 Percentage of Popular Vote by State, 2008 Presidential Election, Democrat, Republican, Third Party 57

4.7 Popular Vote by County, 2008 Presidential Election 58

4.8 Obama Victory Margin by County, Presidential Election 2008 60

4.9 McCain Victory Margin by County, Presidential Election 2008 61

4.10 Did You Vote for McCain in 2008? by Income, Ethnicity, and State 66

4.11 Early Voting Status, 2008/Date of Adoption for Early Voting 70

4.12 Emergence of the Urban-Rural Gap in Voting for Presidential Candidates, 1972–2008 73

4.13 2008 Presidential Election Vote Margin 74

4.14 Average Democratic Vote, 1948 to 1960 Presidential Elections 79

4.15 Average Democratic Vote, 1964 to 1976 Presidential Elections 80

4.16 Average Democratic Vote, 1980 to 1992 Presidential Elections 81

4.17 Average Democratic Vote, 1996 to 2008 Presidential Elections 82

4.18 Democratic Vote Variability, 1948 to 1960 Presidential Elections 83

4.19 Democratic Vote Variability, 1964 to 1976 Presidential Elections 84

4.20 Democratic Vote Variability, 1980 to 1992 Presidential Elections 85

4.21 Democratic Vote Variability, 1966 to 2008 Presidential Elections 86

4.22 Average Republican Vote, 1948 to 1960 Presidential Elections 87

4.23 Average Republican Vote, 1964 to 1976 Presidential Elections 88

4.24 Average Republican Vote, 1980 to 1992 Presidential Elections 89

4.25 Average Republican Vote, 1996 to 2008 Presidential Elections 90

4.26 Republican Vote Variability, 1948 to 1960 Presidential Elections 91

4.27 Republican Vote Variability, 1964 to 1976 Presidential Elections 92

4.28 Republican Vote Variability, 1980 to 1992 Presidential Elections 93

4.29 Republican Vote Variability, 1996 to 2008 Presidential Elections 94

4.30 Change in Turnout Percentage, 2004 to 2008, Virginia and North Carolina 99

4.31 Change in Turnout Percentage, 2004 to 2008, Indiana and New Mexico 100

4.32 Change in Turnout Percentage, 2004 to 2008, Colorado and Florida 101

4.33 Voter Turnout 2008 Presidential Election by County 102

4.34 Voter Turnout 2004 and 2008/Change in Voter Turnout, 2004 to 2008 103

4.35 Electoral College Vote, 2008 Presidential Election/Cartogram 105

4.36 Proportional Electoral College Vote Outcome, 2008 Presidential Election, Obama and McCain 106

4.37 2008 Popular Presidential Vote in Metropolitan Areas with Populations Two Million or More 108

4.38 Micropolitan Results by County, 2008 Presidential Election 111

4.39 Voter Persistence and Change across Presidential, U.S. Senatorial, and/or Gubernatorial Elections from 2004 to 2008, by State 113

4.40 Persistence and Change by County, 2004 to 2008 116

4.41 Change in the Democratic Vote by County, 2004 to 2008 117

4.42 Change in the Republican Vote by County, 2004 to 2008 118

4.43 Voter Consistency across Elections, 2004 to 2008 119

5.1 Northeast Region Presidential Elections 125

5.2 Southeast Region Presidential Elections 128

5.3 Midwest Region Presidential Elections 137

5.4 Great Plains Region Presidential Elections 141

5.5 Mountain West Region Presidential Elections 145

5.6 Pacific Region Presidential Elections 148

5.7 Colorado County-Level Democratic Growth, Correlated with In-Migration from More Liberal Counties and the Rise of the Creative Class 150

5.8 Democratic Percentage of Total Popular Presidential Vote 2008, Florida and Indiana 153

5.9 Persistence and Change from 2004 to 2008, Florida and Indiana 154

5.10 Democratic Percentage of Total Popular Presidential Vote 2008, Missouri and Montana 157

5.11 Persistence and Change from 2004 to 2008, Missouri and Montana 158

5.12 Democratic Percentage of Total Popular Presidential Vote, North Carolina 160

5.13 Democratic Percentage of Total Popular Presidential Vote, Ohio and Pennsylvania 163

5.14 Persistence and Change from 2004 to 2008, Ohio and Pennsylvania 164

5.15 Democratic Percentage of Total Popular Presidential Vote, Tennessee and Virginia 167

5.16 Persistence and Change from 2004 to 2008, Tennessee and Virginia 168

6.1 Creative Class Occupations, 2000 173

6.2 Craft Occupations, 2008 175

6.3 Female Labor Force, 2008 177

6.4 Percentage of Employment in Farming, 2008/Top 200 Counties 179

6.5 Percentage of Employment in Construction, 2008/Top 200 Counties 181

6.6 Percentage of Employment in Manufacturing, 2008/Top 200 Counties 183

6.7 Unemployment, 2008/Top 200 and Bottom 200 Counties 185

6.8 Population Change, 2000 to 2008/Top 200 and Bottom 200 Counties 187

6.9 Percentage of Population Age under 18, 2008/Top 200 Counties 189

6.10 Percentage of Population Age 25 to 44, 2008/Top 200 Counties 190

6.11 Percentage of Population Age 65 and Older, 2008/Top 200 Counties 191

6.12 Net Migration, 2000 to 2009/Top 200 Net In-Migration Counties and Bottom 201 Out-Migration Counties 193

6.13 Median Household Income, 2007/ Top 200 and Bottom 200 Counties 195

6.14 Husband-Wife Households, 2000 or 2006–2008/Top 246 and Bottom 200 Counties 197

6.15 Poverty, 2007/Top 200 Counties below the Poverty Threshold 199

6.16 Population Age 25 or Over with a B.A. Degree or Higher, 2000 or 2006–2008/Top 201 and Bottom 259 Counties 201

6.17 Counties with Major Colleges or Universities 203

6.18 Counties with Military Bases 205

6.19 Dissimilarity Index Values, 2000/Top 200 and Bottom 200 Counties 208

6.20 Environmental Group Membership Location Quotient, 2008/ Top 198 and Bottom 200 Counties 210

6.21 Federal Expenditures per Dollars Received 212

6.22 Asian Population, 2008/Top 200 Counties 220

6.23 Hispanic Population, 2008/Top 200 Counties 221

6.24 Black Population, 2008/Top 200 Counties 222

6.25 American Indian Population, 2008/ Top 200 Counties 223

6.26 Non-Hispanic White Population, 2008/Top 200 224

6.27 Foreign-Born Population, 2000 or 2006–2008/Top 201 and Bottom 217 Counties 228

6.28 Catholic Adherents, 2000/ Top 200 Counties 230

6.29 Baptist Adherents, 2000/ Top 200 Counties 231

6.30 Jewish Adherents, 2000/Top 200 Counties 232

6.31 Methodist Adherents, 2000/Top 200 Counties 233

6.32 Mormon Adherents, 2000/Top 200 Counties 234

6.33 Muslim Adherents, 2000/Top 133 Counties 235

6.34 Pentecostal Adherents, 2000/Top 133 Counties 236

6.35 Bible Belt Denominations Adherents, 2000/Top 200 Counties 238

7.1 Support for Christine Gregoire, 2008 Washington Gubernatorial Election 243

7.2 2008 Minnesota Senatorial Election 246

7.3 2008 Oregon Senatorial Election 249

7.4 2008 Georgia Senatorial Election 251

8.1 Total Number of Initiatives, 1978 to 2008/Number of Initiatives on Ballot, 2008 256

8.2 Arizona Proposition 2, Ban Same-Sex Marriage, 2008 259

8.3 Florida Proposition 2, Ban Same-Sex Marriage, 2008 259

8.4 Proposition 7, Renewable Energy Generation, 2008 Referendum/ Proposition 10, Alternative-Fuel Vehicles and Renewable Energy Bonds, 2008 Referendum 261

8.5 California Proposition 2, Prevention of Farm Animal Cruelty, 2008 Referendum 263

8.6 California Proposition 8, Eliminate Same-Sex Marriage, 2008 Referendum 265

8.7   Medical Use of Marijuana,
Michigan 2008 Referendum   269

8.8   Stem Cell Research, Michigan
2008 Referendum   271

8.9   Initiative 1000, Physician-Assisted
Suicide   274

9.1   Presidential Vote versus
Congressional Vote by Congressional
District, 2008   278

9.2   Democratic Presidential Vote by
Legislative District, 111th House,
2008   279

9.3   Fuel-Efficient Car Voucher Program,
111th Congress, 2009   282

9.4   Health Care Overhaul/Abortion
Funding Ban, 111th Congress,
2009   285

9.5   Health Care Overhaul Passage,
111th Congress, 2009   288

9.6   Greenhouse Gas Emissions Passage,
2009   291

9.7   Americans for Democratic Action
Ratings, 111th House, First Session   296

9.8   American Conservative Union Ratings,
111th House, First Session   297

9.9   AFL-CIO Ratings, 111th House,
First Session   298

9.10   Environment America Ratings,
111th House, First Session   299

9.11   Gun Owners of America Ratings,
111th House, First Session   300

9.12   *National Journal's* Foreign Policy
Ratings, 111th House, First Session   301

TABLES

4.1   Percentage Point Increases in Democratic
Share of the Two-Party Vote   63

4.2   Mean Democratic Share of the
Two-Party Vote, 1980–2008   64

4.3   Comparisons of Average
Socioeconomic and Political
Characteristics of Residents
of Urban and Rural Counties   72

4.4   Obama and McCain Votes within
and without the Electoral College   104

4.5   Metropolitan, Micropolitan, and Rural
Voting by Region in the 2008
Presidential Election   110

5.1   Ideological Identification of
Americans over Age 18 in 2009   122

5.2   Table of Results: Weighted Least-
Squares Estimation of Obama's
Percentage of the Two-Party
Vote in 2008   132

8.1   Ballot Measure Description and
Vote Percentage   255

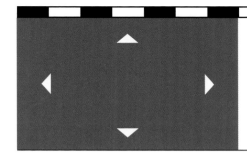

PREFACE

In November 2008 the coeditors met at the annual meeting of the Southeast Division of the Association of American Geographers in Greensboro, North Carolina, to discuss the possibility of an atlas of the presidential election held earlier that month. We were enthusiastic about the opportunity and possibility to present to our colleagues in political geography, political science, and the visual and print media an atlas that would illustrate maps of the primaries, general election, and also selected nonpartisan referenda in states. We also agreed that it would be important and appropriate to contact a number of political scientists who understand geographic processes and regional patterns.

In the weeks immediately following this meeting, we circulated a prospectus and also contacted Susan McEachern at Rowman & Littlefield, a publisher with a strong tradition in geography of publishing books for classroom use. Our initial proposal to Susan was for two books, an atlas and a separate chaptered volume on key components of the election. She convinced us to merge these ideas into a single volume with a focus on the atlas, an idea, she believed, and rightly so, that would have broader appeal to scholars, the media, and those in the general public interested in maps, politics, and elections. We contacted a number of well-known political scientists and invited them to contribute; most responded enthusiastically and were pleased with the contents we planned for the atlas.

In the ensuing months all editors worked on various facets of the project. The total emails exchanged among the editors and with authors approached 3,000. We channeled all of our maps to Clark Archer and Steve Lavin, both of whom had previous experience in preparing quality atlases. We also exchanged ideas on maps for the atlas, ideas that expanded beyond the 2008 primaries and general election to include nearly fifty maps of "top 200" counties of the wealthiest, poorest, those with the highest percentages of employment in creative class occupations, fastest and slowest growing, most religious (specific denominations) as well as votes in predominantly military and university counties, and those with the most elderly. We examined how these counties voted in 2008 as well as 2004 (Bush versus Kerry). The atlas includes maps and analyses of the votes in seven key swing states, states where the margin between Obama and McCain was slight and where the Democrats won in 2008 but had lost in 2004. Eight statewide nonpartisan referenda are examined; these address the medical use of marijuana and stem cell research in Michigan, farm animal cruelty, alternative energy use, and same-sex marriage in California, and physician-assisted suicide in Washington. The narratives accompanying each map are written by the editors and by other geographers and political scientists interested in electoral patterns at the state, metropolitan, and regional scales. In the latter part of the atlas we include maps of four crucial votes by the first session of the 111th House of Representatives (health care, abortion funding, fuel-efficient cars, and greenhouse gas). We also map and discuss the ratings of House members by six different groups with various political agendas. Finally, in chapter 10 we explore with readers some bold and creative ideas about the U.S. electorate and electing presidents.

There are a number of individuals we wish to acknowledge for their assistance in the execution and production of this project. First, we want to thank Susan McEachern for her interest and her vision of a product that would appeal to various scholarly communities and the general public. Susan has always been supportive of creative ventures in geographic publishing and we thank her for her unstinting support. We also want to thank Jehanne Schweitzer and Carrie Broadwell-Tkach for their work with the atlas editors and authors on their narratives, both production tasks that enhance the quality of the final product. Several specific individuals provided the financial support for the color maps. These include Dean Mark Kornbluh in the College of Arts and Sciences at the University of Kentucky, Dean Oliver Walter, Dean of Arts and Sciences at the University of Wyoming, and deans at the University of Nebraska, Lincoln: Donald Wilhite, School of Natural Resources, Gregory Snow, College of Arts and Sciences, and Susan Fritz, Agricultural Resources Division, as well as the University of Nebraska-Lincoln Research Council for their financial support. Two University of Kentucky geography alumni, Brad Loar and Martin Birkenthal, also generously provided funds for the color reproduction. Others who played important roles in seeing this product through to its conclusion were Dick Gilbreath, Director of the Gyula Pauer Cartographic Laboratory at the University of Kentucky, who designed the final atlas pages of bumper stickers (purchased from www.zazzle.com) and stamps (from larryphillips@comcast.net), Mark Peffley in the Department of Political Science at the University of Kentucky, who provided the names of political science contributors to the volume, Lori Tyndall, Business Manager in the Department of Geography at the University of Kentucky, who administered the financial contributions, and, finally, Sue Roberts, Department Chair, who recognized the importance of this product for geographers and other social science communities.

Dedicated to the memory of Stephen J. Lavin (1943–2011)
Friend, scholar, and supercartographer

CHAPTER ONE

INTRODUCTION

ELECTIONS

In political geography we recognize that there are three different contexts within which we can study elections or political behavior. Most obvious is the demographic-economic context or characteristics of the population, that is, the tendencies of women and men, the young and the old, the rich and the poor, the well-educated and less well-educated who have different preferences and values and thus vote differently. Second is the nature of human settlement or where people live; many people in rural areas and small towns have different worldviews from those living in metropolitan areas. A third context is geographical; it overlaps somewhat with both the demographic-economic context and where people live. Different parts of the United States contain many residents whose attitudes are more likely to be progressive, while others contain large numbers of people with more conservative, traditional outlooks. Sharp differences in religious preference, attitudes toward families, new ethnicities, acceptable lifestyles, and the role of women can be found among people living in different regions.

Underlying all three of these contexts is a further geographic principle, that of proximity or nearness. People tend to make voting decisions similar to those of people living nearby. We can observe this at a very local scale. For example, neighborhoods adjacent to colleges and universities inhabited by large numbers of young voters often reported large majorities for Obama. Nearby suburban neighborhoods with older residents reported Republican majorities. At a larger scale, voting percentages in adjacent states with similar demographic patterns tended to report results that were similar to each other. Thus Obama did very well in Maine and neighboring New Hampshire, in Iowa and neighboring Minnesota, and in Washington and neighboring Oregon. On the other hand, McCain won large majorities in Kentucky and West Virginia; Idaho and Utah; and Alabama and Mississippi. We observe evidence of these three contexts in more than 200 maps and discussions that follow.

These three distinctive features underline the well-known cliché of a "red" or a "blue" America, defined on dual (but not necessarily orthogonal) dimensions of rural to metropolitan and traditional to modern. The maps and narratives below reveal that this paradigm is broadly true, that the nation is somewhat polarized and that it also has distinct regional or sectional patterns of voting and behavior. They also show that there is much middle ground along these continua, that is, spaces that are balanced between the parties jockeying for different positions. In this context the 2008 elections can be viewed as a repudiation of Republican rule, ushering in a new era. However, the analysis and histories reported in this atlas illustrate that the electorate is fickle, and the coalition that elected Obama, including the young, ethnic minorities, and the educated and affluent, remains somewhat fragile.

The U.S. presidential election of 2008 was one of the most significant presidential elections in recent American history. For the first time, American voters elected a candidate of African ancestry, Senator Barack Obama of Illinois, to the presidency. The election was marked by unprecedented interest among voters and the mass media, by very high turnouts throughout the country, and by widespread use of the Internet and social media. In defeating his Republican opponent, Senator John McCain of Arizona, Obama and the Democrats ended eight years of

Republican control of the White House. Moreover, the decisive Democratic victory stood in sharp contrast to the closely contested presidential elections of 2000 and 2004.

The purpose of the atlas is to examine the U.S. presidential election of 2008 from a geographical perspective using maps covering many aspects of the campaign and the election results. Because American presidential politics is fundamentally geographical in nature, the geographic perspective presented in the maps, along with the commentary accompanying the maps, provides a unique and important perspective on the election that complements the many verbal accounts of this watershed campaign prepared by journalists.

THE 2008 PRESIDENTIAL ELECTION

In the largest total voter turnout in American history, on November 4, 2008, Obama won about 69.5 million popular votes to about 60 million for McCain. In December, Obama was formally elected president by an Electoral College margin of 365 to 173. On January 20, 2009, he was inaugurated as the forty-fourth president of the United States.

The 2008 campaign was especially engaging because both parties held spirited contests for their presidential nominations. For the first time since 1952, neither the incumbent president nor the incumbent vice president ran for the presidency. Republican president George W. Bush, who had been elected in 2000 and reelected in 2004, was ineligible to run for another term. Vice President Dick Cheney made clear that he was not interested in running for the presidency. Thus it was clear that both parties

would choose new faces to head their national tickets. Several candidates began campaigns for their parties' nominations in 2007. The Democratic field quickly narrowed to two major candidates, Obama and Senator Hillary Clinton of New York. The Republican field was quickly winnowed to three major candidates, including McCain, former governor Mitt Romney of Massachusetts, and former governor Mike Huckabee of Arkansas. By winning narrow but decisive victories over Romney and Huckabee in several early primaries, McCain secured the Republican nomination relatively early in the campaign. In contrast, Obama and Clinton waged a long campaign that was resolved only after all fifty states had held primary elections or caucuses.

Obama and McCain were nominated formally at their respective parties' national conventions in August. Obama selected Senator Joseph Biden of Delaware as his vice-presidential running mate. McCain chose Governor Sarah Palin of Alaska. Palin became the second woman, and the first Republican woman, to run for vice president on a major-party ticket. Although the two candidates ran evenly in the polls through September, by Election Day Obama had pulled ahead of McCain in public opinion surveys, especially in swing states that were critical to the outcome of the election. Most pollsters predicted an Obama victory.

When the votes were counted, it became clear that Obama had won after making substantial inroads into normally Republican territory. For example, Obama carried Virginia and Indiana, although neither of these states had gone Democratic since 1964. Nationwide, Obama won popular vote majorities in nine states that Bush had carried in 2004: Colorado, Florida, Indiana, Iowa, Nevada, New Mexico, North Carolina, Ohio, and Virginia. McCain carried

the other states that had gone Republican in 2004, but he won no states that the Democrats carried four years previously. Thus Obama succeeded in winning the presidency by carrying most of the closely contested states that had been carried by Bush during the two previous elections.

Although Obama's decisive win in 2008 stands in sharp contrast to the Democrats' narrow defeats in 2000 and 2004, close examination of the geographic patterns of the popular vote reveals substantial similarities among these elections and others in the recent past. Across the country, Obama won about 5 percent more of the popular vote than did his predecessor as the Democratic nominee, Senator John Kerry of Massachusetts, four years earlier. Obama outpolled Kerry in most areas of the country. Only in a few areas, most notably in counties across the upper South eastward from northwestern Texas to West Virginia, did McCain win higher percentages of the popular vote than did Bush in 2004.

At the same time, however, the results reveal an increasing split between metropolitan areas and their suburbs. Historically, central cities in the United States have been predominantly Democratic, whereas their rural hinterlands have been primarily Republican. By 2008, however, many suburban counties had become more and more Democratic. At the same time, small cities and rural areas trended more and more toward the Republicans. In fact, Obama owed his victory to his large popular vote margin in large metropolitan areas. He carried twenty-two of the twenty-six metropolitan areas in the United States with populations of two million or more, compiling a popular-vote margin of nearly ten million votes in these cities and their suburbs. Elsewhere, Obama and McCain divided the popular vote almost evenly; McCain claimed a majority of popular votes in rural areas.

INSIGHTS FROM A GEOGRAPHICAL PERSPECTIVE

The American political system, and therefore American politics, is inherently geographic. The United States is a federal state, with power shared formally between the federal government and those of the fifty states. Each state has clearly defined boundaries, and these boundaries stipulate control of all locations within the fifty states.

Moreover, the U.S. electoral system emphasizes and privileges territory. Even before the American Revolution, representation has been based on territory, with legislators selected from territorially defined districts. The Electoral College system articulated in the Constitution and amended by the Twelfth Amendment in 1804 specifies the role of geography in selecting the president of the United States. Technically, voters casting presidential ballots in any state are not voting for the presidential candidates themselves; rather, they are voting for members of the Electoral College, who are pledged, if selected, to vote for the presidential nominees of their respective parties. As a result, it is possible for a presidential nominee to be elected by the Electoral College despite getting fewer popular votes than his or her opponent. Although this situation is unusual, three presidents, John Quincy Adams in 1824, Benjamin Harrison in 1888, and George W. Bush in 2000, were elected without winning a plurality of popular votes.

The structure of the Electoral College means that parties and their candidates pay close attention to the location of voters. Campaign resources are concentrated in those states that are perceived as evenly divided between the two candidates. Heavily Democratic and heavily Republican states are largely ignored by both parties. Prior to World War II, both parties ignored the "Solid South," which was uniformly Democratic in every election. Instead, they concentrated on the evenly divided Middle Atlantic and Great Lakes states, knowing that whichever party won many or all of these states would win the election. Today, neither party pays much attention to the heavily Democratic Northeast or the heavily Republican Great Plains and Rocky Mountain states (except for Colorado and New Mexico). Rather, both concentrate their resources, including campaign funds and personal appearances by the candidates and their prominent supporters, in states perceived to be evenly divided between the two major parties. In 2008, Obama won the election by winning the electoral votes of most of these swing states.

As specified in the Constitution, the number of electoral votes in each state is determined by its number of representatives in Congress, including both the Senate and the House of Representatives. Although this practice is not required by the Constitution, by the middle of the nineteenth century most of the states had begun to award their electoral votes to the candidate who got the most popular votes in that state. (Today, only Maine and Nebraska allocate one electoral vote to the winner in each Congressional district, with the other two going to the candidate with a statewide majority. In 2008, Obama carried one of Nebraska's three House districts; winning one of Nebraska's five electoral votes, while McCain won a statewide plurality as well as majorities in the state's other two districts.) The winner-take-all system used in the other states in allocating their electoral votes has meant that candidates concentrate on large as well as evenly divided states. Thus states such as Ohio, Florida, and Pennsylvania, which have large numbers of electoral votes and a relatively even division of Republicans and Democrats, have been targeted by both major parties. On the other hand, the Obama and McCain campaigns paid little attention to heavily Democratic California and New York or to strongly Republican Texas. Not only does geography affect the organization of U.S. politics, but as this atlas illustrates, it influences many other aspects of the electoral process.

ORGANIZATION OF THE ATLAS

The atlas is divided into ten chapters. Each, except for this introduction, contains maps and accompanying narratives. There are more than 200 maps; most depict voting patterns at the national level. Accompanying both the national and state maps are narratives or essays about the maps or about major features of the national election. These map descriptions and lengthy narratives are written by both junior and senior political geographers and political scientists who have interests in state, regional, or national voting patterns.

Chapter 2 deals with the primary election process that led up to the nominations of Obama and McCain by the Democratic and Republican parties, respectively. The presidential and vice-presidential nominees are formally selected by national nominating conventions. Delegates from each state vote for their party's nominees, with a candidate who receives a majority of votes being nominated. Over the course of U.S. history, the process by which parties select their nominees for president and vice president has changed considerably. In general, these changes have granted increased participation in the nomination process to rank-and-file voters. By the 1970s, each state had begun to hold some form of electoral contest through which that state's delegates to the national nominating conventions are selected. However, the electoral process varies between states. Some states hold open primaries, in which any voter can vote in either party's primary. Some hold closed primaries, in which participation is restricted to previously registered party members. Others hold caucuses.

The timing of the primary elections and caucuses also varies. In 2008, the primary election season began with the Iowa precinct caucuses on January 3 and did not end until primary elections in Montana and South Dakota on June 10. In general, voters who live in states with earlier primaries and caucuses have more influence on the nomination process than do voters who live in states that hold later primaries and caucuses. Candidates who do poorly in early primaries drop out of the race, leaving a smaller field of candidates from whom voters in later-primary states can select. Moreover, in many cases a candidate clinches enough delegate voters to secure his or her party's nomination before all states have held their primary elections. In 2008, for example, McCain wrapped up the Republican nomination by mid-February, and his last remaining rival, Huckabee, dropped out of the race in March. Republicans voting in states that held primary elections after March, therefore, had no chance to influence their party's choice of a presidential nominee.

The voting patterns of primaries and caucuses are shown for Iowa, New Hampshire, North Carolina, Oklahoma, Tennessee, Pennsylvania, Missouri, and Michigan. Chapter 2 concludes with maps showing the outcomes of primary elections in individual states. For many years, the primary season has been kicked off by precinct caucuses in Iowa, followed by a primary election in New Hampshire. Obama and Huckabee won Iowa unexpectedly on January 3, while Clinton and McCain won the New Hampshire primary five days later. The pivotal day was "Super Tuesday," February 5, when twenty states held primary elections or caucuses. McCain won narrow victories in several key states, helping him wrap up the Republican nomination. On the Democratic side, Obama and Clinton split the Super Tuesday primaries, but Obama surged into the lead during the next several weeks by winning key primaries in Virginia, Maryland, Wisconsin, and other states. Although Clinton won a majority of the later primaries, Obama's margins in the early part of the campaign were sufficient for him to secure the Democratic Party's nomination.

Chapter 3 focuses on the electoral process and the election campaign. Voting policies and procedures vary from state to state. For example, many states allow early voting, but how early a voter can cast his or her ballot differs among states. Of course, those who vote early will not be influenced by events taking place at the end of the campaign. As a result, the percentage of voters who cast early ballots varies substantially among the states.

Many of the maps in chapter 3 illustrate the campaign itself. Each party raises millions of dollars from campaign donors. However, these funds are not spent randomly, and they are not spent uniformly from state to state. Rather, they are concentrated in those places where party leaders believe that they will make a difference in the Electoral College. Thus, neither party advertised in heavily Republican states such as Utah and Oklahoma, and neither advertised in heavily Democratic Vermont or Maryland. Similarly, the major-party candidates spent most of their campaign time making appearances in evenly divided swing states. The chapter also examines the pattern of daily newspaper endorsements of the two major candidates. Even a casual reading of the maps reveals some distinct geographic variations in campaign contributions, newspaper endorsements, and campaign stops in the months following the party conventions and during the last week and month of the campaign. The maps also reveal some interesting patterns, especially when comparing those appearances with the actual votes of individual counties and states.

Chapter 4 focuses on the outcome of the election itself. Of particular interest is the map of the election results at the county level. One unfamiliar with the United States might conclude that McCain, who carried a substantial majority of the counties in the United States, had won the election. While Obama carried fewer counties than McCain, many of the counties that Obama did carry were large metropolitan counties. Moreover, he carried very large counties such as Cook County, Illinois (Chicago), and Los Angeles County, California, by very large margins. Largely because many of the counties carried by McCain have small populations, McCain's average margin of victory in those counties that he carried was much less than Obama's average margin of victory.

Maps showing the results of the 2008 election at the state and county level are followed by maps in which Democratic and Republican performances in 2008 are compared with their performances in previous elections, including changes in average Democratic and Republican votes since 1948. In general, the geographical pattern of Democratic and Republican support has changed relatively little over the past three decades. The most Democratic places in the 1980s, including large cities and counties with large minority populations, remain the most Democratic places in the country today. Similarly, strongly Republican areas have remained strongly Republican over the past quarter century. However, the electoral pattern of the late twentieth and early twenty-first centuries stands in sharp contrast to electoral patterns of the period between the Civil War and World War II. During that time, the South was uniformly Democratic while the northern tier of states from New England to the Upper Midwest was dominated by Republicans. Today, this pattern has reversed. For example, Vermont went Republican in every presidential election between 1860 and 1960. However, Vermont has gone Democratic, by larger and larger margins, in each election since 1992, and today it is one of the most solidly Democratic states in the country.

Additional maps in chapter 4 identify the bellwether counties, that is, those at the national and state level where the margin of victory was less than 3 percent. Also the absolute vote margins for Obama and McCain are shown at the county level. One can also visually compare these patterns and the actual votes for Obama and McCain. Note especially the different voting results in the major metropolitan areas and the small counties in the Plains and Middle West. This theme is discussed by a number of authors in their descriptions of individual maps. This chapter also contains maps that can be used to interpret the impact of various voter characteristics such as age, race, and gender on electoral outcomes in different areas. In some cases, such interpretation is possible by comparing maps of election outcomes such as those presented in the early portion of chapter 4 with maps showing these voter characteristics. Thus, it is easy to demonstrate Obama's appeal among nonwhite voters in areas such as heavily Hispanic south Texas, the predominantly African American areas of the Mississippi Delta and the Alabama Black Belt, and American Indian reservations in otherwise Republican Great

Plains and Rocky Mountain states. However, interpretation of this sort is much more difficult in the case of gender, because there are relatively few geographic differences among counties in the percentages of men and women residing in each.

Given this difficulty, we rely on exit polls to interpret the impacts of race, age, and gender on the outcome of the election. The impact of nonwhite voters on the outcome of the election is quite clear; Obama would have lost had only white voters cast ballots across the country. However, the gap between white and nonwhite support for Obama declines steadily from south to north; in places like New England and the Upper Midwest, whites and nonwhites were equally likely to have voted Democratic. Age and gender had some impact on the outcome, but this impact was not decisive as was the case with the voter's race. Obama won the support of voters under thirty by a two-to-one margin, but he would have won the election even without their support. Women were more likely to vote Democratic than were men, especially in large blue states; the gender gap was much smaller in Republican-dominated regions. Turnout also proved to be a major factor contributing to Obama's victory, especially in major metropolitan areas and in swing regions in swing states.

The significance of the 2008 vote as being similar to previous elections or as a distinct and watershed election is a theme discussed by a number of political scientists and geographers. Their consensus is that while the election was a major departure from previous ones in the context that an African American was elected, the major national and regional voting patterns were not that different from 2004 and 2000. This point is also illustrated when correlating the 2008 results with previous elections. Most places that were strongly Republican in 2000 and 2004 remained

strongly Republican in 2008, and places that were heavily Democratic in the 2000 and 2004 elections went Democratic, often by larger margins, in 2008. In fact, Obama won every state that the 2000 and 2004 Democratic nominees won. By winning several other states that the Democrats had lost in these previous elections, Obama achieved a comfortable majority in the Electoral College. The final maps in this chapter look at the turnout levels, which exhibit some distinct regional patterns, and the persistence of party affiliation in 2008 for president, gubernatorial, and senatorial votes. The patterns reveal party loyalties as well as split voting.

In chapter 5, we examine the 2008 election returns at a regional level, again with reference to recent and past electoral history. The six regions discussed include the Northeast, Appalachia and the American South, the Middle West including the Rust Belt, the Great Plains, the Rocky Mountain states, and the Pacific Coast states. Electoral patterns in each of these regions were distinctive. The Northeast and the Pacific Coast regions, which had been dominated by the Democrats in recent years, remained heavily Democratic. The South remained predominantly Republican, although Democrats made substantial inroads relative to the recent past. Democratic gains were especially evident in metropolitan areas and in areas containing large numbers of young voters and professionals. The Democrats' success in the Northern Virginia suburbs of Washington, D.C., and in the Research Triangle area of North Carolina were instrumental in swinging these states into the Democratic column for the first time since 1964 (Virginia) and 1976 (North Carolina).

In the central part of the country, the Midwest was an especially significant swing region. Obama outperformed Kerry throughout the region, especially in large cities and their suburbs. He did well both in declining Rust Belt cities such as Detroit, Flint, and Youngstown while also winning easily in more upscale, growing metropolitan areas, including his home town of Chicago and the Twin Cities of Minnesota. The Great Plains remained Republican, although Obama's percentage increased in much of this region relative to that of Kerry in 2004. The historically Republican Rocky Mountain states remained predominantly Republican, although Obama won Colorado and New Mexico and lost Montana by a small margin. He might also have won Arizona had McCain, an Arizona resident, not headed the Republican ticket.

Also in chapter 5, we focus on key swing states in the November election. The states examined include Colorado, Indiana, Florida, Missouri, Montana, North Carolina, Ohio, Pennsylvania, Virginia, and Tennessee. These were all hotly contested states until Election Day. Some of these were strong Republican states in previous elections but went to Obama in 2008; others were states where McCain won by a small percentage. In many of these states, Obama benefited from a high turnout relative to 2004, including an influx of new voters, as well as increasing success in metropolitan areas. Close examinations of the county-level election results in these states illustrate sharp differences, for example, between an upstate and downstate region or between major urban centers and rural areas.

The maps and narratives in chapter 6 examine the distribution of various types of indicators including measures of ethnicity, religion, demography, occupational structure, population growth and decline, income and wealth, education, and mobility. We specifically look at the extremes, that is, the two hundred counties with the highest and lowest rankings

on selected variables. This perspective enables us to examine various contemporary social, economic, and cultural trends on the outcome of the election. For example, it enables us to assess the effect of the U.S. economic crisis of 2007–2008, including increased unemployment and widening levels of housing foreclosure. Questions that were raised in looking at these variables include: how do members of the creative class vote? What about counties with major military bases? And Bible Belt counties? Comparing these and other maps provides insights about the importance of various issues affecting voters' attitudes in different areas of the United States. We inquire specifically into how the poorest, wealthiest, and fastest and slowest growing counties, the largest Asian, African American, and Hispanic populations, and those with high unemployment voted. We also include bar graphs that provide a comparison of results in 2008 with those in 2004.

While the presidential election commanded most of the country's attention during the 2008 campaign, many state and local elections were also closely contested. In chapter 7 we focus on selected campaigns for various statewide offices, including elections for Senate seats and state governorships. Along with its success in the presidential election, the Democratic Party experienced a net increase in its number of seats in both houses of Congress. Although Obama's theme of "hope and change" may have influenced these state and local races, several Democrats took over previously Republican seats in the House despite the fact that their districts gave majorities to McCain. These results in various parts of the United States reinforce the late House speaker Tip O'Neill's oft-quoted remark that "all politics is local." In the chapter, we examine closely contested elections for the Senate in Virginia, North Carolina, Georgia, and Minnesota.

The Minnesota election was so close that the eventual winner, Democrat Al Franken, was not seated until several months after ballots were cast. The Minnesota race illustrates the importance of split tickets: while Obama won Minnesota comfortably, only a few hundred ballots separated Franken and his Republican opponent, incumbent senator Norm Coleman. Georgia and Washington are two gubernatorial races we examine closely. We also discuss how these voting patterns for senators and governors compared with presidential votes. Answers to these questions would help answer whether Obama and McCain had any coattail effect or whether voters were voting independently for these offices.

The United States, like most large and industrialized countries, is a representative democracy. Voters elect representatives to Congress, state legislatures, and local councils, and the representatives enact legislation. A voter thus influences the legislative process indirectly by voting for candidates who support and against candidates who oppose desired legislation. However, in some cases voters make legislative decisions directly by voting on state constitutional amendments and other issues. Several referenda are examined in chapter 8. Many of these referenda involve highly controversial social issues, including animal cruelty (California), physician-assisted suicide (Washington), same-sex marriage (Arizona, California, and Florida), medical marijuana (Michigan), and stem cell research (Michigan). In this chapter, we examine the geography of voting on referenda on controversial issues in several states.

In chapter 9 we examine congressional issues. There are two main foci for this chapter. One focus is on the geographic patterns of major selected votes in the 111th House of Representatives in 2009. These include votes on health care, abortion, fuel-efficient cars, and greenhouse gas emissions. The second focus is on ratings of members of the House of Representatives by groups that regularly monitor votes on issues important to their constituencies. We include the ratings by groups on a wide spectrum, including Americans for Democratic Action, American Conservative Union, Environmental Action, AFL-CIO, Gun Owners of America, and a foreign policy rating by *National Journal*. We compare not only the geographic patterns of those they give high and low ratings, but also how these congressional districts voted in November 2008. Depending on the group and its position on social and economic issues, some gave strong support for Obama while others gave strong support for McCain

Chapter 10 looks toward the future. What is likely to happen in 2012 and future elections? What can be learned from this campaign that will enhance our understanding of the democratic process in the United States and in other countries? We present ten scenarios about American politics and future elections. We emphasize that the geographic perspective underlying the maps and commentary throughout the atlas provide vital insights into twenty-first century democracy as practiced in the United States and throughout the world. The one certainty that exists in the future is that there will continue to be elections where personalities, parties, territories, and regions will play important roles. While the configuration of parties and regions may be different in 2050 than in 2000 or 1950, there will continue to be intense party and regional competition for the nation's highest elected office.

The final pages include examples of bumper stickers that appeared in the fall 2008 campaign and a representative sample of postage stamps issued following Obama's election. Many of the bumper stickers illustrate famous and catchy slogans used by or attributed to the candidates, including some that are humorous. Many more bumper stickers appeared than those selected. About thirty countries issued stamps about Obama and his family. Some depicted Obama and his inauguration, others showed him with past presidents, and still others alongside current world leaders.

REFERENCES

Archer, J. C., S. J. Lavin, K. C. Martis, and F. M. Shelley. 2002. *Atlas of American Politics*. Washington, D.C.: CQ.

Archer, J. C., S. J. Lavin, K. C. Martis, and F. M. Shelley. 2006. *Atlas of U. S. Presidential Elections, 1789–2004*. Washington, D.C.: CQ.

Archer, J. C., and P. J. Taylor. 1981. *Section and Party. A Political Geography of American Presidential Elections from Andrew Jackson to Ronald Raegan*. Crofts House: Gower.

Brunn, S. D. 1974. *Geography and Politics in America*. New York: Harper & Row.

Gelman, A. 2008. *Red State, Blue State, Rich State, Poor State: Why Americans Vote the Way They Do*. Princeton, N.J.: Princeton University Press.

Gimpel, J. G., and J. E. Schuknecht. 2004. *Patchwork Nation: Sectionalism and Political Change in American Politics*. Ann Arbor: University of Michigan Press.

Martis, K. C. 1982. *Historical Atlas of U. S. Congressional Districts, 1789–1983*. New York: Free Press.

Shelley, F. M., J. C. Archer, F. Davidson, and S. D. Brunn. 1996. *America's Political Geography*. New York: Guilford.

CHAPTER TWO

THE 2008 PRIMARIES

■ PRESIDENTIAL NOMINEES

FRED M. SHELLEY

The election of Barack Obama as the forty-fourth president of the United States began with the selection of presidential nominees in both major parties. Initially, several Democrats and several Republicans put themselves forward as candidates for the presidential nominations of their respective parties. The Democratic field included Senators Joseph Biden of Delaware, Hillary Clinton of New York, Christopher Dodd of Connecticut, and Barack Obama of Illinois, former senator John Edwards of North Carolina, Governor Bill Richardson of New Mexico, and Representative Dennis Kucinich of Ohio. The major Republican candidates included Senator John McCain of Arizona, former New York City mayor Rudolph Giuliani, former governor Mike Huckabee of Arkansas, former governor Mitt Romney of Massachusetts, former senator Fred Thompson of Tennessee, Representative Ron Paul of Texas, Senator Sam Brownback of Kansas, and Representatives

Duncan Hunter of California and Tom Tancredo of Colorado. After primary election contests in all fifty states as well as in U.S. territories, Obama and McCain emerged as their parties' presidential nominees.

PRIMARY SELECTION OVERVIEW

The United States is unique among the world's democracies in that the process of selecting presidential nominees represents the culmination of a process lasting several months and conducted using different election methods in each state. In each state, primary contests are used to select that state's delegates to the parties' national nominating conventions. The process began with caucuses in Iowa on January 3, and concluded with primary elections in Montana and South Dakota on June 8, especially on "Super

Tuesday," February 12, when twenty of the fifty states held their primary contests. The maps in this chapter show the county-level winners of the most important Democratic and Republican primaries and caucuses.

Traditionally, Iowa and New Hampshire are the first states to hold their primary contests. These were followed by contests in South Carolina and Nevada. Leaders of both parties recognized that these four states represented a reasonable geographic cross-section of the American public, with Iowa representing the Midwest, New Hampshire representing the Northeast, South Carolina representing the South, and Nevada representing the West. All of these states held their primaries in January. It is generally recognized that states holding their primary elections early have an advantage over those holding primaries later. In early primaries, all of the announced candidates are on the ballot. After the early primaries are concluded, candidates who perform poorly drop out of the race. By the end of the primary season, only a small number of candidates remain in the running.

The pace of the campaign stepped up in February, especially on February 12, which was known as Super Tuesday. On Super Tuesday, twenty of the fifty states held their contests. After Super Tuesday, McCain had all but wrapped up the presidential nomination of his party. Thus, Republican voters in states that had not yet held their primaries on or before Super Tuesday had no say in choosing the Republican nominee. On the Democratic side, only Obama and Clinton remained viable candidates by Super Tuesday. Obama led in the delegate count after Super Tuesday. Although Clinton made up some ground in the later stages of the campaign, Obama wrapped up a majority of delegates by June, and Clinton suspended her campaign.

There are three basic types of primary contests in the United States. In open and semiopen primary elections, a voter can request the ballot of either party at the polls. This process allows a voter to choose whether to vote in the Republican or Democratic primary. If one party's nomination is wrapped up by the time of the state's primary, voters may opt to vote in the primary of the other party. Because McCain had wrapped up the Republican nomination on Super Tuesday, some normally Republican voters undoubtedly chose a Democratic ballot. Other states hold closed primaries. In a closed primary, a voter must be a registered member of his or her party prior to the primary election, and the voter can only vote in the primary of the party of which he or she is a registered members. Still other states use caucuses rather than primary elections to select their national convention delegates. Caucuses are public meetings of party members, at which voters generally must declare their preferences for their party's nominee publicly. Caucuses often last for several hours. This reduces attendance, and party activists are more likely to participate than are rank-and-file members of the party.

Obama and Huckabee won their respective parties' caucuses in Iowa on January 3 (map 2.5). On the Democratic side, Obama won a plurality of the caucus vote, whereas Clinton and Edwards finished in a virtual tie for second. The remaining candidates garnered little support and soon dropped out of the race. Five days later, Clinton and McCain won the New Hampshire Democratic and Republican primaries, respectively. Edwards dropped out of the race after losing in his native state of South Carolina. By Super Tuesday, only Clinton and Obama among the major candidates remained in the race. On the Republican side, the early primaries were split between McCain, Huckabee, and Romney. By narrowly winning pivotal primary elections in Missouri and Oklahoma over his two main rivals, McCain achieved a nearly insurmountable lead on Super Tuesday. Huckabee remained in the race for a few more weeks, although McCain soon secured the minimum number of delegates needed to clinch the Republican nomination. Paul, like Kucinich on the Democratic side, stayed in the race until the end while the remaining Republican candidates dropped out of the race shortly after Super Tuesday.

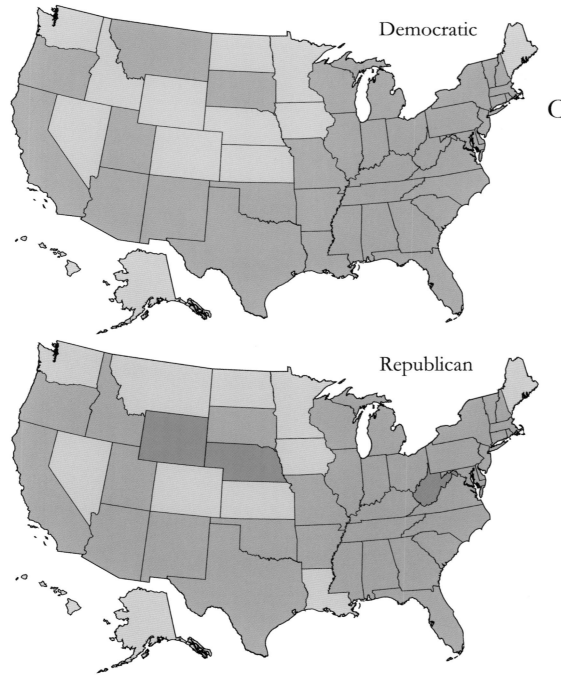

Democratic

Republican

MAP 2.1

Candidate Selection Method
2008

Method

Primary

Caucus

Convention

MAP 2.2

Democratic

Republican

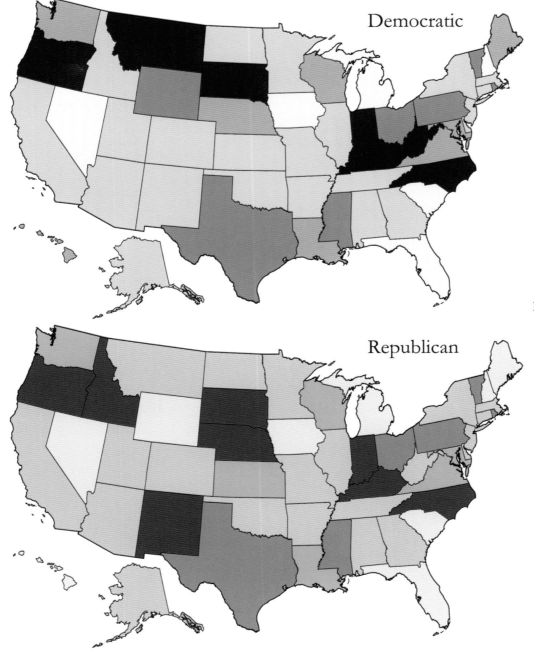

Primary Schedules
2008

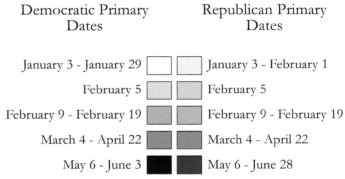

Democratic Primary Dates			Republican Primary Dates
January 3 - January 29			January 3 - February 1
February 5			February 5
February 9 - February 19			February 9 - February 19
March 4 - April 22			March 4 - April 22
May 6 - June 3			May 6 - June 28

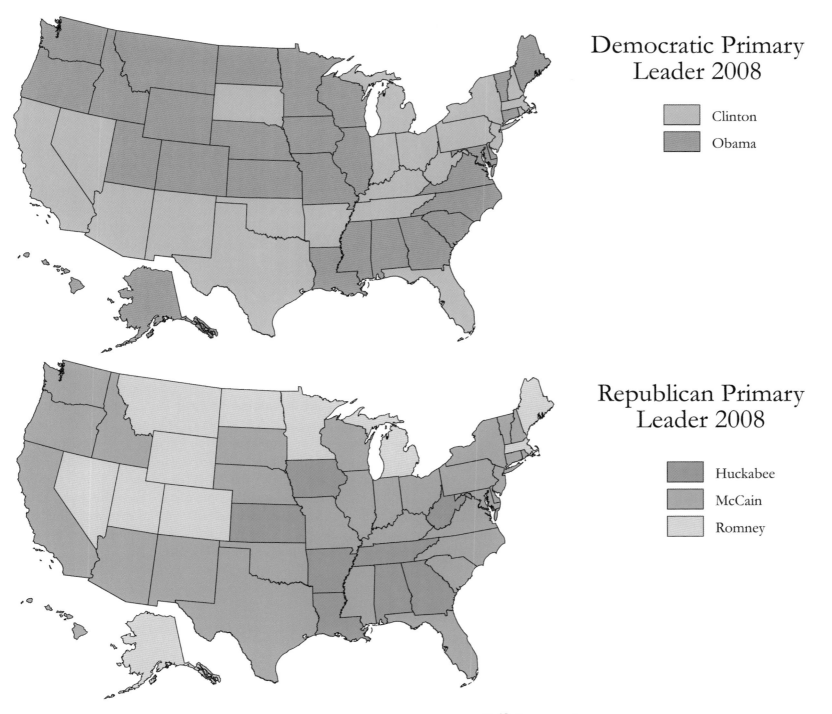

Democratic Primary
Leader 2008

Clinton

Obama

Republican Primary
Leader 2008

Huckabee

McCain

Romney

■ NEW HAMPSHIRE PRIMARY

HEATHER HOLLEN and FRED M. SHELLEY

The first primary election of the 2008 election season took place on January 8, five days after the Iowa precinct caucuses. Neither Mike Huckabee nor Barack Obama (the Iowa caucus winners) won the New Hampshire primaries for their respective parties. Thus, the results of the New Hampshire primaries threw the entire nominating process into confusion.

New Hampshire has held the country's first presidential primary election each year since 1952. In 1977, the New Hampshire legislature passed a law requiring New Hampshire's primary to precede those of any other state (Iowa is not included as "another" state because it holds precinct caucuses rather than a primary election). The two major parties were authorized to move the New Hampshire primary to an earlier date if another state announced plans to hold its primary earlier than that of New Hampshire. Critics have pointed out that Iowa and New Hampshire with their small populations, few minority voters, and lack of large metropolitan areas are unrepresentative of the U.S. electorate as a whole. Yet New Hampshire has retained its long-standing status as the country's first primary election.

Success in previous primaries and caucuses generates momentum for candidates of both parties heading into later primaries. Thus Huckabee on the Republican side and Obama on the Democratic side headed into New Hampshire with momentum associated with their unexpectedly strong showings in the Iowa precinct caucuses. Huckabee, John McCain, and Mitt Romney were expected to compete for the most votes in the New Hampshire primary. Romney was seen as having a possible advantage because he had served as governor of neighboring Massachusetts.

Among Democrats, Obama emphasized his opposition to an unpopular war in Iraq. Combining this theme with a message of "hope and change," he won large majorities in college communities such as Hanover and Lebanon (Dartmouth College) and Durham (University of New Hampshire). He carried many rural communities across the state, and he also won the upscale communities of Concord, the state capital, and Portsmouth. However, Clinton won blue-collar Manchester by 3,110 votes. She also won Nashua and Salem, which are essentially suburbs of Boston, Massachusetts. These three cities alone gave Clinton a margin of 6,585 votes, or most of her statewide margin of 7,481 votes.

McCain won the New Hampshire Republican primary by an unexpectedly large margin over Romney, with Huckabee finishing a distant third. Romney won the densely populated southeastern portion of New Hampshire by a narrow margin, but McCain won the primary with much larger pluralities elsewhere in the state, outside the range of Boston news media. Nearly every city and town north and west of the state capital of Concord gave McCain a plurality, giving him enough votes to secure a comfortable victory.

New Hampshire's presidential primary is an open primary, in which a voter can choose to vote in either party's primary at the polls. Thus, some voters may not have chosen the primary in which they would vote until Election Day. Shortly before Election Day, published public opinion polls showed Obama with a lead over Clinton in the Democratic primary, while McCain and Romney were tied statistically on the Republican side. Because many people who supported Obama among Democrats also supported McCain among Republicans, it is possible that as many as several thousand people who supported both Obama and McCain chose Republican ballots in the belief that McCain would need their votes more than would Obama. If even a few thousand people did so, then this may explain McCain's unexpectedly strong showing along with Obama's unexpectedly weak showing relative to public opinion poll results.

New Hampshire Primary
2008

MAP 2.4

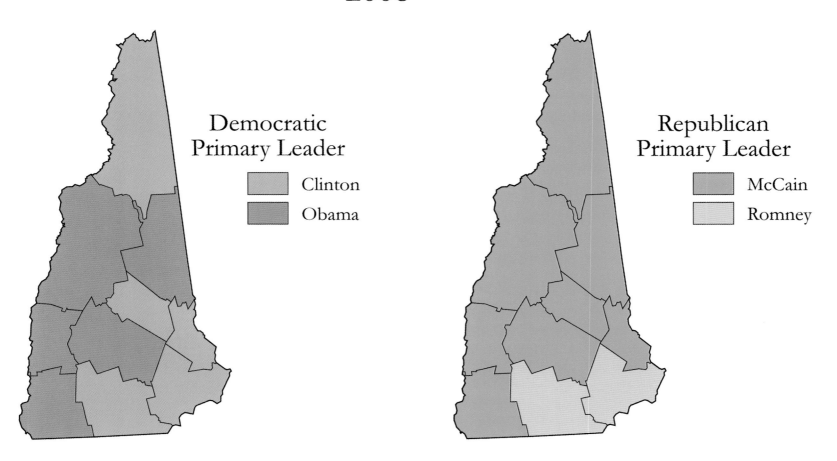

Democratic
Primary Leader

Clinton

Obama

Republican
Primary Leader

McCain

Romney

■ IOWA CAUCUSES

HEATHER HOLLEN AND FRED M. SHELLEY

During the 1970s, Iowa initiated a system of precinct caucuses in which Democratic and Republican voters in each precinct across the state meet to elect delegates to county conventions. Delegates pledged to that potential nominee at the precinct level are allocated proportionally on the basis of support levels within the precinct. The county conventions select delegates to congressional district conventions, which in turn select delegates to statewide conventions. The Iowa caucus system gained nationwide attention in 1976, when then little-known Jimmy Carter, the former governor of Georgia, won a plurality. Carter's success in Iowa helped propel him to victory in the New Hampshire primary and eventually to the Democratic Party nomination and the presidency. Since then, Iowa has been the first state in the country to select its delegates to the national nominating conventions for both major parties. Because the Iowa precinct caucuses represent the first test of voter support for potential presidential nominees of both major parties, candidates and journalists spend large amounts of time campaigning in Iowa.

Both parties had wide-open contests for their presidential nominations. For only the second time since 1928, both parties knew going into the 2008 presidential election campaign that neither the incumbent president nor the incumbent vice president would be on the general election ballot. President George W. Bush was ineligible to run for a third term in keeping with the Twenty-Second Amendment; Vice President Richard Cheney announced that he did not wish to seek his party's 2008 presidential nomination. With neither Bush nor Cheney on the ballot, the race for the Republican nomination was wide open. During 2007, several candidates announced plans to run. These included Senator John McCain of Arizona, former New York City mayor Rudolph Giuliani, former governor Mike Huckabee of Arkansas, former governor Mitt Romney of Massachusetts, former senator Fred Thompson of Tennessee, and Representative Ron Paul of Texas. In addition to these potential nominees, several other candidates, including Senator Sam Brownback of Kansas and Representatives Duncan Hunter of California and Tom Tancredo of Colorado, also initiated campaigns. None of these campaigns generated momentum, however, and all three dropped out before the caucuses took place.

During the precinct caucuses on January 3, 2008, Huckabee was strongly supported by evangelical Christians across Iowa. With strong support from evangelical voters, Huckabee won the most votes and delegates in the Republican caucuses in Iowa. Huckabee won 34 percent of the vote and carried seventy-four of Iowa's ninety-nine counties. Romney finished second with 25 percent of the vote and carried twenty-four counties. Paul carried the remaining county. For the most part, Romney's support was concentrated in more urbanized areas of the state, including counties near the Mississippi River on the east and the Missouri River on the west. He won Cedar Rapids, Davenport, Iowa City, and Dubuque in the east, and Sioux City and Council Bluffs in the west. The concentration of support for Huckabee in rural areas with older populations would continue throughout the primary season. However, Huckabee won Polk County, which contains Iowa's capital and largest city of Des Moines.

On the Democratic side, throughout most of 2007 many commentators and party professionals expected Senator Hillary Clinton of New York to receive the Democratic nomination. However, the perceived likelihood of a Democratic victory in 2008 induced several other candidates to contest the Democratic Party's presidential nomination. The Democratic field included Senators Joseph Biden of Delaware, Christopher Dodd of Connecticut, and Barack Obama of Illinois, former senator John Edwards of North Carolina, Governor Bill Richardson of New Mexico, and Representative Dennis Kucinich of Ohio.

As 2007 ended, public opinion polls showed that Clinton, Obama, and Edwards were most popular among Democratic voters with the others well behind. The Obama and Edwards campaigns in particular emphasized the need for change, and it became clear as the campaign continued that the desire for change relative to the unpopular Bush administration resonated more with many voters than did the experience factor. Obama also emphasized his opposition to the war in Iraq. At the caucuses, Obama surprised observers by winning the Iowa precinct caucuses with 38 percent of the vote. Edwards, with 29.7 percent, edged Clinton, with 29.4 percent, for second place. Richardson, Biden, and Dodd split less than 3 percent of the vote and dropped out of the race shortly thereafter.

Iowa's counties were divided roughly evenly between Obama, Edwards, and Clinton. Obama carried forty-four counties, Edwards carried twenty-nine, and Clinton carried twenty-two, with the other four counties being tied. As was the case throughout the primary season, Obama did best among younger, more upscale, and metropolitan voters. He won more than half of the votes in Johnson County, which contains Iowa City and the University of Iowa. He also carried Des Moines as well as the next-largest cities in the state, Cedar Rapids and Davenport. Clinton and Edwards did best in less upscale and rural areas. Edwards did particularly well in rural southern Iowa, where per capita incomes and farmland quality are somewhat lower than in other parts of the state. Clinton's best counties were in normally Republican north-central and southwestern Iowa. Throughout the primary season, in fact, Clinton did best in Republican-oriented counties that would give popular vote majorities to McCain in November.

MAP 2.5

Iowa Caucuses
2008

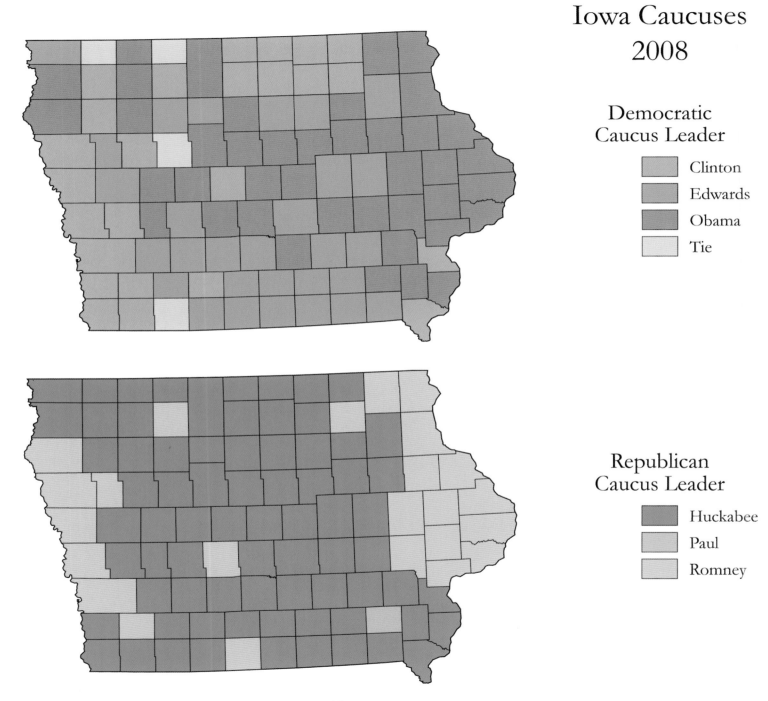

Democratic
Caucus Leader

- Clinton
- Edwards
- Obama
- Tie

Republican
Caucus Leader

- Huckabee
- Paul
- Romney

■ PENNSYLVANIA PRIMARY

HEATHER HOLLEN AND FRED M. SHELLEY

By late February, more than half of the fifty states had held their primary elections or caucuses. Between early March and April 22, however, there were no primary elections at all. While the Republican contest was over, Senators Barack Obama and Hillary Clinton continued their spirited contest for the Democratic Party's nomination.

On April 22, a crucial contest took place in Pennsylvania. Pennsylvania is a blue state, but relative to other strongly Democratic states, many of Pennsylvania's Democratic voters are culturally conservative, older, and more likely to have blue-collar backgrounds. The Appalachian Mountain range, which extends across the width of Pennsylvania from southwest to northeast, divides the Keystone State culturally as well as physically. Southeastern Pennsylvania, including the city of Philadelphia and its suburbs, is part of the Northeastern metropolitan corridor extending from Washington to Boston. West of the mountains, Pittsburgh and other areas are more industrialized, more blue-collar, and more oriented to Appalachia and the Middle West than to Megalopolis.

The preponderance of blue-collar and older voters in Pennsylvania was an essential component in Clinton's victory in the Pennsylvania Democratic primary. Clinton won Pennsylvania easily, getting 1,275,039 votes (55 percent) to 1,061,441 (45 percent) for Obama. Clinton won sixty of Pennsylvania's sixty-seven counties. The seven Obama-majority counties included Philadelphia County, suburban Delaware and Chester Counties, Centre County (State College and Pennsylvania State University), and Dauphin County (the state capital of Harrisburg). Obama's strength among young voters, African Americans, and upscale voters—a pattern prevailing across the United States—was thus evident in Pennsylvania. In contrast, Clinton won 72 percent or more of the vote in 12 counties, many of which were located in rural central Pennsylvania or in the Pittsburgh metropolitan area. With one exception, each of these counties had more elderly people in 2000 than the statewide total of 15.2 percent. Moreover, all but one of these counties had lost population since 2000, and all twelve had less than the statewide African American percentage of 10.7 percent. All twelve counties also have lower per capita incomes than the state per capita income of $20,880. Thus, Clinton did best among older, white, lower-income, blue-collar voters, whereas Obama did best among younger voters, professionals, and African Americans.

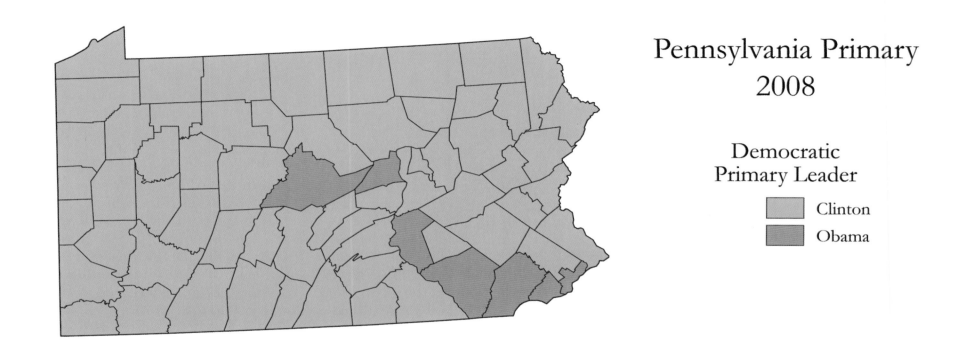

MAP 2.6

Pennsylvania Primary
2008

Democratic
Primary Leader

Clinton
Obama

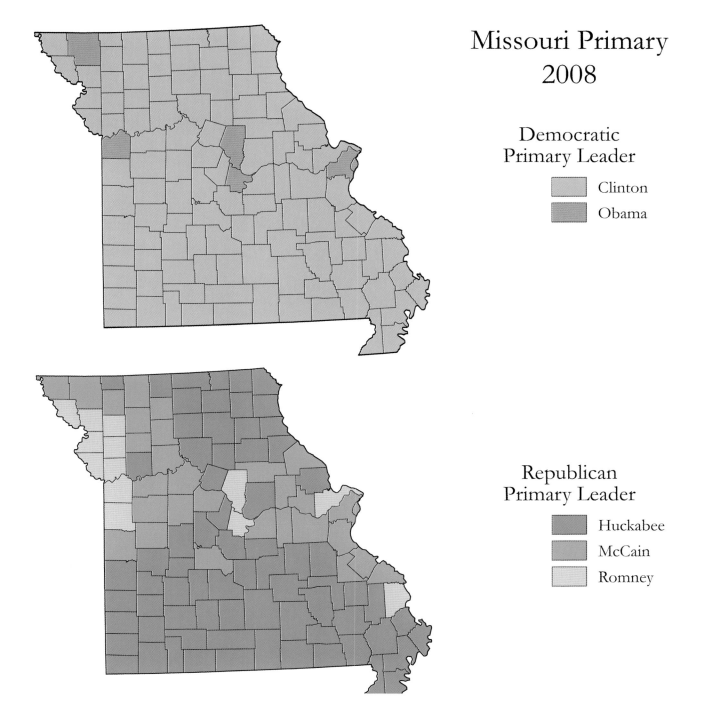

Missouri Primary 2008

MAP 2.7

Democratic Primary Leader

- Clinton
- Obama

Republican Primary Leader

- Huckabee
- McCain
- Romney

MAP 2.8

North Carolina Primary
2008

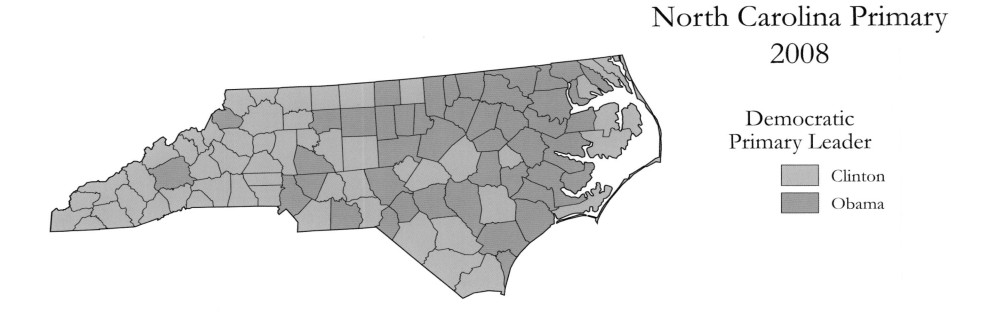

Democratic
Primary Leader

Clinton

Obama

MAP 2.9

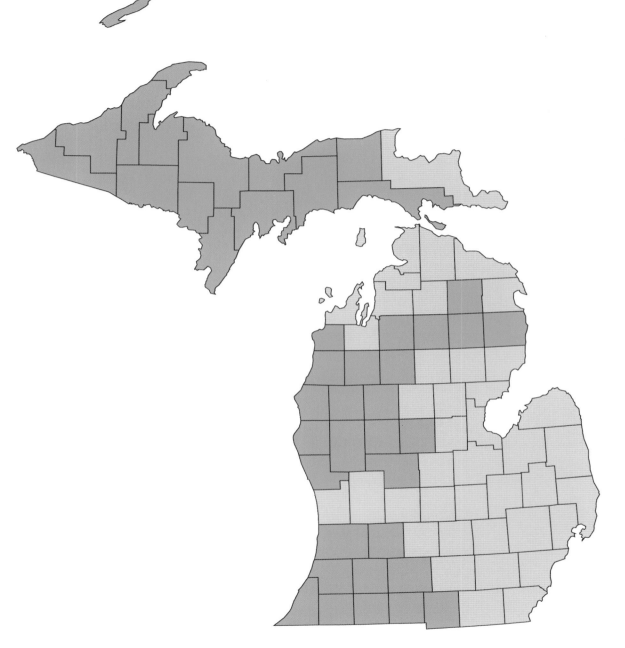

Michigan Primary
2008

Republican
Primary Leader

McCain

Romney

MAP 2.10

Oklahoma Primary
2008

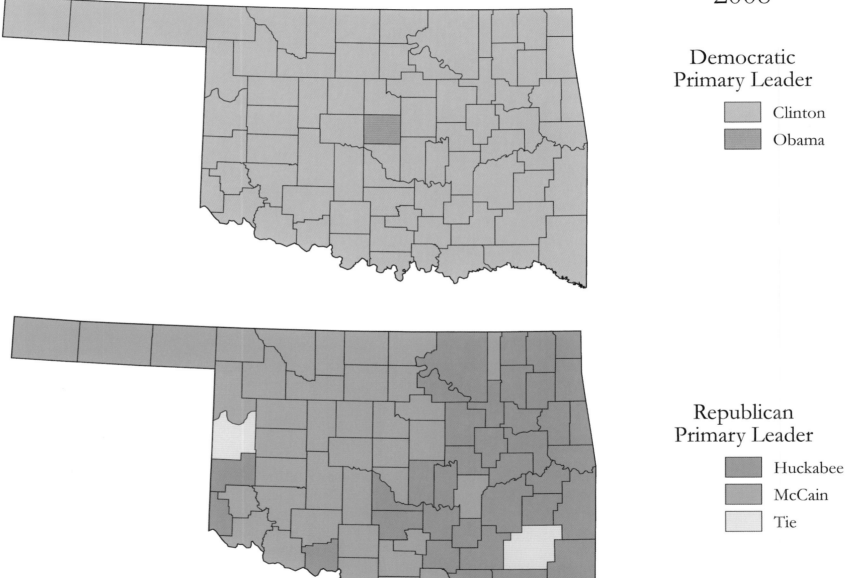

**Democratic
Primary Leader**

Clinton

Obama

**Republican
Primary Leader**

Huckabee

McCain

Tie

MAP 2.11

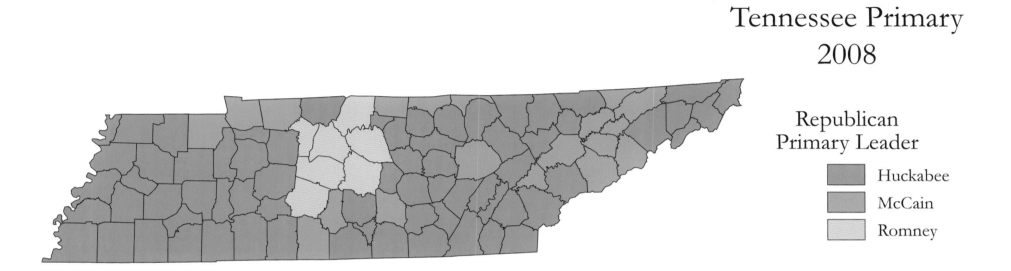

Tennessee Primary
2008

Republican
Primary Leader

Huckabee
McCain
Romney

CHAPTER THREE

CAMPAIGNS

■ ESTIMATED MEDIA ADVERTISING OUTLAYS

GERALD R. WEBSTER

The University of Wisconsin Advertising Project calculated that $1.2 billion was spent to air 2.1 million television ads in the 2008 elections. In total, over three-quarters of the ads were paid for by campaigns of the candidates, with the political parties and interest groups accounting for the remainder. Ads for gubernatorial races ($38 million) accounted for 5 percent of the spending in the general election, followed by Senate campaigns ($162 million, or 20 percent) and House contests ($194 million, or 25 percent). The presidential race accounted for half of the total sum spent in the general election, with 783,000 ad airings costing $396 million. In addition, $201 million was spent on ads in the primaries, meaning $606 million was spent to air 1.1 million ads from the beginning to the end of the presidential race, a new spending record.

A central reason for the new record was Barack Obama's success in fund-raising, which allowed him to forgo federal campaign funds and the limits they impose on total campaign expenditures. John McCain accepted the $84 million potentially available to either campaign in federal funds and could not spend above that sum. Obama, on the other hand, was limited only by the magnitude of the donations to his campaign, and he expended 2.3 times more dollars on television campaign ads than McCain. In fact, in those states in which ads were aired, Obama outspent McCain in every state except Illinois, Minnesota, and West Virginia.

How important are television ads to the success of candidates? Research addressing this question is mixed over whether such ads can generate shifts in voter support for candidates or increase turnout. Regardless, candidates for the presidency spend enormous sums to introduce themselves to the electorate and, at times, in attempts to sully the image of their opponent. There is further a distinct geography to the airing of campaign ads, with candidates actively targeting the electorates of some states while all but ignoring those in others.

When considering all expenditures for television ads in both the primaries and general election, Obama spent funds in every state except Delaware, New Jersey, Vermont, the District of Columbia, and Wyoming. Arguably, the Obama campaign felt confident about wins in the first four and believed that Wyoming's three electoral votes could not be moved from McCain's column. McCain did not air ads in Connecticut, Delaware, Massachusetts, Rhode Island, Maryland, Vermont, New Jersey, the District of Columbia, Hawaii, Kentucky, and Wyoming.

Similar to Obama, McCain likely viewed Kentucky and Wyoming as easy wins and the remaining nine states as strong Obama territory.

Reflecting its importance to the nominating process, both campaigns spent more funds during the primaries and general election per voting-age resident in New Hampshire than in any other state. While McCain spent $6.22 per voting-age resident, Obama spent $10.59. Republican McCain also had high rates of expenditure per voting-age resident in Colorado ($2.18), Iowa ($2.19), Nevada ($2.87), New Mexico ($2.14), and Pennsylvania ($2.26)—all states that he eventually lost to Obama. Democrat Obama's television ad expenditures were not only far larger, but also more broadly distributed. Obama spent more than $2.00 per voting-age resident in Colorado ($2.75), Florida ($2.57), Indiana ($3.48), Iowa ($5.79), Missouri ($2.50), Montana ($2.26), Nevada ($4.74), New Mexico ($2.75), North Carolina ($2.17), Ohio ($2.94), Pennsylvania ($4.10), and Wisconsin ($2.88). Notably, he won all of these states except Missouri and Montana, with particularly important wins in Indiana, Ohio, and North Carolina.

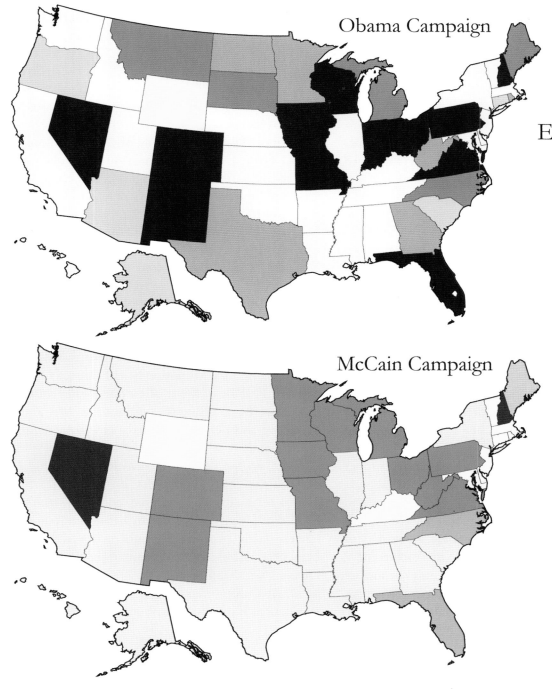

Obama Campaign

McCain Campaign

MAP 3.1

Estimated Media Advertising Outlays

Average Advertising Expenditure
per Voting Age Resident, in Dollars

Obama Campaign	McCain Campaign	
	0	
	.01 to .24	
	.25 to .49	
	.50 to .99	
	1.00 to 2.49	
	2.50 or more	

■ DONOR-SHEDS: INDIVIDUAL CONTRIBUTIONS TO MCCAIN AND OBAMA

CARL T. DAHLMAN

Record-breaking campaign funds were an important part of the 2008 presidential race. The combined total receipt for all candidates and parties topped $1.7 billion. This was 80 percent higher than the amounts in the 2004 cycle and almost three times the total of the 2000 contest. Individual donors remain the major source of campaign finances for major candidates, and in 2008 their contributions were more than $1.3 billion, or 79 percent of all sources. Small donations ($200 or less) accounted for about 32 percent of all contributions, and large contributions ($2,000 or more) were the source of about 31 percent.

Barack Obama's campaign financing was notable for his refusal of public election funds, the first time such money was refused by a major presidential candidate since the system was created in 1976. Doing so allowed Obama to exceed the federal spending limits. Obama raised a total of $748 million, of which 88 percent was from individual contributors. Obama's campaign was also notable for the large number of small donors who gave to his campaign, contributing one-third of his total receipts. Some $659 million came from individuals, of which $246 million were from contributions of $200 or less. By contrast, large donations accounted for only 18.3 percent of his total.

John McCain accepted public financing and so was limited to $84.1 million in total expenditures. Loopholes in the campaign law, which he co-wrote, nevertheless allowed him to use much of the $352 million raised by his campaign. Individual donors contributed $199 million, about 56.7 percent of his total receipts. Small donors and large donors each accounted for about 18 percent of all funds.

Identifying the distribution and size of individual contributions allows us to see clusters of donors. Shown here are individual contributions summed for each three-digit zip code; for example, all zip codes in the Seattle area that begin with 981 are grouped together. These data are limited in one important way: Federal disclosure laws do not require information on donors whose contributions are small, two hundred dollars or less. These small donations are not insignificant. Based on figures released by the Obama campaign, some 2.5 million small donations to his campaign are not included in these data. Shown here, then, are contributions above two hundred dollars, about two-thirds of all funds to either candidate.

Mapping "donor-sheds" reveals a pattern similar to a map of the U.S. population weighted by income. Most contributions come from individuals living in professional and wealthy neighborhoods of major metropolitan areas. These donors are a key part of national political campaigns, yet they represent a small fraction of the population and an even smaller cross-section of American communities. What is, perhaps, more surprising is how both major-party candidates have very similar donor-sheds, even if the actual level of support for McCain was a fraction of that for Obama.

Donors in New York, one of the largest donor-sheds, favored Obama almost five to one over McCain. So, too, did the greater Chicago area, Obama's "hometown," where donors gave Obama at least $50 million but only $11 million to McCain. Northern California donated $66 million to the Obama campaign and only $9 million to McCain. Southern Florida also favored Obama, giving him $18.8 million compared with McCain's $11.9 million. Texas donor-sheds were Obama country, raising three dollars for every two sent to McCain. Obama did very well in the other large donor-sheds, including the metropolitan areas around Boston, Washington, D.C., Atlanta, Minneapolis, and Denver. Obama even led in some of the smallest donor-shed areas of the Upper West, raising twice as much as McCain in Wyoming and performing nearly as well in the rest of the region.

McCain led Obama in several areas, including parts of the Deep South. McCain raised $1.4 million in Mississippi, for example, compared with the $973,000 given to Obama. In his home state, the senator from Arizona did only marginally better than Obama, raising $7.98 million compared with Obama's $7.33 million.

Data source: Federal Election Commission, 2008 Presidential Election, Contributor Data Files.

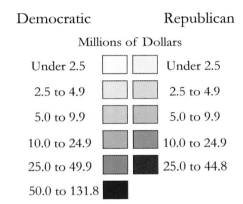

MAP 3.2

Democratic

Republican

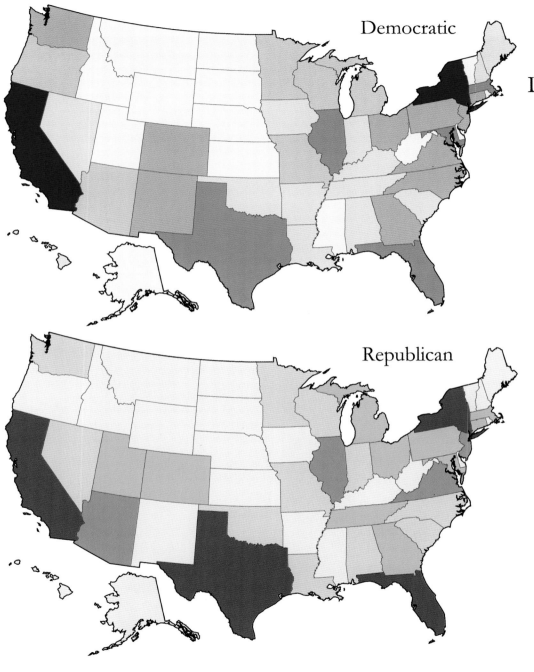

Donor-sheds: Reported Campaign
Contributions to Candidates
Jan. 1, 2007 to Dec. 31, 2008

Democratic   Republican

Millions of Dollars

Under 2.5   Under 2.5

2.5 to 4.9   2.5 to 4.9

5.0 to 9.9   5.0 to 9.9

10.0 to 24.9   10.0 to 24.9

25.0 to 49.9   25.0 to 44.8

50.0 to 131.8

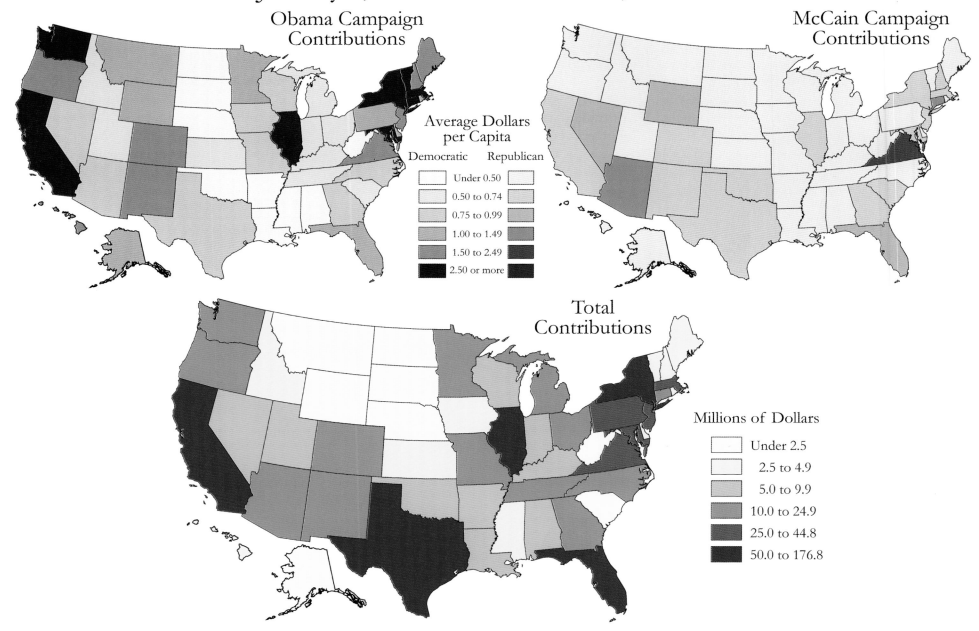

MAP 3.3

Donor-sheds: Reported Campaign Contributions
January 1, 2007 to December 31, 2008

Obama Campaign
Contributions

McCain Campaign
Contributions

Average Dollars
per Capita

Democratic   Republican

	Under 0.50	
	0.50 to 0.74	
	0.75 to 0.99	
	1.00 to 1.49	
	1.50 to 2.49	
	2.50 or more	

Total
Contributions

Millions of Dollars

	Under 2.5
	2.5 to 4.9
	5.0 to 9.9
	10.0 to 24.9
	25.0 to 44.8
	50.0 to 176.8

CAMPAIGN STOPS

GERALD R. WEBSTER

The Democratic and Republican Party conventions to select their respective presidential and vice presidential nominees typically are scheduled in July and August prior to the November general election. To avoid conflicts with the 2008 Summer Olympics, both conventions were scheduled later than is typical, with the Democratic Party's convention concluding on August 28 in Denver, Colorado, and the Republican Party's convention concluding on September 4 in Minneapolis, Minnesota. The Republican convention was the latest ever scheduled.

At the conclusion of the Republican Party convention, both tickets began active campaigning with dozens of campaign stops in different states. The full impact of campaign events remains unclear with respect to the ability of candidates to persuade voters supporting the opposing candidate to switch parties. While such efforts may have a limited ability to alter the proportion of support enjoyed by a ticket, campaign stops can increase enthusiasm among a ticket's supporters and thereby increase voter turnout and campaign donations. Clearly, an increase in voter turnout among a ticket's supporters is critical in close contests, and a rise in campaign donations can increase the purchase of print, radio, and television ads.

In the aggregate, the Republican and Democratic presidential and vice presidential candidates had 380 campaign events from September 1 through November 3 in twenty-eight different states. Republican presidential nominee John McCain had the largest number, with 109 campaign events in twenty different states. He had twenty campaign events in Ohio, nineteen in Pennsylvania, and fourteen in Florida. Thus, 49 percent of all of John McCain's campaign events were in only three states, suggesting he believed Ohio, Pennsylvania, and Florida were critical to an electoral success.

Republican vice-presidential nominee, Sarah Palin, had the second-largest number of campaign events, with ninety-seven from early September through November 3, 2008. Palin visited nineteen different states and like McCain focused heavily on Ohio (nineteen events), Pennsylvania (fourteen events), and Florida (nine events). Thus, in total, 43 percent of Palin's campaign events were in these three swing states. Notably, Palin was the only candidate to visit Arkansas, Maine, New Jersey, and her home state of Alaska.

Between them, Democratic presidential nominee Barack Obama and vice-presidential nominee Joe Biden had 174 campaign events—significantly fewer than the 206 events scheduled by the Republican ticket. Obama had ninety-five events in nineteen different states from September 1 through November 3. He had sixteen events in Florida, thirteen in Ohio, and ten in Virginia. These three states accounted for 41 percent of Obama's ninety-five campaign events. While Virginia would appear to have been targeted by Obama, in response McCain visited Virginia only three times (both Palin and Biden visited the commonwealth six times). Obama was the only candidate to visit Joe Biden's home state of Delaware as well as his home state of Illinois.

Of the four candidates, Democratic vice-presidential nominee Joe Biden had the fewest campaign events at seventy-nine. He also visited the fewest states at seventeen. Biden's events were concentrated in Ohio (nineteen events), Florida (twelve events), Missouri (eight events), Pennsylvania (seven events), Virginia (six events), and North Carolina (six events). Interestingly, Biden visited North Carolina more than any of the other three candidates. While McCain had two events in the state, Palin did not have a single event in North Carolina from early September through November 3. While 39 percent of Biden's campaign events were in hotly contested Ohio and Florida, he had more events not only in North Carolina than any of the other candidates, but also in Missouri, and he was the only candidate to visit West Virginia and Texas.

Twenty-two states had no events by any of the four candidates from early September through November 3. These states tended to be in the South and the West, where Republican victories were highly likely, and in the Northeast and Pacific Coast, where Democratic victories were all but assumed. Hence, generally Republican states such as Alabama, Kentucky, Louisiana, and South Carolina in the South had no events. Strongly Republican states in the West such as Wyoming, Utah, Oklahoma, Nebraska, and Kansas also were not visited by any of the four candidates. Similarly, generally strong Democratic northeastern states such as Connecticut, Massachusetts, Vermont, and Rhode Island, and Pacific Coast states, including California, Washington, Oregon, and Hawaii, were not visited by either the Democratic or Republican nominees. Arguably, both campaigns made judgments about where their monetary and time investments would generate the greatest return.

The final week of the campaign witnessed a flurry of campaign events by all four candidates. Eighty-six (23 percent) of the total 380 campaign events from early September through November 3 occurred in the seven days prior to the election (October 28 through November 3). John McCain and Sarah Palin had a total of fifty campaign events, as compared to the thirty-six scheduled by Barack Obama and Joe Biden. Not surprisingly, given the above discussion, the states most targeted were Ohio (twenty-three campaign events), Florida (fifteen campaign events), and Pennsylvania (thirteen campaign events). McCain and Palin had fifteen campaign events in Ohio to only eight by Obama and Biden. The Republican ticket scheduled eleven campaign events in Pennsylvania, while Obama and Biden each had a single campaign event in the state. It is also interesting, given the competitiveness of Virginia and North Carolina, that McCain visited each state only once in the final week of the campaign. In comparison, Obama had three events in Virginia and two events in North Carolina. At the end, the Democratic ticket won Ohio, Florida, Pennsylvania, North Carolina, and Virginia.

Presidential Election Campaign Stops
September - November 2008

MAP 3.4

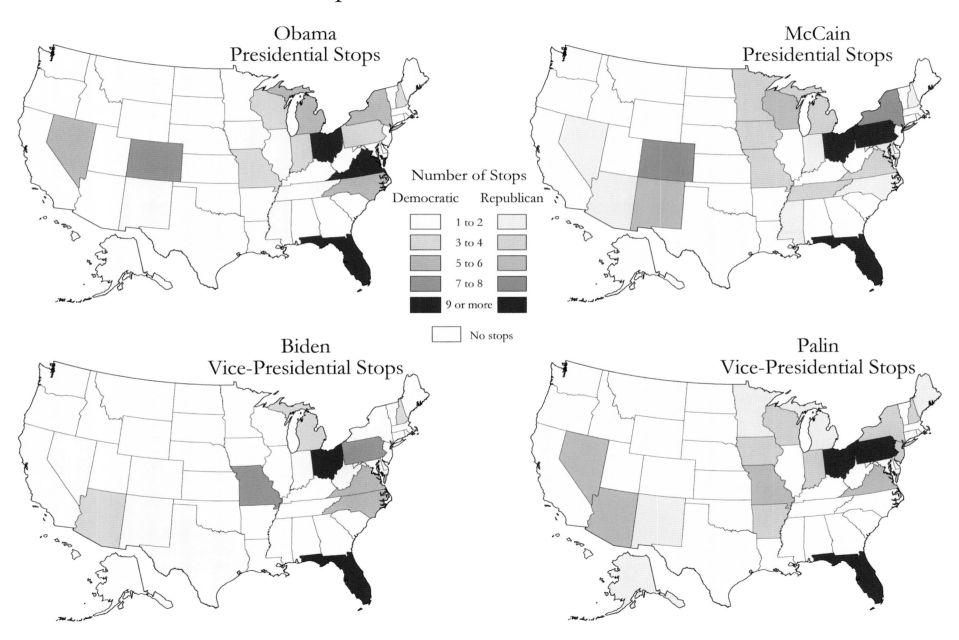

Obama
Presidential Stops

McCain
Presidential Stops

Number of Stops

Democratic   Republican

1 to 2
3 to 4
5 to 6
7 to 8
9 or more

No stops

Biden
Vice-Presidential Stops

Palin
Vice-Presidential Stops

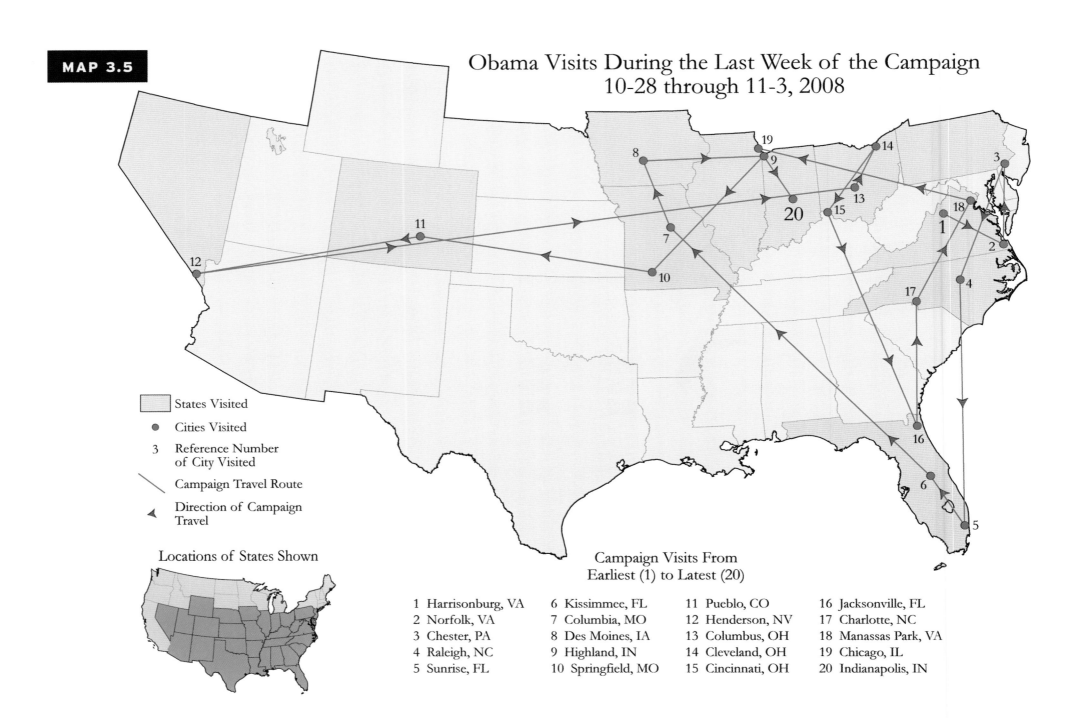

MAP 3.5

Obama Visits During the Last Week of the Campaign 10-28 through 11-3, 2008

States Visited

● Cities Visited

3 Reference Number of City Visited

Campaign Travel Route

◄ Direction of Campaign Travel

Locations of States Shown

Campaign Visits From
Earliest (1) to Latest (20)

1 Harrisonburg, VA	6 Kissimmee, FL	11 Pueblo, CO	16 Jacksonville, FL
2 Norfolk, VA	7 Columbia, MO	12 Henderson, NV	17 Charlotte, NC
3 Chester, PA	8 Des Moines, IA	13 Columbus, OH	18 Manassas Park, VA
4 Raleigh, NC	9 Highland, IN	14 Cleveland, OH	19 Chicago, IL
5 Sunrise, FL	10 Springfield, MO	15 Cincinnati, OH	20 Indianapolis, IN

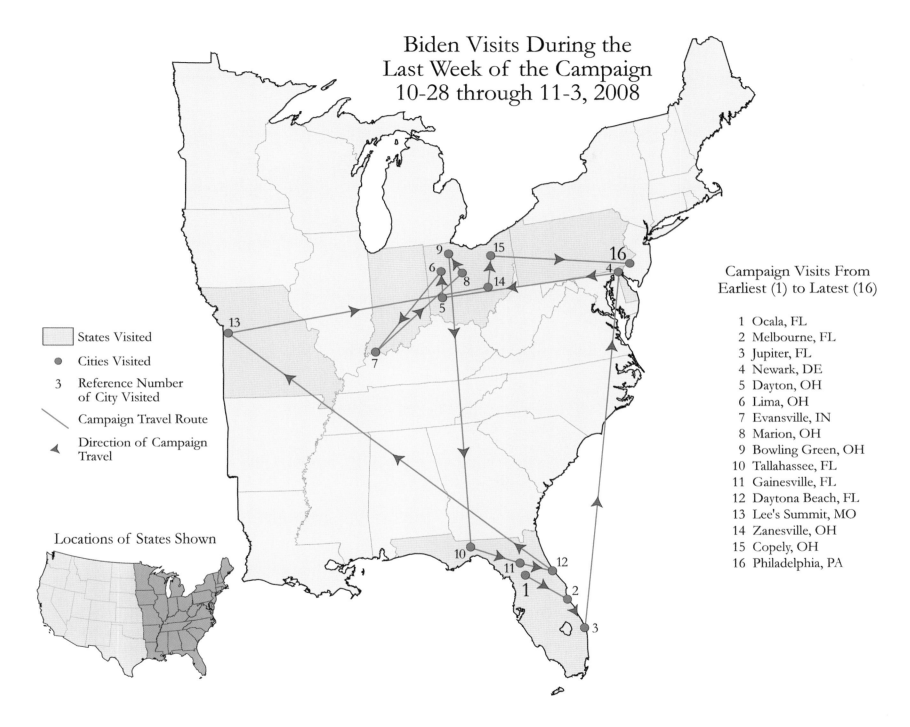

Biden Visits During the Last Week of the Campaign 10-28 through 11-3, 2008

MAP 3.6

States Visited

● Cities Visited

3 Reference Number of City Visited

Campaign Travel Route

▲ Direction of Campaign Travel

Locations of States Shown

Campaign Visits From Earliest (1) to Latest (16)

1 Ocala, FL
2 Melbourne, FL
3 Jupiter, FL
4 Newark, DE
5 Dayton, OH
6 Lima, OH
7 Evansville, IN
8 Marion, OH
9 Bowling Green, OH
10 Tallahassee, FL
11 Gainesville, FL
12 Daytona Beach, FL
13 Lee's Summit, MO
14 Zanesville, OH
15 Copely, OH
16 Philadelphia, PA

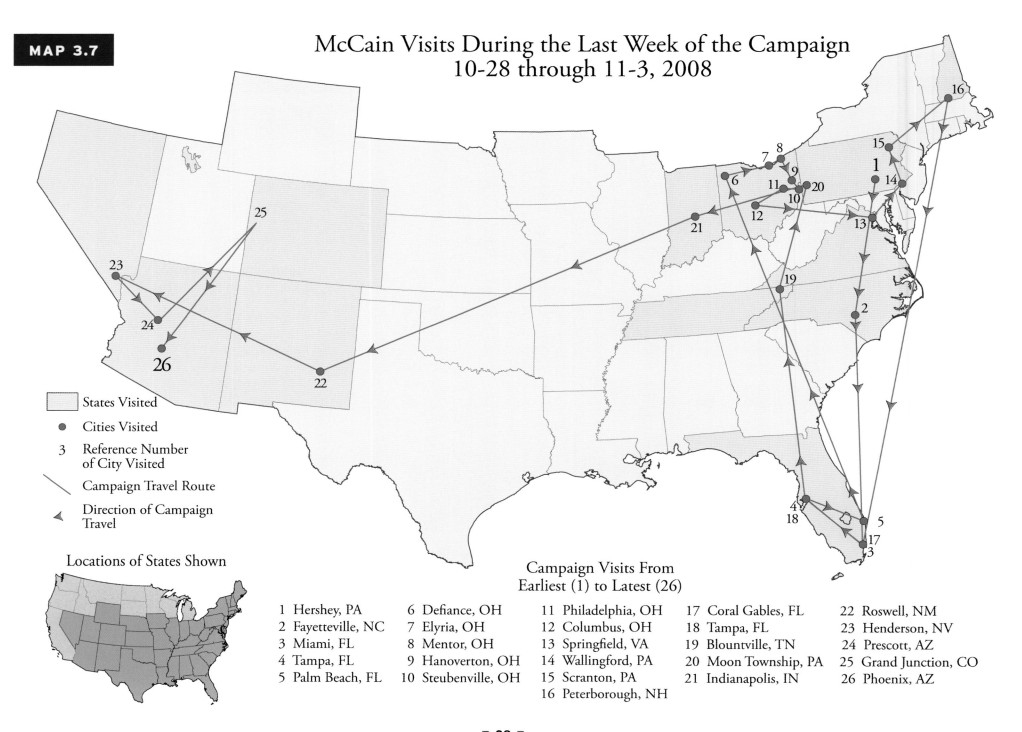

MAP 3.7

McCain Visits During the Last Week of the Campaign
10-28 through 11-3, 2008

States Visited

Cities Visited

3 Reference Number of City Visited

Campaign Travel Route

Direction of Campaign Travel

Locations of States Shown

Campaign Visits From
Earliest (1) to Latest (26)

1 Hershey, PA	6 Defiance, OH	11 Philadelphia, OH	17 Coral Gables, FL	22 Roswell, NM
2 Fayetteville, NC	7 Elyria, OH	12 Columbus, OH	18 Tampa, FL	23 Henderson, NV
3 Miami, FL	8 Mentor, OH	13 Springfield, VA	19 Blountville, TN	24 Prescott, AZ
4 Tampa, FL	9 Hanoverton, OH	14 Wallingford, PA	20 Moon Township, PA	25 Grand Junction, CO
5 Palm Beach, FL	10 Steubenville, OH	15 Scranton, PA	21 Indianapolis, IN	26 Phoenix, AZ
		16 Peterborough, NH		

Palin Visits During the Last Week of the Campaign
10-28 through 11-3, 2008

MAP 3.8

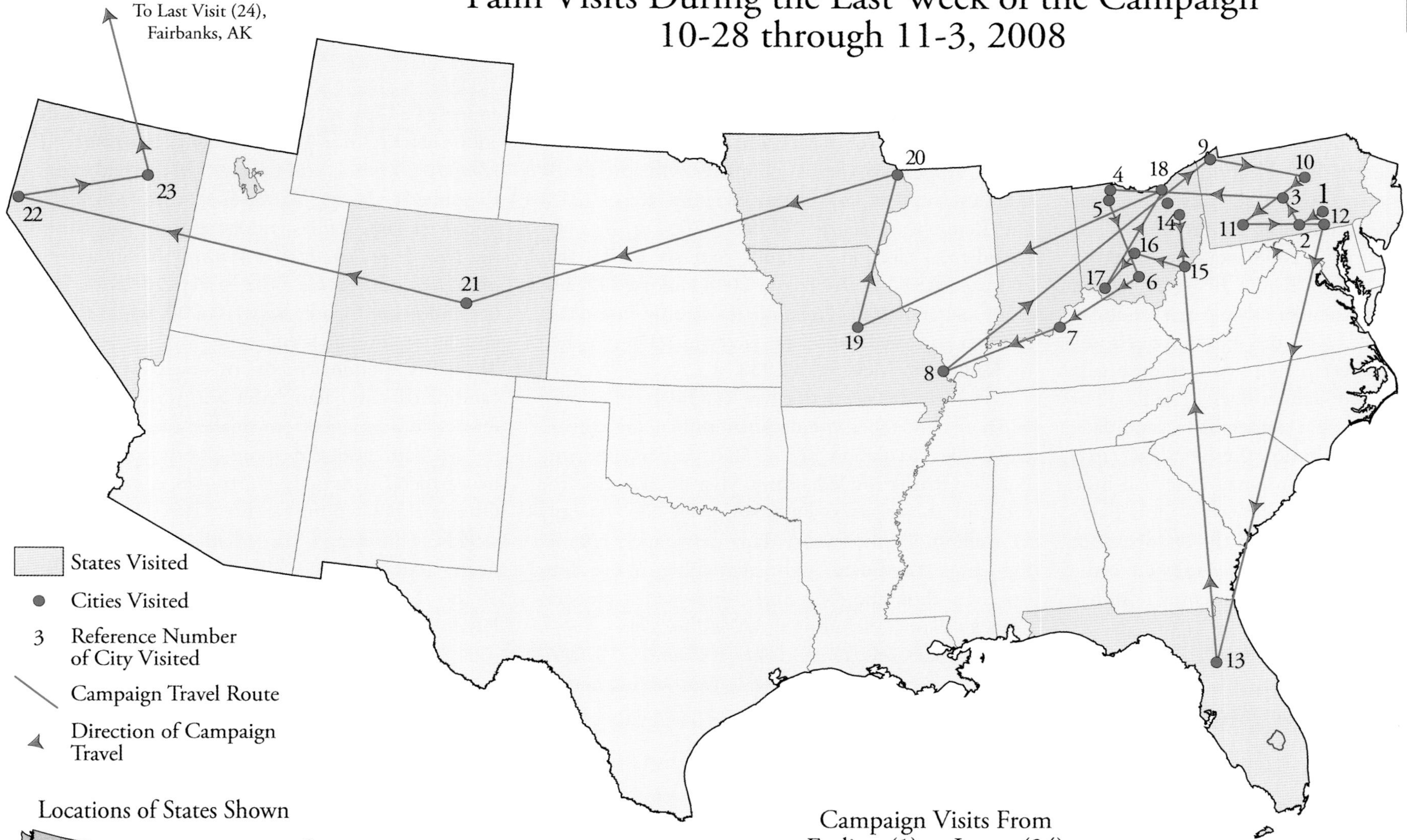

To Last Visit (24),
Fairbanks, AK

States Visited

● Cities Visited

3 Reference Number
of City Visited

Campaign Travel Route

◄ Direction of Campaign
Travel

Locations of States Shown

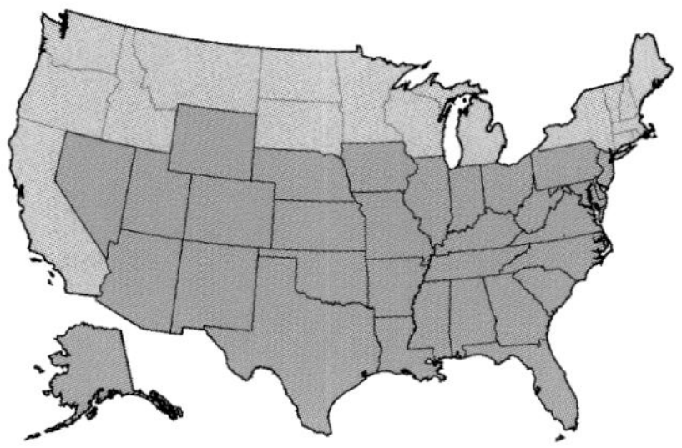

Campaign Visits From
Earliest (1) to Latest (24)

1 Hershey, PA	6 Chillicothe, OH	11 Latrobe, PA	16 Columbus, OH	21 Colorado Springs, CO
2 Shippensburg, PA	7 Jeffersonville, IN	12 York, PA	17 Owensville, OH	22 Reno, NV
3 University Park, PA	8 Cape Girardeau, MO	13 Ocala, FL	18 Lakewood, OH	23 Elko, NV
4 Toledo, OH	9 Erie, PA	14 Canton, OH	19 Jefferson City, MO	24 Fairbanks, AK
5 Bowling Green, OH	10 Williamsport, PA	15 Marietta, OH	20 Dubuque, IA	

■ NEWSPAPER ENDORSEMENTS

GERALD R. WEBSTER

There is a long-standing tradition for the editorial boards of many newspapers to endorse candidates for various election races in the days prior to the election. Do such endorsements have an effect on the outcome of an election? While surely a debatable issue, a 2008 working paper by Brian G. Knight and Chun-Fang Chiang concluded that in certain circumstances, newspaper endorsements can have an effect on the selections of some voters. The greatest effect pertains to a traditionally conservative paper's endorsing a liberal candidate or a liberal paper's endorsing a conservative candidate. Thus, while in the 2008 election the *New York Times* endorsement of Barack Obama may have had little influence on voter decision making, it is more likely that some influence emerged from the endorsement of Obama by the *Anchorage Daily News* since it is the largest daily in Republican vice-presidential nominee Sarah Palin's home state.

Using tallies released by *Editor and Publisher* magazine and added to on Wikipedia, a total of 296 daily newspapers endorsed Democrat Barack Obama

for president as compared with 180 dailies supporting Republican John McCain. This wide differential in support of Obama compares with the nearly identical support for Democrat John Kerry (213) and Republican George W. Bush (205) in the 2004 presidential election. Notably, sixty-six dailies that endorsed Republican Bush in 2004 endorsed Democrat Obama in 2008. In comparison, only eleven dailies that endorsed Democrat Kerry in 2004 switched to Republican McCain in 2008.

The gap between the two candidates was even wider if newspaper circulation numbers are considered. The circulation of the 296 dailies endorsing Barack Obama totaled nearly 31 million, while the total for those papers endorsing McCain was only 12 million. Of the twenty daily newspapers endorsing either candidate with circulations above four hundred thousand, seventeen endorsed Democrat Barack Obama, including the *New York Times, Boston Globe, Los Angeles Times, Chicago Tribune, Philadelphia Inquirer, Houston Chronicle, Denver Post,* and *St. Louis Post-Dispatch*. The *Los Angeles Times* had never

endorsed a Democrat for president and had made no endorsement since 1972. Notably, the *Denver Post, Houston Chronicle,* and *Chicago Tribune* had endorsed Republican George W. Bush in the 2004 election. The three large dailies endorsing John McCain were the *New York Post, Dallas Morning News,* and Phoenix's *Arizona Republic*. The mean circulation of dailies endorsing Obama was 103,000, while the mean circulation for dailies endorsing McCain was 66,000. Thus, if the endorsements of newspapers can aid a candidate's campaign, McCain was hampered by fewer endorsements from smaller-circulation dailies.

McCain also did more poorly among weekly newspapers, with only thirty-two endorsements to Obama's 111 endorsements. The 111 newspaper weeklies endorsing Obama had a total circulation of nearly four million, while the aggregate circulation of the thirty-two endorsing McCain was 333,000. Finally, seventy-eight college newspapers, with a total circulation of 768,000, endorsed Obama; only two college newspapers, with a total circulation of 179,000, endorsed McCain.

Daily Newspaper Endorsements
Obama 2008 Presidential Campaign

MAP 3.9

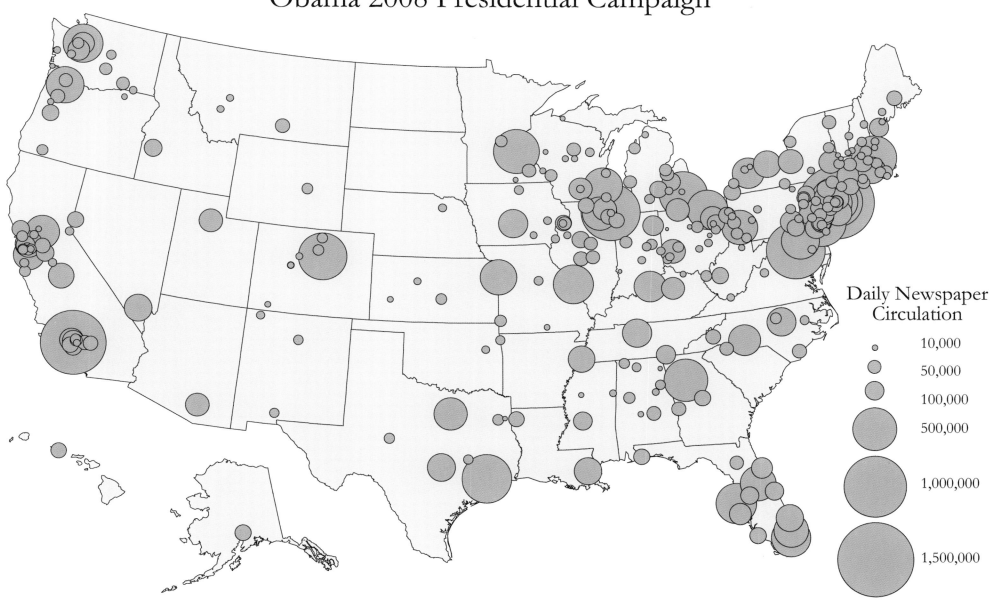

Daily Newspaper
Circulation

· 10,000

· 50,000

· 100,000

· 500,000

· 1,000,000

· 1,500,000

MAP 3.10

Daily Newspaper Endorsements
McCain 2008 Presidential Campaign

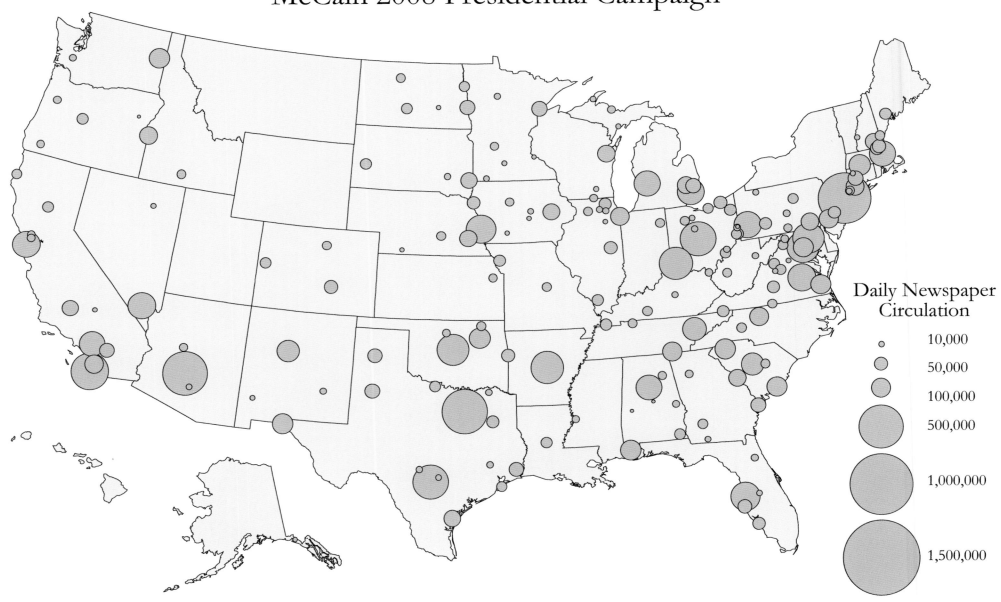

Daily Newspaper
Circulation

10,000

50,000

100,000

500,000

1,000,000

1,500,000

■ THE PRESIDENTIAL PLACEMARK POLL

MATTHEW ZOOK, MARK GRAHAM, AND TAYLOR SHELTON

In August 2008 a Google Maps search was conducted on a quarter-degree grid of all the land mass in North America (roughly 47,000 points) for the keywords "Barack Obama" or "John McCain." For every search, the number of user-generated (as opposed to Google-generated) placemarks containing each keyword was collected. A Google Maps placemark is data in cyberspace (e.g., a piece of text, a digital image, etc.) that are georeferenced to a particular location. At the time the data were collected, user-generated placemarks were a relatively new and innovative use of the Internet.

This visualization represents the aggregation of myriad decisions of Internet users (versus mainstream political, media, or corporate interests) to associate the name of a presidential candidate with a specific place. Common examples of these placemarks include locations of campaign rallies, campaign headquarters, documentations of volunteer activities, or simply positive or negative declarations for a candidate. The difference between the two terms was mapped onto every point in North America with blue and red circles used to indicate a larger number of references for either Obama or McCain, respectively (larger circles indicate a larger degree of difference). An analysis of these differences sheds light on how the two candidates were represented in the emerging user-driven, georeferenced Internet.

Obama clearly dominates this virtual electoral landscape. In North America 71 percent of all references are to Obama, and only 29 percent are to McCain (a statistic that contrasts sharply with the 53 percent–46 percent split in the popular vote). Obama's highest margin of difference is in Chicago, a city he served for four years as an Illinois senator. He not only had a strong showing in most of the traditionally Democratic-leaning areas of the country, but also in many areas considered to be solidly Republican states (e.g., Texas, Oklahoma, and much of the Southeast). In Wyoming, for instance, there are more references to Obama than McCain at every single point. This is despite the fact that John McCain won 65 percent of the popular vote in Wyoming. Clearly, the online representation of interest in the candidates for the 2008 election does not mirror the offline results.

There are, however, places where online presence corresponds well to key locations for the election. For example, the highest margin of difference favoring John McCain is in Rochester, New Hampshire.

Indeed, McCain is far more visible than Obama throughout the state. This fact likely owes much to McCain's strong grassroots support in New Hampshire, which ultimately helped him to win the state's crucial Republican presidential primary. Also of interest is that two of the other states in which McCain also has a high degree of visibility are the other early primary states of Iowa and Michigan. Likewise, key locations for Barack Obama such as Portland, Oregon, where 70,000 people rallied for him in May 2008, and Denver, the site of the Democratic convention, contain disproportionally large numbers of placemarks.

Much media coverage was devoted to the Obama campaign's innovative uses of the Internet to rally supporters; these results provide evidence for those claims. In most places Barack Obama has a level of visibility in the virtual landscape that is unmatched by John McCain. This map further demonstrates that georeferenced cyberspace, or "Geoweb," is neither a simple reflection of the physical places it references nor simply disconnected from material realities. Instead it represents a new layer of place that will ultimately become an important political battleground for any aspiring candidate.

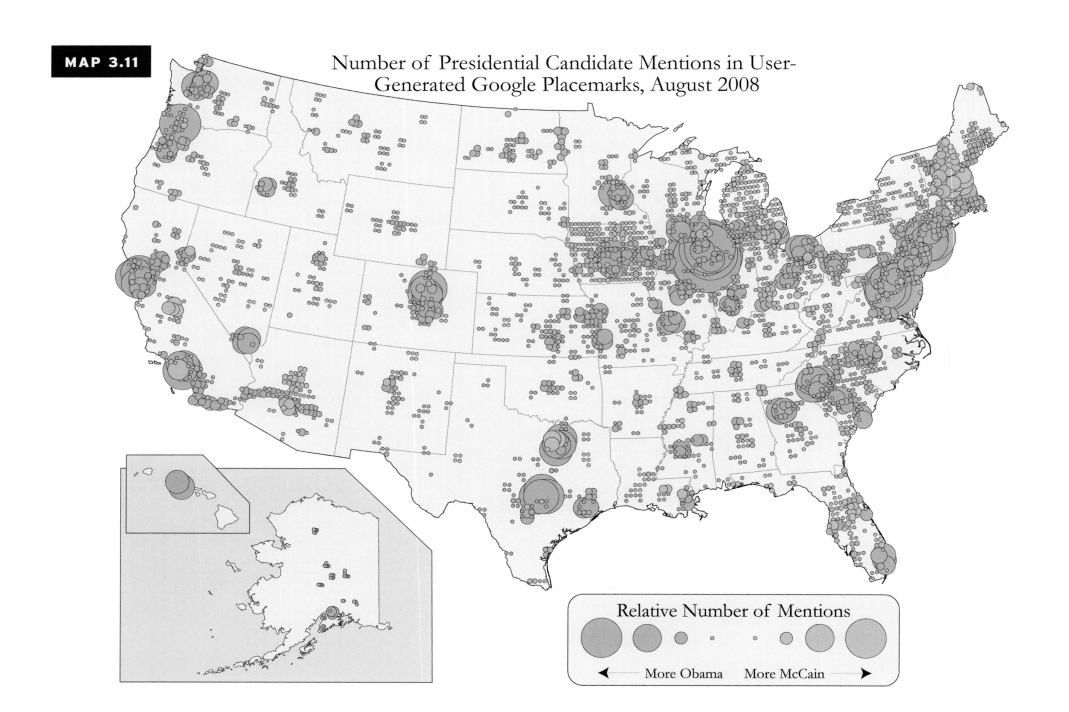

MAP 3.11

Number of Presidential Candidate Mentions in User-
Generated Google Placemarks, August 2008

Relative Number of Mentions

◀ ⋯⋯ More Obama   More McCain ⋯⋯ ▶

CROWDSOURCING DEMOCRATIC TRANSPARENCY: THE TWITTER VOTE REPORT

SEAN P. GORMAN AND ANDREW J. TURNER

The Twitter Vote Report map illustrates crowd-sourced responses from voters of the average wait times at polling stations across the United States during the 2008 presidential election between Barack Obama and John McCain. The Twitter Vote Report platform is an open public reporting system to track election conditions as citizens cast their ballots. The project's goal is to make it easy for anyone to send in a report describing the wait time, overall rating, and any complications that are impairing the person's ability to participate in an election.

In preparing this map, wait time was chosen as the variable to visualize, using proportional symbols with five categories of equal interval classifications. Wait times ranged from one minute and fifteen seconds to a little over seven and a half hours. Participation in Twitter Vote Report had an urban bias, which is reflected in the map, but the 9,148 volunteered measurements provide a large, if biased, sample. Since the data are volunteered, there is an inherent bias in the sample, but several approaches were used to minimize bias in the data. Voters could report polling conditions through email, phone calls, Twitter, iPhone, and Android applications as well as SMS text messages. A group of volunteers cleaned and validated the information as well as produced a Web feed of the data that was publicly consumable. The success of the project spawned the development of several crowdsourced data collection tools such as Ushahidi and Swift River.

The map shows some distinct patterns of locations experiencing long wait times. The Boston-to-Washington corridor illustrates several long wait times, which are especially prominent in Boston, New York City, and Washington, D.C. There is also a belt of long waits through the Midwest in St. Louis, Detroit, Chicago, and Kansas City. The third noticeable concentration of long wait times runs through the South, including Memphis, Birmingham, Atlanta, Columbia, Charleston, Charlotte, and Virginia Beach. Also notable are the states that have consistent short wait times and significant number of observations, consisting of Colorado, Oregon, Washington, Texas, Iowa, Idaho, and Maine.

Crowdsourced data have inherent bias but also provide a new source of information with the ability to create massive data samples of the population. The potential to combine crowdsourced data with other traditional survey and statistical data is just beginning to be understood. In the area of vote monitoring there is a great opportunity for looking at issues of equality and access. Examining the relationship between wait times and voting conditions across the spectrum of race, gender, and income holds the promise of new insight into election fairness and equality.

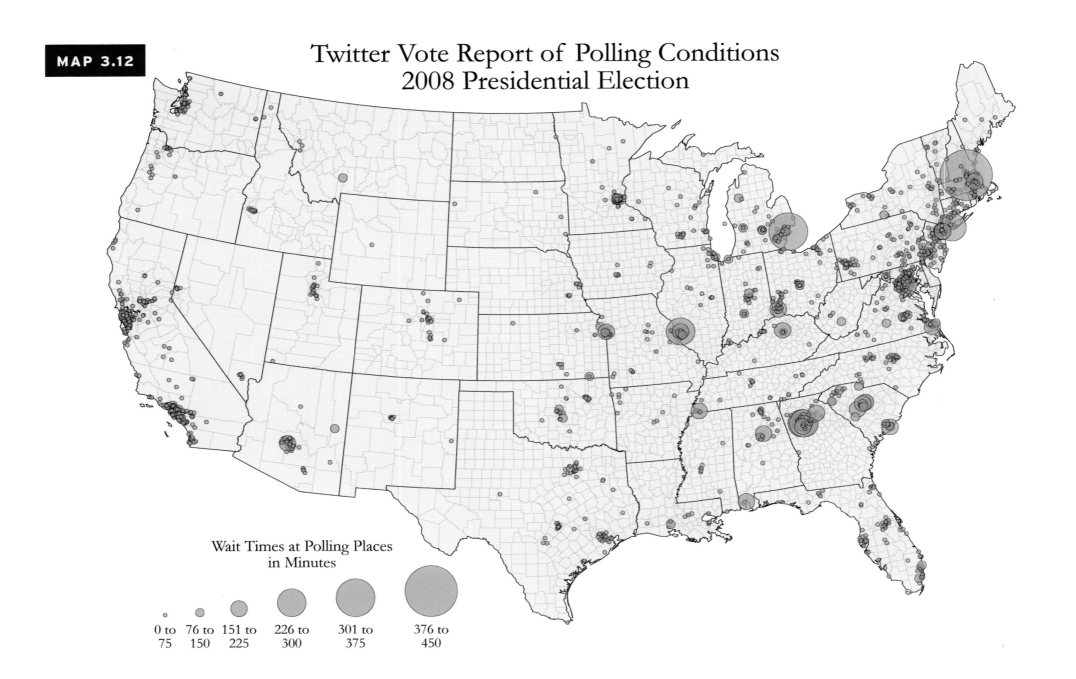

MAP 3.12

Twitter Vote Report of Polling Conditions
2008 Presidential Election

Wait Times at Polling Places
in Minutes

0 to 75   76 to 150   151 to 225   226 to 300   301 to 375   376 to 450

CENTERS OF PARTISAN VOTING: MEDIAN CENTERS OF DEMOCRATIC AND REPUBLICAN VOTES, 2000, 2004, AND 2008

RICHARD L. MORRILL

Where are the foci of the Democratic and the Republican vote? Map 3.13 maps the orthogonal median centers for the past three elections. All the centers are in southern Indiana, as is indeed the median center of the U.S. population. This observation should surprise those who have followed the much farther westward progression of the center of population as reported in the press. The difference is that the popular center is bivariate mean center, or center of gravity, which has the property of minimizing the sum of squares of the population, while the bivariate median center minimizes the simple travel, that is, is the true point of minimum aggregate travel. We, following the U.S. Census Bureau, calculate the simpler orthogonal median centers, defined as the point from which one-half the relevant population is north, half east, half south, and half west, rather than an intuitively simple and straightforward measure. We identify those measures for the Democratic and the Republican votes for three elections.

It may again surprise the observer that these centers are so far north and east. But they are accurate, despite the rapid long-term growth of the population in the South and West. Even today the population is denser in the northeast corner of the nation (the home of Megalopolis) than in any other quadrant.

The reader may also be surprised at how close together the centers are over the past three elections and between the two major parties. In 2008, the center of the Democratic voting was near Rugby, Indiana, near the boundary between Bartholomew and Decatur Counties, east of Columbus and southeast of Indianapolis. The Republican center was in the Tillery Hill State Recreation Area, in southwest Orange County, which is west of Louisville, Kentucky. The Democratic center was just 66 miles (106 km) north and east of the Republican center. While the two centers do show that the national Republican vote is moderately south and west of the Democratic, especially in 2008, their closeness also shows that there are many Democrats in the South and West and many Republicans in the Northeast. This observation is noted on the map, which shows the geography of the absolute vote instead of the familiar red and blue map of counties carried by Democrats or Republicans.

Between 2000 and 2008 the Democratic vote center moved just a few miles west and about 20 miles (32 km) south. The slight southward move reflects, despite Republican domination of the South, Obama's success in turnout and margins among black and Hispanic voters in the South. The Republican center also moved, about 45 miles (72 km) east and 30 miles (48 km) south over the past eight years, probably reflecting the lesser role of Texas in 2008 compared with 2000 and 2004. Both the Democratic and Republican centers, however, are in Republican territory.

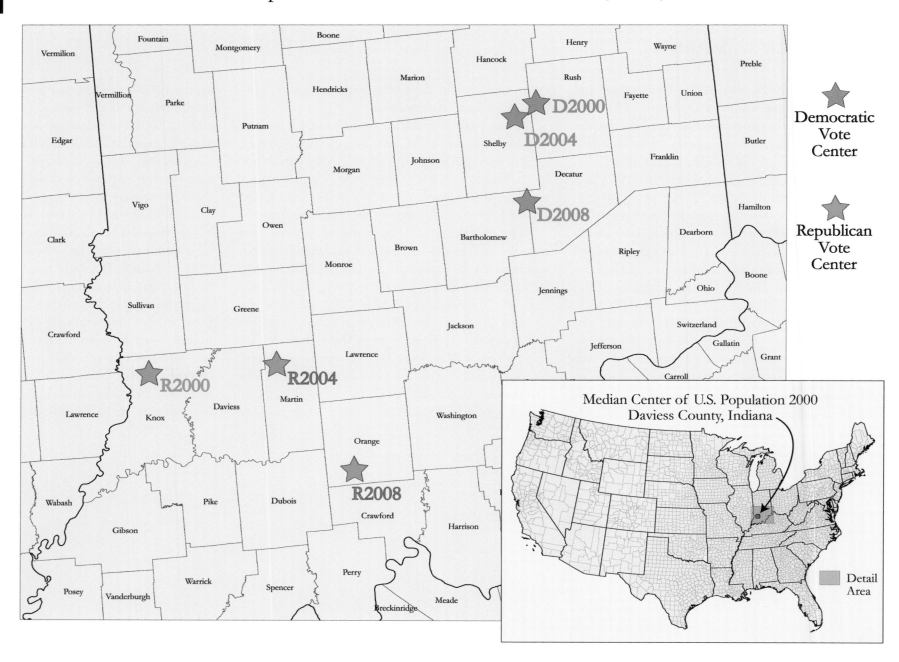

MAP 3.13

Median Centers of Republican and Democratic Votes 2000, 2004, and 2008

D2000

D2004

D2008

R2000

R2004

R2008

Democratic
Vote
Center

Republican
Vote
Center

Median Center of U.S. Population 2000
Daviess County, Indiana

Detail
Area

REFERENCES

Ansolabehere, S., L. Lessem, and J. M. Snyder. 2006. "The Orientation of Newspaper Endorsements in U.S. Elections, 1940–2002." *Quarterly Journal of Political Science* 1 (4): 393–404.

CNN. 2008. "Media Expenditures by Obama and McCain Campaigns." http://www.cnn.com/ELECTION/2008/map/ad.spending, accessed June 12, 2009.

Dahlman, C. T. "At Last Count: Outside Influence." *Atlantic Monthly*, January 2001, 57.

Federal Election Commission. 2009. "2008 Presidential Campaign Financial Activity Summarized: Receipts Nearly Double 2004 Total." Washington, D.C.

Freedman, P., and Goldstein, K. 1999. "Measuring Media Exposure and the Effects of Negative Campaign Ads." *American Journal of Political Science* 43 (4): 1189–1208.

"FRIDAY Final (?) Tally Of Newspaper Endorsements— Obama In Landslide, at 287–159." EditorandPublisher .com. http://www.editorandpublisher.com/eandp/news/article_display.jsp?vnu_content_id=1003875230, November 7, 2008.

Holbrook, Thomas M. 2002. "Did the Whistle-Stop Campaign Matter?." *Political Science and Politics* 35 (1): 59–66.

Kahn, K. F., and P. J. Kenney. 2002. "The Slant of the News: How Editorial Endorsements Influence Campaign Coverage and Citizens' Views of Candidates." *American Political Science Review* 96 (2): 381–94.

Knight, Brian G., and C-F. Chiang. 2008. "Media Bias and Influence: Evidence from Newspaper Endorsements." National Bureau of Economic Research, Working Paper No. W14445, http://papers.ssrn.com/sol3/papers.cfm?abstract_id=1289679.

Krasno, Jonathan S., and Green, Donald J. 2008. "Do Televised Presidential Ads Increase Voter Turnout?" *Journal of Politics* 70 (1): 245–61.

"Newspaper Endorsements in the Unites States Presidential Election, 2008." *Wikipedia*, http://en.wikipedia.org/wiki/Newspaper_endorsements_in_the_United States presidential_ election,_2008.

O'Loughlin, John. 1981. "The Neighborhood Effect in Urban Voting Surfaces: A Cross-National Analysis." In *Political Studies from Spatial Perspectives*, edited by Alan D. Burnett and Peter J. Taylor, 357–88. New York: Wiley.

Shaw, Daron R. 1999. "The Effects of TV Ads and Candidate Appearances on Statewide Presidential Votes, 1988-96." *American Political Science Review* 93 (2): 345–61.

University of Wisconsin Advertising Project. 2008. "Political Advertising in 2008." http://wiscadproject.wisc.edu/wiscads_report_031710.pdf, accessed July 28, 2009.

CHAPTER FOUR

GENERAL ELECTIONS

■ OVERVIEW

Geographers and others with interests in elections are interested in a variety of ways, and the results are evident in the geographical landscape. The patterns of the popular vote for president are very important in any cartographic or geographic analysis, but so are the various other measures about the results themselves. The nearly fifty maps in this chapter illustrate the ways we look at elections and election results.

The first maps look at the 2008 county results (who won the county) for Obama and McCain and also the results of those voting for another party, such as the Libertarian Party and Ralph Nader's party. Even though these minor parties were not significant in any state's final results, still one can observe cities and counties where they achieved some successes. Supplementing the countywide voting patterns are maps that show the popular vote for Obama and McCain for each state. A deeper examination into the Obama and McCain results can be obtained by looking at the voting margin and the differences between the 2004 and 2008 elections. We

also include graphs that show how Obama and McCain performed in the largest metropolitan areas and in the "micropolitan" (small populated counties). These latter maps illustrate the point made elsewhere in this chapter, that one major area of Obama support was in these largest cities and counties.

Interpreting the cartographic patterns and geographic results of any presidential election requires looking at previous elections. It is for this reason that we include county-level votes for Republican and Democratic candidates from 1948 to 2004. The average Democratic and Republican votes are presented, and from these one can compare the county, metropolitan area, or regional results from one election to another. When elections are compared, one is struck by the strong similarity in the way many counties, cities, and regions vote. Very few counties change their party voting pattern significantly over three or four election cycles.

Also included are maps of voter turnout, that is, what percentage of the voters actually voted for

president. Social scientists, including geographers and political scientists, look for meaningful patterns and relate them to income, education level, and population change. Surprising to many readers may be the low turnouts in some regions, especially the South and in major large metropolitan areas. High voter turnout is more a feature of a region's political culture than heritage or party affiliation. The overall turnout in 2008 is not that different from four years earlier.

The final maps look at the 2008 presidential results in ten crucial or "swing" states, that is, those where the political parties and their campaign staffs thought the final outcome would be decided. Maps are included for Colorado, Indiana, Florida, New Mexico, North Carolina, and Virginia, all states that Obama won but that Bush won four years earlier. One can compare the 2004 and 2008 county votes in each state to identify those counties that switched their party allegiance from four years earlier.

MAP 4.1

Democratic Popular Vote
2008 Presidential Election

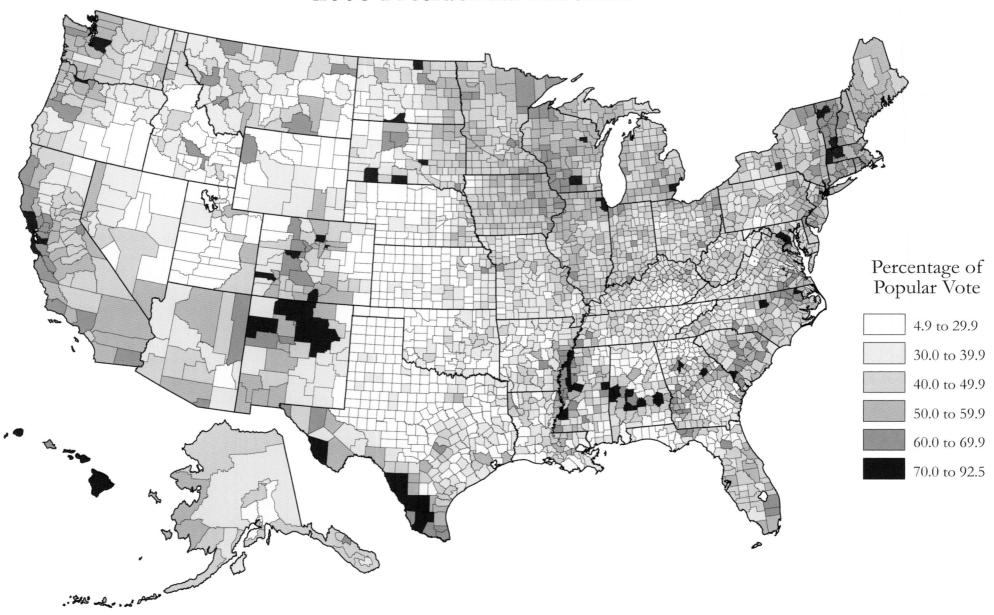

Percentage of
Popular Vote

4.9 to 29.9

30.0 to 39.9

40.0 to 49.9

50.0 to 59.9

60.0 to 69.9

70.0 to 92.5

Republican Popular Vote
2008 Presidential Election

MAP 4.2

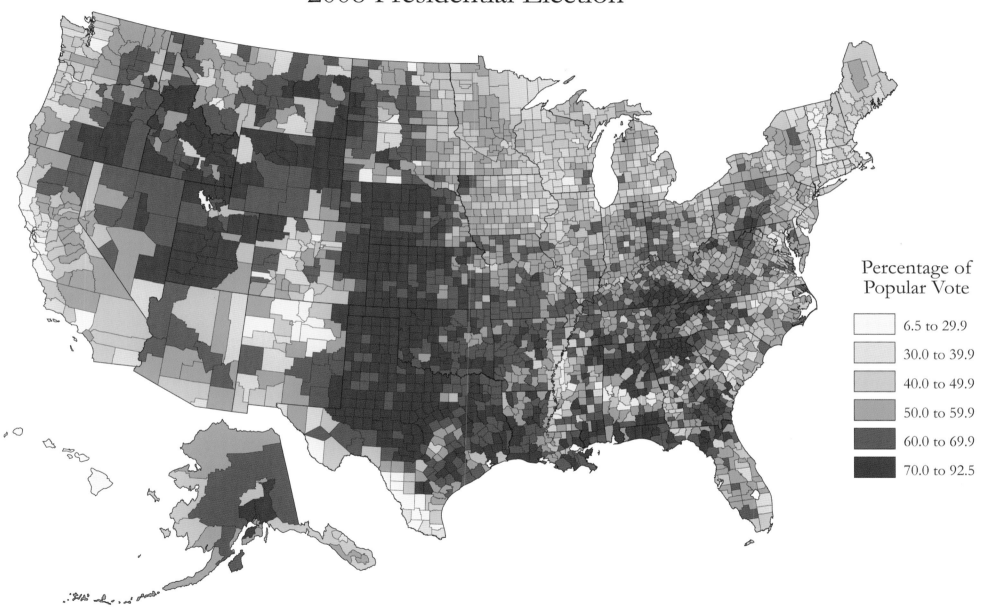

Percentage of
Popular Vote

	6.5 to 29.9
	30.0 to 39.9
	40.0 to 49.9
	50.0 to 59.9
	60.0 to 69.9
	70.0 to 92.5

MAP 4.3

Third Party Popular Vote
2008 Presidential Election

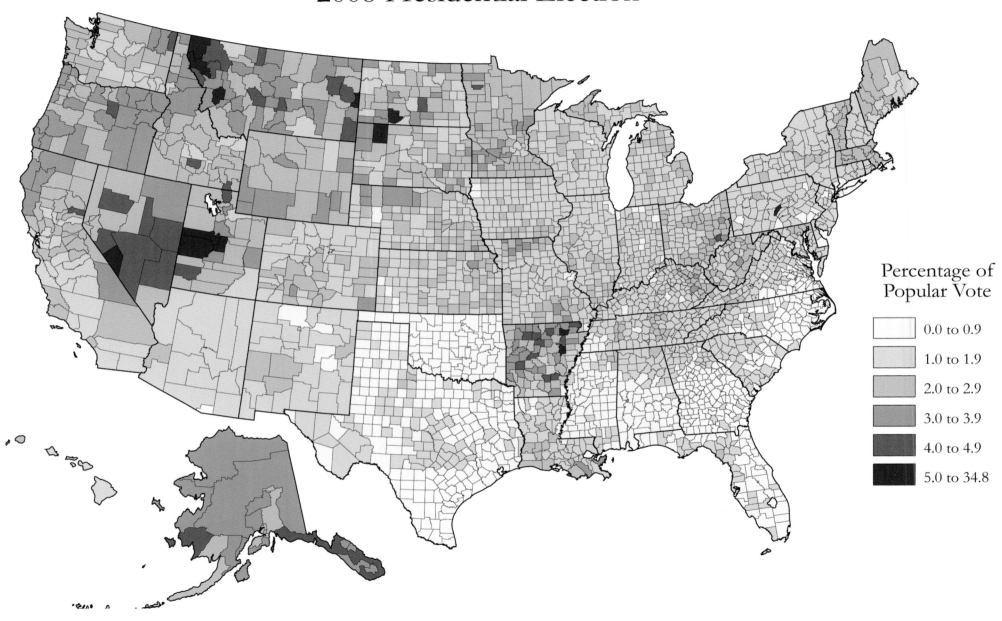

Percentage of
Popular Vote

0.0 to 0.9

1.0 to 1.9

2.0 to 2.9

3.0 to 3.9

4.0 to 4.9

5.0 to 34.8

Bob Barr, Libertarian Party Popular Vote
2008 Presidential Election

MAP 4.4

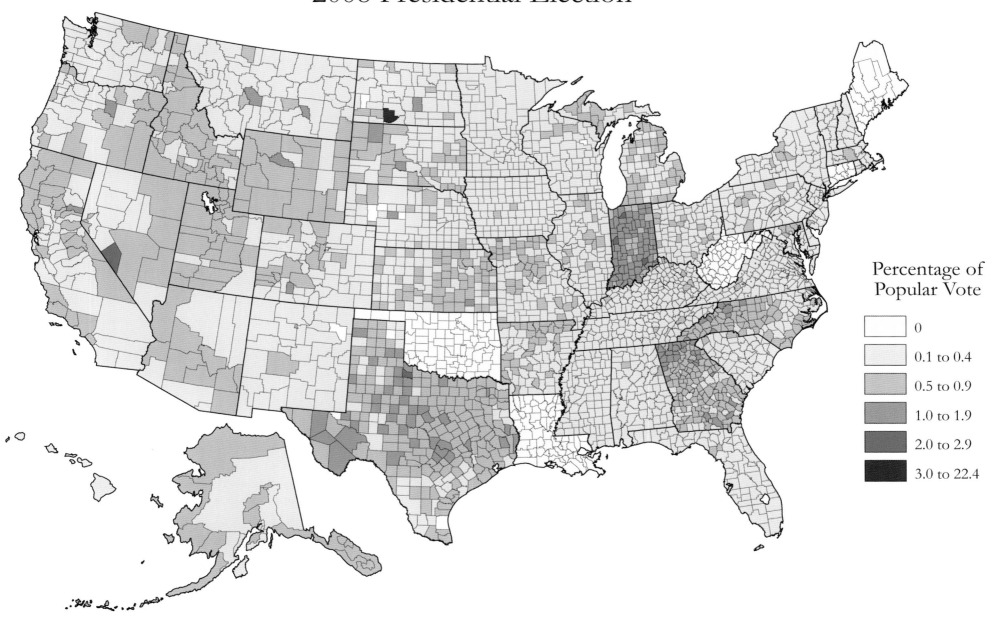

Percentage of
Popular Vote

	0
	0.1 to 0.4
	0.5 to 0.9
	1.0 to 1.9
	2.0 to 2.9
	3.0 to 22.4

MAP 4.5

Ralph Nader, Independent Candidate Popular Vote
2008 Presidential Election

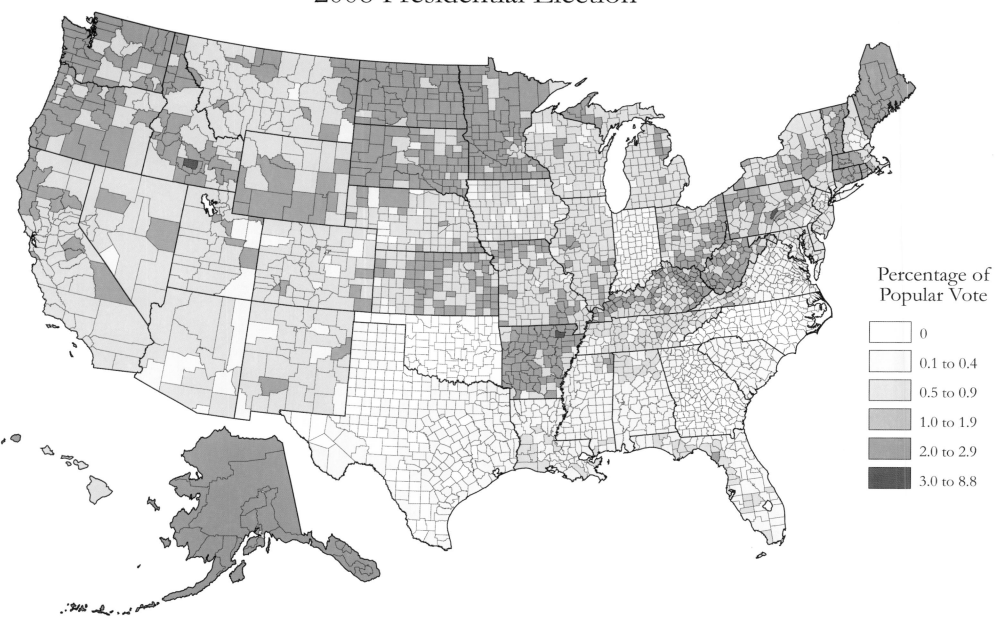

Percentage of
Popular Vote

0

0.1 to 0.4

0.5 to 0.9

1.0 to 1.9

2.0 to 2.9

3.0 to 8.8

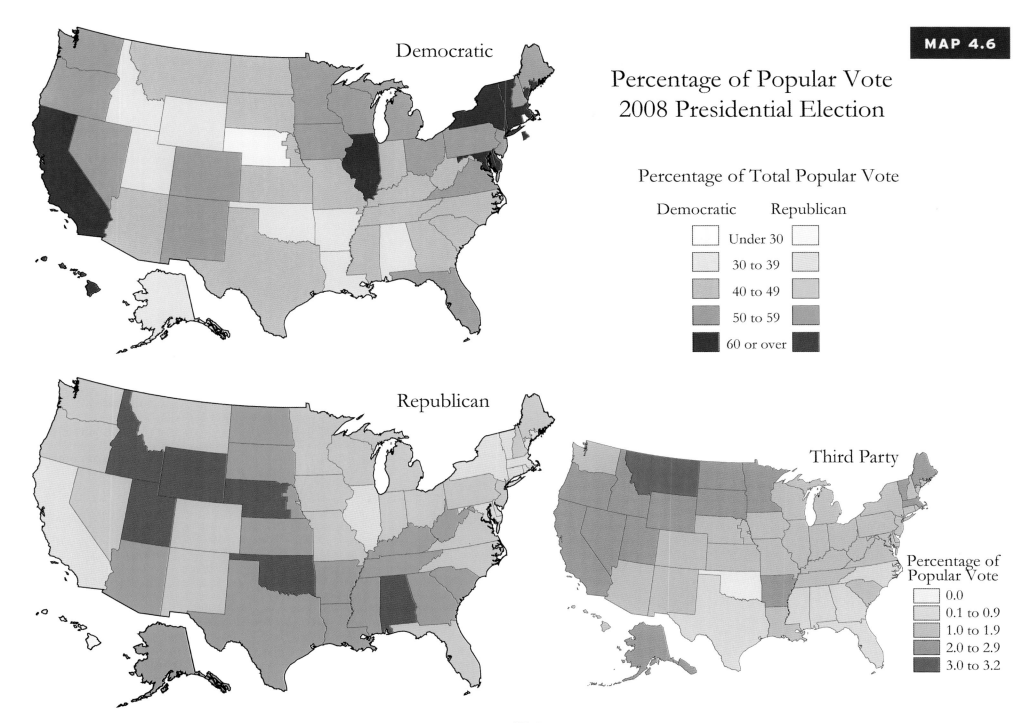

Democratic

Republican

Third Party

MAP 4.6

Percentage of Popular Vote
2008 Presidential Election

Percentage of Total Popular Vote

Democratic   Republican

Under 30

30 to 39

40 to 49

50 to 59

60 or over

Percentage of
Popular Vote

0.0

0.1 to 0.9

1.0 to 1.9

2.0 to 2.9

3.0 to 3.2

Presidential Election Popular Vote
2008

MAP 4.7

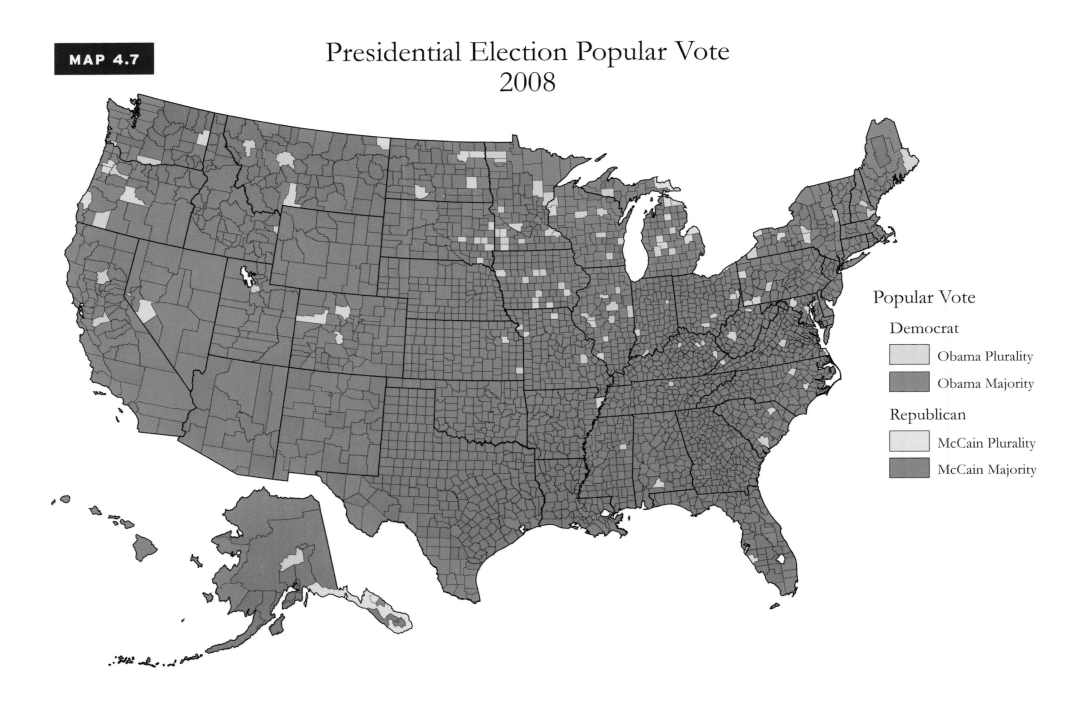

Popular Vote

Democrat

Obama Plurality

Obama Majority

Republican

McCain Plurality

McCain Majority

TRUE BELIEVER COUNTRY: AREAS WITH THE HIGHEST AND LOWEST DEMOCRATIC OR REPUBLICAN MARGINS

RICHARD L. MORRILL

This set of maps looks at the two hundred counties with the highest Democratic margins (percentage for Obama minus the percentage for McCain) and Republican margins in the 2008 election. Republicans have far more counties, mostly small in population, with quite high margins, their two hundred counties ranging from 56 to 90 percent, while the Democratic two hundred counties have margins from as low as 28 percent to as high as 86 percent (Washington, D.C.).

The Democratic high-margin counties are of six types. From the map, the most visible type is where a racial or ethnic minority is dominant—black majority counties across the South, from Arkansas and Mississippi through Alabama, Georgia, and South and North Carolina, to Virginia, to Washington, D.C.; American Indian reservations in Montana, Arizona, New Mexico, North and South Dakota, and Wisconsin; and Hispanic majority counties in New Mexico, Colorado, and mainly Texas. The second type are counties dominated by a college or university, sometimes the state capital as well, as in Arizona, Colorado, Georgia, Indiana, Iowa, Kansas, Massachusetts, Michigan, New Hampshire, New York, North Carolina, Ohio, Oregon, Texas, and Wisconsin. Third are similarly "progressive" counties in high environmental amenity areas in California, Colorado, Hawaii, Idaho, Oregon, and Washington. Fourth is, well, Vermont. Fifth are a very few remaining traditionally Democratic "worker" counties such as Deer Lodge and Silver Bow (Butte), Montana, St. Louis-Douglas (Duluth-Superior), and Muskegon, Michigan. Sixth, and with the vast majority of the population, are large metropolitan counties, as in California (Los Angeles, San Francisco, Santa Clara, and Sacramento), Colorado (Denver), Delaware (Newcastle), Florida (Broward), Georgia (Fulton-Atlanta), Hawaii (Honolulu), Illinois (Cook), Indiana (Indianapolis), Louisiana (Orleans), Maryland (Baltimore, suburban Washington), Massachusetts, Michigan (Wayne-Detroit, Genesee-Flint), Minnesota (Hennepin and Ramsey, Minneapolis-St. Paul), Missouri (St. Louis), New Jersey (Trenton, New York, and Philadelphia suburbs), New York (New York), Ohio (Cuyahoga-Cleveland, Lucas-Toledo), Oregon (Multnomah-Portland), Pennsylvania (Philadelphia), Rhode Island (Providence), Washington (King-Seattle), and Wisconsin (Milwaukee).

The Republican high-margin counties are of four types. The largest share are those of the rural, small-town, and city Great Plains, from Texas (fifty-nine counties), through Oklahoma (twelve), Kansas (twenty-nine), eastern Colorado (four), and Nebraska (twenty). Second are counties in the Mormon cultural realm, centered on Utah but extending into Nevada, Wyoming, and Idaho. Third are selected counties across the South, from Texas, through Louisiana, Mississippi, Alabama, and a belt across northern Alabama to northern Georgia, with an outlying set in southeastern Kentucky. Fourth is perhaps a variant of the first set, a series of resource-dependent sets of counties in Wyoming into Montana, centered on Gillette.

The northeast quarter of the United States does not have a single high-share Republican county (the closest is Sioux County, Iowa), nor does the Pacific Coast. The Mountain States, Great Plains, and South have a mixture, owing to the high percentages of African and Hispanic Americans. States with no extreme counties include Connecticut, Missouri, and West Virginia.

There is a strong degree of continuity among the true believer counties. Of the 201 Democratic counties, 197 simply increased their Democratic share from 2004; two decreased in the Democratic share—Apache County, Arizona (a Navajo reservation) and Gadsden County, Florida (predominantly African American), which experienced a small outmigration of conservative white voters from adjacent Leon County (Tallahassee). Two Hispanic majority counties in Texas, Cameron and Culbertson counties, actually shifted from Republican to Democratic, on the strength of an almost 40 percent shift in margins.

Of the Republican counties, ninety-four experienced declines in their very high shares of 2004, while an even larger number (107) increased in Republican share, despite the overall Democratic shift of the election. Republican gains were dominant in Alabama, Georgia, and Oklahoma, declines in Nebraska and Utah, while Kansas and Texas were mixed.

MAP 4.8

Obama Victory Margin
2008 Presidential Election

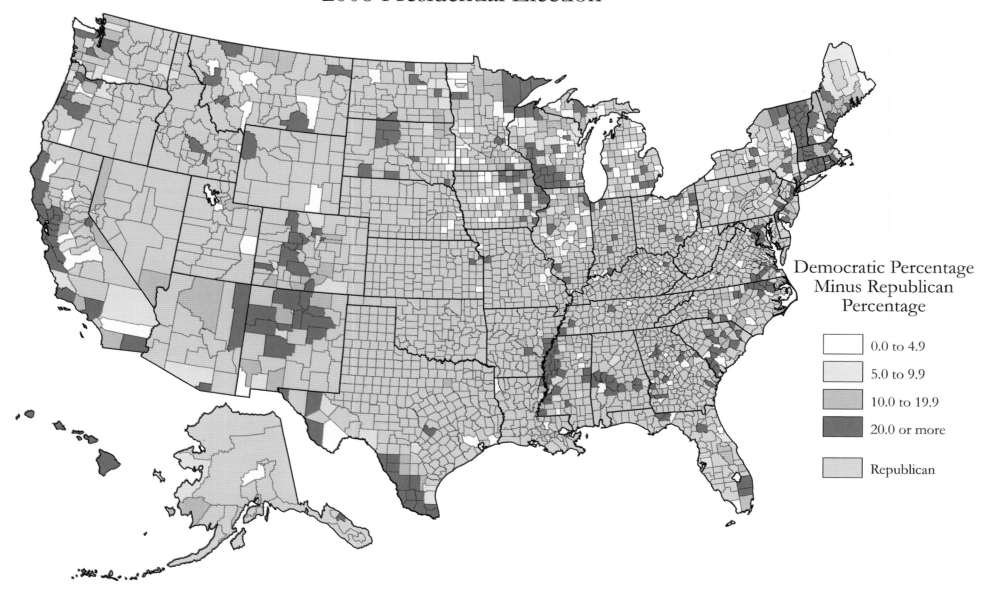

Democratic Percentage
Minus Republican
Percentage

0.0 to 4.9

5.0 to 9.9

10.0 to 19.9

20.0 or more

Republican

McCain Victory Margin
2008 Presidential Election

MAP 4.9

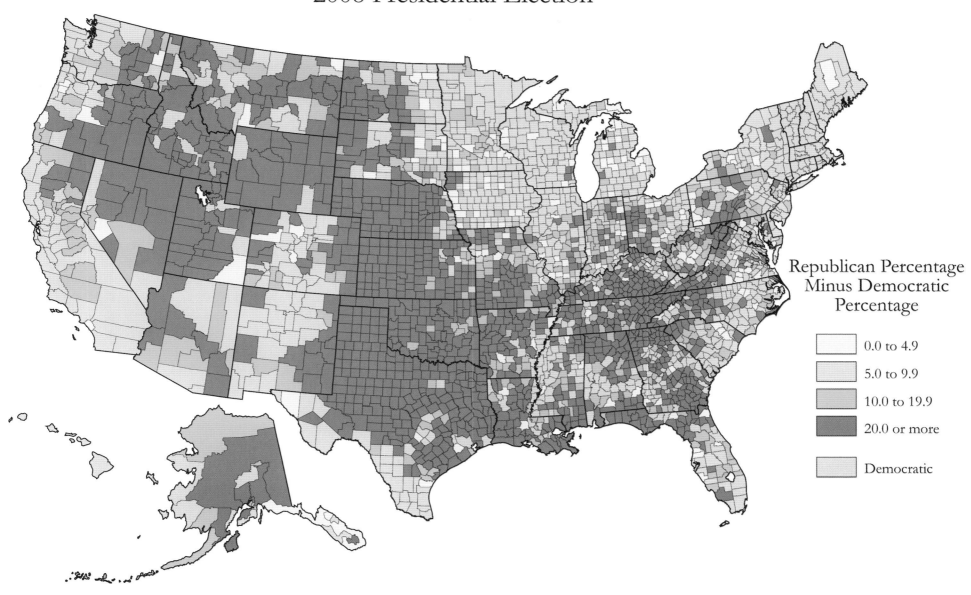

Republican Percentage
Minus Democratic
Percentage

- 0.0 to 4.9
- 5.0 to 9.9
- 10.0 to 19.9
- 20.0 or more

Democratic

TOWARD A REALIGNMENT? THE 2008 ELECTION IN HISTORICAL PERSPECTIVE

DAVID DARMOFAL

As V. O. Key (1955) recognized, realignments are marked by sharp, broad, and enduring changes in the partisan balance. In the wake of the 2008 election, commentators debated whether the election of Barack Obama reflected a realignment in favor of the Democratic Party. As this narrative will discuss, there is little evidence of a realignment in 2008. The Democratic gains in 2008 were only a fraction of the gains the party experienced in the consensus realignment in American history, the New Deal realignment of 1932. In fact, the partisan change in the 2008 election was much more modest than in many elections that are not regarded as realignments by scholars. The 2008 election instead simply returned the Democratic Party to the share of the two-party vote that it had experienced in the 1990s.

The mean county-level Democratic share of the two-party vote increased by 17.97 percentage points in the realigning election of 1932.[1] In contrast, this mean Democratic share increased by only 4.63 points in the 2008 election. As Table 4.1 shows, the Democratic gains in 1932 were sharp and broad: in all six locale types in the United States (counties with large cities, counties with smaller cities, counties surrounding large cities, counties surrounding smaller cities, smaller urban counties, and rural counties), and the Democrats enjoyed large double-digit gains in the two-party vote in 1932.[2] In smaller cities, they enjoyed an average 23.92 point gain; in the counties surrounding these smaller cities, they enjoyed

an average 25.11 point gain. In contrast, the Democratic gains in 2008 in these six locale types ranged from only 3.16 points to 6.48 points.

Similarly, the Democratic gains in the various sections[3] of the country were generally much larger in 1932 than in 2008.[4] The Democratic Party's increase in its share of the two-party vote in 1932 in the Plains was nearly five times its increase in the same counties in 2008. The Democratic gain in the South in 1932 of 29.8 points was nearly seven times its gain in the same section in 2008 of just 4.36 points. Its increase in support in the border states of Kentucky, Maryland, Oklahoma, Tennessee, and West Virginia in 1932 of 22.74 points was more than twelve times its gain of 1.86 points in the same section in the 2008 election.

There is, in short, no evidence of a realignment in 2008 like that which occurred in 1932. The Democratic Party's gains in the 2008 election pale in comparison to its gains in the 1932 New Deal realignment. Franklin Roosevelt was swept into office on partisan gains that were much more sharp and broad than those enjoyed by Barack Obama.

Although 2008 does not appear to have been a realigning election, perhaps the Democrats' gains in 2008 were still large in comparison with other nonrealignment elections. I examined this question using data for each presidential election since the advent of Jacksonian democracy and mass voter participation in the United States. Specifically, I regressed county-level differences in the margin of victory in

consecutive presidential elections on dummy variables for each presidential election from 1832 to 2008.[5] The excluded category in this analysis is the 1884 presidential election, which had the median difference in margin of victory (+ .005) from the preceding presidential election. As with all but four of the presidential elections in the analysis, the dummy variable for the 2008 election was statistically significant at a $p < .01$ level, indicating a statistically significant difference from the median election of 1884. In absolute terms, however, the partisan change in 2008 (a coefficient of .090) pales in comparison to such nonrealignment elections as 1912 (a coefficient of .275), 1920 (− .292), 1964 (.216), 1968 (− .221), 1972 (− .221), and 1976 (.258). In all, twenty-one presidential elections since 1832 exhibited more partisan change than did the 2008 election. The 2008 presidential election ranks only one category above the median election in amount of partisan change. The partisan change in the 2008 election is commonplace, not out of the ordinary, when compared with the partisan change in presidential elections since the advent of mass participation in the United States.

Rather than marking a fundamental realignment, the partisan change in 2008 reflects a much more modest improvement for the Democratic Party. Specifically, the gains for the Democrats in 2008 largely return them to the standing they had during the 1990s. Table 4.2 presents the mean Democratic percentage of the two-party vote for each of the six locale types and each of the eight sections for each presidential election from 1980 through 2008. The most consistent patterns that emerge from table 4.2 are the strong similarities between the 2008 election and the two Clinton victories of 1992 and 1996 and the divergence of these three elections from the two presidential elections in between.

The 2008 election, with its Democratic share of the two-party vote at 53.24 percent, resembles the two Clinton elections much more closely than it resembles any other presidential election during this period. This is also true when we dig below the national surface to examine specific locale types and sections. For example, the Democratic Party's performance in 2008 was nearly identical to its performance in 1996 in counties with large cities, counties surrounding large cities, and smaller urban counties, and much better than its performance in these counties in the elections of 2000 and 2004. The two principal points of divergence in 2008 from the 1990s are counties with smaller cities (where the Democratic Party performed better than it had in the 1990s) and rural counties (where the Democratic Party performed markedly worse than it had in the 1990s).

We also see very similar performances to the 1990s by the Democratic Party in 2008 in many sections of the country. For example, the Democrats' performance in New England, the mid-Atlantic, the Midwest, the Plains, and the Mountain states was very similar to its performance in these sections in 1992 and 1996 and was stronger than in these sections in the 2000 and 2004 elections. The two principal points of divergence from the 1990s are in border states (where the Democratic Party's performance in 2008 was worse than in the 1990s) and on the West Coast (where the Democratic Party's performance in 2008 was better than in the 1990s).

Overall, there is no evidence that the Democratic Party enjoyed a fundamental realignment in its favor in the 2008 election. Instead, the election served principally to return the party to the share of the two-party vote it enjoyed in the Clinton wins in 1992 and 1996. The Democratic Party's ability to solidify these gains is likely to depend significantly on the Obama administration's governing performance.

TABLE 4.1. Percentage Point Increases in Democratic Share of the Two-Party Vote

	1928-1932	2004-2008
By Locale:		
Counties with large cities	12.65	3.93
Counties with smaller cities	23.92	6.48
Counties surrounding large cities	12.90	4.74
Counties surrounding smaller cities	25.11	4.70
Smaller urban counties	17.09	4.91
Rural counties	22.96	3.16
By Section:		
New England	3.89	3.14
Mid-Atlantic	10.54	3.85
South	29.80	4.36
Border	22.74	1.86
Midwest	17.59	6.57
Plains	22.85	4.72
Mountain	22.09	5.87
West Coast	27.06	6.59

TABLE 4.2. Mean Democratic Share of the Two-Party Vote, 1980-2008

	1980	1984	1988	1992	1996	2000	2004	2008
Continental United States	44.49	40.64	45.96	53.29	54.61	50.12	48.61	53.24
By Locale:								
Counties with large cities	49.95	49.34	53.92	61.72	63.93	61.10	59.82	63.75
Counties with smaller cities	45.10	40.43	45.32	51.83	53.30	50.38	49.90	56.38
Counties surrounding large cities	39.68	36.99	42.46	50.76	53.63	50.54	48.45	53.19
Counties surrounding smaller cities	41.76	35.00	40.65	46.52	46.97	41.57	41.57	43.84
Smaller urban counties	43.37	38.87	43.91	51.14	52.67	48.26	48.26	51.66
Rural counties	43.47	37.66	43.94	50.71	50.37	41.91	41.91	43.14
By Section:								
New England	47.43	43.59	49.93	58.37	64.66	60.30	58.58	61.72
Mid-Atlantic	46.45	44.60	48.96	56.41	61.13	58.37	55.21	59.06
South	46.07	37.00	41.14	48.83	49.95	44.22	42.76	47.12
Border	46.73	39.73	44.04	51.91	51.77	46.70	43.29	45.14
Midwest	45.00	41.61	46.45	53.58	55.45	50.79	50.22	56.79
Plains	43.42	41.55	49.14	52.75	51.90	46.35	45.65	50.37
Mountain	32.19	33.06	41.41	48.86	47.89	42.00	42.47	48.34
West Coast	41.28	42.19	48.96	58.27	56.97	55.06	54.49	61.08

■ BREAKING DOWN THE 2008 VOTE

ANDREW GELMAN

As political scientists, we typically try to understand public opinion and voting by using least squares, logistic regression, and other statistical tools for estimating the effects (predictive if not always causal) of demographic factors (such as age, sex, income, education), political affiliation and ideology, and aggregate variables (most importantly, economic trends and presidential approval). We sometimes look at exit poll results or at color-coded maps of national elections but typically consider such descriptive summaries as amusements for the newspapers rather than as adjuncts to serious research.

Recently, however, there has been a renaissance in descriptive analysis of electoral data, accompanying the widespread availability of large datasets, free high-quality statistical graphics software, and outlets for rapid dissemination of color graphics on the Internet. In many ways, this new wave of political graphics harkens back to the classic descriptive work of political scientists such as V. O. Key in the middle of the twentieth century. Along with this, the work of technologically savvy outsiders such as Nate Silver (www.fivethirtyeight.com) has bridged the gap between journalism and political science.

In this article we give some examples from our recent analyses of polling and electoral data from the 2008 presidential election (Gelman, Park, Shor, and Cortina 2009; Gelman and Ghitza 2010; Gelman, Lee, and Ghitza 2010; Gelman and Su 2010). We present two displays: a grid of maps (map 4.10) and a grid of line plots (graph 4.1), each summarizing a different breakdown of the vote in the general election. The maps show vote by ethnicity, income, and state; the line plots show vote by education, within categories defined by age and ethnic groups.

The two displays address different aspects of class-based voting. The maps dramatically reveal the different national voting patterns of rich, middle-income, and poor Americans. Separate rows of maps for each ethnic group make clear the distinctive voting patterns of poor whites, who were somewhat Democratic-leaning in most of the country but strongly Republican in the Deep South. African Americans and Latinos, in contrast, showed little variation by state of residence or income level.

The line plots expand upon the well-known pattern in recent years that Democrats do best among the least- and most-educated voters, with Republicans being most successful with the voters in the middle. (This is *not* the same as the pattern with income; richer voters consistently vote more Republican.) Education is highly correlated with ethnicity and also with age, hence the separate plots for each category, which reveal, among other things, that the Obama vote was strongly correlated with education among the young but not among older voters.

We next briefly discuss some of the choices involved in the statistical modeling and graphical display. For the maps we used hierarchical Bayesian inference to get stable estimates for all states and categories, whereas the line plots were simple enough that we worked with simple weighted means, using error bars to indicate the large uncertainties for some of the smaller groups. We used the technique of small multiples (Bertin 1967; Tufte 1990) to allow a large number of quick comparisons. For the maps, we used a continuous blue-to-gray-to-red color scale to display estimated vote proportions; for the line plots, we put all graphs on a common scale for ease of interpretation.

The two displays shown do not represent the future or even the current state of the art in political mapping or analysis. What they do indicate, we hope, is the way in which current technology allows us to prepare simple maps and graphs to directly summarize important aspects of demographic and geographic variation in public opinion and voting.

We thank the National Science Foundation, Department of Energy, and Institute of Education Sciences for financial support of this work and the Pew Research Center for its survey data. Further graphs of a similar nature appear at our blog: www.stat.columbia.edu/~cook/movabletype/archives/political-science/.

MAP 4.10

Did you vote for McCain in 2008?

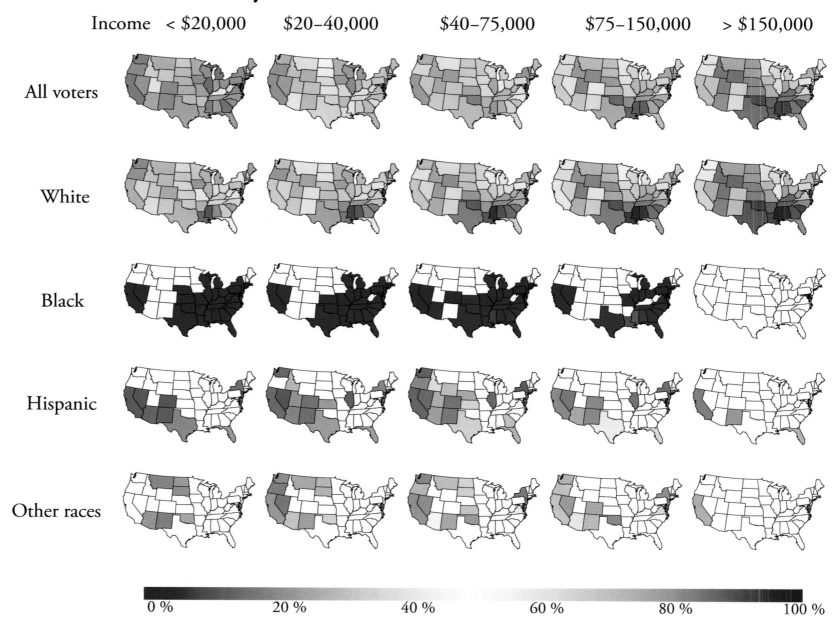

Income   < $20,000 $20–40,000 $40–75,000 $75–150,000   > $150,000

All voters

White

Black

Hispanic

Other races

0 %   20 %   40 %   60 %   80 %   100 %

When a category represents less than 1% of the voters in a state, the state is left blank.

Republican Vote in 2008 by Education, Age, and Ethnic Group　**GRAPH 4.1**

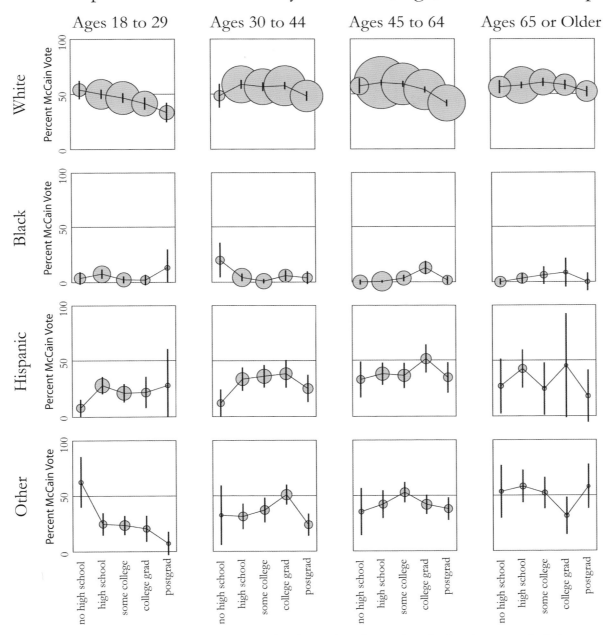

Area of circles is approximately proportional to the number of voters in each education, age, and ethnic group. Vertical error bars show + or - 2 standard errors. Estimates based on PEW Research pre-election polls.

WHAT CAN WE LEARN FROM 2008 EXIT POLLS?

HEATHER HOLLEN AND FRED M. SHELLEY

In American elections, some voters are interviewed immediately after they cast their ballots. These exit polls are conducted by private firms that contract with television networks to interview voters about their decisions.

Voters participating in these polls are asked for whom they voted. They are also asked to provide some demographic and other information about themselves, including their age, gender, race, income, employment status, religion, and political party identification. They are also asked why they voted as they did. Answers to these questions allow researchers to examine the impacts of demographic factors and to issue analyses on voters' decisions and, therefore, on the outcome of the election.

The interpretation of exit polls can sometimes be problematic. Voters answering questions may lie or misrepresent their views in their interviews. Another problem with these polls is that an increasing percentage of voters vote early or by absentee ballot. To the extent that early voters vote differently from those who vote on Election Day, this problem can introduce bias into the interpretation of exit poll results. Moreover, it is possible that the exit polls may not sample enough people to provide meaningful interpretations of the results. In 2008 CNN. com interviewed 17,836 voters in its exit polls, as described below (www.cnn.com/ELECTION/2008/results/polls.main/). One example illustrates this point. What if one wanted to find out whether American Indians in each state supported Obama or McCain? Because only 1 percent of the U.S. voting public is of American Indian ancestry, most states have too few American Indians to allow any meaningful comparison.

Despite these problems, exit polls are often useful in helping researchers understand why different types of voters voted in different ways. The analysis presented in this atlas is based on exit polls conducted by CNN and available through its website at cnn.com. Comparison of exit poll results from one state to another provides valuable geographical insights.

VOTER AGE AND EXIT POLL RESULTS

During the 2008 campaign, considerable attention was paid to the popularity of Obama among voters under thirty. As expected, Obama won a large majority of votes among people under thirty. According to exit polls, Obama won about 66 percent of those under-thirty voters nationwide, as compared with about 32 percent for McCain. Voters over thirty were divided about evenly between Obama and McCain. On a statewide level, a majority of voters under thirty supported McCain in only eight states (Alaska, Idaho, Utah, Wyoming, Oklahoma, Louisiana, Georgia, and West Virginia). Young voters were decisive in Florida, Indiana, Ohio, and North Carolina. In these states, a majority of voters over thirty voted for McCain. The difference between Obama's percentage of under-thirty voters and his overall percentage was greatest in metropolitan blue states (Connecticut,

18 percent; Massachusetts, 16 percent; California, 15 percent; New York, 14 percent) and in the South (North Carolina, 24 percent; Tennessee, 13 percent; and Mississippi, 13 percent). In Utah and Alaska, young voters were more Republican than these states' voters overall.

RACE AND GENDER IN EXIT DATA

Did nonwhite voters give Obama higher percentages than white voters? Some states do not have large enough nonwhite populations to allow for comparisons among racial and ethnic groups within these states. However, comparing percentages of white voters with the overall percentages in each state provides insight into the impact of race and ethnicity. Exit polls confirm that the votes of people of color, including African Americans, Latinos, Asian Americans, and American Indians were critical to Obama's election. Nationwide, the exit poll results reveal that 43 percent of whites voted for Obama. Had people of color not voted, Obama would have lost several mid-Atlantic states (New Jersey, Pennsylvania, Maryland, and Virginia), the four closest Obama states (Ohio, Indiana, Florida, and North Carolina), and two of the Mountain states (New Mexico and Nevada). The "race gap," or the difference between these percentages, was greatest by far in the Deep South and decreased from south to north. In the bluest states, there was little or no difference between white vote for Obama and statewide vote for Obama. Obama's statewide percentage of white voters was below 30 percent in most of the Deep South but rose above 50 percent in the Northeast, the Upper Middle West, and the Pacific Coast states.

Over the past several elections, a "gender gap" has been identified by political analysts. Women have been more likely to vote Democratic since 1980. Exit poll data from the 2008 election confirm the continuing existence of the gender gap. If men alone had voted, McCain would have won Colorado, Indiana, North Carolina, and New Hampshire in addition to the states that he actually won. If only women had voted, Obama would have won Missouri, Georgia, and Montana in addition to the states that he actually won. The gender gap was highest in the Northeast (more than 12 percent in Rhode Island, Delaware, Connecticut, Maine, and Massachusetts). It was lowest in the West, the most closely contested states, and the upland South. In Nebraska and Arkansas, men were more likely than women to have voted for Obama.

■ EARLY VOTING

DANIEL ERVIN AND NATHANIEL HADLEYDIKE

With the exception of those voters formally requesting absentee ballots well in advance of an election, traditionally voters could cast their ballots only on Election Day during set polling hours, such as 7:00 a.m. to 7:00 p.m. Since Election Day is generally a workday for most citizens, a set, limited window of opportunity to vote can act as an obstacle that may reduce turnout.

Beginning with Idaho in 1970, thirty-two states have modified their election laws to allow early or advance in-person voting with no excuse required. This option is also sometimes termed convenience voting. Fourteen additional states allow early voting in-person with an excuse. In these states, voters can cast ballots on a voting machine at a polling station days or even weeks in advance of Election Day. In general, the goal of early voting is to increase citizen voting participation and to reduce the long lines that some voters encounter on Election Day. An estimated 32 million ballots were cast by early voters in the 2008 election.

The length of time available for early voting is variable, based upon the jurisdiction. In Iowa, voters can cast their ballot at the county commissioner's office up to forty days in advance of a primary or general election. In North Carolina, citizens can cast early ballots beginning on the third Thursday prior to the election through the last Saturday before the election. In Virginia, voters can cast in-person ballots up to forty-five days prior to November elections and up to thirty days for all other elections.

In-person early voting is nearly universal in the western half of the United States, with only Washington and Oregon not allowing voters to cast early ballots at a polling station in person. Oregon has pioneered all mail-in voting, negating the need to have polling stations at all. And while Washington does not have in-person early voting, it does provide for no-excuse absentee voting.

Traditionally, political campaigns have focused efforts to encourage their supporters to vote in the few days prior to the election, with such efforts reaching a peak on Election Day itself. The growth in early voting options has changed this cycle since voters may have two or three weeks to visit the polls.

Thus, campaigns with excellent local organizations that can work to get their supporters to the polls over the course of two, three, or even four weeks have an advantage. With a consistent effort over the course of the early voting period, a campaign may have a large number of votes "banked" well before Election Day.

North Carolina provides an excellent example of the importance of early voting to the 2008 election. Barack Obama won the state of North Carolina with 50.2 percent, with a margin of 13,459 votes. While John McCain received 291,595 more votes on Election Day than Barack Obama, Obama received 305,054 more early votes than John McCain. Similarly, Barack Obama won Colorado with 50.3 percent of the vote and a margin of only 9,479 ballots. John McCain actually received 18,022 more votes on Election Day than Barack Obama. But Obama had received 17,845 more early votes and 9,656 more no-excuse absentee ballots than McCain. Thus, while voting on Election Day was clearly critical to the outcomes of the 2008 election contests, Barack Obama's campaign effectively used the early voting options available in many states.

MAP 4.11

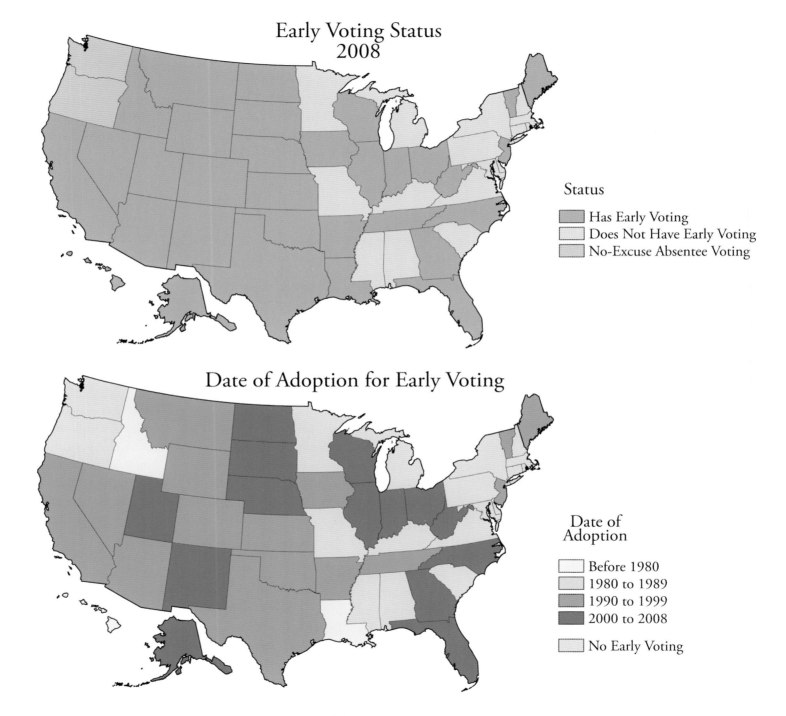

Early Voting Status
2008

Status

Has Early Voting
Does Not Have Early Voting
No-Excuse Absentee Voting

Date of Adoption for Early Voting

Date of
Adoption

Before 1980
1980 to 1989
1990 to 1999
2000 to 2008

No Early Voting

URBAN-RURAL GEOGRAPHY, VOTING, AND THE 2008 PRESIDENTIAL ELECTION

KIMBERLY KARNES AND JAMES G. GIMPEL

An increasingly clear electoral division that remained mostly ignored by press coverage of the 2008 election outcome was the choice urban and rural voters made on Election Day, perhaps because this gap has been so wide in recent elections that no one questioned who would win these distinctive locations. As postelection statistics indicate, Obama came out far ahead of McCain in the most urban counties—more than half of his total victory margin came from only seven large counties, with Los Angeles County, California, alone awarding Obama a 1.2 million vote margin. Taken collectively, in counties with populations of 25,000 or fewer, Obama won 40 percent of votes cast, compared with McCain's 58.1 percent. Summing the vote in all counties containing 10,000 people or fewer, McCain's share jumps to 60.7 percent, and Obama's drops to 37.5 percent.

Although social scientists have long noted that urban and rural can be defined in different ways (Deavers 1992; Theobald 2001; Woods 2005, 5–7), table 4.3 shows that certainly at the poles of population size, a widening gap has emerged only recently in the presidential vote choice of urban and rural voters. The 2008 presidential election saw the most gaping difference between the two locations in recent history.

The locations of the most urban and rural counties as shown on the map exhibit familiar patterns of present-day national population distribution. The political divide between the urban and rural electorate is most often described as having its roots in who

has happened to settle in the two locations and the cultures that have taken root there. The divide, then, is one that separates lifestyles, cultures, and, increasingly, political visions. As such, the rural/urban gap can be described chiefly as a function of the compositional differences between the two populations (Johnston, Shelley, and Taylor 1990; Huckfeldt 1986; Gimpel and Schuknecht 2004). The socioeconomic, demographic, and religious differences separating the two geographic areas have been identified before, and we summarize a few of them in the table below, relying on both U.S. census data and religious survey data.

In addition to a higher propensity to find observant evangelical Christians and older people among the rural population, studies have shown for several decades now that rural residents are more likely than their urban counterparts to hold more conservative beliefs when it comes to social issues, such as abortion, gay marriage, and the second amendment right to bear arms (see Abramowitz and Saunders 2005; Glenn and Hill 1977; Knoke and Henry 1977). Rural and small-town Americans have also been found to be more frugal and risk averse on financial matters, have very high rates of self-employment and entrepreneurship, and are more suspicious of the role of government in the economy (Chinni and Gimpel 2010).

All of these differences combined play some role in turning rural Americans toward the Republican Party and urban dwellers toward the Democrats,

producing the wide gap in 2008 (as well as in the two previous presidential contests). Two points are worth noting in particular about 2008. First, the economic crisis that emerged in the fall to shape the outcome of the 2008 election did not hit rural Americans nearly as hard as it did urbanites. This was especially true of the foreclosure crisis, which rural America managed to escape almost entirely. But also, unemployment and layoffs were not the problem in rural areas that they were in the nation's major metropolitan areas. What this means is that rural Americans had less reason to vote against their party preference than those living in other locations did.

Second, it is certainly possible that rural and small-town voters were particularly suspicious of a Democratic candidate who was different in so many respects from themselves. This is not just a comment about Barack Obama's race, as it has yet to be shown that rural whites are any more racist than white voters living in other geographic locations. It was the entire package that candidate Obama presented: big-city origins, ambiguity about religious beliefs and background, and liberal views on a host of issues ranging from the Gulf War to abortion rights.

Going back any number of election cycles, it is impossible to pick out a candidate who represents big-city life and culture as well as Obama. John McCain's background was typically vague with respect to place. While he did not seem as promising to rural Americans on the issues as his Alaskan running mate, Sarah Palin, he wound up running up record percentages of support in the hinterlands due largely to his highly placed, distinctive opponent. Barack Obama is probably the most thoroughly urban candidate the Democratic Party has ever nominated.

Increasingly, some argue, contemporary partisans are gravitating toward politically friendly turf as they make their residential choices, a development that will likely enhance geographic divisions in the electorate and probably augment the urban-rural division in the electorate (Bishop 2008). Even if not all voters are highly selective about their migration patterns in the way Bishop has described, there is complementary evidence that voters are increasingly lining up their ideological preferences with their partisan ones, as described in the work of Levendusky (2009) and Fiorina and Abrams (2008). Certainly the widening urban-rural gap in table 4.3 is partly attributable to rural Democrats becoming rural Republicans, consistent with their long-held conservative policy views, while urban Republicans have drifted toward the Democratic Party, aligning their party preference with their policy views. The result of the continued alignment of policy preference and party, among both residentially mobile voters and those who remain in place, will be to widen geographic divisions in American political behavior well into the future.

TABLE 4.3. Comparisons of Average Socioeconomic and Political Characteristics of Residents of Urban and Rural Counties

	10,000 and Fewer	25,000 and Fewer	300,000 and More	1,000,000 and More
N of counties	696	1,557	201	37
Sum of population	3,808,885	18,267,440	169,780,994	77,636,435
Average population size (2006)	5,473	11,733	844,682	2,098,282
Pop. density (2006)	22.5	48.5	2315.0	6162.3
Median household income (2006) ($1,000s)	32.0	32.8	51.8	52.8
% over age 65 (2006)	17.1	16.4	13.4	12.8
% black (2006)	4.7	8.0	15.0	17.0
% Hispanic (2006)	7.5	6.6	17.1	25.8
% in agriculture (2000)	16.3	11.3	1.0	0.5
% self-employed (2000)	15.0	12.1	5.9	6.0
% professional (2000)	3.6	4.0	10.7	12.0
% four-year college degree (2000)	14.6	13.9	28.1	28.7
% for Gore 2000	33.3	37.7	51.3	57.6
% for Kerry 2004	32.6	36.2	51.4	57.6
% for Gore 2008	35.3	38.2	56.9	62.7
Residing in South (2006)	1,365,022	9,233,516	44,084,930	17,940,663
% Southern	35.8	50.5	25.9	23.1
Catholic adherence per 1000	148.9	123.8	250.6	284.4
Evangelical adherence per 1000	230.5	252.5	108.1	82.3
Total religious adherence per 1000	612.4	569.4	497.2	504.3

Sources: U.S. Census 2000, and 2006 estimates. For religion estimates, Glenmary Research Center, *Religious Congregations and Membership*, 2000.

Emergence of the Urban-Rural Gap in Voting for Presidential Candidates 1972 to 2008

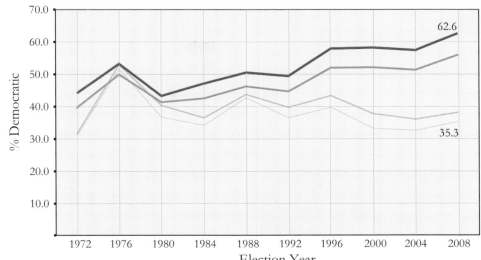

County Population

— 1 Million and more
— 300,000 and more
— 25,000 and less
— 10,000 and less

MAP 4.12

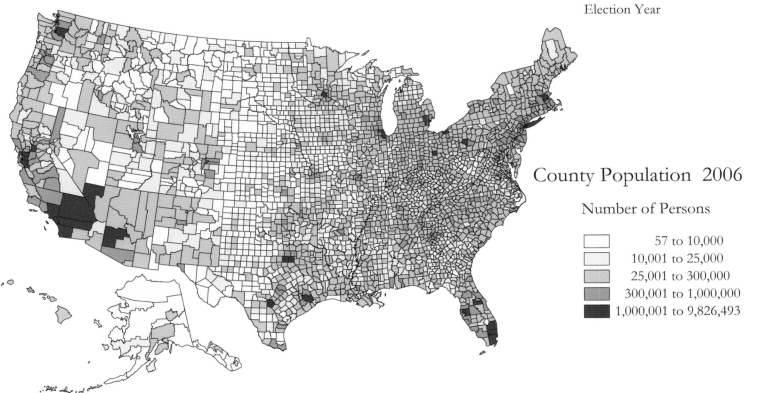

County Population 2006

Number of Persons

☐ 57 to 10,000
☐ 10,001 to 25,000
☐ 25,001 to 300,000
☐ 300,001 to 1,000,000
☐ 1,000,001 to 9,826,493

2008 Presidential Election Vote Margin

MAP 4.13

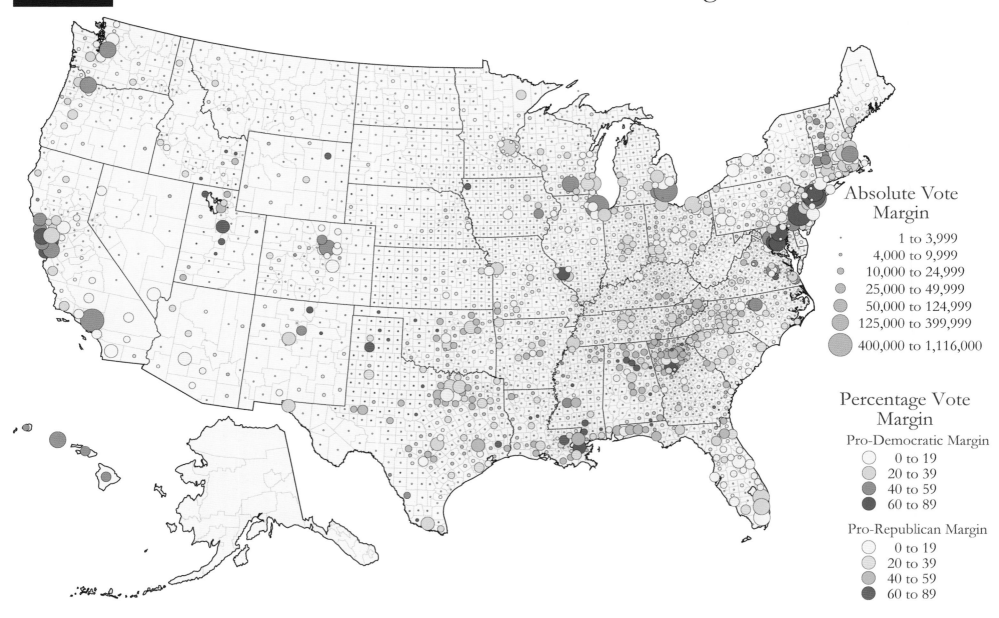

Absolute Vote Margin

· 1 to 3,999
· 4,000 to 9,999
○ 10,000 to 24,999
○ 25,000 to 49,999
○ 50,000 to 124,999
○ 125,000 to 399,999
○ 400,000 to 1,116,000

Percentage Vote Margin

Pro-Democratic Margin
○ 0 to 19
○ 20 to 39
○ 40 to 59
○ 60 to 89

Pro-Republican Margin
○ 0 to 19
○ 20 to 39
○ 40 to 59
○ 60 to 89

■ COMPARISON WITH PREVIOUS ELECTIONS

FRED M. SHELLEY

Obama's decisive victory in 2008 contrasted sharply with the relatively close elections of 2000 and 2004, both of which were won narrowly by the Republicans. The presidential elections of 2000 and 2004 were closely contested in the Electoral College. In the bitterly contested 2000 election, Republican George W. Bush won Florida by a mere 537 popular votes, thereby winning Florida's electoral votes and thereby winning an Electoral College majority despite receiving approximately 500,000 fewer popular votes than his Democratic opponent, Al Gore. Large numbers of disputed ballots in Florida induced Democrats to challenge the result, and the election was not decided until the U.S. Supreme Court ruled in favor of the Republicans several weeks after the election. Bush was reelected more comfortably in 2004. However, a shift of approximately 65,000 popular votes in Ohio would have given the election to his Democratic opponent, John Kerry.

COMPARING 2008 WITH THE 2000 AND 2004 PRESIDENTIAL ELECTIONS

In contrast to 2004, Barack Obama defeated John McCain by comfortable margins in the Electoral College as well as the total popular vote in 2008. Every state carried by Kerry in 2004 gave its electoral votes to Obama in 2008. In addition, Obama won nine states that Bush had carried in 2004: Colorado, Florida, Indiana, Iowa, Nevada, New Mexico, North Carolina, Ohio, and Virginia. He also won one of Nebraska's five electoral votes for a total of 365 versus 173 electoral votes for McCain.

Many of the nine states that Obama carried in 2008 but that Kerry lost in 2004 had gone Republican in most recent elections. Virginia and Indiana went Republican for the first time since Lyndon B. Johnson's landslide victory in 1964. North Carolina had given Jimmy Carter a narrow majority in his successful bid for the presidency in 1976 but had gone Republican in every election since that time. Florida had gone Democratic only twice since 1964, in 1976 and 1996.

The other six of these nine newly Democratic states have had a history of more even division between Democrats and Republicans in recent years. The Western states of Colorado, Nevada, and New Mexico were carried by George W. Bush in 2004 but were won by the Democrats in 1992 and 1996. The Republicans won Colorado and Nevada in 2000 but narrowly lost in New Mexico in that year. Similarly, Bush narrowly won Iowa in 2004, but Iowa went Democratic in 1988, 1992, 1996, and 2000. Ohio, which is long regarded as an important bellwether state, has supported the winning candidate in every election since 1960, and the 2008 election was no exception.

At a county level, Obama's vote percentages were higher than those won by Kerry in many parts of the country. McCain's percentages exceeded those of Bush in only a few places. The largest area in which McCain did consistently better than Bush was in a large group of counties stretching from the central and southern Appalachians westward to northwestern Texas. In Oklahoma, for example, Obama exceeded Kerry's percentages in only five of the state's seventy-seven counties. However, these five counties included Oklahoma and Tulsa counties, which contain the state's two largest cities—Oklahoma City and Tulsa, respectively. Cleveland and Payne counties, where Obama also saw more support than Kerry, contain the state's two largest universities, the University of Oklahoma and Oklahoma State University. The other county in Oklahoma that gave Obama a higher margin than Kerry was Comanche County in the southwestern part of the state. Comanche County contains the city of Lawton and includes a large army installation at Fort Sill. Throughout the country, counties with large army bases tended to give Obama higher percentages of the vote than they did Kerry. Examples include Fort Campbell, Kentucky, and Fort Riley, Kansas. This seemingly counterintuitive outcome likely reflects the fact that more than 40 percent of enlisted personnel in the army are African Americans or members of other minority groups. McCain also exceeded Bush's percentages in his home state of Arizona. Indeed, Arizona might have gone Democratic had McCain, who has represented Arizona in the Senate for many years, not headed the Republican presidential ticket.

LONG-RUN COMPARISONS WITH PREVIOUS ELECTIONS, 1948-2004

Over the longer run, the geographic patterns of support for Democrats and Republicans in the 2008 election are generally similar to those of previous elections dating back to 1980. The Northeast, the Upper Midwest, and the Pacific states with the exception of Alaska have been the most Democratic states in the country for the past thirty years. Republican support has been concentrated in the South, the Great Plains states, and the Mountain states. This geographical divide between Democratic-oriented blue states and Republican-oriented red states has characterized American politics, in both the Electoral College and the popular vote, for the past three decades.

In geographical terms, the elections of 1980 through 2008 contrasted sharply with the presidential elections that took place between 1948 and 1976. Maps 4.14 through 4.29 show average county-level percentages of popular votes by county from 1948 through 1960, 1964 through 1976, 1980 through 1992, and 1996 through 2008, respectively. Thus each of these maps shows averages over a period of four elections taking place during a twelve-year period. (Note that Alaska and Hawaii are not included in earlier time periods because they were not admitted to the Union until 1959. Alaska is treated as a single unit because it is not formally divided into counties.)

For the most part, the elections of 1948 through 1960 represent an extension of geographical polarization that dates back to the end of Reconstruction in the 1870s. After Reconstruction ended, the "Solid South" became uniformly Democratic. Democratic nominees captured every electoral vote in the old Confederacy between 1880 and 1916. The Republicans won the electoral votes of Tennessee in 1920 and won five Southern states in 1928. However, Franklin D. Roosevelt won every electoral vote in the South in all four of his presidential elections between 1932 and 1944. The Democratic dominance of the South during the eighty years after Reconstruction was matched by Republican domination of the North, particularly New England and the Upper Midwest. A belt of states stretching from New York westward to Missouri was generally key to election outcomes. The 1948–1960 span was no exception. Democrat Harry Truman won Missouri, Illinois, and Ohio in 1948; Democrat John F. Kennedy won Missouri, Illinois, Pennsylvania, New Jersey, and New York in 1960. Republican Dwight D. Eisenhower won easily in 1952 and 1956, losing electoral votes only in the South (along with Missouri in 1956).

The geographically polarized electoral politics of the late nineteenth and early twentieth centuries ended abruptly in 1964, when Democrat Lyndon Johnson swept the entire country except for the Deep South. The South continued to swing Republican in 1968 and 1972, going Democratic in 1976 when Jimmy Carter of Georgia, the first candidate from the Deep South nominated by either major party, swept his native region. In those elections, the South along with the West were trending Republican while the Northeast was trending toward the Democratic.

Carter's defeat by Ronald Reagan in 1980 ushered in the contemporary geographic pattern of presidential elections. Although Reagan won the electoral votes of all but seven states, his highest percentages of popular votes were found in the South, with the exception of those counties with large nonwhite populations. The Great Plains states and the Rocky Mountain West were also heavily Republican; the Republicans have won the electoral votes of every state from North Dakota southward to Texas at each election since 1980 (with the exception of one electoral vote from Nebraska in 2008). Meanwhile, the Democrats began to pick up strength in the Pacific Coast states. The nation's largest state, California, went Democratic in 1992 for the first time since 1964, and the Golden State has been solidly Democratic in each subsequent election.

Although the Democratic and Republican parties each won two elections between 1996 and 2008, the geographic pattern of votes in all four elections was very similar. The Democrats continued to gain strength in metropolitan areas, not only in central cities but in their suburbs. Large suburban counties such as Montgomery County, Maryland, Fairfax County, Virginia, Westchester County, New York, Macomb County, Michigan, DuPage County, Illinois, Adams County, Colorado, and Marin County, California, gave solid majorities to Obama in 2008. Many of these and other suburban counties that gave Obama majorities, including DuPage and Adams counties, had enjoyed a long history of Republican support. On the other hand, Republican strength has tended to increase outside metropolitan areas.

Because nonmetropolitan areas are more sparsely populated than central cities and suburbs, a large majority of the more than three thousand counties and county-equivalent units across the United States gave majorities of their popular votes to McCain. In closely contested states, McCain carried a large majority of the counties, even though Obama won the electoral votes of these states; for example, Obama carried only thirteen of Indiana's ninety-two counties. He carried only two of Nevada's sixteen counties, but these two counties include the cities of Las Vegas and Reno, and between them are home to more than half of Nevada's population. McCain carried nearly all of the counties in heavily Republican states. For example, he carried all seventy-seven counties in Oklahoma, all but two in Wyoming, and all but three each in Idaho and Utah. These results reinforced a trend that has developed in these and other peripheral areas of the United States over the past several decades.

In interpreting these maps with an eye to the future, it should be recognized that during the 1990s and in the elections of 2000 and 2004, counties supporting Republican nominees grew faster than those supporting Democratic nominees. Counties that went Republican in 2000 grew by a total of 14 percent between 1990 and 2000, whereas those that went Democratic grew by about 5 percent during that decade. As a result, the reapportionment of 2000 resulted in a shift of about eight seats in the House of Representatives, and therefore in the Electoral College, from the Democrats to the Republicans. This shift slowed down considerably in 2008, when Obama carried rapidly growing and previously Republican Virginia, North Carolina, Florida, Colorado, and Nevada. After the 2010 census, only a slight shift in the Electoral College from the Democrats to the Republicans is expected on the basis of the 2008

results, although whether states such as Indiana and Virginia, both of which had been in Republican hands since the 1960s, will remain Democratic in the 2012 election remains to be seen. Both parties can be expected to pay considerable attention to rapidly growing and closely contested states in the years ahead. These include not only Virginia, North Carolina, Florida, and Colorado but also rapidly growing states that McCain carried narrowly, including Arizona and Georgia.

VOTER TURNOUT IN TEMPORAL AND GEOGRAPHICAL PERSPECTIVE

Voter turnout is defined as the percentage of eligible voters who actually cast ballots in any given election. Relative to previous U.S. presidential elections, voter turnout in the 2008 election was relatively high, reflecting the intense interest shown by many Americans in the campaign. Many precincts throughout the United States reported long lines and delays at polling places on Election Day, despite the fact that the number of people who cast their ballots early has continued to increase, as discussed in chapter 2.

Increased turnout in 2008 relative to 2004 and previous elections has reversed the long-standing historical trend of declining voter turnout, as shown in the graph (graph 4.2). Voter turnout in the United States peaked in the nineteenth century and declined steadily throughout the twentieth century. There are

some exceptions to this general trend. Voter turnout tends to be higher in a given election that is expected to be closely contested, for example, in 1960 and 1968. On the other hand, elections that are not expected to be closely contested generally have relatively low turnouts. Turnout was also relatively low in 1944, not only because the incumbent president, Franklin D. Roosevelt, was expected to win easily, but also because large numbers of eligible voters were serving in the armed forces outside the United States at the time of the election and found it difficult or impossible to cast absentee ballots. Turnout reached a low in 1996, when for the first time in U.S. history less than 50 percent of America's eligible voters cast ballots. Since that time, voter turnout has rebounded and continues to increase.

As in previous elections, voter turnout in the 2008 presidential election varied considerably among various regions of the United States. Generally speaking, voter turnout declines from north to south. Historically, these geographical differences in voter turnout have been related to differences in political culture across the United States. Political culture is defined as the attitudes and beliefs about the nature of politics and government. Political scientists and geographers have long recognized and identified three major political cultures in the United States—the Moralistic political culture of New England and the northern tier of states, the Individualistic political culture of the mid-Atlantic and Great Lakes states westward to California, and the Traditionalistic political culture of the South. Each of these political culture regions originated in colonial days in response to differing political-economic relationships between the various groups of colonies and England, and each spread westward over the course of U.S. history in response to prevailing migration patterns.

New England's political culture is Moralistic, based on the belief that the purpose of politics and government are to promote the common good. In this view, political participation is seen as a civic duty. The political culture of the mid-Atlantic states is Individualistic. Individualistic political culture sees politics and government as businesses, with successful participation rewarded. The political culture of the South is Traditionalistic, and politics and government are seen as a means of preserving and protecting the power of the elite. Political participation and activity among nonmembers of the elite is discouraged.

The influence of these political cultures remains evident in rates of voter turnout even today. Throughout American history, voter turnouts have been highest in the North, whose Moralistic political culture emphasizes the importance of political participation. Voter turnout declines from the North to the South, where political participation has not been encouraged. The 2008 election is no exception; voter turnout was highest in the northern Great Plains and northern New England and lowest in several southern and southwestern states.

Average Democratic Vote
1948 to 1960 Presidential Elections

MAP 4.14

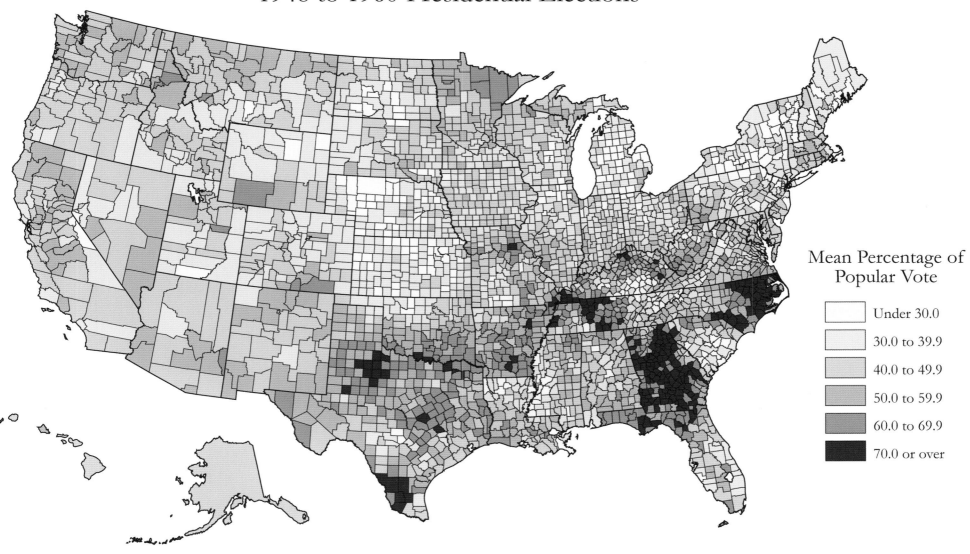

Mean Percentage of
Popular Vote

Under 30.0

30.0 to 39.9

40.0 to 49.9

50.0 to 59.9

60.0 to 69.9

70.0 or over

MAP 4.15

Average Democratic Vote
1964 to 1976 Presidential Elections

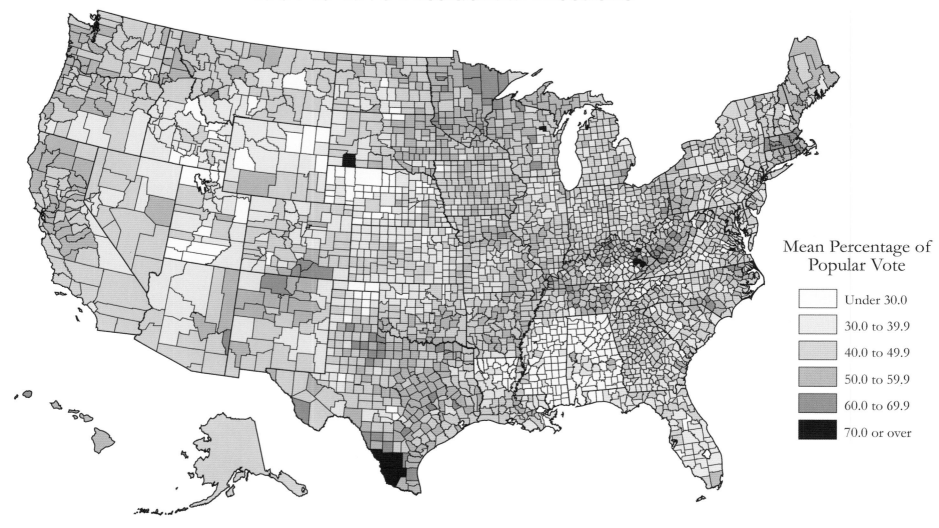

Mean Percentage of
Popular Vote

Under 30.0

30.0 to 39.9

40.0 to 49.9

50.0 to 59.9

60.0 to 69.9

70.0 or over

Average Democratic Vote
1980 to 1992 Presidential Elections

MAP 4.16

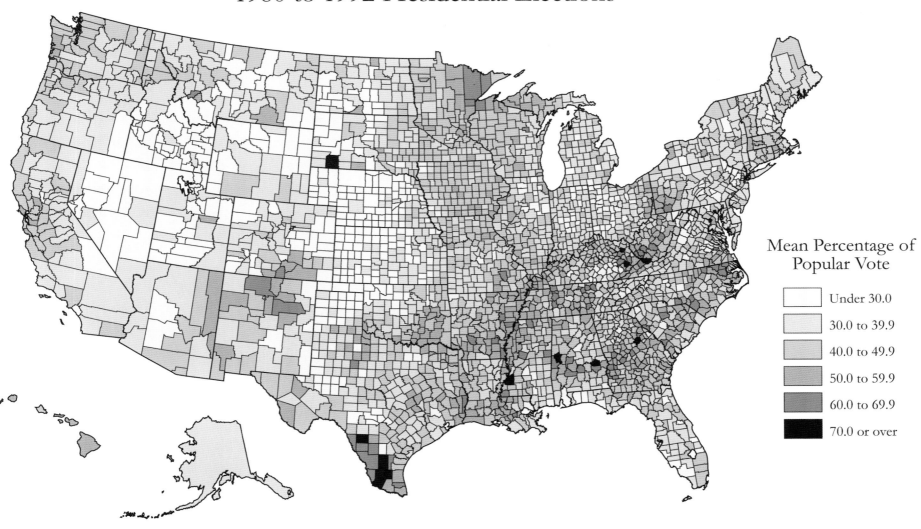

Mean Percentage of
Popular Vote

	Under 30.0
	30.0 to 39.9
	40.0 to 49.9
	50.0 to 59.9
	60.0 to 69.9
	70.0 or over

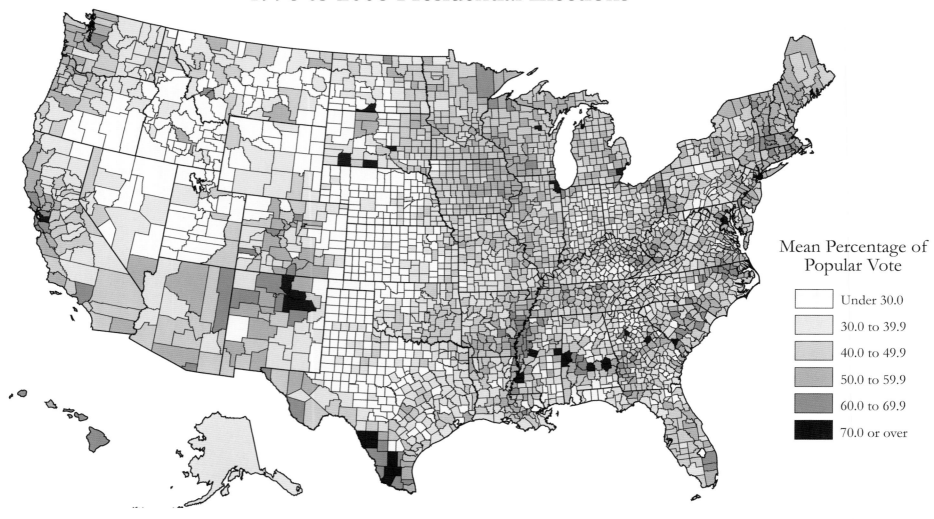

Average Democratic Vote
1996 to 2008 Presidential Elections

MAP 4.17

Mean Percentage of
Popular Vote

Under 30.0
30.0 to 39.9
40.0 to 49.9
50.0 to 59.9
60.0 to 69.9
70.0 or over

Democratic Vote Variability
1948 to 1960 Presidential Elections

MAP 4.18

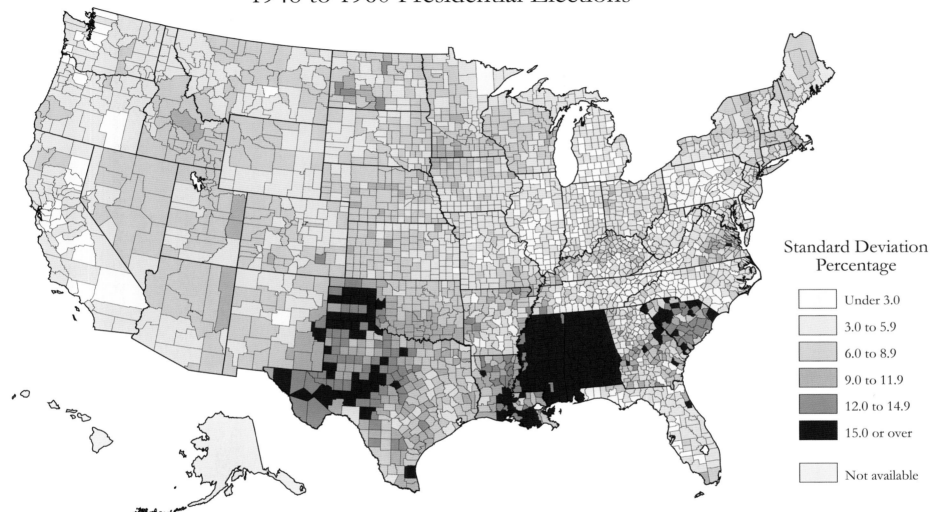

Standard Deviation
Percentage

Under 3.0

3.0 to 5.9

6.0 to 8.9

9.0 to 11.9

12.0 to 14.9

15.0 or over

Not available

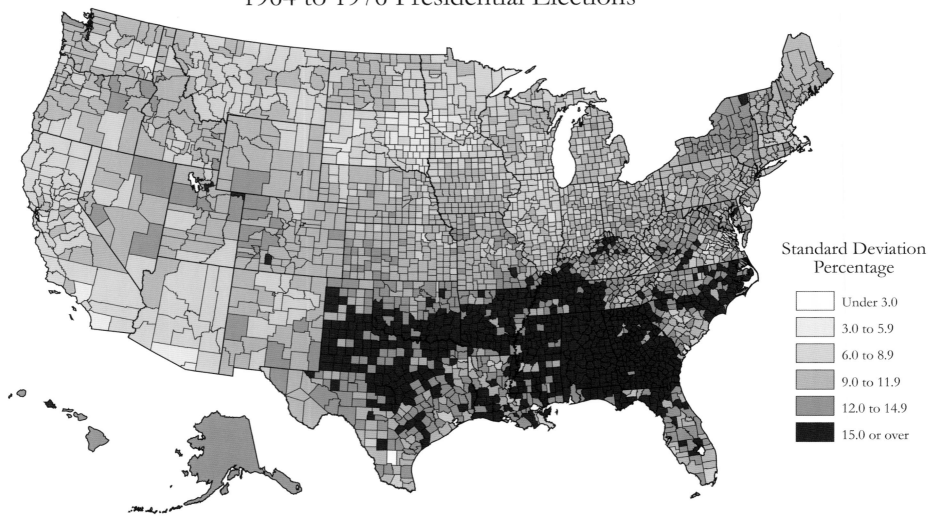

MAP 4.19

Democratic Vote Variability
1964 to 1976 Presidential Elections

Standard Deviation
Percentage

Under 3.0

3.0 to 5.9

6.0 to 8.9

9.0 to 11.9

12.0 to 14.9

15.0 or over

Democratic Vote Variability
1980 to 1992 Presidential Elections

MAP 4.20

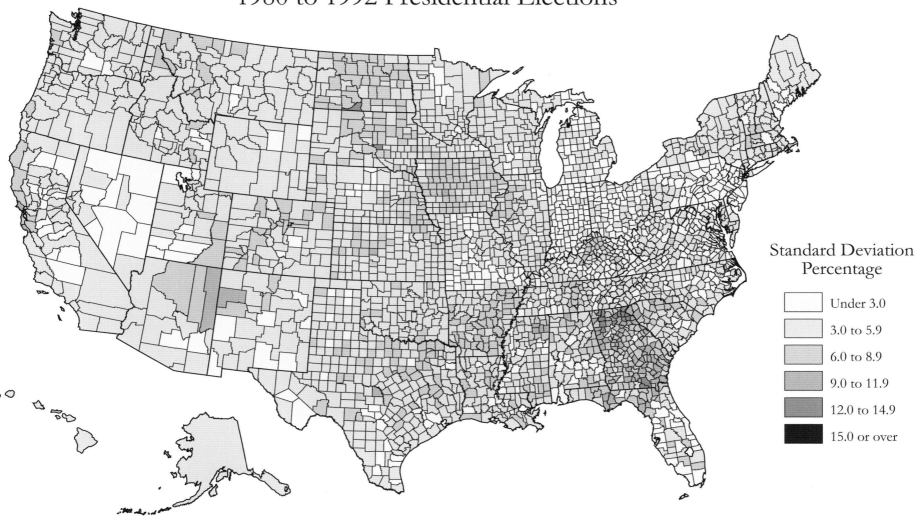

Standard Deviation
Percentage

	Under 3.0
	3.0 to 5.9
	6.0 to 8.9
	9.0 to 11.9
	12.0 to 14.9
	15.0 or over

MAP 4.21

Democratic Vote Variability
1996 to 2008 Presidential Elections

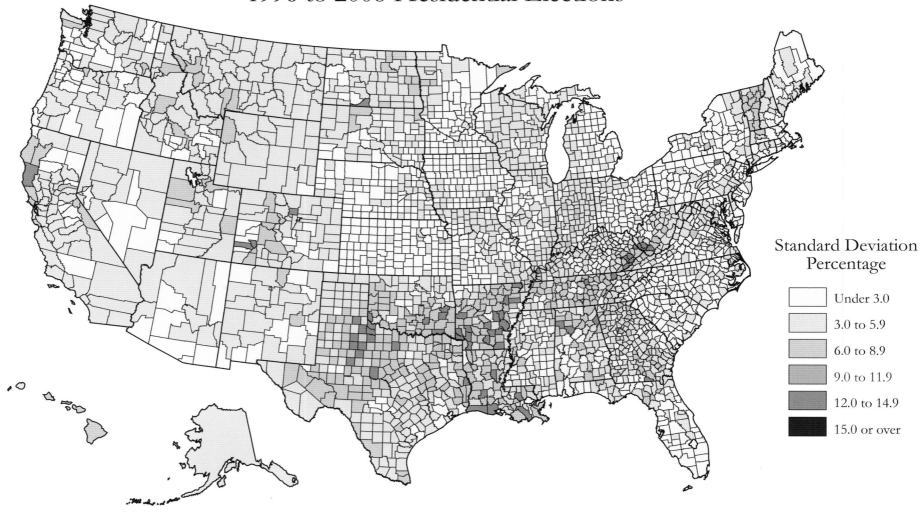

Standard Deviation
Percentage

	Under 3.0
	3.0 to 5.9
	6.0 to 8.9
	9.0 to 11.9
	12.0 to 14.9
	15.0 or over

Average Republican Vote
1948 to 1960 Presidential Elections

MAP 4.22

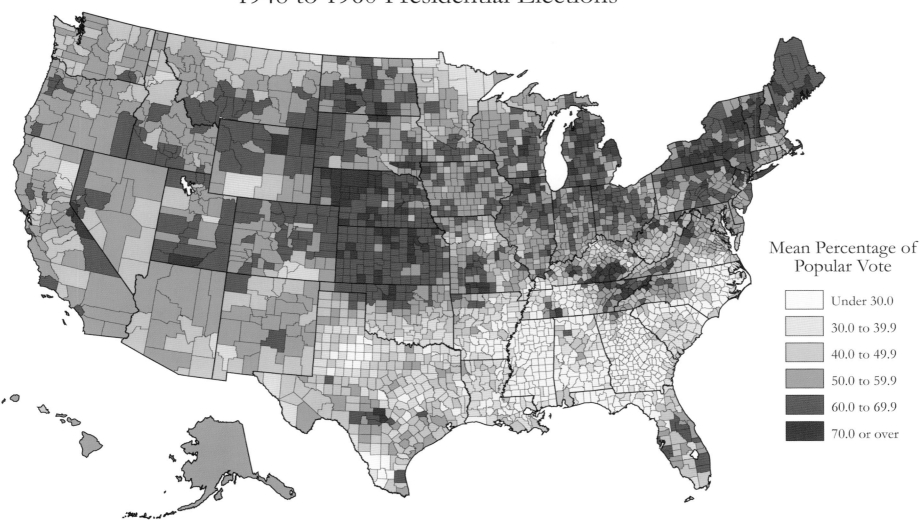

Mean Percentage of
Popular Vote

Under 30.0

30.0 to 39.9

40.0 to 49.9

50.0 to 59.9

60.0 to 69.9

70.0 or over

MAP 4.23

Average Republican Vote
1964 to 1976 Presidential Elections

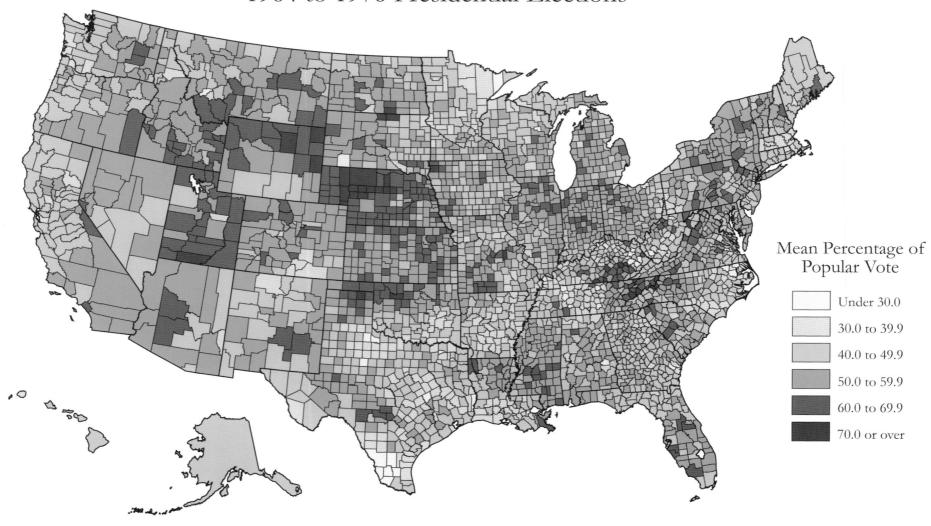

Mean Percentage of
Popular Vote

Under 30.0

30.0 to 39.9

40.0 to 49.9

50.0 to 59.9

60.0 to 69.9

70.0 or over

Average Republican Vote
1980 to 1992 Presidential Elections

MAP 4.24

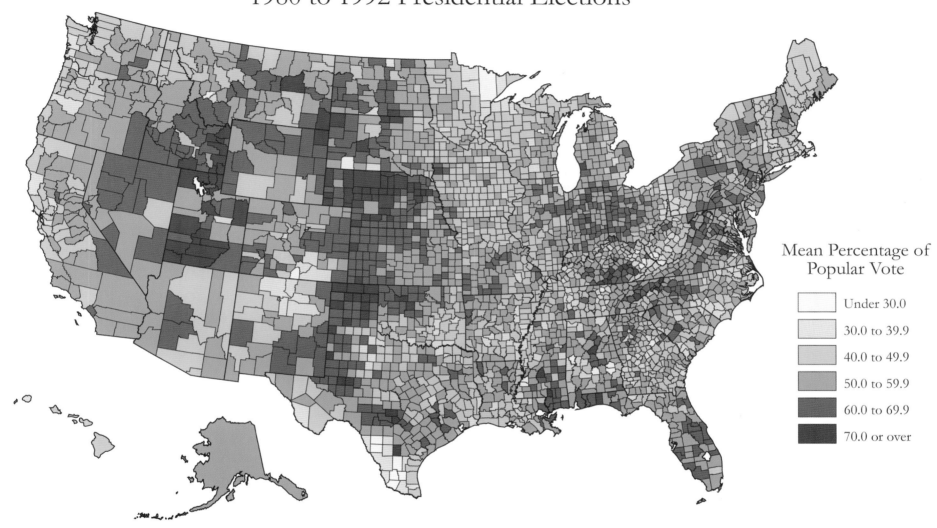

Mean Percentage of
Popular Vote

- Under 30.0
- 30.0 to 39.9
- 40.0 to 49.9
- 50.0 to 59.9
- 60.0 to 69.9
- 70.0 or over

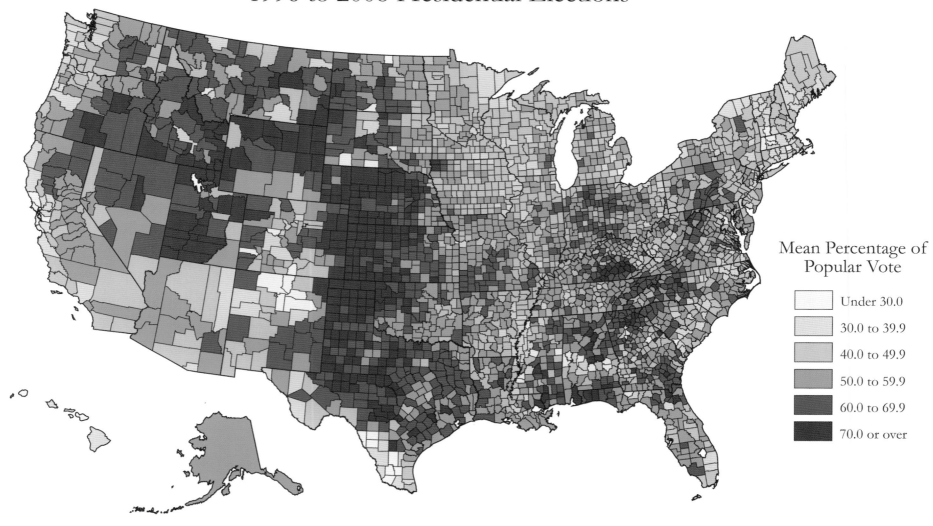

Average Republican Vote
1996 to 2008 Presidential Elections

MAP 4.25

Mean Percentage of
Popular Vote

Under 30.0

30.0 to 39.9

40.0 to 49.9

50.0 to 59.9

60.0 to 69.9

70.0 or over

Republican Vote Variability
1948 to 1960 Presidential Elections

MAP 4.26

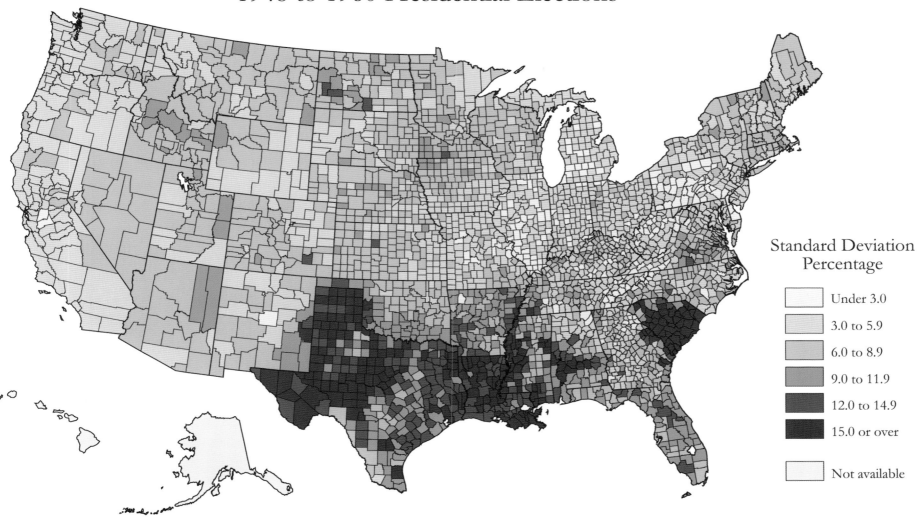

Standard Deviation
Percentage

Under 3.0

3.0 to 5.9

6.0 to 8.9

9.0 to 11.9

12.0 to 14.9

15.0 or over

Not available

MAP 4.27

Republican Vote Variability
1964 to 1976 Presidential Elections

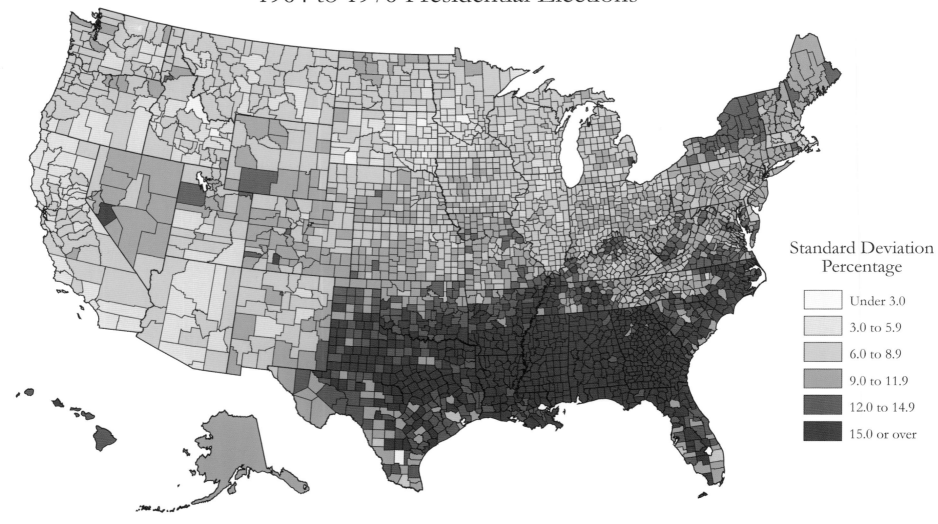

Standard Deviation
Percentage

Under 3.0

3.0 to 5.9

6.0 to 8.9

9.0 to 11.9

12.0 to 14.9

15.0 or over

Republican Vote Variability
1980 to 1992 Presidential Elections

MAP 4.28

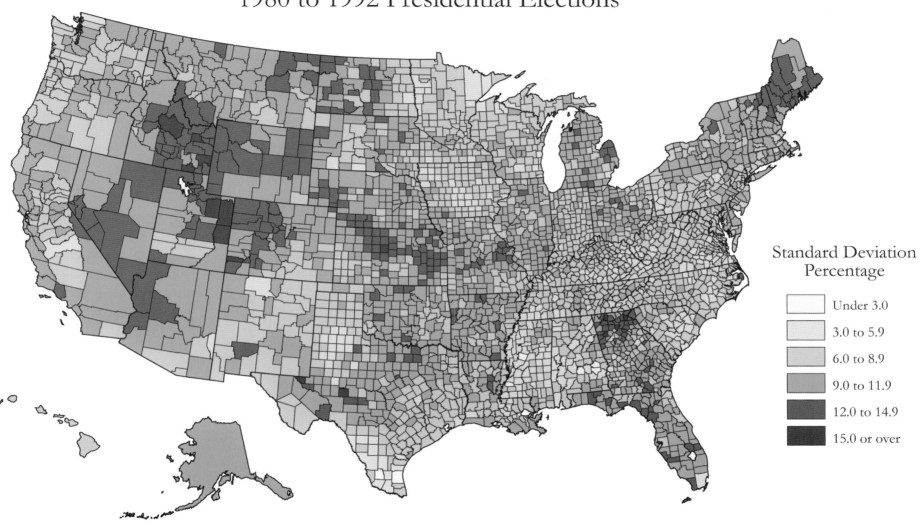

Standard Deviation
Percentage

Under 3.0

3.0 to 5.9

6.0 to 8.9

9.0 to 11.9

12.0 to 14.9

15.0 or over

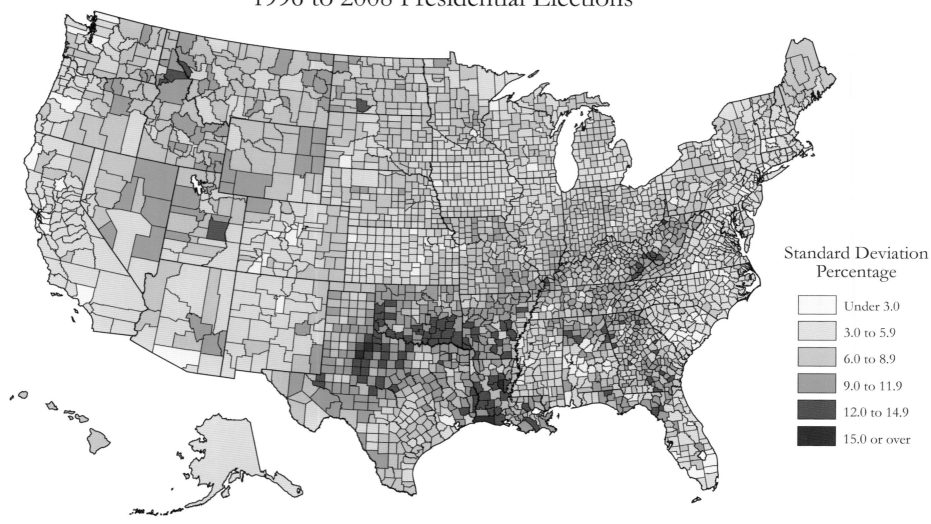

Republican Vote Variability
1996 to 2008 Presidential Elections

MAP 4.29

Standard Deviation Percentage

- Under 3.0
- 3.0 to 5.9
- 6.0 to 8.9
- 9.0 to 11.9
- 12.0 to 14.9
- 15.0 or over

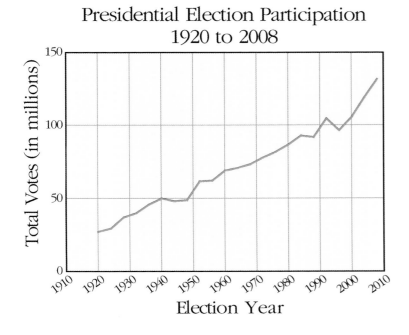

Presidential Election Participation
1920 to 2008

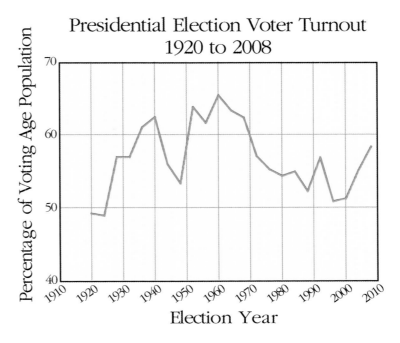

Presidential Election Voter Turnout
1920 to 2008

GRAPH 4.2

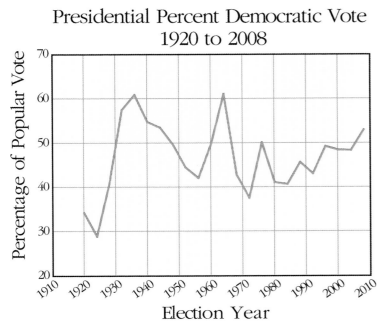

Presidential Percent Democratic Vote
1920 to 2008

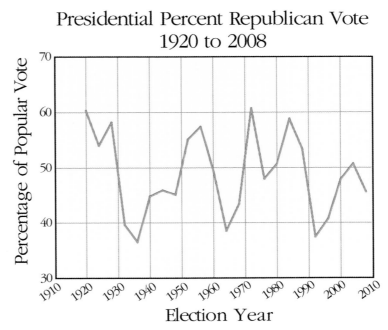

Presidential Percent Republican Vote
1920 to 2008

GRAPH 4.3

County-Level Democratic Vote Correlation with 2008 Election, 1920 to 2008

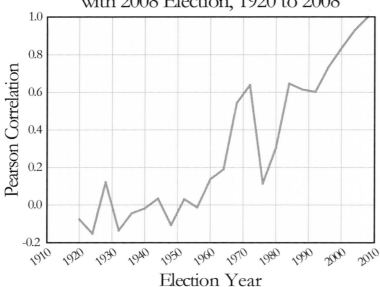

County-Level Republican Vote Correlation with 2008 Election, 1920 to 2008

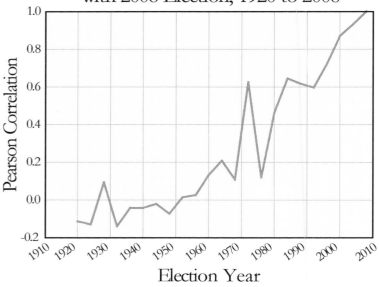

County-Level Democratic Vote Correlation with Previous Election, 1924 to 2008

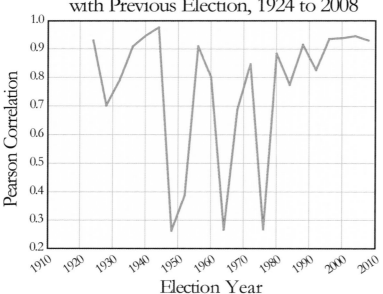

County-Level Republican Vote Correlation with Previous Election, 1924 to 2008

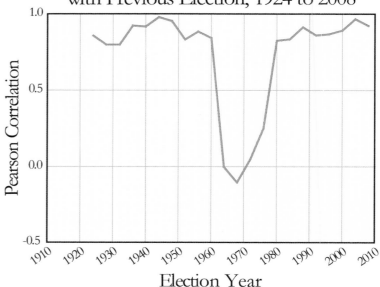

■ THE ROLE OF TURNOUT IN SELECTED STATES

RICHARD L. MORRILL

State level analyses have demonstrated the significance of higher turnout in Obama's victory in 2008. Here I look at six example states: North Carolina, the state with the highest increase in turnout, at 8 percent, Indiana, Virginia, New Mexico, Florida, and Colorado, using county-level data. Short narratives and a few maps highlight the relations between turnout increases and improved elections results for the Democrats.

NORTH CAROLINA

Among these six states, North Carolina had the greatest turnout increases, sufficient to shift the state from Republican to Democratic, as Democrats won a majority of the total vote only in the counties with over an 8 percent increase after losing both sets in 2004 (map 4.30). The regions of highest turnout change are the counties with high shares of black population east and northeast of Raleigh, but two other areas are of interest—the counties around Fayetteville and Fort Bragg, and those around Camp Lejeune—with large shifts toward the Democrats, but still safely Republican. Moderate but still high turnout increases cover much of the central and southeast part of the state, including many major metropolitan counties (Mecklenburg-Charlotte), Forsyth and Guilford (Winston-Salem, Greensboro). Most counties with a low increase in turnout

or a decline are in Appalachia. Wake (Raleigh) had a high turnout before, but also a big shift to the Democrats. Democratic counties, continuing or newly Democratic, had much higher turnout and turnout change than Republican counties.

VIRGINIA

Virginia is the most dramatic case of our six states in the relation between turnout increase, Democratic voting, and increase in the Democratic share (map 4.30). The highest turnout-increase counties were the only set voting Democratic in 2004—mainly counties with high black shares, as well as Richmond, the Norfolk area, and university areas (Charlottesville, Montgomery [Blacksburg]), switching to Democratic in 2008. Counties with turnout increases of 4–9 percent had a Republican majority in 2004, the set registering a Democratic majority in 2008, and including many counties switching from Republican to Democratic. They blanket most of the eastern part of the state, including Washington and Richmond suburbs. The latter are also the highest increase in the Democratic share, often over 10 percent. Thus the counties with lower turnout increases or declines remained Republican, with the declining counties showing a lower Democratic share, not surprisingly along the western Appalachian edge of the state.

INDIANA

Indiana experienced the greatest increase in the Democratic share among these six states, sufficient to shift the state from Republican to Democratic (map 4.31). The higher shifts were indeed for the sets of counties with over a 2 percent turnout increase, but it was only among the counties with over a 4 percent turnout increase that, even in 2008, a Democratic majority was achieved. These include such large metropolitan counties as greater Indianapolis (Marion and surrounding counties), sizable Democratic increases but that still remained safely Republican, Lake (Gary), St. Joseph (South Bend), Vanderburgh (Evansville), and even Republican Allen (Fort Wayne), plus university counties (Monroe-Bloomington, Tippecanoe-Lafayette—the county with the highest increase in Democratic share). The counties with declines in turnout remained strongly Republican and were mainly rural and small town.

NEW MEXICO

Counties with the highest turnout increase, over 5 percent, also had the highest increase in the Democratic share (10 percent). (See map 4.31.) The greatest turnout increases, shares for Obama, and increases in the Democratic share are for the counties north of Santa Fe, both Hispanic and American Indian and environmental, and west of Albuquerque (Cibola—the most extreme in the state). The counties with decreases in turnout, and still largely Republican, dominate the four corners of the state, for example, San Juan County, with the "four corners" small metropolitan area of Farmington.

FLORIDA

Areas with the highest turnout increases did tend to have the highest increases in the share voting Democratic, but from a low level (40 percent) to just over 50 percent, and including several counties that switched from Republican to Democratic, for example, Hillsborough (Tampa), Pinellas (St. Petersburg), and Orange (Orlando). (See map 4.32.) Even the extreme western panhandle (Escambia-Pensacola and Okaloosa-Eglin AFB) had big Democratic gains associated with higher turnout, but remained safely Republican. Areas with the lowest turnout increases and the lowest shift to Democrats, or even increases in the Republican share, cover much of the central panhandle and the western Florida resort and retirement area, beyond Tampa-St. Petersburg.

COLORADO

The highest turnout increases and increases in the Democratic share are in the north central part of the state, centered on Denver, including many environmental amenity counties in the Rockies, but also small metropolitan Fort Collins (Larimer) and Greeley (Weld County). (See map 4.32.) While the total vote of the region is strongly Democratic, many counties remain strongly Republican, even though several Republican counties moved in the Democratic direction—for example, even El Paso (Colorado Springs). The western and eastern edges of the state remained Republican and often had turnout declines.

MAP 4.30

Change in Turnout Percentage 2004 to 2008
Virginia and North Carolina

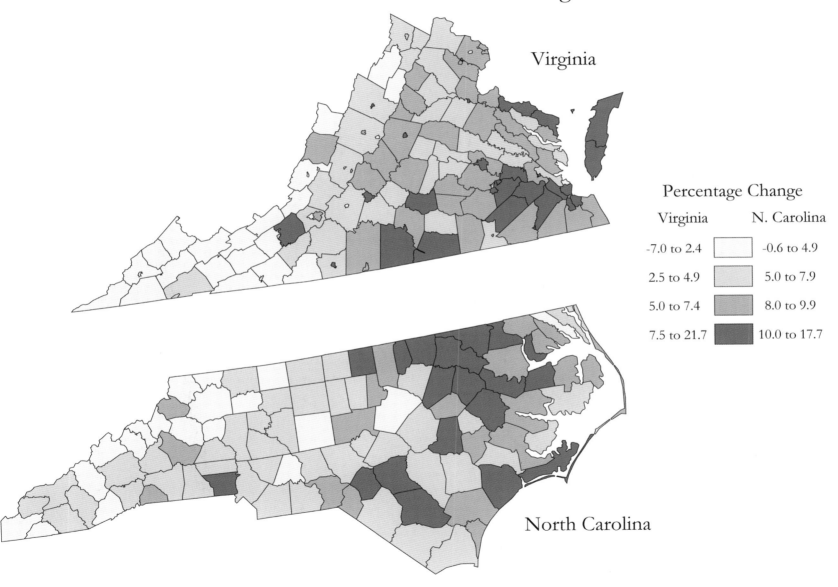

Virginia

Percentage Change

Virginia		N. Carolina
-7.0 to 2.4		-0.6 to 4.9
2.5 to 4.9		5.0 to 7.9
5.0 to 7.4		8.0 to 9.9
7.5 to 21.7		10.0 to 17.7

North Carolina

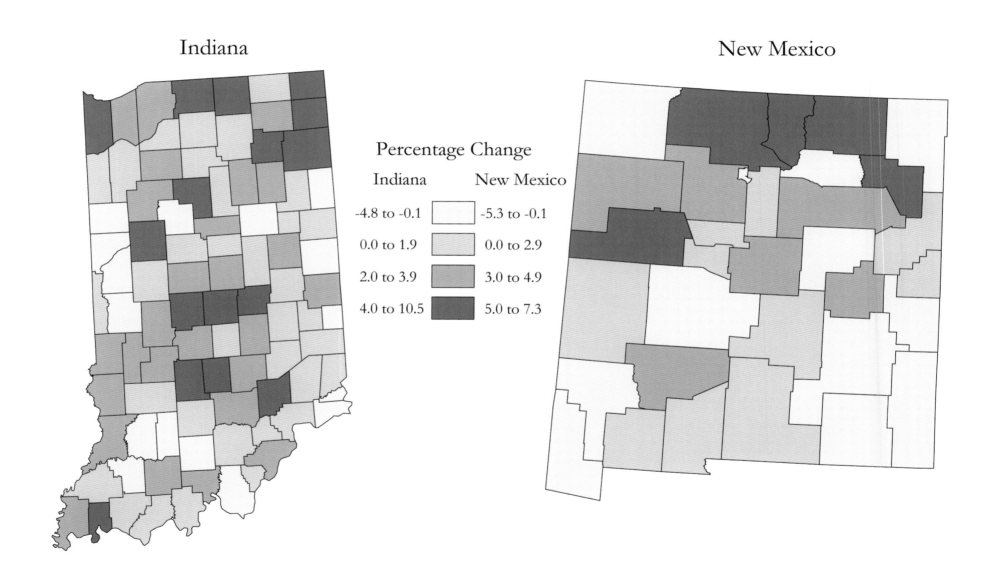

MAP 4.31

Change in Turnout Percentage 2004 to 2008
Indiana and New Mexico

Indiana

New Mexico

Percentage Change

Indiana		New Mexico
-4.8 to -0.1		-5.3 to -0.1
0.0 to 1.9		0.0 to 2.9
2.0 to 3.9		3.0 to 4.9
4.0 to 10.5		5.0 to 7.3

Change in Turnout Percentage 2004 to 2008
Colorado and Florida

MAP 4.32

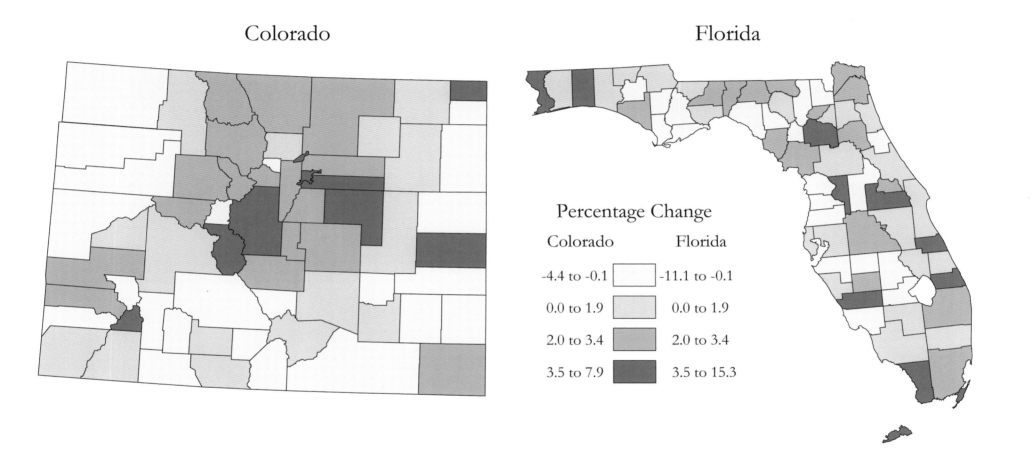

Colorado

Florida

Percentage Change

Colorado		Florida
-4.4 to -0.1		-11.1 to -0.1
0.0 to 1.9		0.0 to 1.9
2.0 to 3.4		2.0 to 3.4
3.5 to 7.9		3.5 to 15.3

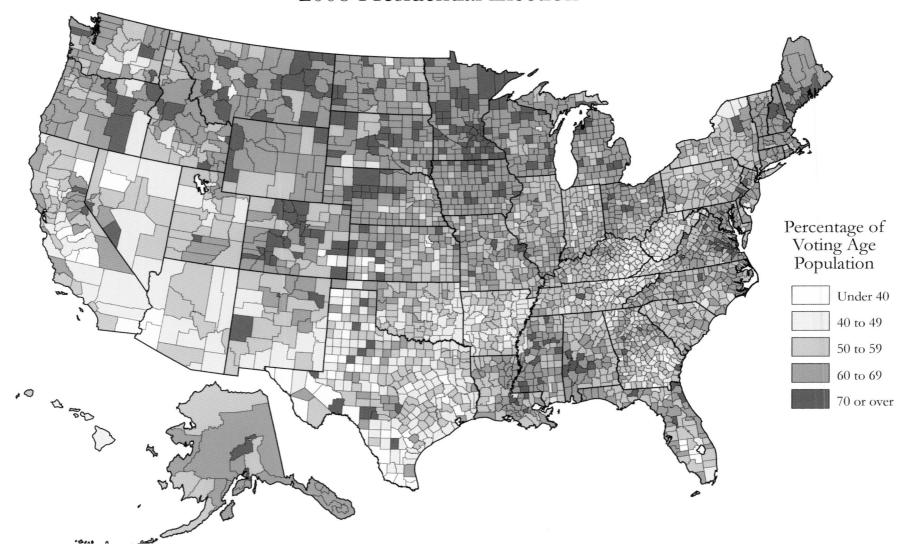

MAP 4.33

Voter Turnout
2008 Presidential Election

Percentage of
Voting Age
Population

Under 40

40 to 49

50 to 59

60 to 69

70 or over

Voter Turnout

MAP 4.34

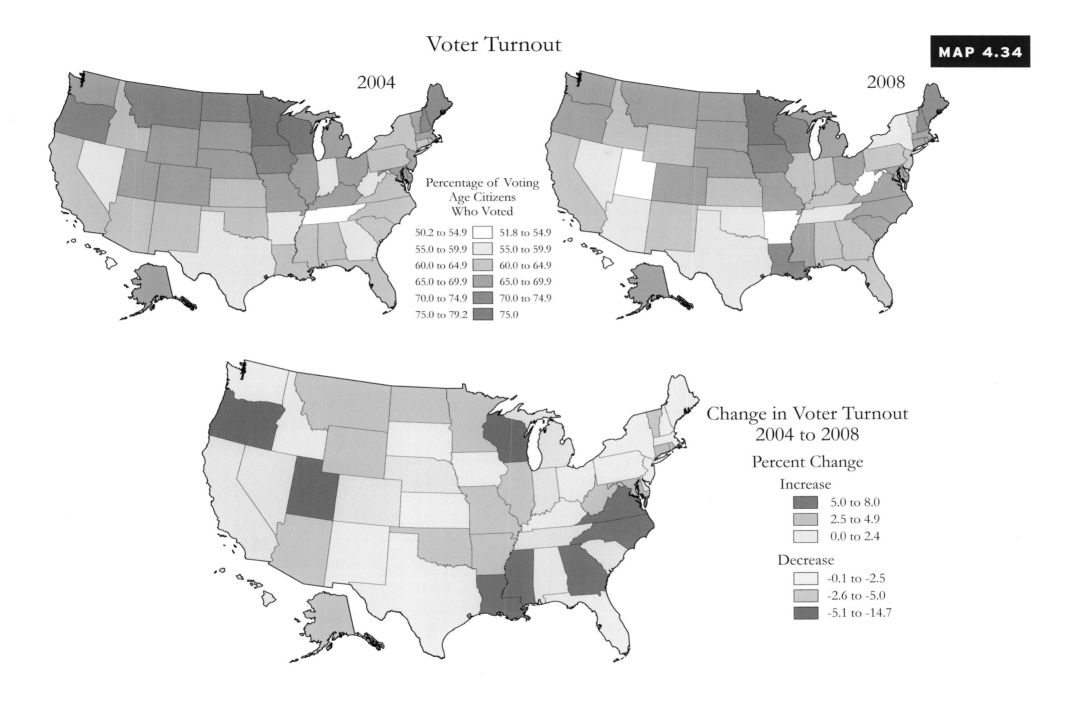

2004

2008

Percentage of Voting
Age Citizens
Who Voted

50.2 to 54.9	51.8 to 54.9
55.0 to 59.9	55.0 to 59.9
60.0 to 64.9	60.0 to 64.9
65.0 to 69.9	65.0 to 69.9
70.0 to 74.9	70.0 to 74.9
75.0 to 79.2	75.0

Change in Voter Turnout
2004 to 2008

Percent Change

Increase

	5.0 to 8.0
	2.5 to 4.9
	0.0 to 2.4

Decrease

	-0.1 to -2.5
	-2.6 to -5.0
	-5.1 to -14.7

■ THE ELECTORAL COLLEGE AND THE 2008 PRESIDENTIAL ELECTION

BARNEY WARF

One of the unique particularities of the American electoral system is its Electoral College: American voters do not directly choose a presidential candidate, but rather vote for representatives to the Electoral College, the body that formally selects the new president and vice president. Enshrined in the Constitution during the Convention of 1787, the Electoral College struck a balance between direct proportional representation, which favors large states, and equal representation by all states, which favors small ones. The number of Electoral College votes for each state equals the size of its congressional delegation, that is, the sum of its senators and representatives, with a minimum of three and the remainder allocated roughly but not directly proportional to its population as assessed by the decennial census. Thus, there are currently 538 electors corresponding with one hundred senators, 435 representatives, and three representatives from the District of Columbia. The minimum number of electoral votes is three, while the maximum is a function of population size; currently California, with 36 million people (12 percent of the national population), has the largest number, 55. To win a presidential election, a candidate must accrue a majority of Electoral College votes, that is, a minimum of 270.

The overriding characteristic of the Electoral College is the "winner-take-all" system, or "unit rule" system, in which candidates who receive a plurality of the popular vote in a state acquire *all* of its Electoral College votes. Maine, starting in 1972, and Nebraska, starting in 1991, are exceptions, giving two electoral votes to the winner of the statewide popular vote and allocating the remainder to the winner of the popular vote within each congressional district. The Electoral College exaggerates the strength of the winner of the popular vote by giving the winner a disproportionately large share of the electoral vote, creating false "mandates" to rule. It is also possible to have a "wrong winner," that is, a presidential candidate who wins a majority of the popular vote but loses in the Electoral College, and hence the election, by winning small states by large margins but losing large states by slim margins, as happened with Al Gore in the 2000 election.

The first two maps (map 4.35) portray the spatial distribution of electoral votes garnered by Obama and McCain, respectively, in the 2008 presidential election. With 53 percent of the popular vote and 365 electoral votes, Obama easily defeated McCain, who won 47 percent of the vote and 173 electoral votes. Obama's largest sources of electoral votes included the Northeast and some Midwestern states (including Nebraska, which gave him one electoral vote), Florida, and the West Coast, particularly California. In contrast, McCain's mother lode of votes was Texas, with others coming from Southern and lightly populated Great Plains states.

In light of these observations, it is instructive to reexamine the 2008 election in light of the question as to how it may have appeared had the electoral votes been allocated in each state proportionately to the popular vote there. Thus, rather than a "winner-take-all" system, presidential candidates could split the vote in each state. The resulting totals of electoral votes would more closely resemble the popular vote, as reflected in the table below and in the proportional representation maps that follow.

Moreover, the spatial distribution of each candidate's electoral votes would shift. Whereas Obama would still have garnered a large number of electoral votes from California, he would have picked up numerous others from Texas and throughout the South, where he frequently won one-quarter or more of the votes (and in some states, such as Missouri, which he lost very narrowly). Conversely, Obama would have lost electoral votes in his greatest areas of strength, that is, in New York and the industrial heartland. John McCain, conversely, would have won more votes from California and New York than he would have from Texas. In short, both candidates' sources of electoral votes would have been considerably more geographically diffuse than they actually were in 2008.

TABLE 4.4. Obama and McCain Votes within and without the Electoral College

	With Electoral College	Without Electoral College
Obama	365	284
McCain	173	245

MAP 4.35

Electoral College Vote 2008 Presidential Election

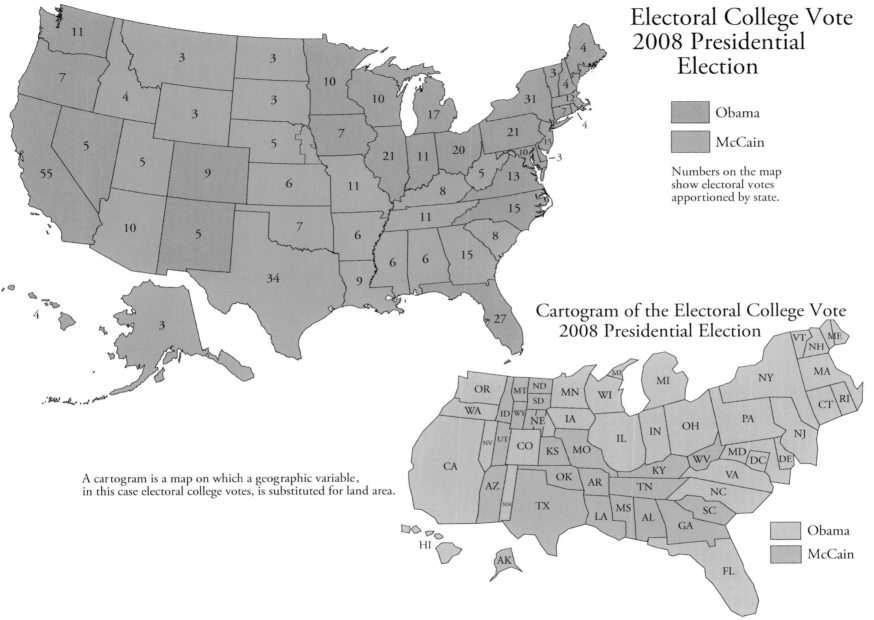

Obama

McCain

Numbers on the map show electoral votes apportioned by state.

Cartogram of the Electoral College Vote 2008 Presidential Election

A cartogram is a map on which a geographic variable, in this case electoral college votes, is substituted for land area.

Obama

McCain

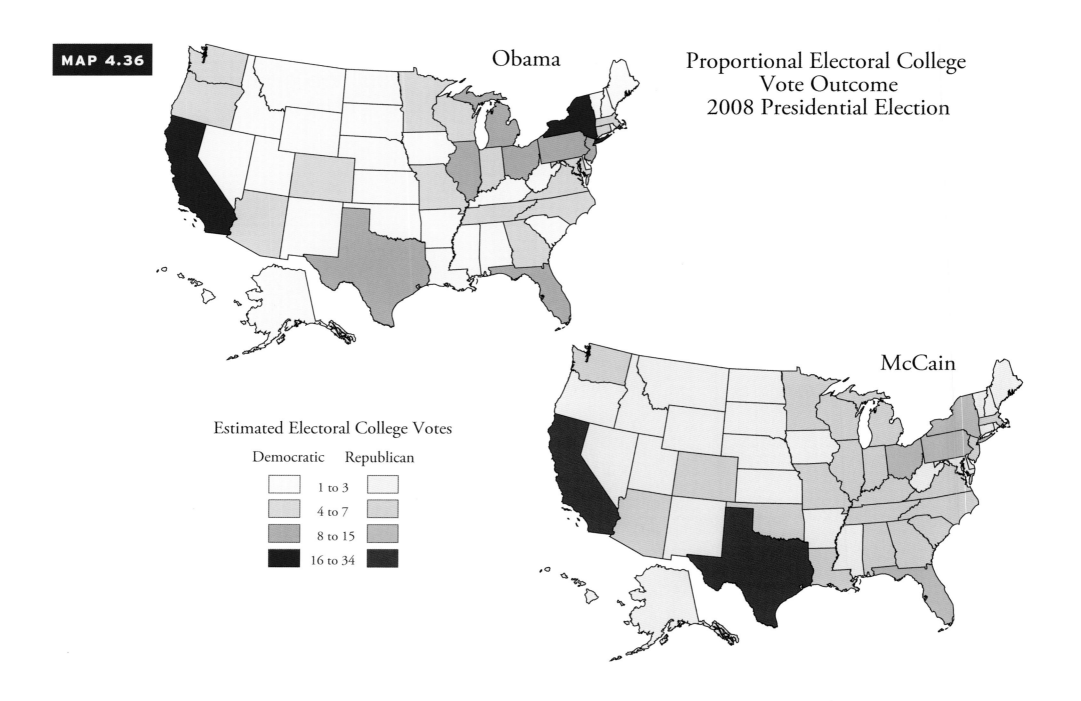

MAP 4.36

Obama

Proportional Electoral College
Vote Outcome
2008 Presidential Election

McCain

Estimated Electoral College Votes

Democratic   Republican

1 to 3

4 to 7

8 to 15

16 to 34

■ METROPOLITAN AREAS OF TWO MILLION OR MORE

FRED M. SHELLEY

Barack Obama's success in the 2008 presidential election was due primarily to the large margins that he amassed in the country's large metropolitan areas. This is evident on the following map, which shows the percentage of votes won by Obama, John McCain, and other candidates for each of the twenty-six metropolitan areas in the United States with more than two million residents. In total, these twenty-six metropolitan areas gave Obama more than 60 percent of the two-party vote in the 2008 election. In contrast, Obama won only a slight majority in smaller metropolitan areas with less than two million residents each, while McCain won majorities in micropolitan counties (defined as counties containing cities with populations between 10,000 and 49,999) and in nonmetropolitan counties. In other words, McCain won a majority of popular votes cast by people who did not reside in metropolitan areas with populations of two million or more. Across the country, Obama outpolled McCain in twenty-two of the twenty-six metropolitan areas with populations of at least two million. McCain carried only the Phoenix metropolitan area, where he resides, along with the Dallas-Fort Worth, Houston, and Cincinnati metropolitan areas. Obama won more than two-thirds of the popular vote in the Seattle, San Francisco-Oakland, Portland, New York, and Washington, D.C., metropolitan areas along with the Chicago metropolitan area, where he resides.

That Obama owed his victory to his strength in metropolitan areas continued a trend dating back to 1992: Democratic Party support has increased in metropolitan areas, whereas Republican strength has increased in nonmetropolitan areas. Thus the Democratic Party has become by far the more metropolitan oriented of the two major parties. This trend dates back to the 1960s and accelerated in the 2000 and 2004 presidential elections. Absent the vote in large metropolitan areas, the Republicans would have won every presidential election since 1964.

An important factor underlying increasing Democratic strength in metropolitan areas has been the fact that Democratic Party strength has increased considerably in suburban areas. Historically, most metropolitan areas were sharply divided between Democratic strength in central cities and Republican strength in suburban counties. For example, Cook County, Illinois, which contains the city of Chicago, has been a Democratic stronghold for many years. On the other hand, neighboring suburban DuPage County has historically been dominated by Republicans. In recent years, however, Democratic Party strength has increased in DuPage County. In 2008, Obama carried DuPage County with 55 percent of the vote, or a higher percentage than he won nationwide.

Increasing Democratic strength in metropolitan areas results from several factors. Throughout the country, suburbs have been growing at much faster rates than either central cities or rural areas since World War II. In many parts of the country, large numbers of nonwhite persons have moved to suburban areas. Metropolitan areas have higher percentages of younger persons, more highly educated voters, and professionals, and all of these demographics gave solid majorities to Obama. Moreover, many parts of the country have seen increased political tension at the local level between metropolitan and rural interests. In some states, city and suburban legislators and voters have joined forces against more conservative interests associated with rural areas, especially on issues associated with social and cultural conservatism such as abortion, gay rights, regulation of alcohol possession, and gun control.

Given that metropolitan areas are growing at faster rates than nonmetropolitan areas, these demographic trends are likely to continue in the years ahead unless the Republicans are able to articulate policy positions more palatable to metropolitan residents. Many newcomers to metropolitan areas are recent college graduates, members of ethnic and racial minority groups, professionals, and immigrants. All of these groups, including immigrants once they achieved U.S. citizenship, were strongly in support of Obama in 2008. The trend toward increasing Democratic dominance of large metropolitan areas poses a dilemma for the Republican Party. By taking more moderate positions on various social and economic issues, the Republicans could pick up support among metropolitan voters but risk alienating their more conservative rural base.

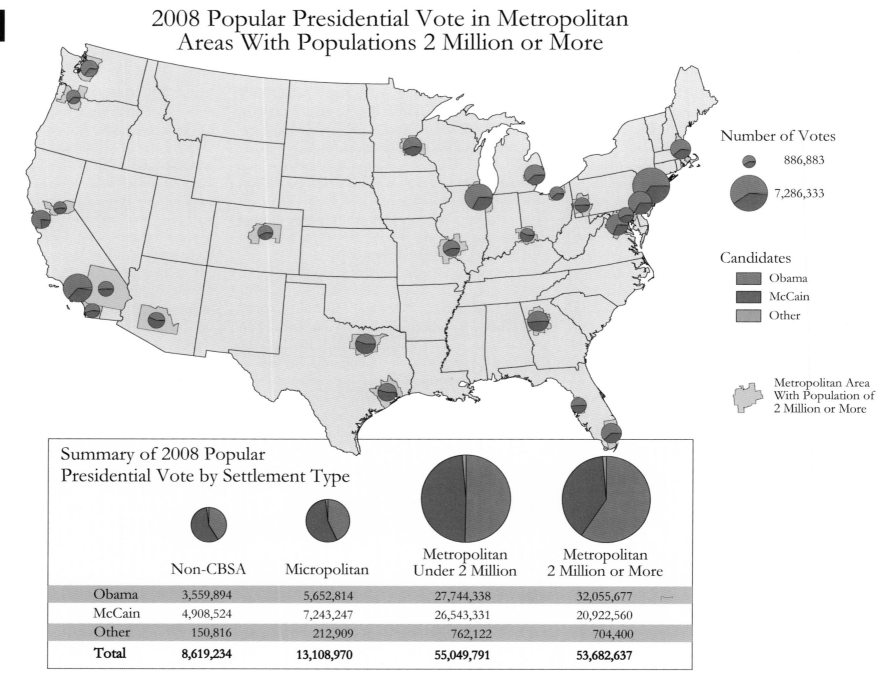

2008 Popular Presidential Vote in Metropolitan Areas With Populations 2 Million or More

MAP 4.37

Number of Votes

886,883

7,286,333

Candidates

Obama

McCain

Other

Metropolitan Area
With Population of
2 Million or More

Summary of 2008 Popular
Presidential Vote by Settlement Type

	Non-CBSA	Micropolitan	Metropolitan Under 2 Million	Metropolitan 2 Million or More
Obama	3,559,894	5,652,814	27,744,338	32,055,677
McCain	4,908,524	7,243,247	26,543,331	20,922,560
Other	150,816	212,909	762,122	704,400
Total	**8,619,234**	**13,108,970**	**55,049,791**	**53,682,637**

■ MICROPOLITAN COUNTY VOTING

ROBERT WATREL

One of the most noticeable differences within the 2008 electorate was increasing polarization between metropolitan and rural counties. While this phenomenon is not new, Democratic Party strength has increased in metropolitan areas while Republican strength has increased outside large cities and their suburbs. In fact, exit polls show that voters outside metropolitan areas gave a majority of their votes to McCain. Obama achieved his margin of victory by winning a substantial majority of the vote in large cities and their suburbs.

What has happened in small metropolitan areas? In 2003, for the first time the U.S. Office of Management and Budget defined a new census category known as the micropolitan county. Micropolitan areas include a central city of 10,000 to 49,999 population plus adjacent outlying counties that are linked economically with the central city. Micropolitan cities are smaller than metropolitan cities, which exceed 50,000 residents.

When comparing voters in micropolitan counties to voters in metropolitan and rural counties in the United States, there is a trend among micropolitan county voters to vote more similarly to voters in rural counties than to voters in metropolitan counties. The large majority of American voters reside in metropolitan areas. Of voters who cast ballots in the 2008 presidential election, 83.15 percent lived in metropolitan counties, 10.06 percent lived in micropolitan counties, and 6.83 percent lived in rural counties. Obama won a majority of 55.0 percent of the vote in metropolitan counties. McCain, on the other hand, received the majority of votes from voters living in micropolitan and rural counties, receiving 54.9 percent and 56.8 percent, respectively. This trend of voters in micropolitan counties to vote more like those in rural counties than voters in metropolitan counties is evident when looking at the vote distribution at the regional level. Table 4.5 shows the distribution of votes among metropolitan, micropolitan, and rural county voters for the six regional designations identified in this atlas. In all six regions, Obama's percentage of the metropolitan vote exceeded his percentage of the micropolitan and rural vote percentages. Except for one region, Barack Obama did not receive a majority of votes from voters in micropolitan and rural counties. The exception was the Pacific Coast region, where micropolitian county voters gave Obama 51.4 percent of the vote.

Although Obama did not fare well in most regions with micropolitan voters, there were some micropolitan counties that gave him a large majority of their votes (map 4.38). Many of these counties contained large minority populations. In fact, of the top five micropolitan counties for Obama, based on percentage of the total vote, all were counties with an overwhelming majority of African American or Hispanic populations. These included Macon County, Alabama, with 86.9 percent, Starr County, Texas, with 84.5 percent, Taos County, New Mexico, with 81.8 percent, Hancock County, Georgia, with 81.2 percent, and San Miguel County, New Mexico, with 79.8 percent. McCain's top five micropolitan counties included Roberts County, Texas, with 92.1 percent, Texas County, Oklahoma, with 85.3 percent, Madison County, Idaho, with 85.3 percent, Gray County, Texas, with 85.1 percent, and Hutchinson County, Texas, with 84.0 percent. All of these counties have large white populations, with the exception of Texas County, Oklahoma, which has a sizable minority Hispanic population.

With the American electorate still polarized along party lines and a demographic shift toward increasing minority populations and a decreasing white population, rural and micropolitan voters will likely continue to vote in a similar manner in supporting the Republican Party.

TABLE 4.5. Metropolitan, Micropolitan, and Rural Voting by Region in the 2008 Presidential Election

Region	County Type	% Obama '08	% McCain '08	Margin of Victory (%)
New England	Metro	61.05	37.74	23.31
	Micro	49.88	48.54	1.34
	Rural	49.62	48.59	1.03
South	Metro	48.79	50.24	-1.45
	Micro	39.19	59.59	-20.40
	Rural	40.08	58.54	-18.46
Midwest	Metro	57.04	41.55	15.49
	Micro	46.85	51.31	-4.46
	Rural	46.04	51.98	-5.94
Great Plains	Metro	44.91	54.17	-9.26
	Micro	34.35	64.56	-30.21
	Rural	31.21	67.50	-36.29
Mountain West	Metro	49.06	49.17	-0.11
	Micro	42.26	55.53	-13.27
	Rural	39.79	57.57	-17.78
Pacific Coast	Metro	61.09	36.90	24.19
	Micro	51.40	45.86	5.54
	Rural	45.70	51.51	-5.81

2008 Presidential Election Micropolitan County Results

MAP 4.38

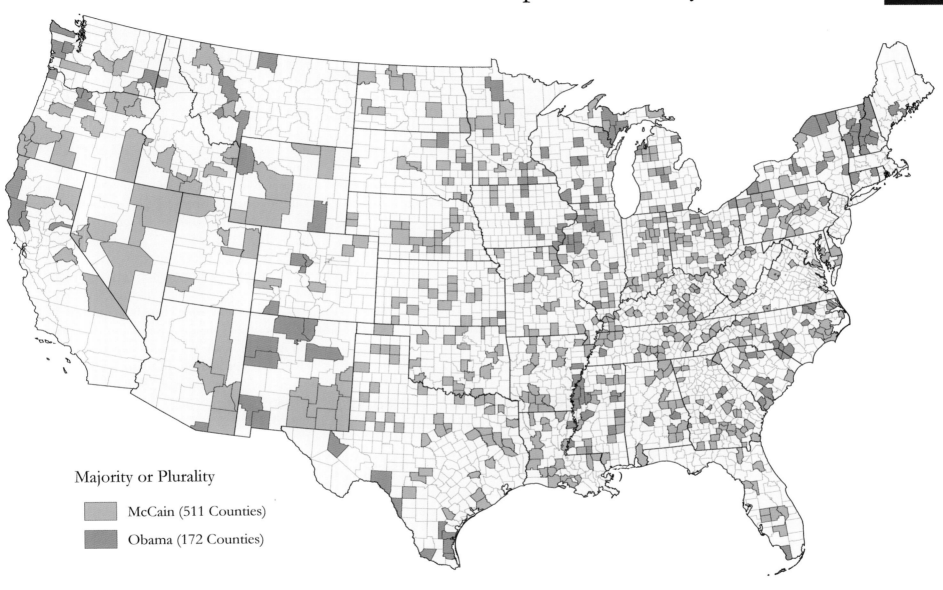

Majority or Plurality

McCain (511 Counties)

Obama (172 Counties)

PERSISTENCE AND CHANGE BY STATE 2004 TO 2008

RICHARD L. MORRILL

Four maps are shown, one each for president, senators, and governors, and a summary map of consistency across these positions.

PRESIDENT

The 2008 election of Barack Obama was a numerical consequence of the shift of nine states: three in the West, three in the South, and three in the Midwest. Those in the West came from the vast expanse of Republican wins in 2004 in the Mountain West and Plains states, those in the South from the south Atlantic coastal states, and those in the Midwest from the "border" states of Iowa, Indiana, and Ohio.

GOVERNORS

There were only eleven gubernatorial races in 2008, and only one, Missouri, shifted between parties. Six states stayed Democratic: Delaware, Montana, New Hampshire, North Carolina, Washington, and West Virginia, and four remained Republican: Indiana, North Dakota, Utah, and Vermont. These results are not indicative of broader trends.

SENATORS

Thirty-four states elected senators. Twelve remained Democratic, fourteen remained Republican, and eight switched from Republican to Democratic. The Republican states seem more predictable—the Mountain West and the South—except for "Democratic" Maine and Vermont. Meanwhile, the Democratic senators are prevalent in all parts of the country, showing that local conditions and perceptions can override national assumptions.

The fourth map addresses these inconsistencies. States that voted Republican for president and senator or governor are as expected, in the South, Plains, and Mountain West, but the states that voted Democratic for all positions are again in all regions. Three Democratic states for Obama elected Republican senators or governors, and six voting Republican for president voted for Democratic senators or governors, especially in several moderately conservative states.

VOTER CONSISTENCY ACROSS ELECTED POSITIONS

How consistent and loyal are voters at the county level in voting straight Democratic or Republican? The answer is not as consistent as might be expected from the rhetoric on polarization of the American electorate, or perhaps the polarization is more on a liberal-conservative continuum than on partisan grounds. This map compares votes for president in 2004 and 2008 and votes for senator and/or governor in 2006 and 2008 (only a few governors were up for election in 2008). The simple coding is blue (415 counties) for consistent Democratic counties voting for president in 2004 and 2008 and for senator or governor in 2006 and 2008; red is used to identify the 1,086 comparable Republican county loyalty. Green indicates the almost 377 counties that switched from Republican to Democratic or from Democratic to Republican between 2004 and 2008. Gold identifies how the 1,236 counties that voted for both Republicans and Democrats, including the positions of senator or governor in 2006 and 2008, voted for president.

Democratic purity is not very common, occurring primarily in black, American Indian, and Hispanic areas and in somewhat larger areas in the Upper Midwest and Northeast. Republican loyalty is more pervasive, at least for these elections. It stretches across the South from Texas to North Carolina; it also includes the Interior West, Kentucky-Indiana (despite Indiana voting for Obama), and central Pennsylvania.

Areas of inconsistency are common, especially across the Border South, even in ostensibly very Republican states, because of the popularity of many Democratic senators and governors (for example, in Oklahoma, Arkansas, Louisiana, Tennessee, and Virginia), in the Plains (Nebraska, North Dakota, South Dakota, Wyoming, and Montana), and in several seemingly Democratic Midwest and Northeast states (Illinois, Ohio, New York, Vermont, and Maine), states with popular and moderate Republican senators and governors.

Voter Persistence and Change across Presidential, U.S. Senatorial, and/or Gubernatorial Elections from 2004 to 2008, by State

MAP 4.39

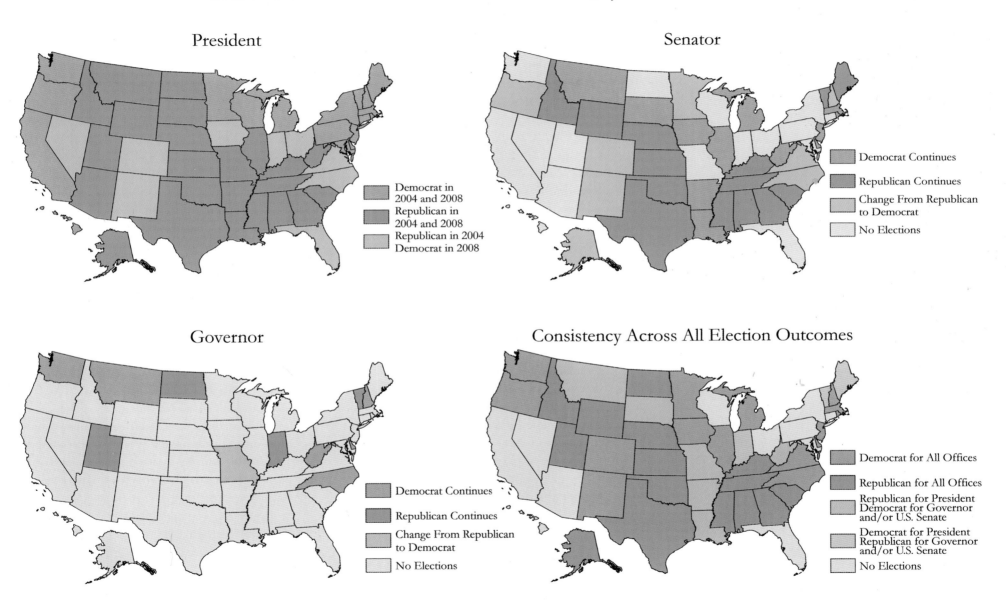

President

- Democrat in 2004 and 2008
- Republican in 2004 and 2008
- Republican in 2004 Democrat in 2008

Senator

- Democrat Continues
- Republican Continues
- Change From Republican to Democrat
- No Elections

Governor

- Democrat Continues
- Republican Continues
- Change From Republican to Democrat
- No Elections

Consistency Across All Election Outcomes

- Democrat for All Offices
- Republican for All Offices
- Republican for President Democrat for Governor and/or U.S. Senate
- Democrat for President Republican for Governor and/or U.S. Senate
- No Elections

■ PERSISTENCE AND CHANGE BY COUNTY 2004 TO 2008

RICHARD L. MORRILL

While the dominant story of the 2008 election was change, great enough to elect a Democratic president, and a black Democrat as well, there was underneath this a great deal of persistence in partisan voting. In this section we look at patterns of change and persistence between 2004 and 2008 (map 4.40).

Three maps are employed (4.41–4.43). Map 4.40 shows counties that voted Democratic in 2004 and 2008 (537 counties), counties that voted Republican in 2004 and 2008 (2,197), then counties that switched from Democratic to Republican (47), and then the much larger number that switched from Republican to Democratic (337 counties). Maps 4.41 and 4.42 show change in the Democratic vote and change in the Republican vote—that is, increases and decreases. The maps are mirror images of each other except for the effect of minor-party candidates in a few counties. However, we show both for balance.

Most striking is the vast extent of the 2,200 Republican counties in both 2004 and 2008, essentially the interior of the country save for the Upper Midwest, the Black Belt of the South, and the Democratic inroads in the Rocky Mountain region. Of course, the great majority of these counties are rural and small town. The less than nine hundred Democratic counties are instead peripheral, on the Pacific Coast, the Upper Midwest, Megalopolis through New England, part of coastal Florida, the above-noted Rocky Mountain islands, and a combination of environmental and American Indian reservations.

The geography of counties switching between the parties is quite remarkable. The relatively small number of Democratic defections are confined to the Border South, from Arkansas, then Tennessee, Kentucky, West Virginia, into western Pennsylvania—Appalachia, the Ouachita uplands, and the Tennessee Valley, plus a couple of similar Louisiana counties. Note that these counties are almost all embedded within a region that was already Republican and that had increased Republican margins between 2004 and 2008 (map 4.42), a kind of remnant of traditional New Deal Democratic loyalty but that came to prefer the more traditional message of today's Republican party over the perceived big-city liberalism and secularism of today's Democratic establishment.

These are almost all rural and small-town counties and are probably lost to the Democrats for president in the current political climate.

The much larger number of counties defecting from the Republicans in 2004 have a very different geography and settlement character. They are overwhelmingly intermingled with or adjacent to already Democratic counties in 2004, those that became even more Democratic in 2008 (map 4.41), and counties that are still Republican but that suffered Republican declines. There are seven kinds of areas of such switches. The largest number by far are in the Upper Midwest, in Illinois, Iowa, Michigan, North and South Dakota, and Wisconsin. What is unusual about these is that most are nonmetropolitan or small metropolitan, a setting not generally favorable to Democrats, as well

as several suburban and exurban switches, especially around Chicago. The second area is along the Pacific Coast, from San Diego, Riverside, and San Bernardino in the south to near the Canadian border, and including many metropolitan switches, such as Medford, Oregon, Reno, Nevada, and Fresno, Merced, Ventura and Stockton, California, as well as suburban counties around Portland, Oregon. Third are in the same Rocky Mountain region of Democratic persistence, but adding many environmental, American Indian, or university-dominated counties, such as Gallatin, Montana, or Albany, Wyoming. Fourth are additional Hispanic counties in New Mexico, southern Colorado, and Texas. Fifth are many black-majority counties in the belt from Mississippi through Alabama, Georgia, South and North Carolina, and into Virginia, a consequence of much increased turnout from and enthusiasm for a black candidate. Sixth is the capture of most of the rest of New England, into eastern New York, and seventh is further success in the suburbs and exurbs of Megalopolis.

Patterns of increase and decrease in Democratic and Republican voting have a similar broad geography to those for switches. The dominant and dramatic pattern is that of Democratic increases (and Republican decreases) over about 90 percent of the country: the West, outside "favorite son" Arizona and Alaska; the northern Plains, especially Nebraska, South and North Dakota, Montana, and even Wyoming, but not Minnesota; the Great Lakes region, the largest area of high Democratic increases, whether the counties voted Republican or Democratic; counties with significant minority populations, from Mississippi through Alabama, Georgia, South and North Carolina, and into Virginia, but not Arkansas, again whether counties were carried by Obama or not; much of Florida; and most of the Northeast, from Virginia to Maine, with the exception of eastern Massachusetts, not quite so strongly Democratic.

As dramatic but much smaller in area are regions of Republican increases (and Democratic decreases). See map 4.42. The belt of Republican increases from Oklahoma and Texas, through Arkansas and Tennessee, northern Alabama and Georgia, Kentucky, West Virginia, and even into southwestern Pennsylvania is amazingly contiguous and intense, a border South, predominantly white, that appears most alienated from the perceived image of a big city, to secular and modern America. Areas of Louisiana and northwest Florida, into Georgia are similar in character. The remaining areas of relative Republican strength include Arizona and Alaska, the expected "favorite son" effect.

High Democratic declines (or high Republican increases) fill the border South belt, while lower Democratic losses are in the wider zone surrounding the Republican core of gain. High Republican decreases are in the West and North and in mixed areas of the South, while lesser decreases are in the

South, beyond the core area of greatest gain, and in selected states such as Wyoming, Minnesota, Kansas, and Missouri, northern Appalachia, and Maine and Massachusetts, some fairly strongly Republican, others (New England) still strongly Democratic.

The numerical impact of these patterns of change is revealing. Counties Democratic in 2004 and with increased margins in 2008 provided 36.8 million votes for Obama against 18.6 million for McCain, a margin of more than 18.1 million. Of this, the metropolitan vote was 33.9 percent and 17 million. Conversely, the Republican counties in 2004 and that became more Republican in 2008 yielded only 5.3 million votes for McCain versus 2.5 million for Obama, for a margin of 2.8 million, 2.2 million of which was nonmetropolitan.

Counties Democratic in 2004 and declining in the Democratic margin by 2008 were not common and voted 977,000 to 720,000 for Obama. But counties Republican in 2004 and declining to 2008 were by far the most frequent, and they voted 24.2 million for McCain versus 16.6 for Obama, to yield a Republican margin of 7.7 million. Metropolitan county decline was about two-thirds of the total, voting 14.8 to 10.4 million for McCain, and thus a serious setback for Republican fortunes in 2008.

Finally, the rather few counties switching from Democratic to Republican voted 525,000 to

563,000 in favor of McCain, symbolically important but numerically small. The many more counties that switched from Republican to Democratic were numerically as well as symbolically important, voting 12.6 to 10.3 million in favor of Obama and providing a sizable Democratic margin of 1.7 million, 1.5 million of which was from metropolitan counties.

Counties with higher Democratic gains provided a margin of 11.9 million on a vote of 25.1 to 13.3 million while slower-gaining Democratic counties had a margin of 8.2 million on a vote of 24.9 to 16.6 million votes. Faster-growing Republican counties yielded a margin of 6.9 million on a vote of 10.7 and 17.6 million, while more slowly increasing Republican counties had a margin of 3.6 million on a vote of 8.7 to 12.3 million. These numbers highlight the particular importance of areas becoming more Republican.

In sum, the pattern of change showed that Democratic gains dominated most of the country, with Republican gains concentrated in the Border South region. Democratic gains were dominantly metropolitan, Republican nonmetropolitan. Finally, Democratic gains were often especially impressive in areas with a more educated and professional population, in suburban and exurban areas, small metropolitan areas, often with universities, and in environmental amenity areas.

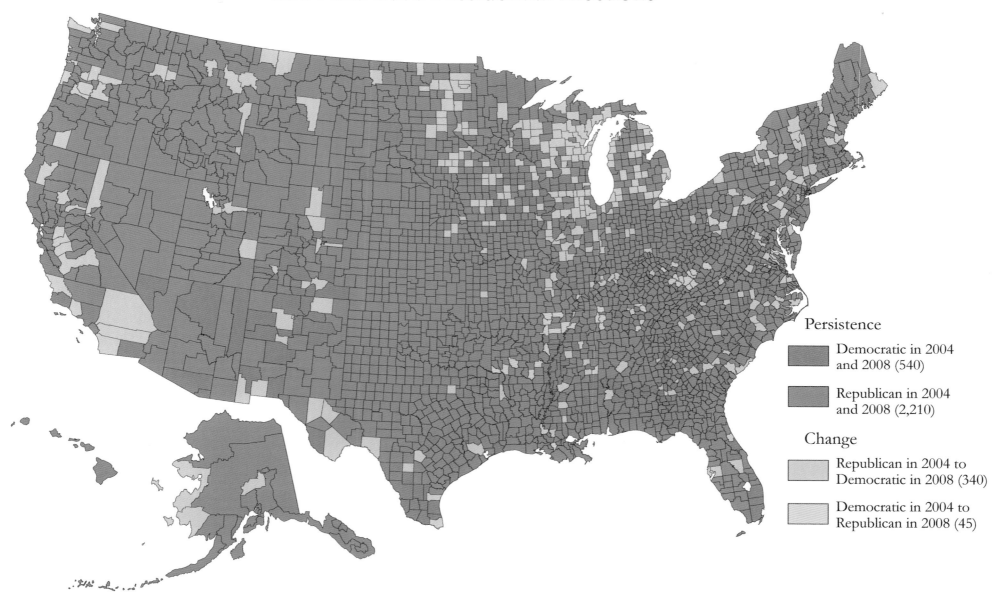

MAP 4.40

Persistence and Change
2004 and 2008 Presidential Elections

Persistence

Democratic in 2004
and 2008 (540)

Republican in 2004
and 2008 (2,210)

Change

Republican in 2004 to
Democratic in 2008 (340)

Democratic in 2004 to
Republican in 2008 (45)

Change in the Democratic Vote
From the 2004 Election to the 2008 Election

MAP 4.41

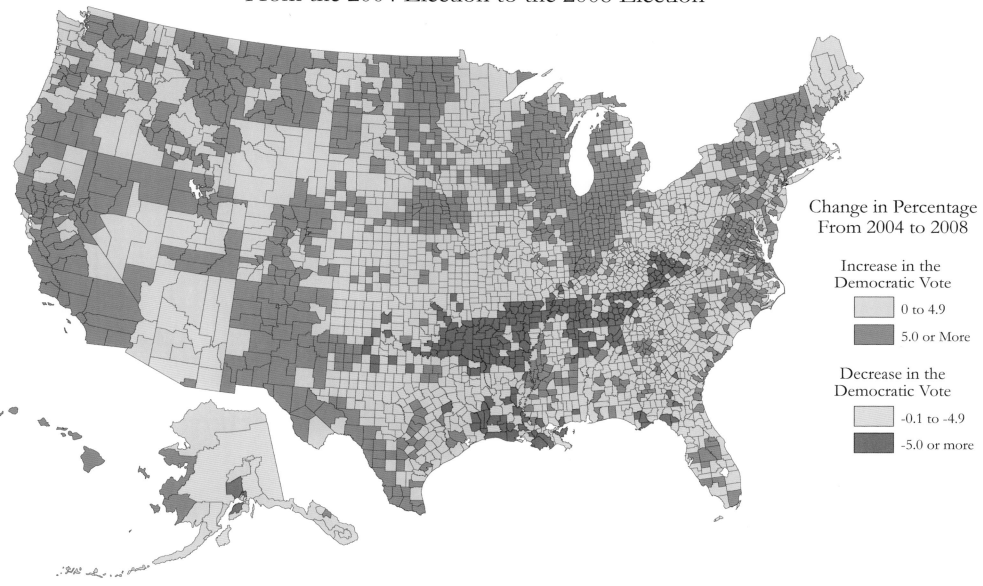

Change in Percentage
From 2004 to 2008

Increase in the
Democratic Vote

0 to 4.9

5.0 or More

Decrease in the
Democratic Vote

-0.1 to -4.9

-5.0 or more

MAP 4.42

Change in the Republican Vote
From the 2004 Election to the 2008 Election

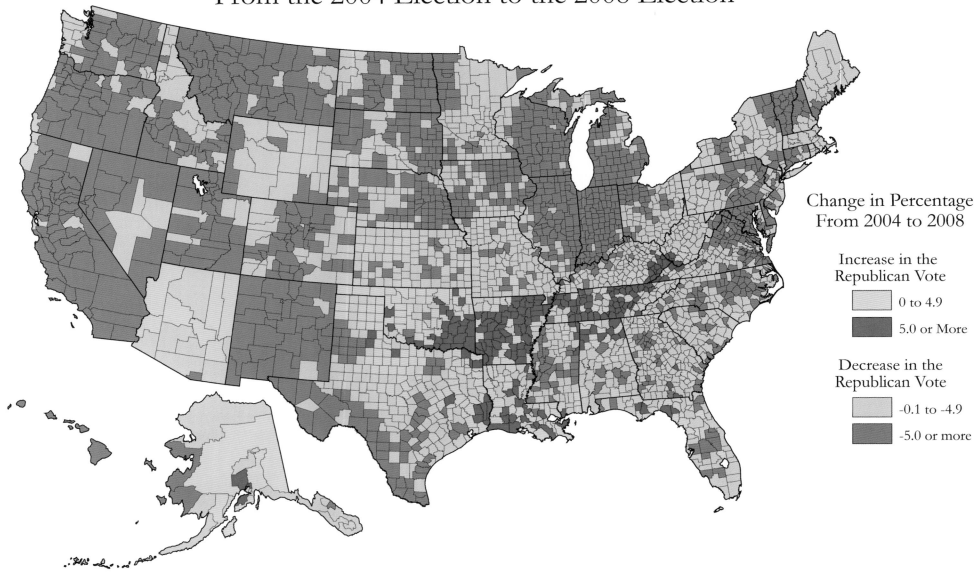

Change in Percentage
From 2004 to 2008

Increase in the
Republican Vote

0 to 4.9

5.0 or More

Decrease in the
Republican Vote

-0.1 to -4.9

-5.0 or more

Voter Consistency across Elections
2004 to 2008

MAP 4.43

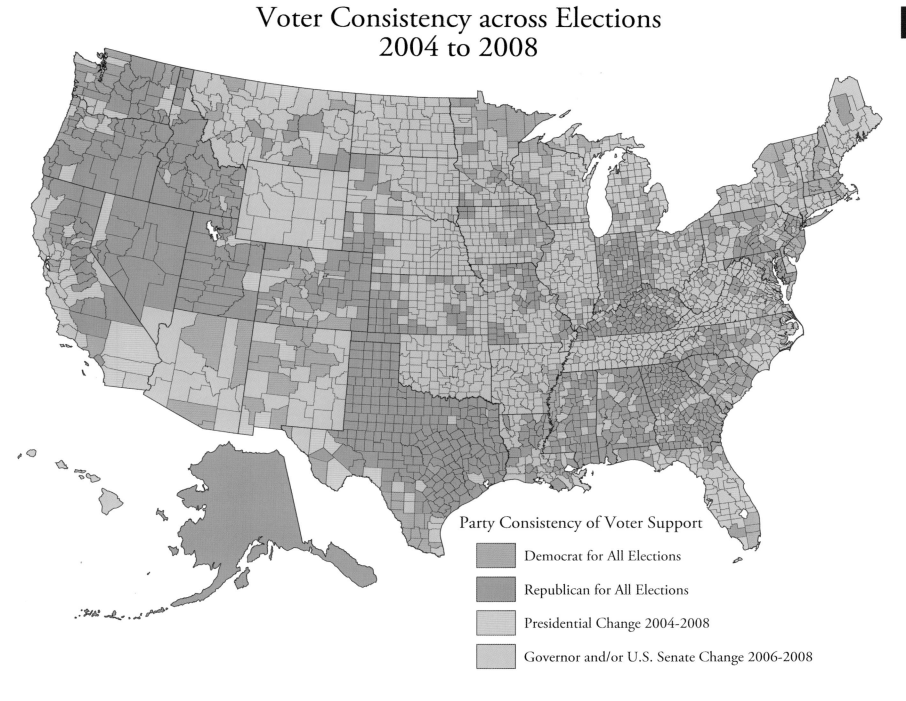

Party Consistency of Voter Support

- Democrat for All Elections
- Republican for All Elections
- Presidential Change 2004-2008
- Governor and/or U.S. Senate Change 2006-2008

NOTES

1. The county-level means in the analysis are weighted by the number of votes cast in the county for the Democratic and Republican Party presidential candidates.
2. The large cities are Atlanta, Baltimore, Boston, Buffalo, Chicago, Cincinnati, Cleveland, Dallas, Denver, Detroit, Fort Worth, Houston, Indianapolis, Kansas City, Los Angeles, Miami, Milwaukee, Minneapolis, New Orleans, New York City, Oakland, Philadelphia, Phoenix, Pittsburgh, Portland, St. Louis, St. Paul, San Antonio, San Diego, San Francisco, and Seattle. The smaller cities are Akron, Albuquerque, Austin, Baton Rouge, Birmingham, Bridgeport, Charlotte, Columbus, Corpus Christi, Des Moines, El Paso, Fresno, Jacksonville, Las Vegas, Lexington, Louisville, Memphis, Mobile, Nashville, Newark, Norfolk, Oklahoma City, Omaha, Providence, Raleigh, Richmond, Rochester, Sacramento, St. Petersburg, Salt Lake City, San Jose, Stockton, Tampa, Toledo, Tucson, Tulsa, Virginia Beach, and Wichita.
3. The states in each section are New England (Connecticut, Massachusetts, Maine, New Hampshire, Rhode Island, Vermont), mid-Atlantic (Delaware, New Jersey, New York, Pennsylvania), South (Alabama, Arkansas, Florida, Georgia, Louisiana, Mississippi, North Carolina, South Carolina, Texas, Virginia), Border (Kentucky, Maryland, Oklahoma, Tennessee, West Virginia), Midwest (Illinois, Indiana, Michigan, Ohio, Wisconsin), Plains (Iowa, Kansas, Minnesota, Missouri, North Dakota, Nebraska, South Dakota), Mountain states (Arizona, Colorado, Idaho, Montana, New Mexico, Nevada, Utah, Wyoming), and West Coast (California, Oregon, Washington).
4. Only in New England were the Democratic gains in the two-party vote in 1932 and 2008 comparable, at 3.89 and 3.14 points, respectively.
5. The dependent variable in the model is thus Margin of Victory$_{t+1}$ − Margin of Victory$_t$, where Margin of Victory = the county-level Democratic proportion of the vote for president minus the county-level Republican proportion of the vote for president and t and $t + 1$ refer to consecutive presidential elections.

REFERENCES

Abramowitz, Alan, and Kyle L. Saunders. 2005. "Why Can't We Just Get Along? The Reality of a Polarized America." *The Forum* 3 (2).

Bertin, J. 1967, 1983. *Semiology of Graphics.* Translated by W. J. Berg. Madison: University of Wisconsin Press.

Bishop, Bill. 2008. *The Big Sort: Why the Clustering of Like-Minded America is Tearing Us Apart.* Boston: Houghton Mifflin.

Chinni, Dante, and James G. Gimpel. 2010. *Our Patchwork Nation.* New York: Gotham.

Darmofal, David. 2008. "The Political Geography of the New Deal Realignment." *American Politics Research* 36 (6): 934–61.

Deavers, Ken. 1992. "What Is Rural?" *Policy Studies Journal* 20 (2): 184–89.

Early Voting Information Center, Reed College, http://www.earlyvoting.net.

Fiorina, Morris, and Samuel J. Abrams. 2008. "Political Polarization in the American Public." *Annual Review of Political Science* 11: 563–88.

Gelman, A., and Y. Ghitza. 2010. *Who Votes? How Did They Vote? And What Were They Thinking?* Technical report. New York: Columbia University, Department of Political Science.

Gelman, A., D. Lee, and Y. Ghitza. 2010. "A Snapshot of the 2008 Election." *Statistics, Politics, and Policy,* forthcoming.

Gelman, A., D. Park, B. Shor, and J. Cortina. 2009. *Red State, Blue State, Rich State, Poor State: Why Americans Vote the Way They Do.* 2nd ed. Princeton, N.J.: University Press.

Gelman, A., and Y. S. Su. 2010. "Voting by Age in 2008." *Chance,* forthcoming.

Gimpel, James G., and Jason E. Schuknecht. 2004. *Patchwork Nation: Sectionalism and Political Change in American Politics.* Ann Arbor: University of Michigan Press.

Glenn, Norval, and Lester Hill, Jr. 1977. "Rural-Urban Differences in Attitudes & Behavior in the United States." *Annals of the American Academy of Political and Social Science* 429 (1): 36–50.

Gronke, P., E. Galanes-Rosenbaum, P. A. Miller, and D. Toffey. 2008. "Convenience Voting." *Annual Review of Political Science* 11: 417–55.

Huckfeldt, Robert. 1986. *Politics in Context: Assimilation and Conflict in Urban Neighborhoods.* New York: Agathon.

Johnston, Ronald J., Fred M. Shelley, and Peter J. Taylor, eds. 1990. *Developments in Electoral Geography.* London: Routledge.

Key, V. O., Jr. 1955. A Theory of Critical Elections. *Journal of Politics* 17: 3–18.

Knoke, David, and Constance Henry. 1977. "Political Structure of Rural America." *Annals of the American Academy of Political and Social Science* 429: 51–62.

Levendusky, Matthew. 2009. *The Partisan Sort: How Liberals Became Democrats and Conservatives Became Republicans.* Chicago: University of Chicago Press.

Nardulli, Peter F. 1995. "The Concept of a Critical Realignment, Electoral Behavior, and Partisan Change." *American Political Science Review* 89 (1): 10–22.

Neeley, G. W., and L. E. Richardson. 2001. "Who Is Early Voting? An Individual Level Examination." *Social Science Journal* 38: 381–92.

Silver, Nate. http://www.fivethirtyeight.com.

Theobald, David M. 2001. "Land-Use Dynamics beyond the American Urban Fringe. *Geographical Review* 91 (3): 544–64.

Tufte, E. R. 1990. *Envisioning Information.* Cheshire, CT: Graphics Press.

Woods, Michael. 2005. *Rural Geography.* Thousand Oaks, Calif.: Sage.

CHAPTER FIVE

REGIONAL PATTERNS AND SWING STATES: REGIONAL ANALYSES

■ NORTHEAST

WILLIAM BERENTSEN

The Northeast was the only major region in the United States in which voters of every state favored the Democratic presidential candidates in both the 2004 and 2008 elections. In fact, since the 1992 presidential election, only once has any northeastern state provided any electoral votes for a Republican candidate (New Hampshire, very narrowly and consequentially, in 2000). However, there were (and are) significant differences in voting patterns in presidential elections within states, particularly between (a) urban and rural and (b) the New England and mid-Atlantic subregions. Also, despite the reputation of the Northeast as a bastion of liberal voters, the region, in fact, is dominated by a combination of political moderates and fiscal conservatives (table 5.1). Many Republicans hold office, especially at the level of state government. Northeastern voters and politicians, including some key Republicans

(notably U.S. senators) are, however, most frequently moderates or liberals on social issues (e.g., on abortion) at a time when national Republican Party leaders and popular spokespeople hold strongly conservative positions on these issues. Overall, the factors above explain much of the geographic patterns of voting in the 2004 and 2008 presidential elections.

The most basic geographic electoral pattern at the county level in the two most recent northeastern presidential elections is that voters in New England consistently chose Democrats, while regional patterns were much more varied among the mid-Atlantic state voters, especially in the larger states, notably New York and Pennsylvania. In New England, Bush won very few counties in 2004, and in 2008 McCain barely carried (by 355 votes) Maine's least populous county (Piscataquis), the only one that he won within the entire region. That dramatic result was matched

by a historic sweep by Democrats of all U.S. representative seats within what was once a major Republican stronghold.

Within the mid-Atlantic states, regional voting patterns for Democratic versus Republican presidential candidates were fairly consistent in both 2004 and 2008. In New York State, urban counties as well as three in the far north voted consistently Democratic; a few counties in eastern New York switched from Republican to Democratic majorities in 2008. In Pennsylvania, Democratic candidates carried most eastern counties, while Republican candidates carried most central and western counties in both elections. In New Jersey, voters in a few counties in the northwest and along "the shore" favored Republicans in both elections, while the counties in the urban-suburban corridor from the New York City suburbs to the Delaware line were won in both elections by the

TABLE 5.1. Ideological Identification of Americans over Age 18 in 2009: A List of the Most "Conservative" and "Liberal" (as well as other northeastern) States (in percentages)

	Conservative	Liberal	Other*
United States	40	21	39
Alabama	49	15	36
Mississippi	48	14	38
Louisiana	48	14	38
Idaho	46	15	39
Oklahoma	46	16	38
Utah	46	16	38
North Dakota	45	16	39
South Dakota	44	16	40
Arkansas	44	16	40
Wyoming	44	16	40
Pennsylvania	39	20	41
Delaware	37	19	44
New Hampshire	38	23	39
Maine	36	24	40
Rhode Island	30	23	47
Maryland	33	24	43
Connecticut	31	24	45
New Jersey	33	25	42
California	33	25	42
Washington	34	26	40
Hawaii	27	26	47
Oregon	33	26	41
New York	32	26	42
Vermont	29	28	43
Massachusetts	30	29	41
District of Columbia	22	36	

Source: Jones, 2010.

* Nationally, 92 percent of those listed as "Other" self-identified as "Moderates."

Democrats. In Maryland, the Baltimore-D.C. corridor counties were carried by Democrats and the rest of the state by Republicans in each election. In Delaware's three counties, there was a consistent north-south split between Democrats and Republicans.

Urban-rural voting patterns also changed little in the Northeast between 2004 and 2008. In both elections, voters were more likely to vote Republican in dominantly rural counties, especially those in northern Maine, upstate New York, and central and western Pennsylvania, though the pattern was somewhat less pronounced in 2008 than in 2004. Rural areas that were dominated by white populations had relatively low incomes and educational levels; also areas with relatively high poverty levels were the most likely to be carried by the Republican candidate, notably areas in the Appalachian Mountain and Allegheny Plateau regions of Pennsylvania, in upstate New York, in parts of northern Maine, and in a few other similar counties in Maryland, Vermont, and New Hampshire. These voting patterns are very much like those in similar counties in adjacent Virginia and West Virginia.

In both the 2004 and 2008 elections, voting in major urban centers was heavily Democratic—notably among the large numbers of voters in the counties containing central Boston, Providence, Hartford, New York, Albany, Syracuse, Rochester, Buffalo, Trenton, Newark, Philadelphia, Pittsburgh, Wilmington, and Baltimore (as well as in adjacent Washington, D.C.). The predominantly suburban and exurban counties that make up most of Massachusetts, Rhode Island, and Connecticut displayed virtual complete Democratic dominance in both 2004 and 2008. Most Vermont counties, though largely rural, experienced

similar electoral results. Voters in suburban counties near Philadelphia also favored Democratic candidates in both elections. Voting patterns in suburban areas near New York City were more balanced between parties, especially in 2004. For example, there was a literal halo of suburban counties around New York City in which most people voted Republican in 2004, though, tellingly, that pattern was much more fragmented in 2008.

Counties with historically high proportions of college students voted heavily Democratic in both 2004 and 2008, notably in and near Boston and Springfield, Massachusetts, and in suburban Washington, D.C. College student voters also probably contributed disproportionately to Democratic gains in most northeastern counties between 2004 and 2008, given President Obama's very high vote totals from young and first-time voters as well as from voters with higher levels of education.

There are few, if any, counties in the Northeast where military activities and personnel dominate life or politics, and, thus, little discernible impact on county-level maps of the 2004 or 2008 elections. The small number of well-known areas (Ft. Drum and West Point, New York, Annapolis, Maryland, and New London-Groton, Connecticut) where the military is prominent did not display an electoral pattern that differed sharply from regional trends.

Similar to the patterns across much of the United States, nearly all counties in the Northeast registered relatively more votes for the Democratic presidential candidate in 2008 than in 2004. There are two intriguing exceptions to the pattern: counties in southwestern Pennsylvania and in suburban Boston. The former overlaps with the late Representative Murtha's district,

about which he lamented racist sentiments during the 2008 election campaign before later apologizing for his remarks. The demographic characteristics of this area—largely white and relatively poor—are similar to large areas of Appalachia and the mid-South, from eastern Oklahoma to Tennessee, which also exhibited increased support for the Republican, McCain, in 2008 in comparison with Bush in 2004. The Boston suburbs that registered lower percentages of votes for Obama in 2008 than for Kerry in 2004 were later key ones for the unexpected senatorial election outcome that sent Republican Scott Brown to Washington, D.C., to replace the late Ted Kennedy. While some people interpret the latter result as a reaction to the policies of the Obama administration, instead (or as well) it may illustrate the importance of conservative views among the electorate of Massachusetts, and indeed all of New England. The largest ideological group in every New England and Northeastern state comprises moderates, not liberals (table 5.1). The relative strength of liberals in New England is real, but it is also sometimes exaggerated by overly generalized accounts of New England politics (table 5.1).

It was a species as endemic to New England as craggy seascapes and creamy clam chowder: the moderate Yankee Republican. Dignified in demeanor, independent in ideology, and frequently blue in blood, they were politicians in the mold of Roosevelt and Rockefeller: socially tolerant, environmentally enthusiastic, people who liked government to keep its wallet close to its vest and its hands out of social issues such as abortion and, in recent years, same-sex marriage (Belluck 2006).

Many Northeasterners are fiscal conservatives, but fewer hold conservative views on social issues.

Republican senators from New England (in Maine, New Hampshire, and Massachusetts [there are now no Republican U.S. representatives]) have more moderate social views than most leaders of the contemporary national Republican Party. And New England and Northeastern Republicans with political platforms similar to these sitting officeholders will likely win national offices in the 2012 midterm elections.

Large numbers of voters in New England and other Northeastern states, in fact majorities in all cases, self-identify as conservatives or moderates. At the same time, polls on important issues, politicians' positions, and state policies indicate that New England (and the Northeast) is quite pro-choice in comparison with the rest of the United States, though, somewhat ironically, "liberal" Massachusetts is a state with much

debate and differing views on abortion and choice. Polls also indicate that more residents in New England, and in the Northeast more generally, support health care reform than in most other U.S. regions. Thus, future support for the Republican Party in the Northeast in national elections may hinge in part on how important social conservatism will be within the Republican Party nationwide.

Northeast Region Presidential Elections

MAP 5.1

Presidential Election Popular Vote Leader

Change in Democratic Vote Percentage From 2004 to 2008

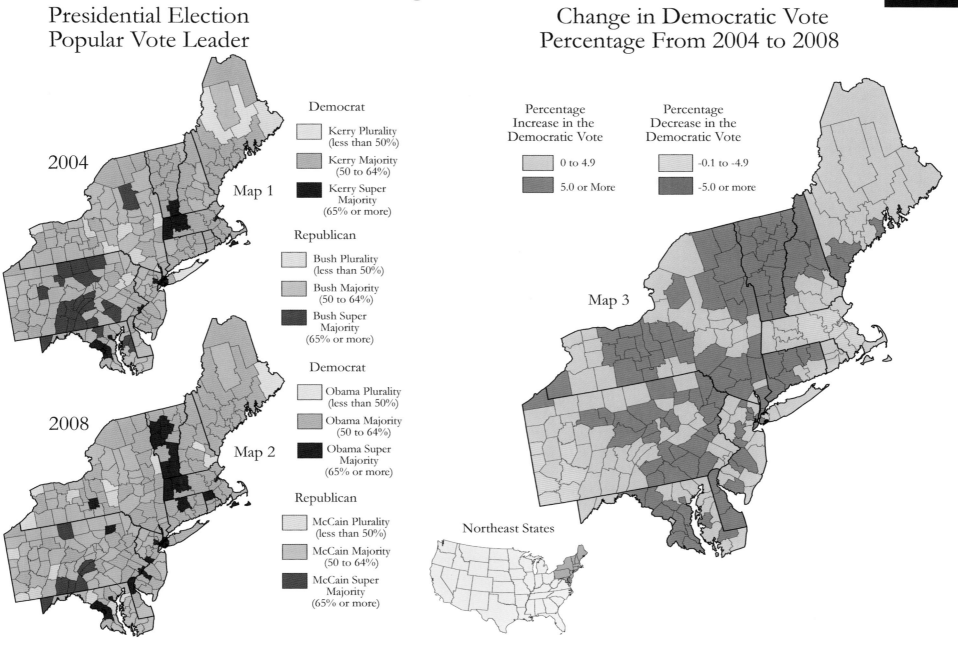

2004

Map 1

Democrat

- Kerry Plurality (less than 50%)
- Kerry Majority (50 to 64%)
- Kerry Super Majority (65% or more)

Republican

- Bush Plurality (less than 50%)
- Bush Majority (50 to 64%)
- Bush Super Majority (65% or more)

2008

Map 2

Democrat

- Obama Plurality (less than 50%)
- Obama Majority (50 to 64%)
- Obama Super Majority (65% or more)

Republican

- McCain Plurality (less than 50%)
- McCain Majority (50 to 64%)
- McCain Super Majority (65% or more)

Percentage Increase in the Democratic Vote

- 0 to 4.9
- 5.0 or More

Percentage Decrease in the Democratic Vote

- -0.1 to -4.9
- -5.0 or more

Map 3

Northeast States

■ APPALACHIA AND THE AMERICAN SOUTH

JONATHAN I. LEIB

Despite losing the popular vote in Appalachia and the American South to Republican John McCain, Democrat Barack Obama made significant inroads in 2008 in a region that in recent decades had been hostile to Democratic presidential candidates. Obama received 46.7 percent of the popular vote cast in the 2008 election in Appalachia and the South, six percentage points fewer than his nationwide vote percentage and 5.6 percentage points less than John McCain won in the region. However, Obama's percentage point total was three points higher than the total that 2004 Democratic candidate John Kerry received in Appalachia and the South, and, combined with an increase in voter turnout over 2004, Obama received nearly three million more votes in the region than Kerry.

Of the region's twelve states, McCain won nine to Obama's three. However, Obama's three victories were in states among the region's largest in population: Florida, North Carolina, and Virginia. As a result, Obama's three states netted him 41.7 percent of the region's electoral votes (55 of 132). Also, Obama's number of states won in the region was the most by a Democratic presidential candidate since Bill Clinton in 1996, and the most by a non-Southern Democratic candidate since John F. Kennedy in 1960. Obama's victory in North Carolina was the first by a Democratic candidate since Jimmy Carter won the state in 1976, and his victory in Virginia was the first by a Democratic candidate since Lyndon Johnson's in 1964.

Examined at the county level, Obama fared well in several categories of places in Appalachia and the American South. His best electoral showings were generally found in the region's largest cities, the rural Black Belt college towns, and some of the largest population clusters located on the margins of the region.

Obama won many of the major urban counties in the region. In Virginia, he won Richmond and all but one of the Hampton Roads cities (barely losing only Virginia Beach, a traditionally Republican city). Obama also won Atlanta and its eastern and southern suburban counties, the south Atlantic coastal cities of Charleston, South Carolina, and Savannah, Georgia, urban areas of south Florida (West Palm Beach, Fort Lauderdale, and Miami), as well as Louisville, Little Rock, Memphis, Nashville, Birmingham, and New Orleans.

He ran very strongly in fast-growing urban and suburban areas in the three states that he won. He performed well in the Northern Virginia suburbs of Washington, D.C., in the three main population centers along the I-85 North Carolina Piedmont conurbation (from Raleigh-Durham to Greensboro, Winston-Salem, and High Point to Charlotte), and cities and counties in central Florida's Interstate 4 corridor (from Daytona Beach to Orlando to Tampa-St. Petersburg). Northern Virginia and the I-4 corridor are considered important "swing" areas in Virginia and Florida, respectively, and all three areas have seen large-scale in-migration in recent decades from outside the region.

Obama also won a majority of counties in the region's traditional Black Belt. These are rural areas running from South Carolina's midlands, through middle Georgia, central Alabama, and into east-central Mississippi, with a western extension in the Delta region of northwestern Mississippi and eastern Arkansas. Named for the rich black soil found in this area, it was the center of the region's antebellum plantation economy and contained large numbers of enslaved persons. The legacy today is that this part of the South contains the highest percentage of the region's rural black population. A Democratic stronghold since the implementation of the Voting Rights Act, this region gave a large share of its votes to Obama.

Obama also won in many (though not all) of the region's counties containing large state universities. He carried the cities and counties containing West Virginia University, the University of Virginia and Virginia Tech, and the universities of North Carolina, Georgia, Florida, and Kentucky. Having said that, his support was not uniform throughout college towns in the region; he lost to McCain in the counties that contain the large state universities of Alabama, Mississippi, Tennessee, and Arkansas.

While Obama did better in the region in 2008 than Kerry had in 2004, and conversely while McCain received a smaller percentage of the vote in 2008 than George W. Bush had in 2004, the changes between 2004 and 2008 in the Democratic and Republican shares of the vote were not uniform throughout the region. There was a geographical divide, with Obama in 2008 doing better in the eastern and southern portions of the region than Kerry did in 2004, and with McCain doing better in parts of the interior and western portions of the region than Bush had four years earlier.

In terms of the increase in the Democratic share of the vote between 2004 and 2008, Obama did better than Kerry in most cities and counties of Virginia and in many counties of North Carolina, South Carolina, and Mississippi, as well as in northern Kentucky, the Atlanta metropolitan area and middle Georgia, central and lower Alabama, and peninsular Florida. He improved significantly on Kerry's percentages in both the largest and fastest-growing population centers of the region. For example, he significantly outperformed Kerry in Washington, D.C.'s fast-growing Northern Virginia suburbs (extending into the eastern panhandle counties of West Virginia), the cities and suburbs of Richmond and Hampton Roads in Virginia, the I-85 North Carolina Piedmont conurbation, metro Atlanta, coastal areas of South Carolina, Georgia, and north Florida, central Florida's Interstate 4 corridor, and also south Florida.

At the same time, McCain outperformed Bush in various parts of the region, receiving a significantly higher percentage of the vote in 2008 than Bush received in 2004 in both central and southern Appalachia (running from southern West Virginia, eastern Kentucky, and southwestern Virginia, through eastern Tennessee and south into north Georgia and north Alabama), rural areas of middle and west Tennessee, and most of Arkansas. Indeed, a majority of the forty-five counties in the United States that switched from Democratic in 2004 to Republican in 2008 are in this region: in central Appalachia (southern West Virginia and eastern Kentucky), Tennessee, and northeastern Arkansas. To a lesser extent, McCain also outperformed Bush in parts of north Florida as well as in much of Louisiana (especially in southern parishes, where many African Americans left in 2005 after Hurricane Katrina and have not returned).

One question that has arisen about these areas where McCain significantly outperformed Bush is this: were these results the consequence of a growing disenchantment among the region's voters with the Democrats at the national level, or was race a critical factor in these results? Indeed, this question of whether white voters would be receptive to voting for the first major-party African American presidential candidate came up repeatedly during 2008 and was raised especially in the context of the American South, given the region's history of racial animosity.

White support for Obama varied considerably in the region. In 2008 nationally, according to data from the media consortium's national exit poll as reported by Todd and Gawiser (2009), 43 percent of white voters voted for Obama (up from Kerry's 41 percent in 2004). While no state in Appalachia or the South achieved the nationwide percentage of white Obama supporters in 2008, six states came within eight percentage points, led by Florida (42 percent), West Virginia (41 percent), and Virginia (39 percent). All three of these states contain large areas that are at the margins of the American South. The percentage of white Obama voters dropped off considerably in the Deep South, with Obama's percentage of the vote among whites at its lowest in Alabama (10 percent), Mississippi (11 percent), and Louisiana (14 percent). These states, by far, represent the lowest percentage of white support for Obama in the country.

However, low percentages of white support in the region may be a result of antipathy toward national Democratic candidates in general, rather than being the result of the race of the candidate per se. Other maps in this atlas show the change in white support for the Democratic presidential candidate from 2004 to 2008, based on the exit poll results. Within Appalachia and the South, white voter support for Obama increased the most over white voter support for Kerry in North Carolina and Virginia, two of the three states won by Obama in the region (both states were targeted by the Obama campaign as "takeover" possibilities). However, white support dropped precipitously in Louisiana, Alabama, and Arkansas between 2004 and 2008. In Alabama, on a percentage point basis, Obama lost nearly half of the white support that Kerry had garnered in 2004, from 19 percent of the white vote in 2004 to only 10 percent by 2008.

In the end, Obama performed better in Appalachia and the American South than any Democratic presidential candidate in more than a decade, and better than any non-Southern Democrat in almost five decades. White reaction to the civil rights movement combined with the Republicans' "Southern Strategy" helped lead, starting in the 1960s, to a nearly half-century GOP domination in presidential elections in the region, long a Democratic bastion. It is yet to be seen whether Obama's success in 2008 is a harbinger of a reversal of Republican domination in the region or whether it is an aberration.

MAP 5.2

Southeast Region Presidential Elections

Presidential Election Popular Vote Leader

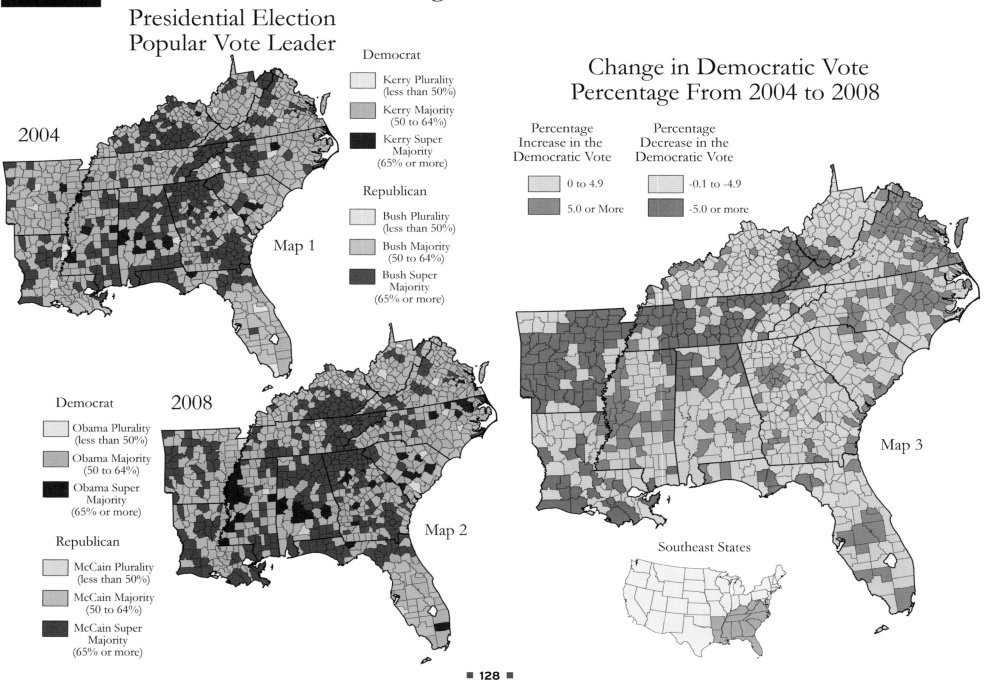

2004

Democrat

Kerry Plurality (less than 50%)

Kerry Majority (50 to 64%)

Kerry Super Majority (65% or more)

Republican

Bush Plurality (less than 50%)

Bush Majority (50 to 64%)

Bush Super Majority (65% or more)

Map 1

2008

Democrat

Obama Plurality (less than 50%)

Obama Majority (50 to 64%)

Obama Super Majority (65% or more)

Republican

McCain Plurality (less than 50%)

McCain Majority (50 to 64%)

McCain Super Majority (65% or more)

Map 2

Change in Democratic Vote Percentage From 2004 to 2008

Percentage Increase in the Democratic Vote

0 to 4.9

5.0 or More

Percentage Decrease in the Democratic Vote

-0.1 to -4.9

-5.0 or more

Map 3

Southeast States

THE "BIGOT BELT" AND THE 2008 ELECTION

J. ERIC OLIVER

The 2008 election of Barack Obama to the presidency of the United States was a historic occasion in many regards, but its greatest significance was in relation to race in America. One hundred fifty years after the end of slavery and a mere two generations after the end of the legalized racial discrimination of Jim Crow, a black man had captured nearly 53 percent of the popular vote and gained election to the United States' highest and most powerful office. Many commentators viewed this historic event as a watershed for American race relations. The Obama victory was propelled by a broad coalition of whites, Latinos, and African Americans. As so many Americans were able and willing to vote for a black president, this victory putatively signaled the ability of all Americans to look beyond their racial biases and embrace their country's new multiethnic future.

While it is tempting to think Obama's election represented a new era of race relations in the United States, such an optimistic reading is confounded by the actual voting patterns. If one examines an electoral map comparing the vote margins between 2004 and 2008 (map 4.42), one will find a broad swath of counties running from Oklahoma and East Texas through Arkansas to Kentucky and West Virginia where the Republican vote margins actually increased from 2004. In other words, Obama actually did worse in these Southern and Appalachian counties in 2008 than the "liberal, flip-flopping, wind-surfing" John Kerry of Massachusetts did in 2004.

By any measure, these results are surprising. Compared with 2004, the election in 2008 was nothing short of a disaster for Republicans, and John McCain had innumerable problems as a candidate: the incumbent president of his party had the lowest approval ratings in modern history, his party lost numerous seats in the House and Senate, the economy was plummeting, unending wars continued in Iraq and Afghanistan, and his campaign was beset by gaffes and missteps. With all of these problems, it seems quite unlikely that the Republican presidential vote share would increase, particularly in those places where the Republican vote margin from the previous elections was already quite high. Nevertheless, in over six hundred counties, the McCain margin of victory over Obama was actually higher than George W. Bush's margin of victory over John Kerry.

Why, in an election year so dominated by Democrats, did these counties go from merely Republican to heavily Republican? The answer to this question highlights the importance of geography to not only electoral politics but also to America's racial attitudes. One should rarely expect to see uniform vote trends across a country as large and diverse as the United States. Not only do different parts of the country have distinct histories, they experience sharp differences in attention from the various political campaigns. In 2008, voters in Missouri, North Carolina, and Virginia, for example, were bombarded with political advertisements, while voters in nearby Tennessee, Kentucky, and Arkansas saw few. Because political campaigns strategically concentrate resources in some place rather than others, geographic differences in voting patterns may grow more pronounced.

Similarly, different parts of the country have very different demographic profiles. According to data from the 2000 census, Republican counties are less affluent and educated, more rural and southern, and have higher unemployment rates than the national average. For example, in heavily Republican counties, only 13 percent of adults hold a college degree, on average, compared with 17 percent for the heavily Democratic counties. Seventy-three percent of the heavily Republican counties are rural, compared with 59 percent of heavily Democratic counties. Interestingly, the heavily Republican counties were not older or more white: their populations average about 85 percent white and 15 percent over age sixty-five, rates nearly identical to the national county averages.

But perhaps the most important factor in explaining these voting patterns is the racial composition of nearby counties. Nearly all of the counties that went Republican were proximate to counties or states with large black populations. In fact, 72 percent of the Republican counties are in states that are more than 10 percent black, compared with only 49 percent of the Democratic Counties (map 6.24). Regression analyses of county-level election data reveal that the best predictor of county-level shifts is the racial percentage of a county relative to its state's black population size. In other words, the counties in which Republican margins grew the largest tended to be predominantly white places in otherwise racially mixed states.

The coincidence between the upward trends in Republican votes in 2008 and the large proximate black populations begs the question of whether large numbers of white Americans were motivated to vote against a black candidate simply because of his race. With such aggregate data like these, we cannot derive any conclusions about individual level voting behavior (something social scientists call an "ecological fallacy"), and there are some alternative hypotheses that might explain these results. For instance, McCain's popular running mate, Sarah Palin, might have mobilized voters in these Republican counties with a campaign style designed to appeal to rural, less-educated voters. But if this were the case, one would expect to see greater Republican gains in rural counties in other parts of the country as well, and one does not. Alternatively, McCain's platform might have had a distinct appeal to voters in these counties. Yet, once again, it is hard to fathom that the policy differences between McCain and Obama were all that much greater than between Bush and Kerry, particularly given the fact that McCain was viewed with suspicion by so many conservatives in his own party. Finally, one might wonder whether

these counties happen to be places where the Republicans actively campaigned and the Democrats did not. Once again, however, the McCain campaign was grossly outspent by Obama's and was not actively mobilizing voters in these areas, particularly because they were largely in areas that were considered "safe" Republican seats.

After eliminating these and nearly all other alternative explanations, one is left with the conclusion that racial resentment was a driving factor in the voting decisions among whites in many parts of the country particularly where there are large black populations. Indeed, these voting patterns correspond to a large body of research demonstrating that regional proximity to minority populations increases whites' racial animosity. Whites who live in white enclaves that are proximate to large minority populations usually demonstrate the highest levels of racial bias and resentment in public opinion surveys (Oliver 2010). Moreover, this map may actually be underrepresenting the amount of white racial voting

in these general areas. Because of unprecedentedly high turnout among African Americans in 2008, the white racial voting patterns in counties with large black populations may be somewhat hidden. It is quite likely that the Republican vote share was also greater among whites in many counties not depicted in this map.

Together these findings suggest that Obama's victory, while undoubtedly a historic milestone in the history of American race relations, does not mean that white racial resentment has faded in the United States. Race is a major divider of the American population, and much of this racial resentment is geographically situated. In those places where whites feel greater political and economic competition with nearby black populations, they typically exhibit more racial resentment. While Obama's performance as president may help further diminish white racial animosity, the election of 2008 shows that race continues to be a very significant determinant of many Americans' social and political views.

■ TRIUMPH OF THE CARPETBAGGERS

JOHN MCNULTY

The election to the presidency of Illinois Senator Barack Obama, an African American, was a tremendous symbol of racial progress in the United States. Making the election especially heartening from the standpoint of racial progress is that Obama made significant inroads in that part of the United States historically most inhospitable to African Americans and more recently in the Democratic Party, namely, the former states of the Confederacy, usually just called "The South" as shorthand. The

2008 presidential election has been hailed by some as the final chapter in the post–Civil War Reconstruction of the Union.

Reconstruction was the effort following the North's victory in the Civil War to restore the rebel states to the union under the terms of the Union's victory; to wit, the end of slavery and the subjugation of the black race. The complicating factor was that those traits that made the region sufficiently distinct to foment secession were still in place;

Southern society remained bifurcated by race and defined by white supremacy and insularity, and its economy was unindustrialized and agrarian. The federal government hoped to capitalize on the societal tumult following the war and transform the "new" South into a more modern, less exceptional region. This effort floundered, and the South maintained backward Jim Crow practices, along with all the peculiar institutions that supported them, for another century.

During the Reconstruction effort, some Northerners moved to the South seeking financial or career opportunities, often as agents of the federal government; they were colorfully nicknamed "carpetbaggers" by the resentful native Southerners (Davidson et al. 1998). Popular travel bags of the day were made of old carpets, and the relocating Yankees would arrive with the carpetbags in tow. These carpetbaggers would collaborate with freed slaves (freedmen) and Northern sympathizers (scalawags) to establish outposts of the Republican Party in the South. Upon the failure of Reconstruction, the Republican Party was effectively dissolved in the South: freedmen were disenfranchised, scalawags went underground, and carpetbaggers retreated north as the South became a one-party Democratic polity, enforced when necessary by the Ku Klux Klan, with the principal party platform being the maintenance of the Jim Crow status quo (Current 1988).

However, the carpetbaggers would come back . . . eventually. Since roughly World War II, a massive population shift has occurred in the United States; citizens relocated from the Northeast and Midwest to the South. This can be explained by many factors; the invention of air conditioning is perhaps the most parsimonious, if glib. Air conditioning made the climate tolerable to Yankees, most stereotypically "snowbird" retirees, but also younger people seeking a vibrant economic environment and a lower cost of living. Regardless of the reasons, these latter-day carpetbaggers moved to the emerging urban and suburban centers in the New South, as simultaneously African Americans were enfranchised and beginning to exercise their electoral power (Polsby 2004).

The activation of African American voting in the South, via the civil rights legislation of the mid-1960s, shattered the teetering Dixiecrat establishment. With the decline of Jim Crow and the integration of the Democratic Party, conservative politicians and voters abandoned their ancestral party and drifted right to the emerging Republican Party, which they found ideologically more simpatico.

Ironically, the first handful of Republican politicians and organizers were Yankee transplants who brought their Republicanism with them as they migrated south. "Main Street" or "country club" Republicans were elected in cities like Tampa, Dallas, Houston, and Norfolk and joined with the rump "mountain Republicans," mainly from the Appalachian Blue Ridge, to create an emergent Southern Republican caucus (Polsby 2004). Over time, however, the ideological progeny of the Dixiecrats enjoyed sufficient electoral success so that they not only dominated the Republican Party politics of the region, but indeed became the predominant voice in the politics of the national GOP.

This shift tended to push Yankee transplants, especially younger ones with weaker partisan ties, away from the Republicans during the Bush-Clinton-Bush era and culminated in 2008, when a uniquely charismatic Democratic nominee for president vied to succeed an exceptionally unpopular Southern Republican president, in terrible economic times and amid the morass of two stalemated overseas occupations. To add extra allure to racially tolerant white voters in the South, the Democratic candidate was black and his candidacy seemed to symbolically proffer a chance for some degree of absolution for the wrongs of the past.

Of the three Southern states Obama won, Florida is by far the state with the most extreme shift in the population due to its massive retiree population. By 1990 over half (50.1 percent) of Florida's residents were born outside of the South (1990 U.S. Census, via Polsby 2004, 90). Virginia was a comfortable second in Southern states at 30.8 percent; growth heavily centered on the rapidly growing Washington, D.C., metropolitan region (1990 U.S. Census). North Carolina has attracted relatively less migration from the non-South; that growth was largely limited to Charlotte and the Research Triangle (1990 U.S. Census).

FLORIDA

Florida's recent rate of migration is impeded by an extreme outlier in Miami-Dade County.[1] The net migration of Miami-Dade was negative[2] at the end of the last century, due to aftereffects from Hurricane Andrew and widespread poverty in the city of Miami.[3] According to the 2000 census, more than 50 percent of Miami-Dade residents were foreign-born, the highest percentage of any U.S. city-county; hence, many of the new migrants that tend to shift electoral outcomes are ineligible to vote. (It should be noted that many foreign-born immigrants eventually become naturalized U.S. citizens.) Miami-Dade was also Obama's primary base of support in Florida, providing more votes than any other county and the eighth-highest percentage of the two-party vote of Florida counties.

When considering the effect of in-migration, the Miami-Dade anomaly must be accounted for in any analysis, and the African American vote, which is so uniformly Democratic that it is immune to migration patterns, must also be addressed. We shall control for these in a weighted least-squares estimation of Obama's percentage of the two-party vote per county as the dependent variable and the net migration from 1995 to 2000 as the primary independent

TABLE 5.2. Table of Results: Weighted Least-Squares Estimation of Obama's Percentage of the Two-Party Vote in 2008

Weight = 2008 population

FLORIDA–67 counties (Log likelihood = –79658110)	Coefficient	Standard Error
Net migration (in millions)	3.32	0.29***
Percentage of population identified as African American	0.70	0.10***
Miami-Dade County	0.65	0.06***
Constant	0.32	0.02***

VIRGINIA–101 units* (Log likelihood = –27851919)	Coefficient	Standard Error
Net migration (in millions)	3.83	0.66***
Percentage of population identified as African American	0.62	0.05***
Close D.C. suburbs (Alexandria, Arlington, Fairfax, Fairfax City, Falls Church)	0.33	0.02***
Virginia Beach	0.10	0.02***
Charlottesville and Albemarle County	0.14	0.04**
Lynchburg and Campbell County	–0.10	0.01***
Constant	0.36	0.01***

NORTH CAROLINA–100 counties (Log likelihood = –40322772.2)	Coefficient	Standard Error
Net migration (in millions)	2.51	0.89**
Percentage of population identified as African American	–0.07	0.11
Cumberland County	0.19	0.03***
Constant	0.47	0.03***

* The U.S. Census aggregates some counties and independent cities together in Virginia.

** Significant at 0.5%.

*** Significant at 0.1% (two-tailed).

variable.[4] The percentage of the county's population that is African American will be a control variable, and Miami-Dade will be treated as a dummy variable. The weight factor will be the population (2008 estimate) of the county.[5]

Obama did much better in counties with more migrants, migrants disproportionately from the Northeast and Midwest. Migration explains roughly half of the variation in the two-party Obama vote in Florida. The percentage of the county's population that is African American is also a strong predictor of the Obama vote, as expected, and the distinctive nature of Miami-Dade is confirmed.

VIRGINIA

Virginia has experienced tremendous growth as well, driven by in-migration. The most prominent destination for incoming Virginians has been in the Washington, D.C., metropolitan area, commonly known as Northern Virginia. Other areas of recent growth are in the greater Richmond and Hampton Roads regions. In Northern Virginia, growth has been so rapid that there is a pattern of resettlement from communities on the Potomac River across from Washington such as Arlington, Alexandria, and Fairfax to more exurban parts of the region such as Loudoun and Prince William counties and the city of Manassas. A likewise phenomenon occurred in the Hampton Roads region, with heavy migration away from the southerly part of Hampton Roads, centered on the coastal cities of Virginia Beach, Norfolk, and Newport News, inland and north to the less-industrialized areas around Williamsburg,

the Northern Neck, and the James River. The cities of Virginia Beach, Alexandria, Fairfax, and Falls Church, and the counties of Arlington and Fairfax are outliers in out-migrants;[6] Loudoun County, the fastest-growing county in the United States, is an outlier for in-migrants.

These outliers are the first-, fourth-, sixth-, and eighth-most-populous units in Virginia, so they account for much of Obama's base of votes. In terms of percentage support, however, there are substantial differences. Arlington/Alexandria represented Obama's biggest two-party percentage in the state (72.5 percent), and Obama's margin of victory in megacounty Fairfax represented nearly half of his statewide margin of victory. However, in Virginia Beach, admittedly a world apart from Northern Virginia, Obama lost by about a percentage point. Both in Northern Virginia and in the city of Virginia Beach, however, Obama surpassed the statistical expectations for his share of the two-party vote based on migration and black population alone.

Loudoun County is the acid test among these outliers; if a county with this many new migrants does not lean toward Obama, then the notion of carpetbaggers tilting the Dixie vote must be terribly suspect. However, Obama won Loudoun County, 54 percent to 45 percent. This is especially noteworthy because this is the first time a Democratic presidential candidate has won Loudoun County since the Voting Rights Act of 1965 fundamentally reordered Southern partisanship patterns; only once (Jimmy Carter, running explicitly as a Southern Democrat in 1976) did a Democrat even narrow the margin to single digits. During this same

period, Loudoun's population exploded, growing from fewer than 25,000 people in 1960 to approximately 300,000 in 2010.

The pattern in Loudoun County applies statewide; net migration is a highly significant predictor for the two-party vote. African American population is also an exceptionally strong predictor. The remaining outliers again are controlled for using dummy variables. The D.C. suburbs are disproportionately federal government workers and new migrants, and Virginia Beach is a community heavily populated by military families and retirees; these populations are expected to favor Obama more than the norm. Also noteworthy were greater Charlottesville, home of the University of Virginia, for unusually high Obama support, and greater Lynchburg, home of the Virginia Military Institute, Washington and Lee University, and Liberty University, for unusually low Obama support.

NORTH CAROLINA

North Carolina is the final former Confederate state taken by Obama, by the narrowest margin. Once again, there is a major outlier county: Cumberland, the home of Fort Bragg, a very large military installation; it has experienced a major decline in population, similar to Virginia Beach, but Obama still scored well there. There seems to be a slight exception in the migration effect regarding communities with large military installations. Presumably, much of the churning of population in these communities is due to exigencies outside the normal course of events in predominantly civilian communities.

One unexpected peculiarity is that the percentage of a county's black population is insignificant in North Carolina; Obama did not benefit from a higher proportion of blacks in the electorate. This paradox is an artifact of the distribution of the African American population in North Carolina; it is concentrated in smaller, rural, low-migration counties, and hence the variation in the Obama vote is consumed by the migration variable and the population weight factor, partially obscured by larger black populations in the very biggest (that is, urban) counties. The Pearson correlation coefficient between net migration and percentage black population is -0.168, which is statistically significant at $p < 0.10$. The suspicion here is that in these smaller counties, the white population votes Republican fairly uniformly, eliding the apparent impact of the black vote in state totals. This is a common pattern in racially (or otherwise) polarized areas. Hood and McKee (2010) demonstrate that on the individual level, African Americans voted Democratic at typically high rates. Regardless of the peculiar outcome regarding the black vote, the effect of net migration is very strongly in Obama's favor once again; he does best in counties where many new voters are on the rolls.

CONCLUSION

One of the ongoing sagas of politics in the United States is the exceptionalism of the culture of the South relative to the rest of the nation. Since the civil rights reforms of the 1960s, a two-party system has emerged in the South; the presumption is that displaced white Dixiecrats fled to the party with which they were ideologically more congenial, especially in the context of Goldwater's opposition to the Civil Rights Act on federalist grounds and Nixon's Southern Strategy. This is true to an extent, but it is not sufficient to explain the evolution in the South.

The South is changing because of a steady stream of in-migration from the Northeast and Midwest since the mid-twentieth century; these latter-day carpetbaggers are pollinating the areas of high growth in the South with political and cultural attitudes that are largely free of the baggage of Jim Crow and Reconstruction. These are the voters who delivered three states of the Confederacy to a half-Kenyan man, brought up in Hawaii and Indonesia, who made his career on Chicago's South Side, a milestone in America's ongoing struggle to overcome the national sin of slavery.

ACKNOWLEDGMENTS

Many of the ideas in this piece germinated when I was a graduate student at afternoon discussions over tea at University of California, Berkeley's Institute of Governmental Studies; the late Nelson W. Polsby hosted those discussions and propounded his "air conditioning" theory, which eventually found its way to his last book (cited at the end of this chapter). I owe Nelson and the other participants at those teas (too many and varied to mention) a great debt.

I also received very helpful comments and criticism from my current colleagues at Binghamton when I presented an early version at our department's Comparative-American Workshop. I am grateful to all who participated, especially to Michael D. McDonald and Gregory Robinson, for particularly attentive and perspicacious suggestions.

Finally I am grateful to the editors of this volume for their invitation and for their support, especially to Stan Brunn, who has been my primary point of contact; his input has improved this contribution substantially. All errors and omissions are, of course, my responsibility alone.

■ MIDWEST

JOHN HEPPEN

The Great Lakes/Midwest states were among the most contested terrain in the 2008 presidential election. Seven of the eight states at one time or another had battleground status. Ohio and Missouri are traditional bellwether states that more often than not side with the winner. In 2008 only Barack Obama's home state of Illinois was not closely contested.

Ever mindful of the electoral importance of this region, and knowing how close the 2000 and 2004 elections were, Republicans held their national convention in St. Paul, Minnesota. John McCain and the GOP had hoped to sway Minnesota and its neighbors to vote for him, since Iowa went Republican in 2004 and Wisconsin and Minnesota were tantalizingly close in 2000 and 2004. The last time the GOP had held a convention in this region was in 1980 in Detroit. In that year the Republicans swept much of the Midwest. But the Obama team struck gold in 2008, winning seven of eight states for a total of ninety-six electoral votes out of a possible 107. Although the Democrats narrowly lost Missouri, they recaptured Iowa and surprisingly won Indiana, which had not gone Democratic since 1964 and is traditionally Republican. Other states in the region had long-standing loyalties to the Democratic Party. Minnesota had not gone Republican since 1972, Wisconsin since 1984, Michigan and Illinois since 1988, and Iowa (except for 2004) since 1984. Despite that history, this region was highly contested. The switch of Ohio, Wisconsin, Michigan, and Iowa could have potentially changed the outcome.

Despite the Obama near sweep in the Midwest, a county-level analysis shows that both campaigns were right in contesting much of this region. County-level analyses revealed some fascinating patterns: urban, suburban, and rural differences; differences between rural counties of the northern Midwest and the southern Midwest; and the appearance of counties that stand out from their neighbors due to the presence of minority populations and universities.

Urban, suburban, and rural differences are discussed first. The large urban counties of the Midwest proved to be fertile ground for Obama. These cities are usually carried by Democrats by large margins and are a vital part of any Democratic strategy in the region. Obama carried the major urban counties of the region housing the cities of: Detroit (Wayne), Cleveland (Cuyahoga), Columbus (Franklin), Dayton (Montgomery), Cincinnati (Hamilton), Gary (Lake), Chicago (Cook), Indianapolis (Marion), Milwaukee (Milwaukee), Minneapolis (Hennepin), St. Paul (Ramsey), St. Louis (St. Louis City), and Kansas City (Jackson). This was expected since liberal, working-class, and minority populations with income levels lower than those in the suburbs dominate these cities. The urban giants provided either majority or supermajority (greater than 65 percent) votes for Obama.

Furthermore, several suburban areas also provided the votes necessary for Obama's victory. Historically, suburban collar counties were Republican bases counteracting Democratic urban advantages. But suburban counties of Detroit (Oakland, Macomb, Washtenaw, and Monroe) gave majorities to Obama. Oakland and Macomb Counties had previously been Republican. In 2004, Macomb and Monroe Counties, home to the quintessential Reagan Democrats, provided George W. Bush with majorities. Cleveland's suburban Lake County went from a Bush majority to an Obama plurality. In Minneapolis-St. Paul, suburban Washington and Dakota Counties switched, as did Chicago's Lake and DuPage Counties. Though not as hurt as Michigan, the mortgage crisis and stock market collapse must have added to suburban economic anxieties.

Likewise, gains in Indiana for Obama provided one of the surprises of the 2008 election. Obama swept industrial and suburban northwestern Indiana, winning majorities in Lake (Gary), Porter, La Porte, and St. Joseph (South Bend) Counties. Other Obama urban counties included Vanderburgh (Evansville), Marion (Indianapolis), Vermillion, and Vigo (Terre Haute), which helped Obama carry Indiana. Obama improved upon John Kerry's percentages in every single county in Indiana, and his increase was greater than 5 percent in eighty-one out of Indiana's ninety-two counties. But the story was different in Missouri.

Unlike Indiana, the Democratic vote declined in a number of rural counties in Missouri from 2004 to 2008. St. Louis area counties, including St. Louis City and Jefferson (Kansas City), provided Obama majorities, but suburban Kansas City counties did not provide Obama any boost. Unlike Indiana, where there was an increase in Democratic percentage from 2004, many rural counties in Missouri showed less enthusiasm for Obama. In fact, Obama lost votes compared with Kerry in southeastern Missouri, including the Bootheel section of the Show Me State. Directly to the north of the Bootheel, Scott and Cape Girardeau Counties remained a consistent site of Republican support. Cape Girardeau was the boyhood home to radio commentator Rush Limbaugh and is where his grandfather and father were prominent attorneys and political leaders. Perhaps this identification explained part of the vote. Southeastern Ohio, which is part of Appalachia, saw a decrease in the Democratic vote between 2004 and 2008. Eastern Ohio bordering Pennsylvania saw decreases, but Obama managed to win more Ohio counties bordering Pennsylvania than those counties bordering West Virginia and Kentucky. In a manner similar to Missouri, the southern reaches of the Midwest showed an affinity for John McCain much like their southern neighbors of West Virginia, Kentucky, and Arkansas.

North-South differences were also evident within the Midwest. Large swaths of rural Michigan, Wisconsin, Minnesota, and Iowa were won by Obama, and his share of the vote increased throughout the region. The Upper Mississippi River valley of Iowa, Wisconsin, and Minnesota was an especially strong area of Obama support. A good number of these rural and smaller town counties switched from Bush to Obama. Many of these northern rural counties have an agricultural base or are forestry and mining counties. By contrast, the rural counties of southern Ohio, Indiana and Illinois, and almost all of Missouri were swept by McCain. McCain's win also included both rural areas and medium-sized urban areas. Rural areas of the lower Midwest, along with medium-sized towns, may have felt the impact of the recession less severely as their economies were less tied to manufacturing. The region also may have escaped some of the harsher impacts of the mortgage crisis in the larger towns and cities. In addition, the prices of soybeans, corn, and ethanol enjoyed a boost during the second term of the Bush presidency. The agribusinesses of staple crops and ethanol present a contrast to the smaller farms and less-prosperous parts of the Upper Midwest.

In the northern reaches of the corn and soybean belt, however, there were a large number of counties that switched from Bush to Obama majorities. This pattern harks back to historical settlement patterns and the political culture thesis advanced by the political scientist Daniel J. Elazar (1984) in *American Federalism: A View from the States*. Many initial Euro-American settlers of the Upper Midwest came from New England and upstate New York; they possessed a distinct political culture different from the earlier American settlers of the lower Midwest. Michigan, Wisconsin, Minnesota, Iowa, and the northern halves of Ohio, Indiana, and Illinois all have, according to Elazar, a Moralistic political culture that believes in government fostering the common good and being a positive force. Missouri and the southern halves of Ohio, Indiana, and Illinois were influenced by this Individualistic political culture. The settlers in this region of the Midwest came from northern Appalachia and the Middle Colonies, where the purpose of government was viewed as aiding individual and commercial economic interests and political patronage. Kevin Phillips (1999), in

The Cousins' Wars, has contrasted the Upper Midwest with the lower Midwest, calling the Upper Midwest part of a "Greater New England." A greater New England can be traced back to the Lincoln election of 1860 as Lincoln, like Obama, swept greater New England and performed better in northern Illinois relative to southern Illinois.

The northern reaches of greater New England (the forestry and mining counties) were hit hard by the Great Recession. It pushed many forestry and mining counties in a new voting direction in 2008. An example can be found in Michigan's Iron County in the Upper Peninsula. Although Iron County has been traditionally Democratic leaning due to the historical legacy of unions and a depressed economy, it gave Bush a plurality in 2004. Iron County had not voted for a Republican since 1972, so the switch to Bush was a surprise in a county where the last iron mines closed in the 1970s. However, this county switched to Obama in 2008. American Indian populations and reservations also dot the forestry and mining counties. American Indian populations historically support Democrats. One good example is Menominee County in northeastern Wisconsin, which contains the Menominee Indian Reservation. Their influence helps produce shades of blue in the Upper Midwest, but given the relatively small numbers of American Indian populations, they are not a deciding factor in presidential elections in the Midwest. In summary, Obama did a better job than McCain of convincing more Midwesterners across the Midwest that he was within the mainstream and would

better stimulate the economy while not endangering the country's security.

A final group of counties were islands of blue in seas of red due to the presence of large universities. In southeastern Ohio, Athens County, the home to Ohio University supported Obama despite being surrounded by red counties. Franklin County is another blue island; it is home to Ohio State University. Other islands of blue were in neighboring Indiana. Delaware County (and neighboring Anderson County) houses the medium-sized city of Muncie and Ball State University. To the west of Ball State is Lafayette County (Purdue University), and to the southeast of Purdue is Monroe County (Indiana University). In Illinois, Champaign County (University of Illinois) pops up as an Obama winner. South of Champaign County is Coles County, home to Eastern Illinois University. Another island of blue in southwestern Illinois is Jackson County (Southern Illinois University, Carbondale). Missouri offered one island of blue in the center of the state in Boone County (University of Missouri). Johnson County, which is home to the University of Iowa, is the only Obama supermajority county in Iowa.

In conclusion, both Barack Obama and John McCain had ample reason to contest this region. While McCain won more counties, in the end it was the population size of the counties won that mattered, as Obama swept the more populous urban giants. Obama swept the large cities and college towns and made strong inroads in the suburbs by winning suburban counties that Bush took, a combination that was successful in all the Midwest states except Missouri.

Midwest Region Presidential Elections

MAP 5.3

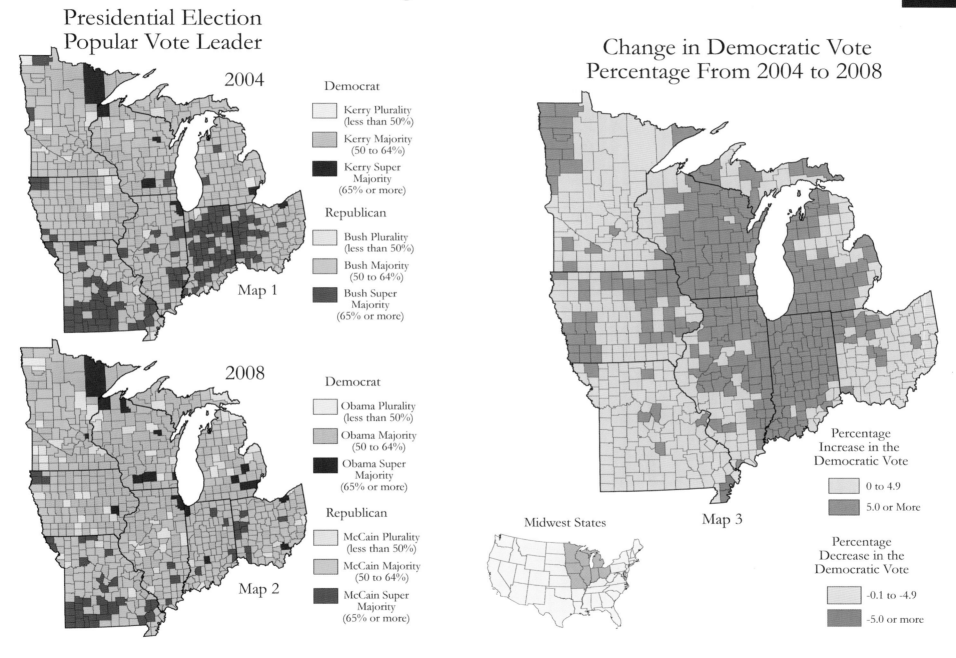

Presidential Election Popular Vote Leader

2004

Democrat

- Kerry Plurality (less than 50%)
- Kerry Majority (50 to 64%)
- Kerry Super Majority (65% or more)

Republican

- Bush Plurality (less than 50%)
- Bush Majority (50 to 64%)
- Bush Super Majority (65% or more)

Map 1

2008

Democrat

- Obama Plurality (less than 50%)
- Obama Majority (50 to 64%)
- Obama Super Majority (65% or more)

Republican

- McCain Plurality (less than 50%)
- McCain Majority (50 to 64%)
- McCain Super Majority (65% or more)

Map 2

Change in Democratic Vote Percentage From 2004 to 2008

Map 3

Midwest States

Percentage Increase in the Democratic Vote

- 0 to 4.9
- 5.0 or More

Percentage Decrease in the Democratic Vote

- -0.1 to -4.9
- -5.0 or more

■ GREAT PLAINS

ROBERT WATREL

From an Electoral College standpoint, the Great Plains states have been strong supporters of Republican presidential candidates for many years. The Great Plains region encompasses six states in the interior of the United States. Running north to south, these states include North and South Dakota, Nebraska, Kansas, Oklahoma, and Texas. Prior to the 2008 presidential election, the last time a Great Plains state did not cast its Electoral College votes for a Republican candidate was in 1976 when Texas cast its electoral votes for Jimmy Carter. Although the Electoral College outcome for the 2008 presidential election was typical for Great Plains states, there was one major exception: Nebraska. In 1992, Nebraska changed its winner-take-all method of distributing electoral votes to the congressional district method of distributing electoral votes, in which one electoral vote was allotted to the candidate who won the most popular votes in each district, with the other two electoral votes going to the popular vote winner statewide.

In the Second District, including the city of Omaha, Democrat Barack Obama got a plurality of popular votes. Democrats got an electoral vote from Nebraska, winning Electoral College support from Nebraska from the first time since 1964.

The results of the 2004 and 2008 presidential elections at the county level reveal a continuing pattern in the Great Plains with voters in large numbers of counties casting 50 percent or more of their ballots for the Republican presidential candidate. Indeed, of the 843 counties that the Great Plains comprises,

576 counties gave 50 percent or more of their votes to John McCain, while only sixty counties did the same for Barack Obama. As bad as these results were for the 2008 Democratic presidential candidate, the results had been even more depressing for the Democrats in the 2004 presidential election. In 2004, only thirty-four counties gave 50 percent or more of their support to John Kerry, the Democratic candidate, while George W. Bush carried 781 counties with a majority of the votes. However, even in the largely conservative region of the Great Plains, the 2008 presidential election, much like the rest of the country, saw some increases for the Democratic candidate compared with the 2004 presidential election.

Although a large number of counties in the Great Plains tend to give a majority of their votes to Republican candidates, there are some localized differences in voting patterns within the region. When looking for these anomalous areas of the Great Plains where Republicans have not done as well, the map of the 2004 presidential election is the place to start. Democratic-majority counties can be grouped into four categories: counties with higher American Indian populations, counties with higher Hispanic populations, several college-town counties, and several other counties that have traditionally voted Democratic. In the northern Great Plains, almost all the counties with Democratic majorities have high American Indian populations, which have historically been strong supporters of the Democratic Party. In North Dakota, Rolette County (Turtle Mountain Indian Reservation), Benson County (Spirit Lake Indian

Reservation), and Sioux County (Standing Rock Indian Reservation) all have American Indian populations of 5 percent or more. In South Dakota, the pattern is similar. Counties with higher American Indian populations such as Corson (Standing Rock Indian Reservation), Dewey and Ziebach (Cheyenne River Indian Reservation), Shannon (Pine Ridge Indian Reservation), Todd (Rosebud Indian Reservation), Buffalo (Crow Creek Indian Reservation), and Roberts (Lake Traverse Indian Reservation) have been strong supporters of the Democratic presidential candidates. In Nebraska, the only county to give John Kerry a majority of votes in 2004 was Thurston County, which contains the Winnebago and Omaha Indian Reservations (Wishart 2004).

Another area of Democratic support is located in the southern Great Plains, close to or along the United States-Mexico border. These are counties with historically high Hispanic populations (De Leon 2009). Some of these counties have been strong supporters of the Democratic Party for many decades. Brooks, Duval, Starr, and Jim Hogg counties have never given a Republican presidential candidate a majority of their votes. All of these counties have Hispanic populations over 75 percent. Not all counties with high Hispanic populations vote Democratic, but these counties have a long history of Democratic support. Counties such as Zavala, Dimmit, Jim Hogg, Starr, Brooks, and Duval gave supermajorities (65 percent or more) to John Kerry in 2004. Of the remaining counties in the Great Plains that gave John Kerry a majority of votes, three had universities: Clay

County, South Dakota (University of South Dakota), Douglas County, Kansas (University of Kansas), and Travis County, Texas (University of Texas, Austin). Another four are either rural or urban counties that tend to lean toward the Democratic Party. The rural counties include Steele County, North Dakota, and Day County, South Dakota, while the urban counties include Wyandotte County, Kansas (Kansas City), and Jefferson County, Texas (Beaumont and Port Arthur).

When looking over the map of the 2008 presidential election, which shows the popular vote leader by county, the pattern is similar to the 2004 election, but there are some noticeable differences. The noticeable areas of increased Democratic support are largely located in the northern Great Plains and in southern Texas. In the middle map, counties shaded in blue represent counties that cast a majority (50 percent or more) of their votes for Barack Obama in 2008. Every county that cast a majority of votes for John Kerry in 2004 did so for Barack Obama in 2008, so only those counties that gave majorities or pluralities to Obama, but not to Kerry, are discussed here. In the northern Great Plains, new counties that gave Barack Obama a majority are located in the eastern halves of North Dakota and South Dakota. These eastern counties tend to be more densely populated and have more urban areas than those in the western parts of these states. They also tend to be oriented to commercial farming and were settled largely by Norwegians, Germans, and other European groups (Sherman and Thorson 1988). These counties are generally more competitive than most western counties. For example, rural counties such as Traill, Eddy, Nelson, Ransom, and Sargent in North Dakota; Marshall, Lake, and Miner Counties in South Dakota; and Saline County, Nebraska, fall in this category. Counties with a larger urban center that gave Barack Obama a majority or plurality include Grand Forks County, North Dakota (Grand Forks and the University of North Dakota), Cass County, North Dakota (Fargo and North Dakota State University), Brown County, South Dakota (Aberdeen and Northern State University), Brookings County, South Dakota (Brookings and South Dakota State University), Minnehaha County, South Dakota (Sioux Falls), Douglas County, Nebraska (Omaha), Lancaster County, Nebraska (Lincoln and the University of Nebraska, Lincoln), and Crawford County, Kansas (Pittsburg and Pittsburg State University).

The other notable area of increased Democratic support is in southern Texas. Along with the sixteen counties that gave a majority to the Democrats in 2004, seven additional counties with larger Hispanic populations gave a majority to Obama. Three other counties in Texas with larger urban populations gave Obama a majority in 2008 but did not give Kerry a majority in 2004. They include Dallas County (Dallas), Harris County (Houston), and Bexar County (San Antonio).

Finally, the vast support for the Republican Party by counties in the Great Plains needs to be addressed. The states of Nebraska, Kansas, especially Oklahoma, western North and South Dakota, and northern Texas tend to be staunch supporters of Republican candidates. In Oklahoma, no counties in either election gave a majority to the Democratic candidate. In Nebraska, one county gave a majority to Kerry, and in 2008, only four counties gave a majority to Obama. These counties tend to be rural, have small towns, depend on farming and ranching, and consist of whites and older people.

In 2004, all the Great Plains states gave a 20 percent or larger margin of victory to the Republican candidate, with Nebraska highest at 33.2 percent and South Dakota the lowest at 27.4 percent. Although McCain won the popular vote in all of the Great Plains states, Obama made significant gains in every state except for Oklahoma. Indeed, all of the Great Plains states except Oklahoma had a 10 percent or more shift in Democratic voting in 2008 compared with 2004. North Dakota had the largest shift in Democratic voting with an 18.7 percent increase, while Oklahoma had a 0.1 percent increase for the Republican candidate relative to the 2004 election. However, when looking at the change in Democratic percentage by county between the 2004 and 2008 elections, the 2008 election had a polarizing effect on Great Plains voters. As previously indicated, counties with large increases in Democratic support were concentrated in the northern Plains and eastern Texas. Counties that had a vote change toward the Republican Party in 2008 are located in northern and eastern Texas and especially in Oklahoma. In Oklahoma, the counties that saw a gain in Democratic support tended to be counties with larger urban areas, military bases, and universities, such as Oklahoma County (Oklahoma City and Tinker Air Force Base), and other counties within the Oklahoma City MSA (Comanche, Logan, and Canadian), plus other urban counties such as Comanche (Lawton and Fort Sill), Tulsa (Tulsa), and Garfield (Enid and Vance Air Force Base). Counties with universities include Stillwater (Oklahoma State University) and Norman (University of Oklahoma). The other military base county was Jackson (Altus Air Force Base). Although all but twelve of the seventy-seven counties saw a shift toward the Republican Party, the counties that gravitated more than 5 percent toward the Republican Party in 2008 were largely located in southeastern Oklahoma, eastern Texas close to the Louisiana border, and a few counties in northern Texas and western Oklahoma. Many of the counties located in southeastern and northeastern Oklahoma are within the Ouachita Mountains and have more cultural linkages to the South than to the Great Plains. This Southern influence would also include the counties of eastern Texas. In many ways this is the western edge of a swath of counties, extending from eastern Oklahoma to eastern Kentucky, and from eastern Texas through Louisiana, that made a more drastic swing toward the Republican Party than anywhere else in the country.

The future of presidential voting trends in the Great Plains will likely follow the patterns described above for the foreseeable future. This trend can be attributed to slow or little demographic change in most of the counties throughout the Great Plains, especially rural counties. As a result, the Great Plains will remain largely white, rural, small town, agriculturally based, and conservative in political outlook. These six states also will most likely be reliable electoral votes for Republican candidates.

Great Plains Region Presidential Elections

MAP 5.4

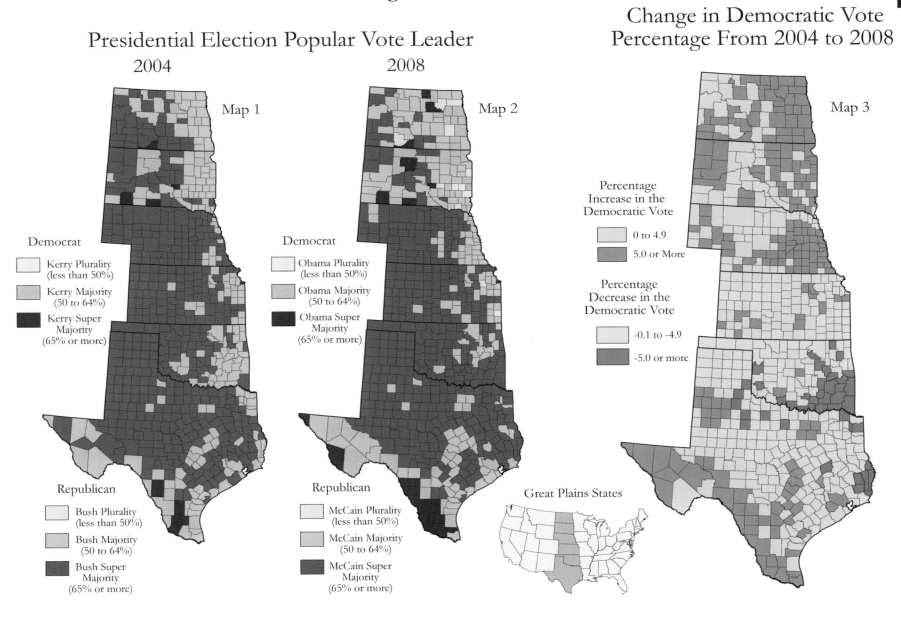

Presidential Election Popular Vote Leader

2004

Map 1

Democrat

- Kerry Plurality (less than 50%)
- Kerry Majority (50 to 64%)
- Kerry Super Majority (65% or more)

Republican

- Bush Plurality (less than 50%)
- Bush Majority (50 to 64%)
- Bush Super Majority (65% or more)

2008

Map 2

Democrat

- Obama Plurality (less than 50%)
- Obama Majority (50 to 64%)
- Obama Super Majority (65% or more)

Republican

- McCain Plurality (less than 50%)
- McCain Majority (50 to 64%)
- McCain Super Majority (65% or more)

Great Plains States

Change in Democratic Vote Percentage From 2004 to 2008

Map 3

Percentage Increase in the Democratic Vote

- 0 to 4.9
- 5.0 or More

Percentage Decrease in the Democratic Vote

- -0.1 to -4.9
- -5.0 or more

■ MOUNTAIN WEST

TONY ROBINSON

Legendary Speaker of the House Tip O'Neill once claimed that "all politics is local." One way of looking at county-level electoral maps of the Mountain West, as elsewhere, is to ponder the hundreds of unique county-level stories that are revealed. What's going on with that blue county in a sea of Republican Red in Idaho's panhandle, for example (map 2 in map 5.5)? That's Latah County, home of the University of Idaho, whose voting habits in 2008 replicated Obama's popularity with college voters nationwide. What's the story behind the single Democratic county in conservative Wyoming in the 2008 election? That's Teton County, home to the affluent Jackson Hole ski-resort area and to thousands of "wired" professionals and migrants from California and the East Coast, typically Democratic constituencies.

Unique county-level stories are fascinating, but these maps also point to broader dynamics playing out across the region. One of the more intriguing of those dynamics suggested by these maps is the recent growth of the Democratic Party across the Mountain West. Though states in this region have voted unanimously Republican in all presidential elections since 1968 (excepting Colorado, Montana, and New Mexico in Clinton's 1992 victory, New Mexico and Arizona in 1996, and New Mexico in 2000), things changed in 2008, when Colorado, New Mexico, and Nevada were all won by the Democrats—and the party almost won Montana. Swaths of Democratic blue across the region in the first map testify to surging Democratic prospects. Across the West, only

Arizona showed Democrats losing ground in the presidential vote between 2004 and 2008—and Arizona would probably have paralleled regional dynamics if not for Arizona Senator John McCain heading the 2008 Republican ticket.

Rising Democratic fortunes in the West go beyond the 2008 presidential election. Once a reliable eight-state Republican region, the Mountain West is electing more and more Democrats to state and national office, leading some to point to the region as the linchpin of future national Democratic majorities (Frey and Teixeira 2008; Schaller 2002). Colorado, a state once dominated by Republican officials, recently elected a Democratic majority to its state legislature, a Democratic governor, two Democratic U.S. senators, and a 2009 U.S. House delegation favoring Democrats five to two. Montana, where Democrats had neither held the governor's office since 1989 nor controlled the state legislature since 1991, turned both chambers of the state legislature and the governor's office over to the Democrats in the 2004 elections and sent a Democrat to the U.S. Senate in 2006 (though Republicans recaptured the state Senate in 2008). In 1998, the eight-state region boasted eight GOP governors. By 2008, there were only three. The GOP's 1990 fifteen-to-nine advantage in congressional House seats reversed to a seventeen-to-eleven Democratic advantage by 2008.

Democrats are making gains across the West, but this claim must be qualified in three important

ways. First, Democratic gains do not mean Democrats are now the majority party in the West. The second and third maps demonstrate that the Republican presidential candidate won a plurality of the vote in a majority of Western counties in both 2004 and 2008. Democratic gains in 2008 were usually the result of the Republican "supermajority" in a county shrinking to a simple majority, rather than the result of red counties suddenly turning Democratic blue. Though Democrats in 2008 were only twenty thousand votes behind Republicans in the regional presidential vote (out of nearly 885,000 votes cast), versus being one hundred thousand-plus votes behind in 2004, the fact remains that Democrats remain the minority party at a regional level.

A second qualifier to surging Democratic prospects is that the gains differ greatly by state. These maps demonstrate that Democrats are growing or are consistently competitive in five Western states (Colorado, Montana, New Mexico, Nevada, and Arizona—discounting the McCain effect in 2008), but Republicans retain a bright red dominance over Utah, Idaho, and Wyoming.

Finally, just as Democratic gains are not regionally uniform, a third qualifier is that gains are not uniform below the state level—they vary by county. The swath of strong Democratic counties across central Colorado, for example, clearly stands out from the Republican-red surrounding counties in each map. The pepper of blue counties in Montana in the second and third maps are isolated Democratic islands in Montana's sea of Republican purple and red. In Nevada, only two blue Democratic counties appear in the 2008 presidential election; the rest of the state voted Republican. One of these counties was Clark County (Las Vegas), which has about 70 percent of the state's population. Elsewhere across the region, Democratic strengths are similarly concentrated in a small number of relatively heavily populated counties. For example, most of Obama's 2008 margin in New Mexico was due to his strong showing in Albuquerque, Santa Fe, and Taos. In Colorado, it came entirely from his large majorities in the Denver-Boulder area. In fact, throw out Denver and Boulder counties and Obama would have lost the state.

These dynamics raise intriguing questions. What accounts for rising Democratic prospects across the West and for continuing Republican strength in Utah, Idaho, and Wyoming? What can be learned about the different kinds of counties where either Democrats or Republicans are strong or growing?

To understand why Democrats are growing across the West, it is necessary to study the kinds of counties where they are doing well. One clear pattern is the urban-rural electoral divide across the West. Though Nevada voted Democratic for president in 2008, the third map reveals that the Democratic majority was entirely driven by only two relatively urbanized Nevada counties (Las Vegas's Clark County and Reno's Washoe County). A majority elsewhere in the state voted Republican. Similarly the second and third maps show that Democratic majority counties often contain a large urban area (such as the Albuquerque/Santa Fe area in New Mexico and the Denver-Fort Collins corridor in Colorado). Many of Montana's Democratic-majority counties in the 2008 election (third map) are home to Montana's larger cities (e.g., Bozeman, Missoula, or Helena). Even conservative Utah showed Democratic strength in the Salt Lake City area. While Democrats dominate many urban counties in the West, the brightest Republican-red areas of these maps, such as in Wyoming, the eastern Colorado plains, or southern Idaho and Utah, are the most sparsely populated, rural areas in the region.

A second dynamic is the tendency of Democratic-leaning counties to have a high percentage of white-collar jobs held by educated professionals (a group some call the "creative class" [Florida 2002]) or to be classified as "recreation-destination" counties, such as mountain ski towns or environmental amenity communities. As a "New West" unfolds along Colorado's Front Range, for example, wired cities of high-tech professionals have exploded, and Democrats perform well with this demographic. Another aspect of the "New West" is that all along the Rocky Mountain spine through Colorado and New Mexico, "recreation-destination" counties are attracting thousands of migrants from other areas of the country, mostly from the liberal West Coast. As these migrants move in, the counties become more Democratic. These same dynamics help account for Democratic strength in northwest Wyoming near the recreation-destination of Jackson Hole and in Montana's increasingly "wired" college counties, such as Missoula and Bozeman. At the same time, traditional rural counties, such as in the eastern plains of Montana, Wyoming, and Colorado, have not attracted many new migrants and are not hot spots of the new "wired economy." These areas remain Republican strongholds (Bishop and Cushing 2008).

A third lesson emerging in these maps pertains to racial voting patterns. Two nonwhite ethnic/racial groups (Latinos and American Indians) are significant in the West. Both have pro-Democratic voting habits. The substantial numbers of blue Democratic counties in New Mexico in each of these maps reflects the very high number of Latino voters in that state (Latinos make up 45 percent of New Mexico's population, and they vote 60 percent-plus Democratic). Heavy Latino concentrations are also present along Arizona's southern border, in Nevada's southern Clark County, and in south-central Colorado, all areas of Democratic strength.

These maps also reveal the tendency of American Indians to vote Democratic at 85 percent-plus levels. Overlaying a map of Western Indian Reservations onto the second and third maps would closely correlate with counties in which Democrats won the presidential vote in 2004 and 2008, especially in Arizona, New Mexico, and Montana. This dynamic becomes most clear by examining Montana, in the second map. In the 2004 presidential election, Democrats won six Montana counties. Of these six counties, three match almost perfectly with Indian reservation boundaries: the Crow Reservation to the south, Blackfeet to the north, and Fort Peck Reservation to the east.

The preceding points explain Democratic strength and ascendance, but what explains continuing Republican dominance in Wyoming, Idaho, and Utah? Part of the explanation is the tendency of rural voters in these sparsely populated states to vote Republican, but it is important to note that in all three states these Republican tendencies are reinforced by the large number of members of the Church of Jesus Christ of Latter-Day Saints (Mormons).

Utah, Idaho, and Wyoming (the three most reliably Republican states in the West) are also the top three U.S. states in the proportion of Mormons in the population (more than 60 percent Mormon in Utah, 25 percent in Idaho, and 10 percent in Wyoming). Bright red Republican dominance throughout Utah and in southern Idaho and southwestern Wyoming correlates with large concentrations of Mormon voters in these counties. A socially conservative segment of the electorate, these voters have responded well to the GOP message of valuing traditional families and the role of God in political life.

All told, these maps demonstrate Democratic ascendance in the West. They reveal a "New West" unfolding in the most heavily populated and "creative class" counties and the related influence of new migrants into the region's lifestyle-amenity counties. Evidence of the Democratic voting tendencies of Latinos and American Indians in the Mountain West is also clear. Still, sparsely populated, rural, and heavily religious counties constitute a good deal of the Mountain West, which largely accounts for the region's enduring (though shrinking) Republican majority.

Mountain West Region Presidential Elections

MAP 5.5

Presidential Election Popular Vote Leader

Change in Democratic Vote Percentage From 2004 to 2008

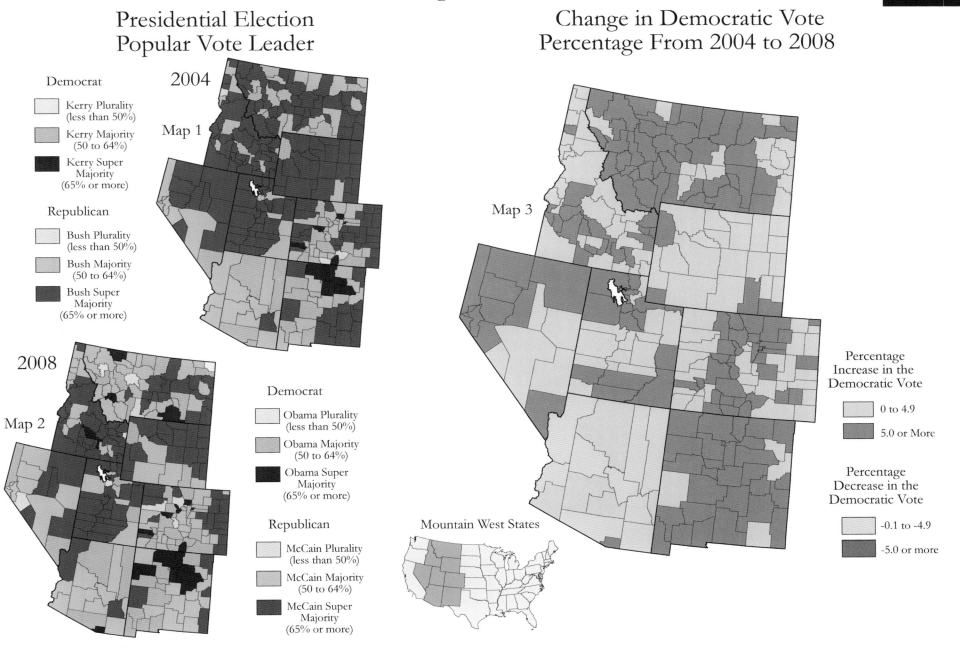

Democrat

Kerry Plurality (less than 50%)

Kerry Majority (50 to 64%)

Kerry Super Majority (65% or more)

Republican

Bush Plurality (less than 50%)

Bush Majority (50 to 64%)

Bush Super Majority (65% or more)

2004

Map 1

2008

Map 2

Democrat

Obama Plurality (less than 50%)

Obama Majority (50 to 64%)

Obama Super Majority (65% or more)

Republican

McCain Plurality (less than 50%)

McCain Majority (50 to 64%)

McCain Super Majority (65% or more)

Map 3

Percentage Increase in the Democratic Vote

0 to 4.9

5.0 or More

Percentage Decrease in the Democratic Vote

-0.1 to -4.9

-5.0 or more

Mountain West States

■ PACIFIC REGION

JOHN AGNEW

The three contiguous coastal states and Hawaii have become strongholds of Democratic Party presidential candidates since the 1990s. Alaska remains apart from the others as a more consistently Republican state in presidential politics. As the county returns from the 2008 presidential election show, however, below the state level there is considerable geographical variation across the region that is not well captured by the popular stereotype of the region in some quarters as the "left coast." Though California, by far the largest of the region's states in population and Electoral College votes, went heavily for Barack Obama, there is a remarkable division across the state between the coastal and interior counties, many of the latter giving majorities to John McCain. Much of this is an urban/rural phenomenon, with the largely agricultural-valley and rural-mountainous counties breaking in the opposite direction from urban-metropolitan counties in Southern California and the Bay Area (Decker 2009). This pattern, very similar to ones in Oregon and Washington State, parallels the ideological and party affiliation patterns long noted in California state politics. An older north/south divide based in issues such as the politics of water and the greater conservatism of the immigrants to Southern California from the U.S. Midwest and South in the 1930s and 1940s has largely disappeared. Just as in the rest of the United States, in the Pacific Region there is a persisting geographical clustering in presidential voting by party, though this does not seem to have increased since 2004 except

in parts of California (Seabrook 2009). Much of the geographical polarization is due to the increased right-wing ideology of the Republican party, narrowing the appeal of the party in this region to very specific cultural-geographical constituencies and producing candidates in statewide and congressional elections who are so extreme that they cannot appeal to moderate voters (Fiorina and Abrams 2008).

An east/west divide now rules in California, and to a degree in the other two contiguous states, not just in presidential elections but also across popular initiative ballots and in state electoral politics (Kousser 2009). Apart from suburban Orange County, to the south of Los Angeles, long a stronghold of the Republican Party across all elections, the Republican Party in the western coastal states has become increasingly a rural and small-town party as it has moved to the right since the 1980s. If in Orange County it is the libertarian and business-friendly face of the Republican Party that has long prevailed, in the interior of the state (and in the interiors of the two northward states) it is the social conservatism of the contemporary party that appeals the most (Douzet et al. 2008). But evangelical Christians and Mormons, wherever they are, both important social groups in the Pacific region, tend to overwhelmingly support Republican candidates. In the major metropolitan areas, the Democratic Party has acquired an electoral predominance reflected in the 2008 presidential vote, with Los Angeles and San Francisco both giving supermajorities to Obama. Adjacent suburban

counties, such as Ventura in relation to Los Angeles, and the city and suburbs of San Diego, swung from being Bush to Obama majority counties between 2004 and 2008. The relatively more affluent voters of coastal California and the smaller numbers of their affluent brethren elsewhere went heavily for Obama rather than McCain in 2008. San Diego, historically a "military" town as the base of the U.S. Pacific Fleet, has undergone something of a social transformation as a result of new industries and immigration from Asia and Latin America. This probably accounts for some of the shift from the Republican to the Democratic column in 2008, as did the collapse of the local housing market in 2007. Even more surprisingly, historically Republican areas to the east of Los Angeles in Riverside and San Bernardino counties also went heavily for Obama, also reflecting both the impact of the 2008 recession. This is the area in California with the highest rate of housing foreclosures in 2007–2008 and an increasingly Latino composition of the population. The Latino vote in California and other Pacific states tends, partly because of Republican views about immigration, to vote Democratic. But it is still a small relative portion of the overall electorate. Its role in the increased support for Democratic candidates across all California elections can be exaggerated (Fiorina and Abrams 2008).

If anything, the rural/urban divide, particularly between the sparsely populated southeast of the state and the population centers in the Willamette valley, is even starker in Oregon than in California and Washington State. In 2008, McCain did nearly as well in southeast Oregon as had Bush in 2004, whereas his vote slipped markedly compared to that of Bush in the interior regions of the other two states. Oregon as a whole has been a more competitive state in recent presidential elections than have California and Washington State. This perhaps reflects the fact that the state is generally less urban and without the major metropolitan areas of the other two states. 2008 represented something of a breakthrough for the Democratic candidate, with Obama advancing considerably in the more populous areas of Oregon compared with Kerry in 2004. In Washington State the pattern between 2004 and 2008 did not change much, with the Seattle-Tacoma metropolitan area remaining the seat of Democratic strength and the Republican vote holding up well in a difficult election nationally for the Republican candidate in the eastern/rural part of the state.

Hawaii and Alaska represent opposite ends of the political spectrum as far as the 2008 presidential election is concerned. Ever since statehood these states have tended to be dominated respectively by the Democratic and Republican parties in just about every type of election. The 2008 presidential election was to prove no exception. Across all of Hawaii, Obama, himself born in the state, acquired a clear majority of the vote. Hawaii remains a difficult state for Republican candidates for all offices (Semuels 2010). With most of the population of native Hawaiian and Asian heritage, Hawaii has a very different ethnic profile from the other states in the region. In Alaska, McCain dominated almost as much as did Obama in Hawaii, perhaps with a major assist from his running mate, the then sitting governor of Alaska, Sarah Palin. He did particularly well in the hinterland of Anchorage (Palin's home turf) and in Alaska's sparsely populated interior.

Conservative Republicans have long done well in these areas. Areas with American Indian majorities, however, tended to go heavily for Obama. This is something of a change. Democratic presidential candidates have not always done well in these areas. Alone of all counties and electoral districts in the Pacific Region as a whole, only in the central Alaskan interior and around Palin's hometown of Wasilla was there a net swing to the Republican candidate in 2008. This looks very much like a classic "friends-and-neighbors" effect, with many voting for McCain because of his running mate. The Alaska panhandle, interestingly because the seat of Alaskan state government is in Juneau, was considerably less enthusiastic for McCain-Palin in 2008 than it had been for Bush-Cheney in 2004. This could be a case of the area of the homeplace of the Republican vice-presidential candidate going in one direction and that of her workplace in another.

Pacific Region Presidential Elections

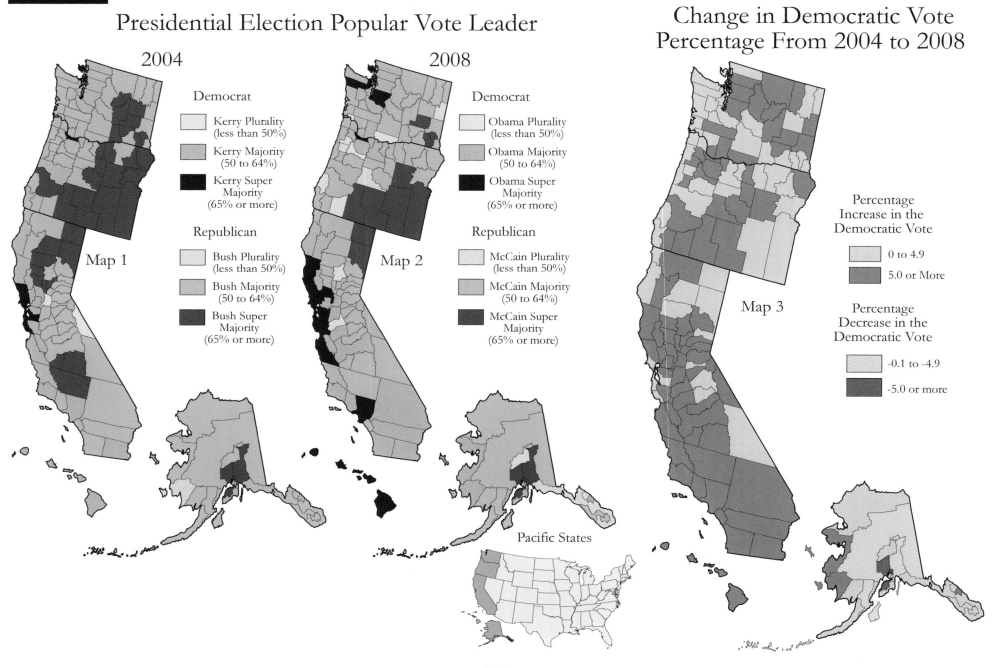

MAP 5.6

Presidential Election Popular Vote Leader

2004

Democrat

- Kerry Plurality (less than 50%)
- Kerry Majority (50 to 64%)
- Kerry Super Majority (65% or more)

Republican

- Bush Plurality (less than 50%)
- Bush Majority (50 to 64%)
- Bush Super Majority (65% or more)

Map 1

2008

Democrat

- Obama Plurality (less than 50%)
- Obama Majority (50 to 64%)
- Obama Super Majority (65% or more)

Republican

- McCain Plurality (less than 50%)
- McCain Majority (50 to 64%)
- McCain Super Majority (65% or more)

Map 2

Change in Democratic Vote Percentage From 2004 to 2008

Map 3

Percentage Increase in the Democratic Vote

- 0 to 4.9
- 5.0 or More

Percentage Decrease in the Democratic Vote

- -0.1 to -4.9
- -5.0 or more

Pacific States

THE CALIFORNIZATION OF COLORADO

TONY ROBINSON

For only the second time in history, the Democrats chose Colorado for their 2008 national convention, and it was no mistake. As Republican strength erodes across the Rocky Mountains, nowhere is the Democratic tilt as dramatic as in Colorado. A once rock-ribbed Republican stronghold boasting the United States' most conservative tax-constraint legislation (TABOR—Taxpayer Bill of Rights), and the headquarters of the conservative Focus on the Family religious organization, Colorado now showcases the changing West: electing a Democratic legislature in 2004, choosing a Democratic governor in 2006, voting Democratic for president in 2008, and selecting a 2008 House/Senate delegation favoring Democrats seven to two. What accounts for this electoral change? The maps presented here highlight two factors behind Colorado's emergence as a swing state: significant in-migration from more liberal areas of the country, and the growth of highly educated and typically socially liberal "creative class" workers.

The first map (in map 5.7) presents the geography of Democratic strength and weakness in Colorado, comparing Democratic performance in all statewide and federal elections between 1992 and 2008. Reflecting their rural weakness nationwide, Democrats continue to flounder in Colorado's eastern plains, the least populated, slowest growing, and most heavily agricultural area of the state. But Democratic gains are dramatic in the rapidly growing Front Range urban corridor (from Fort Collins to Pueblo) and in scenic mountain counties. Almost every county that displays Democratic blue in the first map is rapidly growing, with several counties (e.g., Douglas, Weld, and Denver) posting census-estimated growth rates in the top ten American counties in the past decade. Something about the dynamics in these booming counties is favorable to Democrats, but what?

The second map suggests one answer: the in-migration of new Colorado residents from more liberal areas of the country. When one considers the level of in-migration into each Colorado county and averages the Democratic strength of counties out of which new residents have moved, the resulting map correlates well with counties where Democrats are posting strong gains. To a large extent, it's because of the Californians. Census and IRS tax-filer data demonstrate that 40 percent of Colorado migrants hail from more liberal California, with the top exporting county into Colorado being heavily Democratic Los Angeles.

The third map suggests a related development. The top-performing Democratic counties in the first map tend also to score high on the percentage of residents employed in "creative class" occupations. These people are classified as well-educated, ethnically diverse, white-collar, environmentally conscious workers who are increasingly replacing Colorado's blue-collar, agriculture, and extraction-economy demographic of previous decades, as they swell the high-tech Front Range, the increasingly wired southwestern Durango area, and recreation-destination mountain ski counties. Scholars have found that "creative class" voters tend to be more socially liberal than traditional Western voters and more supportive of "green" environmental policies, which generally aligns them as Democrats.

Together, these maps suggest that as well-educated, "creative class" migrants pour out of liberal areas of the country and into Colorado, they are catalyzing rising Democratic power. Call it the Californization of Colorado, and it is fueling the emergence of a new American swing state.

MAP 5.7

Colorado County-Level Democratic Growth Correlated with In-Migration from More Liberal Counties and the Rise of the Creative Class

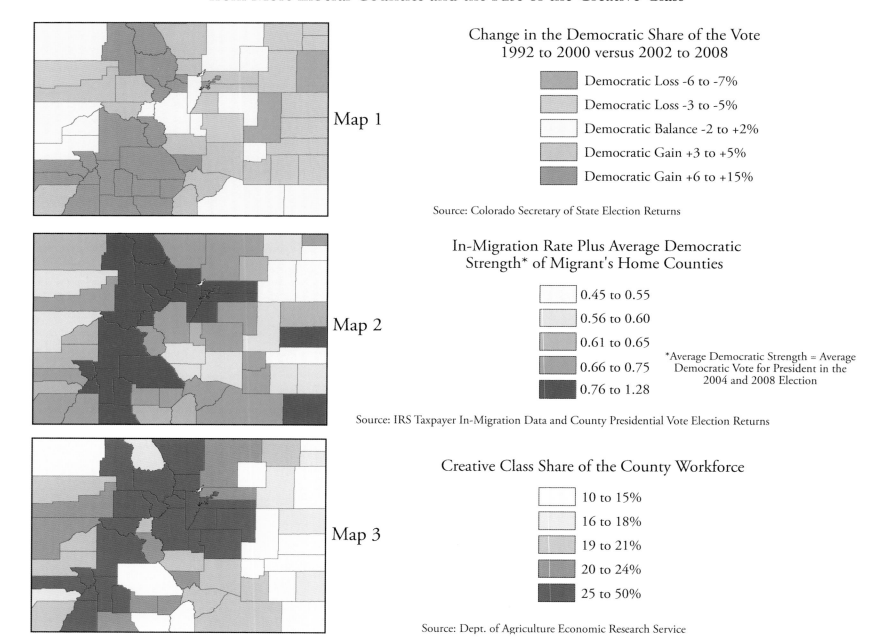

Map 1

Change in the Democratic Share of the Vote 1992 to 2000 versus 2002 to 2008

Democratic Loss -6 to -7%

Democratic Loss -3 to -5%

Democratic Balance -2 to +2%

Democratic Gain +3 to +5%

Democratic Gain +6 to +15%

Source: Colorado Secretary of State Election Returns

Map 2

In-Migration Rate Plus Average Democratic Strength* of Migrant's Home Counties

0.45 to 0.55

0.56 to 0.60

0.61 to 0.65

0.66 to 0.75

0.76 to 1.28

*Average Democratic Strength = Average Democratic Vote for President in the 2004 and 2008 Election

Source: IRS Taxpayer In-Migration Data and County Presidential Vote Election Returns

Map 3

Creative Class Share of the County Workforce

10 to 15%

16 to 18%

19 to 21%

20 to 24%

25 to 50%

Source: Dept. of Agriculture Economic Research Service

FLORIDA

NICK QUINTON

Florida plays a significant role in U.S. presidential politics due to its relatively large number of Electoral College votes (twenty-seven). In both the 2000 and 2004 presidential elections, George W. Bush's margin of Electoral College victory necessitated a win in Florida. The state's decisive role in the Electoral College in these two recent presidential elections contributed to its being a "must win" state for presidential aspirants.

Florida's appeal to prospective presidential candidates, however, is not limited to the size of its electorate. Candidates are also drawn to the general competitiveness associated with the state's electorate for candidates from either political party. Partisan volatility associated with Florida's electorate has led to its being classified as a swing state. Electorates in swing states routinely shift their Electoral College votes between the two major political parties in successive elections. Florida's electoral votes have swung from one political party to the other three times in the past five presidential elections. This includes the most recent presidential election, where Florida swung from the Republican candidate in 2004 to the Democratic candidate in 2008.

Any shift in Electoral College votes is predicated upon members of the particular state's electorate shifting their preferences in successive elections. In 2008, 51 percent of Floridians cast ballots in favor of the Democratic candidate, an increase from 47 percent in 2004. Thus, it was a single-digit gain in the proportion of the electorate that produced the 2004–2008 swing.

This 4 percent swing from Republican to Democrat in 2008 suggests a small shift in only part of Florida's electorate. That being said, the 2008 partisan swing is evident in all of Florida's counties but is also a substantial swing throughout the state. On one hand, voters in forty-two of Florida's sixty-seven counties cast higher proportions of their ballots in favor of the Democratic candidate than in 2004. These forty-two counties are clustered in particular areas. The most prominent swing region for increased Democratic support was in the central part of the state along the I-4 corridor. This region stretches across the central peninsula and includes Orlando and Tampa, both major urban locales. The positive Democratic swings included gains between 5 and 13 percent in Hardee, Hillsborough (Tampa), Orange (Orlando), Osceola, Polk, and Seminole counties. On the other hand, Florida's partisan volatility in 2008 also included areas of intensified Republican support. The most marked shifts to greater Republican votes were counties in the predominantly rural central panhandle. This area show shifts between 5 and 8 percent to the Republican candidate in Calhoun, Franklin, Lafayette, Liberty, and Taylor counties.

Rural and urban distinctions provide one axis on which to interpret Democratic gains in Florida. However, this claim must be tempered since some major urban locales provided only slight gains for the Democratic candidate, such as Miami-Dade County (less than 5 percent) and much of south Florida. Florida's swing to Democrat Barack Obama in 2008, thus, is composed of significant regional shifts in favor of both the Republican and Democratic candidates with net gains for the Democratic candidate due largely to the intensity of the urban I-4 Democratic swing.

INDIANA

JOHN HEPPEN

Indiana was a swing state in 2008, albeit one that did not emerge until well into the 2008 presidential campaign. Indiana is historically Republican in presidential elections and has been written off by Democrats. What was different for Indiana in 2008 was the state of the economy and the presence of Barack Obama from neighboring Illinois since northwestern Indiana is part of the Chicago metropolitan area and northern Indiana is part of the North American Manufacturing Belt. While most people consider Indiana as farm country and part of the American heartland, the 2008 election showed that under the right circumstances Indiana can be a swing state.

Places like Gary, East Chicago, Hammond, South Bend, Terra Haute, Fort Wayne, and Muncie are more dependent on manufacturing; they attracted immigrants from Eastern, Southern, and Central Europe like many other parts of the North American Manufacturing Belt. African Americans also moved to Indiana during the Great Migration of last century. For example, the Jacksons (Michael Jackson's family) were from Gary, Indiana. Their father, who was from Arkansas, worked in a steel mill. Gary is still home to one of the largest steel mills in the country, and South Bend was home to Studebaker. The primary settlers of northern Indiana were New Englanders and upstate New Yorkers, but southern Indiana was settled by upland Southerners from Virginia and Kentucky. Abe Lincoln, who was from Kentucky, spent his boyhood in Perry County along the Ohio River.

Whereas the popular image of Indiana is agrarian with Indianapolis as a hub of an agricultural and service-based economy, the economic circumstances of Gary and Fort Wayne can impact elections under the right circumstances. But what makes Indiana different from Ohio, Michigan, and Illinois is that it never developed an urban-industrial base on par with those neighboring states, which was beneficial in providing for a more diversified economy. However, that base reduced Indiana's ability to be a swing state. Northern Indiana, though heavily industrialized, never developed a large enough population at the mercy of economic fluctuations in the world economy that could consistently swing elections. Those swing regions and counties are not large enough to make the state a consistent swing state. But the regions are still there, and under the right economic circumstances these voters can be supplemented by those in other regions. Thus swing counties and regions of Indiana are based in places where the boom and bust circumstances of industrial Indiana are most pertinent. The 2008 election and a comparison with the 2004 election clearly illustrate this change. Porter and St. Joseph Counties in the northwest swung to Obama. Vermillion and Vigo counties of Terre Haute and Vanderburgh County of Evansville represent medium-sized urban areas, as do Madison and Delaware counties. While those counties alone did not shift the election in Obama's favor, it appears that enough voters throughout the state swung toward Obama in larger than expected margins. This observation was especially pronounced in northwestern Indiana and in some medium-sized metropolitan areas. In short, under the right circumstances these places can constitute swing areas in Indiana.

MAP 5.8

Democratic Percent of Total Popular Presidential Vote 2008

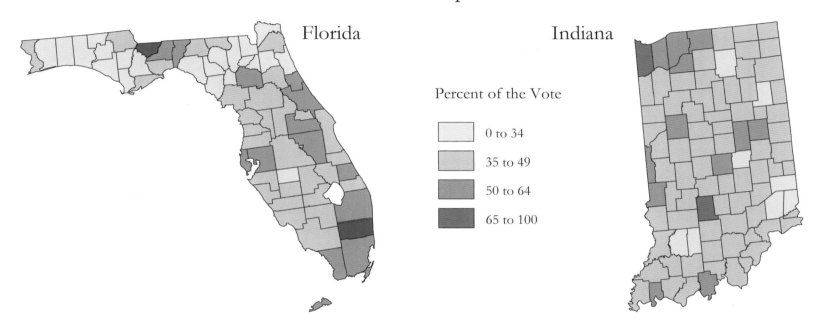

Florida

Indiana

Percent of the Vote

0 to 34

35 to 49

50 to 64

65 to 100

MAP 5.9

Persistence and Change From 2004 to 2008

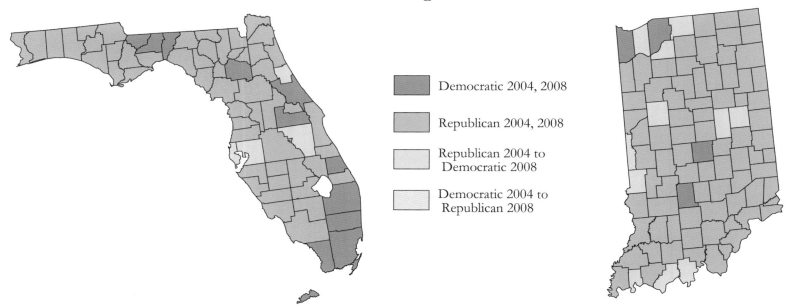

Democratic 2004, 2008

Republican 2004, 2008

Republican 2004 to
Democratic 2008

Democratic 2004 to
Republican 2008

■ MISSOURI

JOHN HEPPEN

Missouri can be considered the best bellwether or swing state in the country. This quintessential border state, Missouri has sided with the winner in every presidential election since 1904, with 1956 and 2008 being the lone exceptions. Missouri's electoral votes will be targeted in every election due to its bellwether status, which comes from its economy and settlement. Many settlers to Missouri came from the upland South and settled in the southern half of the state and along the Missouri River Valley. Midwesterners settled in the northern and western portions. It is also worth remembering that Missouri entered the Union as a slave state, the result of a famous compromise that bears its name. Missouri remained in the Union since plantation agriculture did not become large enough to change its political moorings, but it did strongly influence its political future.

The middle part of Missouri along the Missouri River is called Little Dixie; there slaveholding was common. Southeastern Missouri was also settled by Southerners and thus it can also be considered Southern. The Ozark region of Missouri became home to "mountain" Republicanism. German immigrants in the Lower Missouri River Valley northwest of St. Louis also tended to vote Republican. Northerners who immigrated to northern and northwestern Missouri also tended to favor the Republican Party. German and Irish immigrants were important, especially in St. Louis and Kansas City, while Italian immigrants gravitated toward St. Louis. European immigrants also historically generally supported Democrats. The Great Migration drew African Americans to St. Louis and Kansas City. But segregation was the norm in St. Louis and elsewhere in Missouri despite the changes brought on by industrialization.

Even though industrialization came to St. Louis and Kansas City and some medium-sized cities, Missouri is generally not considered part of the North American Manufacturing Belt in the same way as Ohio, Illinois, and Pennsylvania. In Missouri, the urban areas of St. Louis and Kansas City usually produce Democratic majorities, while most of the rest of the state votes Republican in presidential elections. This generalization applies to suburbs, medium-sized cities, and small-town and rural counties. Even though Missouri did not change from red to blue in 2008, Obama increased the Democratic vote total and had the best showing for a Democrat since Bill Clinton. Clinton won suburban areas and northern Missouri, which can be considered the swing parts of the state. The vote disparity between Democrats and Republicans went from 196,542 in 2004 to only 3,903 in 2008. These counties switched allegiances: Iron, Boone, Buchanan, Jefferson, and Washington. Jefferson County is part of the St. Louis metropolitan area. Gains in these swing counties, however, were not large enough to swing the entire state or vote to the Democratic side. There were widespread gains through swing counties in northern Missouri and increases in St. Louis and Kansas City. Compared with the 2004 Democratic results, Obama gained about 19,900 votes in the City of St. Louis, almost 33,000 votes in Jackson County (Kansas City), and about 61,103 votes in St. Louis County. Since the margin in 2008 was less than 4,000 votes, Missouri and its swing areas will be hotly contested in 2012.

■ MONTANA

FRED M. SHELLEY

Aside from Missouri, the election in Montana was the closest of any state that was carried by McCain in 2008. McCain won 243,882 popular votes in Montana (50 percent) to 232,159 for Obama (47 percent), with the remaining popular votes going to minor candidates.

Montana straddles the Great Plains and the Rocky Mountain West. The eastern two-thirds of Montana is part of the Great Plains, with flat to rolling topography and large tracts of land given over to farming and ranching. The Rocky Mountains stretch across the western third of the state. Here the economy is based on mining and tourism rather than on agriculture. Unlike most other states in the Rocky Mountain West, Montana's urban population is not concentrated in a single metropolitan area such as Denver, Las Vegas, Salt Lake City, Phoenix, or Boise. Rather, Montana includes several small, widely separated metropolitan areas including Great Falls, Billings, the college communities of Missoula and Bozeman, and the state capital of Helena.

Historically, the majority Great Plains section of Montana has been predominantly Republican, and the mining-oriented western part of the state has been oriented toward the Democrats. The politics of both parts of Montana have been influenced over the years by populist impulses. The Republicans have carried Montana in the majority of presidential elections since Montana became a state in 1890, but since World War II Montana's electoral votes have gone to Democratic nominees in 1948, 1964, and 1992.

The historical split between the more Republican eastern portion of Montana and the more Democratic western portion of the state remained evident in the presidential election of 2008. McCain carried forty-three of Montana's fifty-six counties, with Obama carrying the remaining thirteen. Obama carried only six counties in eastern Montana. Of these, four—Blaine, Bighorn, Roosevelt, and Rosebud—contain large American Indian reservations, and in each case at least a third of the county's residents are American Indians. Although their populations are small, McCain won very large majorities in most eastern Montana counties with few American Indian residents. For example he won 80 percent in Carter County and 74 percent in Fallon County, both in the southeastern corner of the state; thus, McCain's strong showing paralleled his strength among rural whites in other portions of the Great Plains.

Obama showed much more strength in western Montana. He carried Glacier County, which contains Glacier National Park, with 69 percent of the vote. He also won 69 percent in Silver Bow County, including the city of Butte, and Deer Lodge County, including the city of Anaconda. Both of these counties have long histories of tension between miners and mine owners, and both have been solidly Democratic since Montana became a state.

Obama also carried four of Montana's five urbanized counties. He lost Yellowstone County, which contains the state's largest city of Billings, by about 4,500 votes. He won Cascade County (Great Falls), Lewis and Clark County (Helena), and Gallatin County (Bozeman) by narrow margins and won Missoula County, which contains the city of Missoula and the University of Montana, by a decisive 62 to 35 percent margin of popular votes. McCain won most of the rural counties in western Montana, but in most cases with lower percentages than he got in eastern Montana.

Demographic change in Montana suggests that Democratic strength in Big Sky Country may increase in the years ahead. The counties carried by Obama include most of the rapidly growing areas of the state and four of the state's five largest cities. The population of Gallatin County, which is adjacent to Yellowstone National Park, has increased by more than 30 percent since 2000, while Missoula County's population has increased by 12 percent and that of Lewis and Clark County by 10 percent. On the other hand, many of the Republican-oriented counties of eastern Montana are losing population. For example, Carter County's population dropped by 12 percent between 2000 and 2009, while that of Fallon County declined by 6 percent. If rural eastern Montana is reminiscent of the Great Plains states to the east, western Montana is more reminiscent of the Front Range of Colorado. Democratic strength may be increasing there and may continue to increase statewide as more and more people move away from rural areas and into the state's metropolitan areas.

MAP 5.10

Democratic Percent of Total Popular Presidential Vote 2008

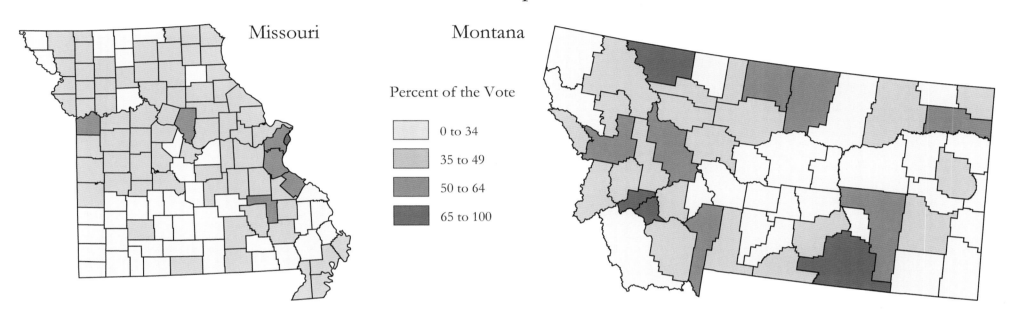

Missouri

Montana

Percent of the Vote

0 to 34

35 to 49

50 to 64

65 to 100

MAP 5.11

Persistence and Change From 2004 to 2008

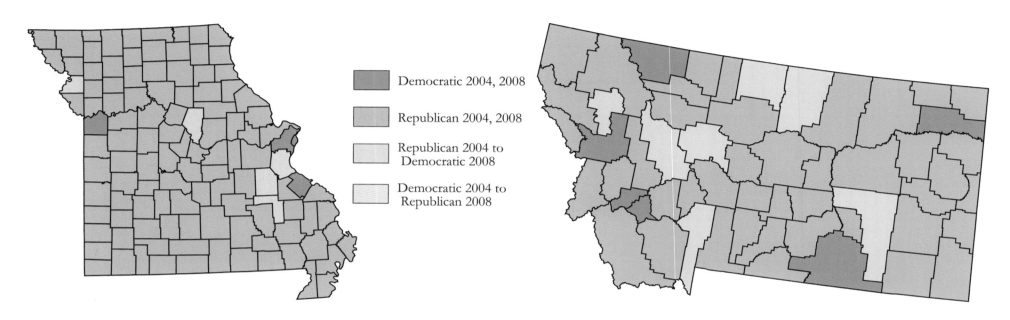

Democratic 2004, 2008

Republican 2004, 2008

Republican 2004 to
Democratic 2008

Democratic 2004 to
Republican 2008

■ NORTH CAROLINA

TOBY MOORE

On November 4, 2008, John McCain claimed 150,000 more votes for president in North Carolina than George W. Bush had in winning handily four years previously. Yet McCain lost the election to Barack Obama, who became the first Democrat to carry the state since Jimmy Carter in 1976.

The reasons Obama succeeded where even the centrist Southerner Bill Clinton failed were in part tactical—Obama campaigned heavily here and invested campaign cash—and in part due to changes in who votes in the state and how they cast their ballots. Unlike many other Southern states, Obama could rely on a vigorous state party: North Carolina's Democrats have remained more viable for state offices than in many other Southern states. Also, a significant African American population presented an inviting demographic target for Obama strategists.

Given the closeness of the final tally, however, Obama's key victory may well have come a year and a half before, when the Democratic-controlled legislature changed the way the state's voters could register and cast their ballots. In 2007, over the objections of most Republican legislators, North Carolina added a provision to the state's early voting law that allowed for a novel form of same-day voter registration: voters could register and vote on any day during the state's two-week-long early voting period. So-called one-stop absentee voting proved immediately popular, with more than half of all voters opting to cast their ballots before Election Day.

Turnout soared 22.6 percent over 2004, one of the largest increases in the country. In an election that would be decided by a mere 14,177 votes, or 0.32 percentage points, the addition of one-stop voting likely tipped the balance in Obama's favor. The Obama campaign made a deliberate effort to get its voters to the polls early. In fact, among voters casting their ballot on Election Day, McCain was an easy winner, garnering 57 percent of those votes.

Obama carried only thirty-five of the state's one hundred counties, and his success was rooted in the traditional bastions of the party's recent success, the heavily African American but sparsely populated counties in the state's northeastern corner, as well as the crown jewels of the state's electoral geography, the rapidly growing string of small cities tied together by Interstate 85 in the state's battleground Piedmont region: Raleigh, Durham, Greensboro, Winston-Salem, and Charlotte. The five counties containing these cities, the most populous in the state, are now home to close to a third of the state's electorate, and here Obama beat McCain three to two. In the rest of the state, Obama lost by nearly 300,000 votes.

How Obama won North Carolina may turn out to be more important than the fact that he won it at all. After all, he would have won the White House without North Carolina's electoral votes, and the narrow margin in such a strong Democratic year suggests Republicans will return to a favorite status in the next several presidential elections. Yet the Obama campaign's ability to leverage new election rules to boost turnout among its supporters and the role played by the still-growing Piedmont counties argue for more close elections ahead as Democrats attempt to encroach on the Republicans' old "Solid South."

MAP 5.12

Democratic Percentage of Total Popular Presidential Vote 2008

2004

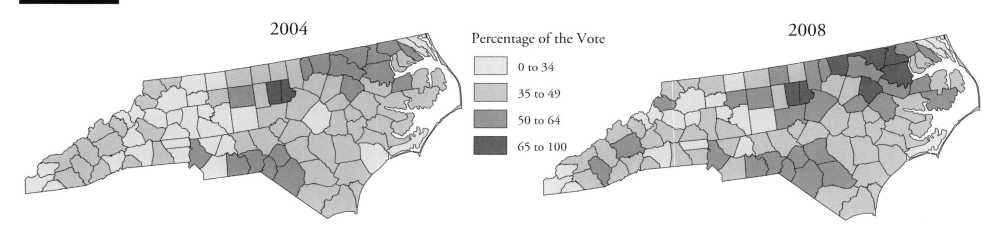

Percentage of the Vote

- 0 to 34
- 35 to 49
- 50 to 64
- 65 to 100

2008

Absentee and One-Stop Voting

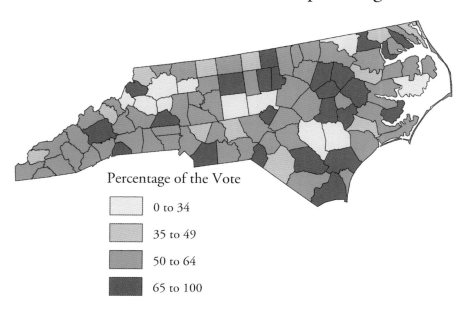

Percentage of the Vote

- 0 to 34
- 35 to 49
- 50 to 64
- 65 to 100

Persistence and Change From 2004 to 2008

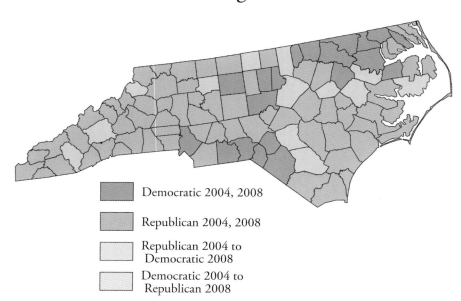

- Democratic 2004, 2008
- Republican 2004, 2008
- Republican 2004 to Democratic 2008
- Democratic 2004 to Republican 2008

■ OHIO

JOHN HEPPEN

Ohio fits the swing state criteria quite well. Its juxtaposition between the East and Midwest, Great Lakes and Ohio River, Michigan and Kentucky, and West Virginia and Indiana places it at a geographic crossroads. In presidential elections, its electoral votes have gone to the winning side in every presidential election since 1964. Furthermore, no Republican has won the White House without Ohio. John F. Kennedy was the last president to win without Ohio. In 2000 and 2004, a switch to the Democratic side would have changed the election, and that made Ohio so vitally important in 2008. In 2004 and 2008 Ohio had twenty electoral votes and twenty-one in 2000. These numbers were enough electoral votes to make a difference in the final electoral vote count for 2000 and 2004. Most counties in Ohio vote rather consistently for Republicans, as evident in the maps of the 2004 and 2008 elections. However, swing counties in urban and industrial northern and northeastern Ohio and Hamilton County (Cincinnati) and suburbs provide the momentum for electoral change. Two Toledo area counties (Wood and Ottawa) swung to Obama from McCain. Northeastern Ohio is another swing area. Lake County swung from red to blue, as did Tuscarawas County south of Canton and Massillon. In addition to counties switching allegiances, a higher vote total for a candidate can also contribute to swinging a state. Northwestern Ohio and the Columbus region saw the biggest gains in Democratic favor. The Columbus metropolitan counties of Franklin, Delaware, and Union saw gains of five percentage points or more for Obama in 2008. Even though the number of counties that swung in Obama's favor was relatively small, the statewide gains propelled him to victory.

Swing regions and counties are made up of swing voters, and in contemporary American electoral geography, swing voters are disproportionally white, suburban, moderate, and lower-middle- to middle-class voters who weigh their votes in terms of current economic conditions. In Ohio these voters are most influential in the suburban industrial areas. Much of rural and medium- to small-town Ohio remains Republican while the cities of Cleveland, Akron, Toledo, Columbus, and Youngstown remain Democratic, so the suburbs and medium-sized urban areas become battleground or swing territories. Urban and industrial Ohio became home to immigrants from Eastern, Central, and Southern Europe from the 1870s to the 1920s. Many white ethnics and their descendants attained middle-class status working in factories, shops, and mills and in providing goods and services. Adding to the immigrant mix was the influx of African Americans during the Great Migration from World War I to the 1970s. Recently, immigration from Latin America and Asia has supplemented the earlier immigrant stock. African Americans and other minority groups support Democrats, even though white ethnic support for Democratic candidates has steadily eroded since the 1970s. Many of the latter supported Ronald Reagan and subsequent Republicans. This group constituted the state's swing voters who, when prompted, would switch allegiances and support the party that best addressed their economic concerns. Thus swing areas in Ohio are those working- to middle-class places in the shadow of urban-industrial economies.

■ PENNSYLVANIA

WILLIAM BERENTSEN

As evidenced by maps in this atlas, the geographical patterns of Pennsylvania's presidential elections are more diverse than in other northeastern states. This pattern reflects, among other things, diversity in the state's ethnic and religious patterns as well as contrasts between its many highly urbanized and rural regions. In recent decades both the Democratic and Republican parties have also had successes in winning presidential, congressional, and statehouse elections. And Pennsylvania's large number of electoral votes (twenty-one in recent elections), eclipsed by only four other U.S. states, underscores its importance as a possible swing state in any presidential or congressional election.

While Pennsylvania's electoral votes have been won by Democratic presidential candidates in each election since 1992, between 1932 and 1992 the Republicans and Democrats each won the state's electoral votes eight times, frequently trading back and forth brief eras of dominance after every third or fourth election. Obama's eleven percentage point win in 2008 was the largest by any presidential candidate dating back to the 1972 election; in 2000 and 2004 there were quite narrow (2.5 and 4.2 percent) wins by the Democratic presidential candidates. The state's congressional delegation has been split fairly evenly between the major parties for decades. It has a relatively even split among voters who view themselves as conservative, moderate, and liberal (see table 5.1 in the overview of voting patterns in the Northeast). In the past two presidential elections covered in this atlas there are stable geographical areas in Pennsylvania that voted both strongly Democratic and Republican, the former largely in the eastern part of the state and in urban areas, and the latter in the more rural central and western regions. In short, both major national political parties have won and can win in Pennsylvania.

On the one hand, it can be argued that Pennsylvania is now leaning more toward the Democrats. The recent switch to the Democratic Party by Senator Arlen Specter has given both Senate seats to the Democrats, but this is only the second time in the past 140 years that the state was represented in the Senate by only one party. Combined with Obama's relatively wide margin of victory and a string of presidential election wins by the Democrats since 1992, there is some evidence of an established trend favoring the Democratic Party in Pennsylvania. On the other hand, these results may simply reflect election outcomes within a quite "middle of the road" Pennsylvania electorate that is not embracing the rise of Republican social conservatism, arguably a new type of electoral pattern across the U.S. Northeast in recent presidential and congressional elections. One could easily argue that a politically moderate Republican presidential candidate would have a good opportunity to win Pennsylvania in 2012, and Republican congressional candidates will most likely continue to compete well within the state in both the 2010 and 2012 elections. In the Northeast, perhaps the smaller New Hampshire (four electoral votes) and New Jersey (fifteen votes) are the only other places that could emerge as swing states in elections in the next few years.

MAP 5.13

Democratic Percentage of Total Popular Presidential Vote 2008

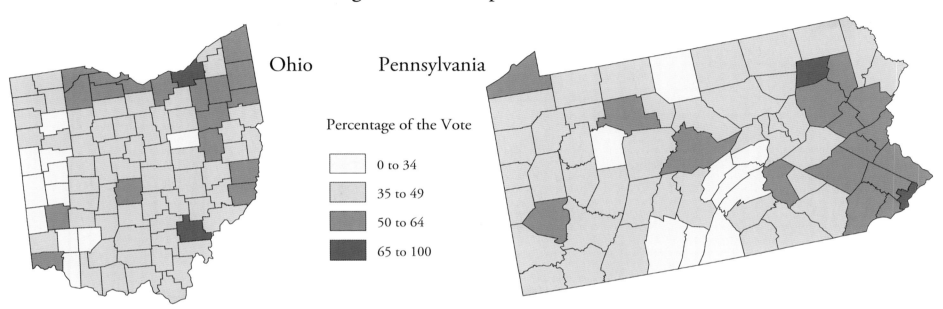

Ohio   Pennsylvania

Percentage of the Vote

0 to 34

35 to 49

50 to 64

65 to 100

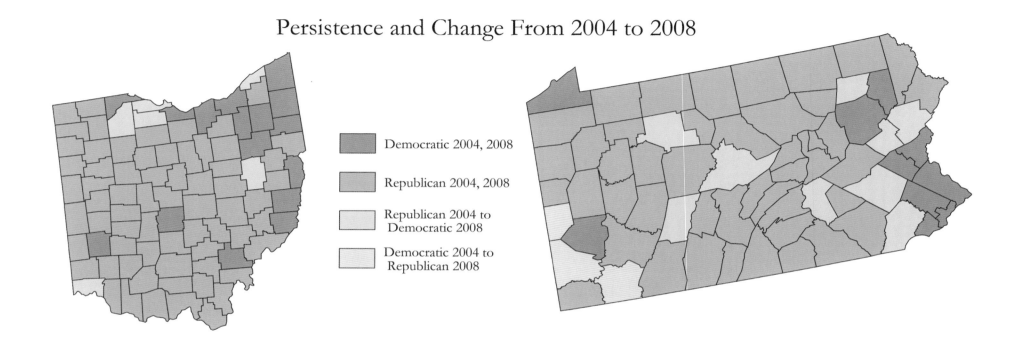

Persistence and Change From 2004 to 2008

Democratic 2004, 2008

Republican 2004, 2008

Republican 2004 to
Democratic 2008

Democratic 2004 to
Republican 2008

MAP 5.14

■ TENNESSEE

NICK QUINTON

Tennessee was one of only six state electorates in the United States to return a higher proportion of support for the Republican candidate for president in 2008 than they did for the Republican candidate in 2004. Republican gains were evident throughout the state, indicating a large-scale shift in voter preference. In fact, eighty-three county electorates of the ninety-five in Tennessee yielded greater proportions of their votes for the Republican candidate in 2008 than in 2004. Still, ten county electorates returned gains for the Democratic Party, suggesting that Tennessee's electorate is diverse.

In terms of Republican gains, the area of traditional Democratic dominance between Nashville (Davidson County) and the Mississippi River provided large gains for the Republican candidate. This includes swings of 9 percent in Lake County and 12 percent in Benton and Decatur Counties. Even Houston County, perhaps the strongest Democratic bulwark in the state, yielded an 8 percent gain for the Republicans. Another area of long-standing Democratic control just east of Nashville, including Jackson, Smith, DeKalb, Putnam, Warren, and Clay counties, also provided Republican gains of between 4 percent and 11 percent. Further Republican gains were made in other regions of the state. The cluster of counties along the Tennessee and Kentucky border that includes Campbell, Fentress, Pickett, and Scott counties returned between 7 percent and 14 percent more Republican votes than in 2004, and the swath of counties along Tennessee's southern border that stretches from Wayne to Marion counties returned between 6 percent and 8 percent gains for the Republicans.

While many county electorates shifted significant support to the Republican candidate between 2004 and 2008, many returned few, if any, gains for the Republicans, and a few county electorates favored the Democratic candidate. The areas that yielded the smallest Republican gains between 2004 and 2008 are those associated with the most long-established Republican support in Tennessee. This includes Hardin, McNairy, and Wayne counties in the southwestern part of the state and much of far eastern Tennessee. Conversely, two county electorates that returned greater proportions of their votes for the Democratic candidate in Tennessee are long-established Democratic bastions. These are the two largest urban centers in Tennessee, Memphis (Shelby County) and Nashville (Davidson County), which each returned 6 percent gains for the Democratic Party in 2008. Further, the Democrats made gains in seven of the ten most populous counties (including Shelby and Davidson) and in rural Haywood County (the state's only majority African American county).

One means of discussing the 2008 presidential election in Tennessee, then, is the gains and losses associated with areas of traditional Republican and Democratic support. Significant Republican gains in Tennessee are evident in both long-standing Democratic bastions and Republican strongholds throughout Tennessee. Alternatively, slight Republican gains were made in many of the most long-standing Republican strongholds in the state. Finally, the Democratic Party made gains in two of the state's traditional Democratic bastions (Memphis and Nashville) and in the other populous county electorates. Thus, significant Republican gains in long-standing Democratic bastions coupled with gains throughout Tennessee's Republican strongholds outweighed Democratic gains made in Tennessee's most populated county electorates.

■ VIRGINIA

JONATHAN I. LEIB

Virginia was an important swing state in the 2008 presidential election. While a Democratic presidential candidate had not won the state since Lyndon Johnson in 1964, Virginia had been trending more Democratic in recent statewide elections. The state's voters elected Democratic governors in 2001 (Mark Warner) and 2005 (Tim Kaine) and a Democratic U.S. senator in 2006 (Jim Webb).

In 2008, Barack Obama defeated John McCain in Virginia by 6.3 percentage points (52.6 to 46.3 percent). Obama's showing was 7.1 percentage points higher than John Kerry's in 2004, when Kerry won only 45.5 percent of the statewide vote. Obama increased his vote percentage over Kerry in most of Virginia's counties and independent cities, with the largest increases coming in the northern third of the state, and in a swath from metropolitan Richmond southeast to Hampton Roads (Norfolk/Virginia Beach/Newport News).

Leading to Obama's statewide victory was his ability to carry the state's large metropolitan areas. Obama won many independent cities and suburban counties in Northern Virginia (the southern part of the Washington, D.C., metro area), metropolitan Richmond, and Hampton Roads. The role of the suburbs in leading to Obama's victory is reinforced in examining the counties that switched from Republican George W. Bush in 2004 to Democrat Barack Obama in 2008, including the outer suburban counties of Northern Virginia (Loudoun and Prince William), Richmond's suburban Henrico County, and the Hampton Roads suburban independent cities of Chesapeake and Suffolk. By contrast, only two Virginia counties that gave a majority of their vote to John Kerry in 2004 switched to John McCain in 2008. Both of these were small Appalachian counties in southwestern Virginia (Buchanan and Dickenson).

As elsewhere, interest in the 2008 election was intense across Virginia, with over 500,000 more votes cast in 2008 than 2004, a 16.3 percent increase in the number of votes statewide. Increased turnout played an important role in the election. To take two places as examples, in Northern Virginia's Loudoun County, while McCain won 3,000 more votes than Bush had four years earlier, Obama won 27,000 more votes than Kerry. As a result, while Bush won 55.7 percent of Loudoun's votes in 2004, Obama won 53.7 percent in 2008. In the state's largest city in population, Virginia Beach (which is predominantly suburban in nature), Bush defeated Kerry by 19 percentage points in 2004, winning 103,752 votes to Kerry's 70,666; a difference of more than 23,000 votes. While McCain did carry Virginia Beach in 2008, he did so by less than one percentage point (49.8 percent to 49.1 percent). McCain's vote total in Virginia Beach was only 3,000 less than Bush's in 2004 (100,319 votes compared with 103,752); however, Obama's vote total in the city was more than 28,000 greater than Kerry's had been four years earlier (98,885 compared with 70,666).

Does Obama's 2008 victory suggest that Democrats now have a strong foothold in Virginia in presidential elections? While Obama and Democratic U.S. Senate candidate Mark Warner won in 2008 (giving the state two Democratic senators for the first time since former Senator Harry Byrd, Jr., left the Democratic party to become an Independent in 1970), Republican Bob McDonnell won the state's 2009 gubernatorial election. Whether Obama's victory in 2008 heralded a shift to the Democrats or whether it was an aberration is unclear. It is likely, however, that Virginia will continue in its new role as an important swing state in 2012 and beyond.

MAP 5.15

Democratic Percentage of Total Popular Presidential Vote 2008

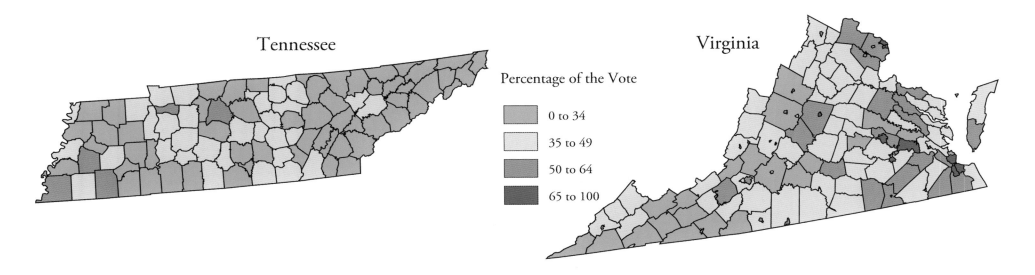

Tennessee

Virginia

Percentage of the Vote

0 to 34

35 to 49

50 to 64

65 to 100

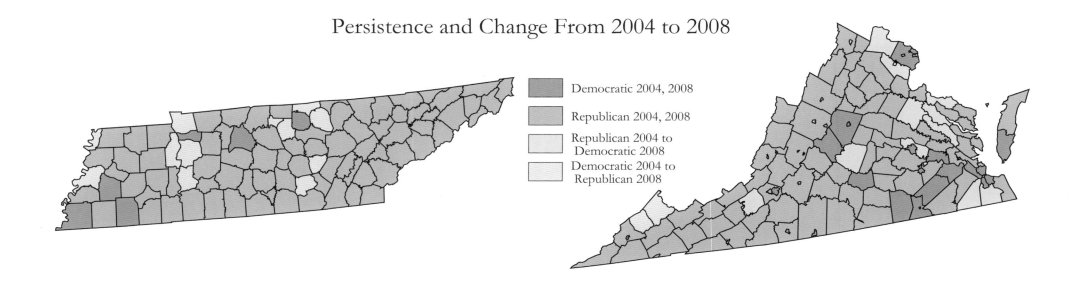

Persistence and Change From 2004 to 2008

Democratic 2004, 2008

Republican 2004, 2008

Republican 2004 to Democratic 2008

Democratic 2004 to Republican 2008

NOTES

1. This was named Dade County until 1997; Miami was attached by a referendum vote.
2. Notably, the overall population did not decline, but the birthrate outstripped net out-migration and deaths.
3. Indeed, the city of Miami itself courted insolvency.
4. Unfortunately, we are rather remote from the 2000 census, where these migration data are collected. The mid-census estimate published by the Census Bureau does not include migration by county. The state-level data appear comparable, however. When the 2010 census data are available, the analysis should be replicated with the expectation that the results will be more robust.
5. There are several generally accepted ways to weight independent variables. I am using *Stata*'s p-weight function, which effectively weights by the value of a variable indicating the size of each unit. I explored other weighting methods, as well as no weighting at all; the choice of weighting method had no effect on the substantive cast of the findings.
6. The census aggregates several independent cities in Virginia into extant counties. Specific to the outliers, Arlington County and the city of Alexandria are treated as one unit, and the cities of Fairfax and Falls Church are treated as if they were part of Fairfax County. The city of Charlottesville and Albemarle County are merged, as are the city of Lynchburg and Campbell County.

REFERENCES

Belluck, Pam. 2006. "A Republican Breed Loses Its Place in New England as Voters Seek Change." *New York Times*, Nov. 26. http://query.nytimes.com/gst/fullpage.html?res=9E05E4DB103EF934A15752C1A9609C8B63&sec=&spon=&pagewanted=3. Last accessed June 13, 2010.

Bishop, B., and R. Cushing. 2008. "The Big Sort: Migration, Community and Politics in the United States of 'Those People.'" In *Red, Blue and Purple America: The Future of Election Demographics*, edited by R. Teixeira, 50–78. Washington, D.C.: Brookings Institute Press.

Current, R. N. 1988. *Those Terrible Carpetbaggers: A Reinterpretation*. Oxford and New York: Oxford University Press.

Davidson, J.W., W. E. Gienapp, C. L. Heyrman, M. H. Lytle, and M. B. Stoff. 1998. *Nation of Nations: A Concise Narrative of the American Republic, Volume I*. 2nd ed. New York: McGraw-Hill.

Decker, C. "Splitting the State Down the Middle. *Los Angeles Times*, November 15, 2009.

De Leon, Arnoldo. 2009. *Mexican Americans in Texas: A Brief History*. 3rd ed. Wheeling, IL: Harlan Davidson.

Douzet, F., et al. (eds.). 2008. *The New Political Geography of California*. Berkeley: University of California, Berkeley, Berkeley Public Policy Press.

Elazar, Daniel J. 1984. *American Federalism: A View from the States*. 3rd ed. New York: Harper & Row.

Fiorina, M. P., and S. J. Abrams. 2008. "Is California Really a Blue State?" In *The New Political Geography of California*, edited by F. Douzet et al. Berkeley: University of California, Berkeley, Berkeley Public Policy Press.

Florida, R. 2002. *The Rise of the Creative Class*. New York: Basic.

Frey, W., and R. Teixeira. 2008. *The Political Geography of the Intermountain West: The New Swing Region*. Washington, D.C.: Brookings Institute Policy Brief.

Hood, M. V., III, and S. C. McKee. 2010. "What Made Carolina Blue? In-Migration and the 2008 North Carolina Presidential Vote." *American Politics Research* 38 (2): 266–302.

Infield, Tom. "It's East vs. West in Battle for Pennsylvania Voters." [Pittsburg] Post-gazette.com, April 26, 2010. http://www.post-gazette.com/pg/10116/1053371-178.stm?cmpid=news.xml. Last accessed June 13, 2010.

Jones, Jeffrey M. 2010. "Ideology: Three Deep South States are the Most Conservative." Gallup, http://www.gallup.com/poll/125480/ideology-three-deep-south-states-conservative.aspx. Last accessed on June 13, 2010.

Kousser, T. 2009. "How Geopolitics Cleaved California's Republicans and United Its Democrats." *California Journal of Politics and Policy* 1. http://www.bepress.com/cjpp.

McMahon, Kevin J. 2009. "The Northeast: Blue, Deep Blue." In *Winning the Whitehouse, 2008*, edited by K. J. McMahon, D. M. Rankin, D. W. Beachler, and J. K. White, 81–102. New York: Palgrave Macmillan.

Oliver, J. Eric. 2010. *The Paradoxes of Integration: Race, Neighborhood, and Civic Life in Multi-Ethnic America*. Chicago: University of Chicago Press.

Phillips, Kevin. 1999. *The Cousins' Wars: Religion, Politics and the Triumph of Anglo-America*. New York: Basic.

Polsby, N. W. 2004. *How Congress Evolves: Social Bases of Institutional Change*. Oxford and New York: Oxford University Press.

Schaller, T. 2002. *Whistling Past Dixie: How Democrats Can Win without the South*. New York: Simon & Schuster.

Seabrook, N. R. 2009. "The Obama Effect: Patterns of Geographic Clustering in the 2004 and 2008 Presidential Elections. *The Forum* 7. http://www.bepress.com/forum/vol7/iss2/aet6.

Semuels, A. "Lonely Times for Hawaii's Republicans." *Los Angeles Times*, January 9, 2010. http://www.latimes.com/news/nation-and-world/la-na-hawaii-gop-jan,0,4400225.story.

Sherman, William C., and Playford V. Thorson. 1988. *Plains Folk: North Dakota's Ethnic History*. Fargo: North Dakota Institute for Regional Studies.

Todd, Chuck, and Sheldon Gawiser. 2009. *How Barack Obama Won: A State-by-State Guide to the Historic 2008 Presidential Election*. New York: Vintage.

U.S. Census. (2000). Washington, DC: Bureau of the Census.

Wishart, David J. 2004. *Encyclopedia of the Great Plains*. Lincoln: University of Nebraska Press.

LEADING COUNTIES: 2004 AND 2008 VOTES AND TURNOUTS: SELECTED ECONOMIC, DEMOGRAPHIC, AND RELIGIOUS CORRELATES

■ CREATIVE CLASS OCCUPATIONS

THOMAS E. CHAPMAN

eveloped by urban theorist Richard Florida[1], the creative class is a diverse, knowledge-intensive workforce that he argues is the fundamental engine for economic growth in a region. The core occupations of the creative class are in the fields of science and engineering, architecture and design, higher education, art, music, and the entertainment industry. This new "economic geography of creativity" revolves around what Florida calls the three *T*'s of economic development: technology, talent, and tolerance. A region must have all three of these *T*'s in order to attract creative people, generate business innovation, and stimulate economic growth. Traditional location theory models of economic development that base their premise on workers following location decisions by business firms are taken to task for their inability to predict economic growth of the twenty-first century postindustrial city. Instead, Florida argues that it is the creative workers themselves that choose to live and work in places where cultural and social amenities best fit their lifestyles, and where economic growth is powered by the sort of social and human capital that places a high value on creativity and human diversity. Corporate location decisions, therefore, are powered not so much by incentives such as tax breaks or offers of low-cost land as they are by places that are diverse, tolerant, and open to new ideas. This is a cycle of economic growth directly tied to even greater and more diverse concentrations of this "creative capital," which in turn leads to even higher rates of innovation, high technology business formation, and job generation. Regions that embrace a wider range of economic talent by valuing diversity in such attributes as nationality, race, ethnicity, and sexual orientation are therefore able to remain competitive in a globalizing world.

Florida uses a variety of indices to describe how members of the creative class are attracted to a city or region, such as markers of innovation (measured as patents per capita) and concentrations of high tech industries. He and others have also found a strong correlation between those cities and regions that embrace a more tolerant atmosphere toward nonconformist groups, such as gay people (exemplified by Florida's "Gay Index"), or artists and musicians (the "Bohemian Index"), and the share of creative class workers who choose to live in these places.

The creative class currently employs about 40 million workers in the United States, roughly 30 percent of the workforce. A number of cities and regions have come to be identified with these economic trends, such as California's Silicon Valley, Boston's Route 128, and the Research Triangle area in Raleigh-Durham, North Carolina. Other cities where there are high concentrations of the creative class include Austin, Seattle, San Francisco, and Denver.

In terms of spatial patterns associated with the 2008 presidential election, there is a strong and significant positive correlation between votes for Barack Obama and members of the creative class $(r = .425)^2$. The accompanying map showing the top two hundred counties with the highest concentration of these workers exemplifies this trend, where Obama received close to 60 percent of the popular vote. Conversely, votes for John McCain were negative and significant $(r = -.442)$, indicating wider support for the GOP candidate in those counties with larger concentrations of blue-collar working class occupations. This is reflected by the "bottom 200 counties" illustrated on the map and where McCain received close to 60 percent of the popular vote. Without exception, these counties also have the highest concentrations of rural population.

MAP 6.1

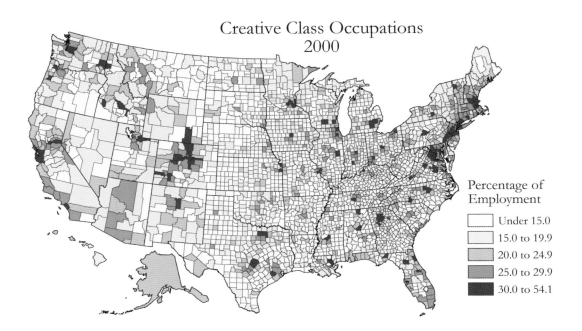

Creative Class Occupations
2000

Percentage of
Employment

Under 15.0
15.0 to 19.9
20.0 to 24.9
25.0 to 29.9
30.0 to 54.1

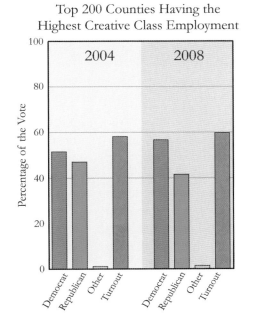

Top 200 Counties Having the
Highest Creative Class Employment

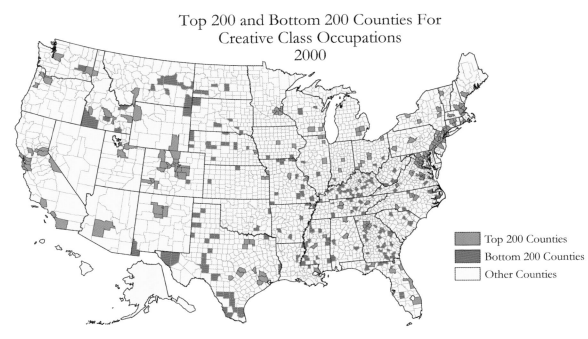

Top 200 and Bottom 200 Counties For
Creative Class Occupations
2000

Top 200 Counties
Bottom 200 Counties
Other Counties

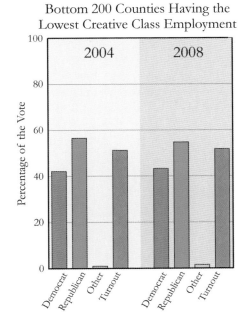

Bottom 200 Counties Having the
Lowest Creative Class Employment

■ PERCENTAGE OF WORKERS IN CRAFT OCCUPATIONS

RICHARD L. MORRILL

Craft occupations are those requiring technical skills and include such fields as carpenters, plumbers, electricians, and others in construction and manufacturing.

Many have traditionally been and still are proprietary, in groups encompassing union workers and the self-employed, with a long tendency to vote Republican, increasingly so since the party realignment following the "Reagan revolution." It is not surprising, then, that these counties highest in craft occupations voted 65.6 percent for John McCain, on a total vote of about 1.7 million.

Craft workers are everywhere, so they rarely reach high shares of the labor force. Thus the geography of their concentration is somewhat unusual, in fact, totally absent across the Northeast and on the Pacific Coast, but strongly represented across the Mountain states, and scattered across the South, especially in Texas-Louisiana and Kentucky-West Virginia-Georgia, often in areas of energy industry development.

Only thirty of the counties voted Democratic. One hundred seventy voted Republican. While ninety-four of these did experience Republican declines from 2004, seventy-six increased, a high share of these two hundred counties, and nine switched from Democratic to Republican. Most were rural and small-town with only small metropolitan areas. The nine counties switching from Democratic to Republican were in Kentucky, Tennessee, West Virginia, and Virginia. The consistently Republican counties were scattered across five regions—the Mountain states Nevada (ten), Colorado (eleven), Utah (three), and Wyoming (eight); Idaho (four) and Montana (two); in Texas (twenty-eight) and Louisiana (six); Kentucky (eighteen); and West Virginia (six); near the switching counties, Alabama (seven), Tennessee (five), and Virginia (ten).

The four declining counties, which remained Democratic counties, were in Kentucky, Tennessee, and West Virginia, again near the switching counties. The five counties that switched from Republican to Democratic are quite different, three environmental counties in western Colorado, Idaho, and New Mexico (also Hispanic), and King, Queen, and Manassas in Virginia. The twelve counties that increased in Democratic share include five environmental amenity counties, Braxton, West Virginia, which defied the general pattern of Democratic nonmetropolitan decline, and six racial minority counties, located in Georgia, New Mexico, Texas, and Virginia.

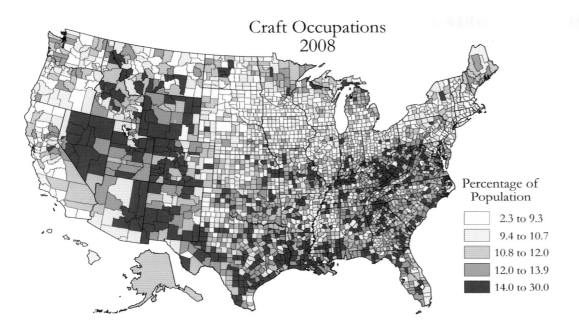

Craft Occupations
2008

Percentage of
Population

	2.3 to 9.3
	9.4 to 10.7
	10.8 to 12.0
	12.0 to 13.9
	14.0 to 30.0

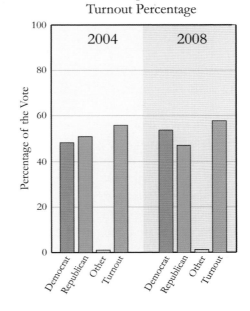

Total U.S. Popular Vote and
Turnout Percentage

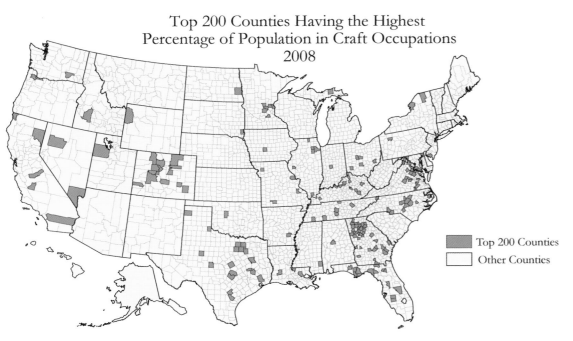

Top 200 Counties Having the Highest
Percentage of Population in Craft Occupations
2008

	Top 200 Counties
	Other Counties

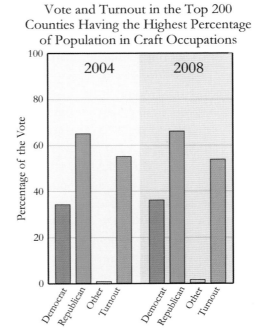

Vote and Turnout in the Top 200
Counties Having the Highest Percentage
of Population in Craft Occupations

MAP 6.2

PERCENTAGE OF FEMALES IN THE LABOR FORCE

RICHARD L. MORRILL

In modern society, women tend to participate in the labor force, even among conservative, traditional populations, often because of economic necessity. Nevertheless there is a marked tendency for areas with higher female work participation to vote Democratic and areas with low participation to vote Republican. Thus in 2008 the high female worker counties voted 56 to 44 percent Democratic, while the low female worker counties voted 56 to 44 percent Republican. The geography of female labor force participation is markedly North versus South, with fewer than twenty low participation counties in the North, and fewer than twenty high participation counties across the South. The high participation counties are not mainly large metropolitan counties, as might be inferred from modern versus traditional arguments. The main large metropolitan concentrations are in and around Minneapolis, Washington-Baltimore, Denver, Dallas-Fort Worth, Nashville, Kansas City, and suburban Atlanta, in several university-dominated metropolitan areas like Austin, Texas; Columbus, Ohio; Madison, Wisconsin; Champaign-Urbana, Illinois; Ann Arbor, Michigan; Ames and Iowa City, Iowa; Missoula, Montana; and Raleigh, North Carolina; and in a number of smaller metropolitan areas, mainly in the Upper Midwest. Nonmetropolitan areas with high participation tend to be environmental, as in Colorado, Montana, Idaho, California, Vermont, Utah, and Wyoming.

Areas with low female participation in the North tend to have high numbers of the elderly. Across the South, there are at least three overlapping kinds of concentrations. The most striking is the almost total saturation in the heart of Appalachia from northeast Tennessee, through eastern Kentucky and West Virginia, and into Pennsylvania and Ohio—areas of tradition and limited job opportunities. The lesser concentration in the Ozarks-Ouachita has some similarity but is more related to large shares of the elderly retired. Large numbers of the elderly retired are even more the story in parts of Arizona, New Mexico, and especially western Florida. The remaining low participation areas are Hispanic and American Indian areas in Arizona, New Mexico, and Texas, and majority black areas in Louisiana, Mississippi, and Alabama.

The patterns of change among the high participation counties favored Democrats, with sixty-seven counties gaining in Democratic strength—sixteen large metropolitan, fourteen small metropolitan, and a high thirty-seven nonmetropolitan, generally "progressive" counties, notably in Colorado (eleven), Iowa (five), Maryland (four), Massachusetts (two), Minnesota (six), North Carolina (Mecklenburg), Ohio (Franklin), South Carolina (Richland), Texas (Travis), Vermont (six), Virginia (four), Wisconsin (ten), and Wyoming (Teton). Only two counties had Democratic declines. A significant forty-three counties switched from Republican to Democratic—a mix of metropolitan counties and university and/or state capital counties—located

in Colorado (four), Illinois (three), Iowa (two), Kentucky (Fayette), Minnesota (six), Missouri (two), Montana (two), Nebraska (two), New Hampshire (two), North Carolina (Wake), North Dakota (two), South Dakota (four), Utah (Summit), Virginia (four), Wisconsin (seven), and Wyoming (one). Fifty-eight counties declined in their Republican share; the party's share increased in only six counties, and no counties switched from Democratic to Republican.

The pattern of change among the low participation counties favored Republicans more, with ninety-four counties increasing their Republican share. The 152 Republican gaining or declining counties were widespread but especially prevalent across the South, as in Florida (eleven), Kentucky (eighteen), Louisiana (twelve), Texas (thirty-four), and West Virginia (seventeen).

Twelve counties switched from Democratic to Republican, in Kentucky (five), Mississippi, Tennessee, Virginia (two), and West Virginia (three)—all "traditionally Democratic" nonmetro counties. Another ten experienced Democratic decline—three racial minority counties (in Arizona, Arkansas, and Georgia) and seven "traditional" counties (in Kentucky, Ohio, and West Virginia). Twenty-nine counties did experience Democratic gains, racially based in Alabama, Arizona, Colorado, Georgia, Louisiana, Mississippi, South Carolina, South Dakota, and Texas, but also in two "traditional" holdouts, Menifee, Kentucky, and Braxton, West Virginia.

Female Labor Force
2008

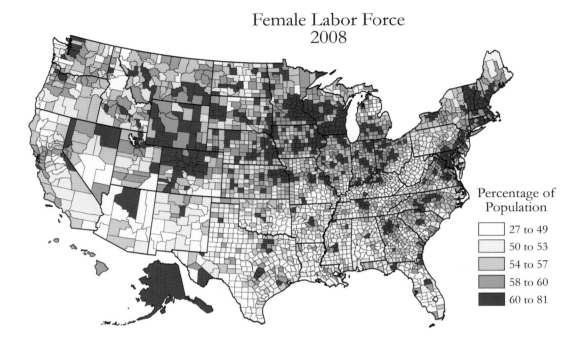

Percentage of
Population

- 27 to 49
- 50 to 53
- 54 to 57
- 58 to 60
- 60 to 81

MAP 6.3

Top 200 Counties Having More Than 64.5% of Women in the Labor Force

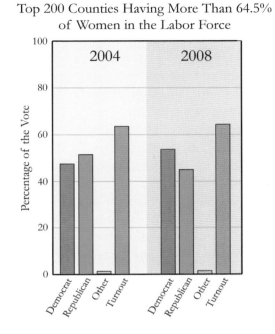

Top 198 and Bottom 200 Counties For
Percentage of Females in the Labor Force
2008

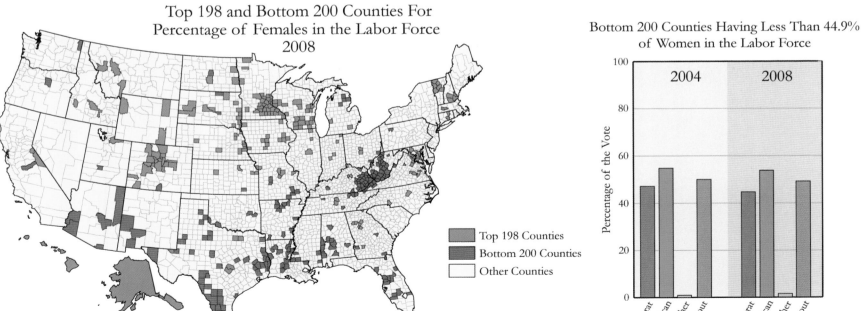

- Top 198 Counties
- Bottom 200 Counties
- Other Counties

Bottom 200 Counties Having Less Than 44.9% of Women in the Labor Force

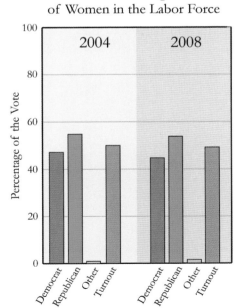

■ FARMING EMPLOYMENT

JEFFREY R. CRUMP

Counties with the greatest dependence on farming employment are found predominantly in the Great Plains states of North and South Dakota, extending south into the High Plains of Oklahoma and Texas. In addition, significant concentrations of farming employment are evident in the Midwestern Corn Belt.

The high proportion of farming employment in the Great Plains is quite apparent on the map illustrating the top two hundred counties having the highest percentage of farm employment. With few exceptions, these counties are found in a north to south band that accurately outlines the regional boundaries of the Great Plains.

It is noteworthy that many of these counties also rank among the highest in per capita federal outlays due to the large number of federal programs intended to support agriculture. Moreover, the federally supported boom in ethanol production helped to fuel increases in corn prices, making the George W. Bush presidency a prosperous one for farmers.

The Great Plains and other agricultural regions vote consistently Republican, and the 2008 presidential election was no exception. In the top two hundred farming counties, Republican McCain garnered over 60 percent of the vote. This Republican margin of victory was quite similar to that achieved by George W. Bush in 2004. It is quite clear that Democratic candidate Barack Obama made little headway in those regions that are heavily dependent on farming employment. Turnout in farming counties was actually lower in 2008 than in 2004. This pattern runs counter to the national trend and may indicate that some farming Republicans chose to stay away from the polls.

Among the top two hundred farming-dependent counties, only seventeen (8.5 percent) voted Democratic, and fourteen of these counties were found in the Midwest. In the Dakotas, counties with American Indian majorities strongly supported Barack Obama. In addition, counties in Colorado and New Mexico with high proportions of Hispanics also supported Obama in 2008. An example of such a county is Costilla County, Colorado. Candidate Obama claimed 73 percent of the vote in Costilla County, where Hispanic voters comprise 68 percent of the population. Costilla County also has a long-standing tradition of supporting Democratic presidential candidates, and the last time a Republican won was in 1924, when Calvin Coolidge was victorious in the county.

Another interesting farming county to vote Democratic was Elliott County, Kentucky, which is overwhelmingly white, with 99 percent of the population of European American extraction. Yet, Barack Obama won 61 percent of the vote. These results reflect a long-standing preference for Democratic presidential candidates as Elliott County has gone Democratic in every presidential contest since 1869.

Percentage of Employment in Farming
2008

Total U.S. Popular Vote and Turnout Percentage

Percentage of Employment

	1.9 or less
	2.0 to 3.9
	4.0 to 7.9
	8.0 to 15.9
	16.0 or more
	No Data

MAP 6.4

Top 200 Counties Having the Highest Percentage of Farm Employment
2008

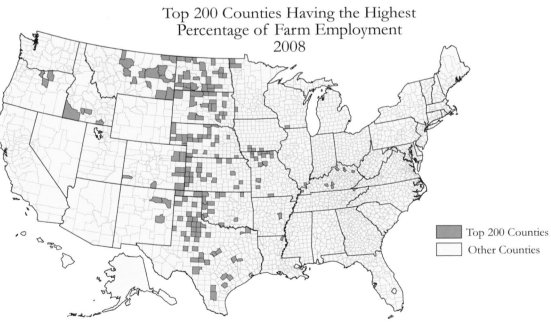

Top 200 Counties
Other Counties

Vote and Turnout in the Top 200 Counties Having the Highest Percentage of Farm Employment

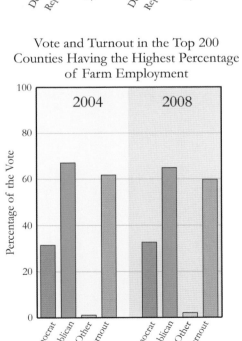

■ CONSTRUCTION EMPLOYMENT

JEFFREY R. CRUMP

Construction employment is closely associated with economic growth. In particular, during the great housing boom of 2000–2007, largely driven by the demand for housing, construction employment in the United States increased rapidly. The map depicting percentage of employment in construction illustrates this nicely. Counties with the highest percentage of employment in construction are found mainly in Colorado and Utah and in Wyoming, where construction employment is likely associated with energy development. Other hot spots of construction employment are found in the Carolinas and in many counties in Georgia. Notably lacking are any counties in Indiana, Ohio, New York, and Pennsylvania.

Quite clearly, regions where construction employment is concentrated remained largely in the Republican camp. Candidate John McCain won over 60 percent of the vote in those counties having the most construction employment. However, Democratic challenger Barack Obama did win Indiana, Ohio, New York, and Pennsylvania, states where construction employment was not a cornerstone of the economy. In terms of voter turnout, there was a small rise in counties where construction employment is important. Overall, turnout rates were very close to the national average.

It certainly appears that those dependent on construction employment were likely to support the antiregulatory philosophy espoused by the Republican candidate. In addition, construction employment is predominantly white male, and approximately 57 percent of white men did vote for Republican McCain in the 2008 presidential election.

Of the top two hundred counties in construction employment, only twenty-eight (14 percent) were tallied in Barack Obama's win column. Of these, twenty were either in the West or North. In terms of regional concentrations, seven of the construction-dependent counties were in the state of Colorado. For example, in Eagle County, Colorado, Barack Obama won 61 percent of the vote, an unusually high proportion for a construction-dependent county. The likely explanation for this is that Eagle County is home to the wealthy resort community of Vail, a city well known for its liberal proclivities. Jefferson Davis County, Mississippi, is one of only eight of the top two hundred construction counties located in the South. Named for the president of the Confederacy, 60 percent of the voters in Jefferson Davis County voted for the first African American President, Barack Obama. A likely explanation is found in the racial composition of the county, which is approximately 57.4 percent African American.

Percentage of Employment in Construction
2008

Percentage of
Employment

	2.4 or less
	2.5 to 4.9
	5.0 to 7.4
	7.5 to 9.9
	10.0 or more
	No Data

Top 200 Counties Having the Highest
Percentage of Construction Employment
2008

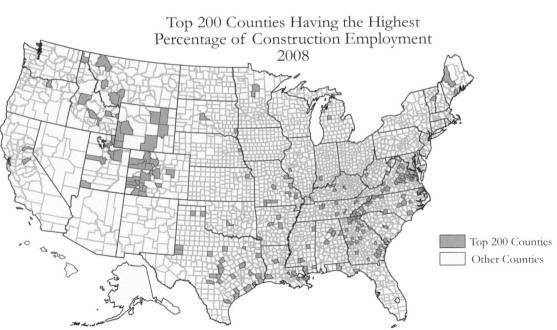

	Top 200 Counties
	Other Counties

Total U.S. Popular Vote and
Turnout Percentage

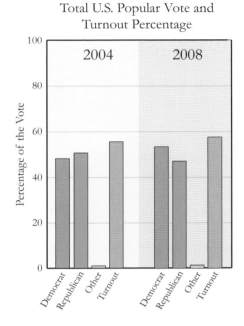

MAP 6.5

Vote and Turnout in the Top 200
Counties Having the Highest Percentage
of Construction Employment

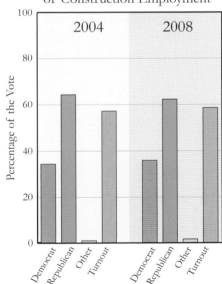

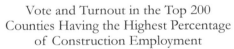

MANUFACTURING EMPLOYMENT

JEFFREY R. CRUMP

As the map depicting percentage of employment in manufacturing indicates, manufacturing employment is particularly important throughout the traditional U.S. Midwest Manufacturing Belt. However, the growth of manufacturing throughout the Southern states is also evident on the map, and counties with relatively high percentages of manufacturing employment extend through the Carolinas and into Tennessee and Alabama.

Further evidence of the dispersed nature of manufacturing employment is provided by the map depicting the top two hundred counties with the highest percentage of manufacturing employment. Here, even though many counties lie within the traditional Manufacturing Belt states of Ohio and Indiana, many are also to be found in the South. The dispersion of manufacturing is closely connected with the decline in the strength of unions within this sector. Although midwestern plants were highly unionized, unions largely failed to make inroads in the South.

Moreover, many manufacturing workers in traditionally Democratic strongholds shifted their allegiances to the Republican Party during the Reagan era.

Evidence of these trends is fairly clear in the U.S. presidential vote. In the 2004 presidential election, George W. Bush garnered over 60 percent of the vote in the top two hundred manufacturing counties. In the 2008 presidential election, Democrat Barack Obama won only 40 percent of the vote in these counties. These results indicate that "Joe Sixpack" remained solidly in the Republican corner during the 2008 presidential election. In terms of turnout, there was only a very slight increase between 2004 and 2008. In both presidential elections, turnout in the top two hundred manufacturing counties was below the national figures.

It is interesting that Barack Obama was victorious in only thirty (15 percent) of the top two hundred manufacturing counties. Almost all of these counties were in the Midwest; twenty-six of the thirty

(87 percent) are located in that region. One Midwestern example is Brookings, South Dakota, home to South Dakota State University. The city also has a significant manufacturing base. A major manufacturing firm is Daktronics, a company that produces high-tech scoreboards for sports stadiums. Brookings is also home to production facilities operated by the 3M Corporation.

In the South, the Democratic candidate won 75 percent of the vote in manufacturing-rich Lowndes County, Alabama. Long recognized for its oppression of African Americans, in the civil rights era "Bloody Lowndes" was the site of a hard-fought battle to secure the voting rights of African Americans. These struggles did succeed, and Barack Obama won handily in Lowndes County. One may conclude that the history of civil rights organizing and the predominantly African American population account for Barack Obama's victory in this Southern county.

Percentage of Employment in Manufacturing
2008

Percentage of
Employment

	2.4 or less
	2.5 to 4.9
	5.0 to 9.9
	10.0 to 19.9
	20.0 or more
	No Data

Total U.S. Popular Vote and Turnout Percentage

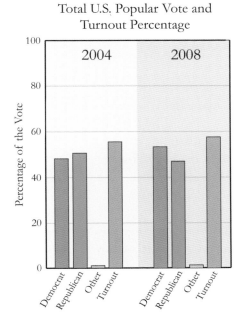

MAP 6.6

Top 200 Counties Having the Highest Percentage of Manufacturing Employment
2008

	Top 200 Counties
	Other Counties

Vote and Turnout in the Top 200 Counties Having the Highest Percentage of Manufacturing Employment

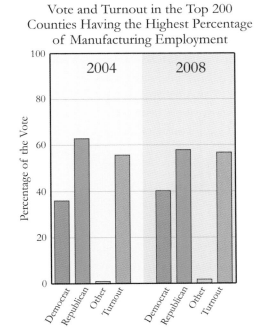

■ UNEMPLOYMENT

JEFFREY R. CRUMP

Pundits argue that the 2008 presidential election was one in which the rapidly deteriorating state of the U.S. economy played an important role in shaping the vote. Certainly the collapse of the U.S. housing market, the costly federal bailout of Wall Street investment banks, and the loss of some eight million jobs was cause for consternation among many voters.

Indicative of economic conditions, these maps of the unemployment rate provide a picture of the regional distribution of joblessness. The state of Michigan stands out as the epicenter of unemployment—fueled by the bankruptcy of General Motors. Unemployment rates were also high throughout the Carolinas and into Alabama and Georgia. In the West, California's Central Valley counties experienced comparatively high unemployment rates as well.

In the second map, we compare the top two hundred counties and the bottom two hundred counties in terms of the unemployment rate. Low unemployment rates are evident in the Great Plains states, where the Republican candidate, John McCain, won handily.

By contrast, high unemployment rates were found in Michigan and in California and Oregon, all states that supported Democratic challenger Barack Obama.

Comparing voting results with unemployment patterns does lend support to the notion that the state of the U.S. economy played an important role in Barack Obama's historic victory. In the top two hundred counties having the highest unemployment rates, the Democratic vote increased significantly. It is quite clear that in the counties most impacted by unemployment, the Democratic challenger made significant inroads into the Republican vote.

Barack Obama also outperformed his 2004 counterpart in the bottom two hundred counties. Here, it is apparent that Democratic support increased significantly, although Republican John McCain still won a higher proportion of the vote.

Turnout rates increased between 2004 and 2008. However, there is little difference between the top two hundred unemployment counties and the bottom two hundred unemployment counties.

Imperial County, California, has one of the nation's highest unemployment rates. In addition, Imperial County is a heavily Hispanic county, with 76 percent of its population of Latino origin. These factors helped to push Barack Obama's vote to 62 percent of the total vote, a strong margin of victory by any measure.

At the other end of the spectrum, Billings County, North Dakota, has one of the lowest unemployment rates in the nation. The voters of this county voted robustly Republican, with 75 percent supporting John McCain. Emblematic of the Great Plains Republican regional stronghold, Billings County is quite homogeneous, with whites accounting for over 98 percent of the population in 2000.

There does appear to be a spatial correlation between voting and unemployment rates. Currently, unemployment remains high throughout the nation, and whether subsequent elections will support the link between the economy and voting patterns remains to be seen.

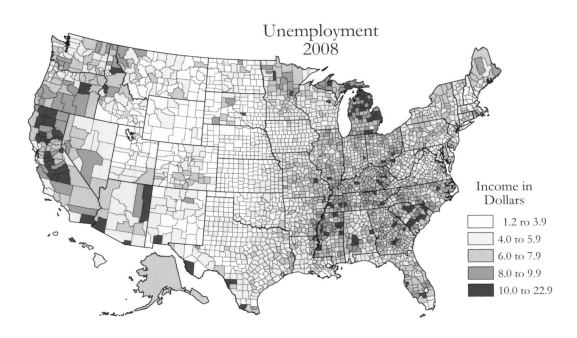

Unemployment
2008

Income in
Dollars

	1.2 ro 3.9
	4.0 to 5.9
	6.0 to 7.9
	8.0 to 9.9
	10.0 to 22.9

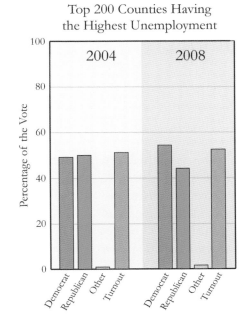

Top 200 Counties Having
the Highest Unemployment

2004   2008

Percentage of the Vote

Democrat Republican Other Turnout   Democrat Republican Other Turnout

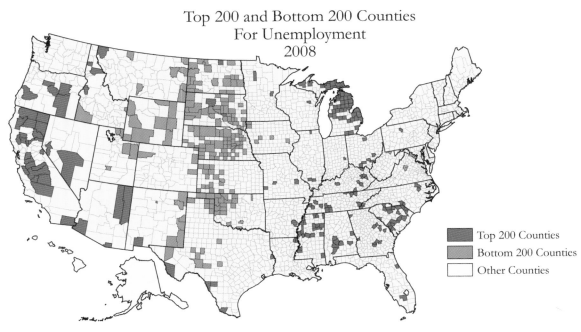

Top 200 and Bottom 200 Counties
For Unemployment
2008

	Top 200 Counties
	Bottom 200 Counties
	Other Counties

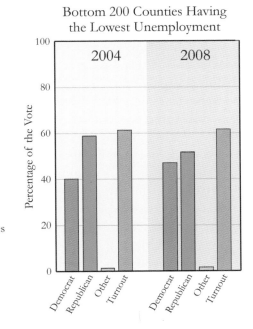

Bottom 200 Counties Having
the Lowest Unemployment

2004   2008

Percentage of the Vote

Democrat Republican Other Turnout   Democrat Republican Other Turnout

MAP 6.7

■ POPULATION CHANGE BY COUNTY

RICHARD L. MORRILL

The largest two hundred counties contain 174 million people, about 57 percent of the U.S. population. Obviously, Obama's 60 to 40 percent margin in these largest metropolitan areas (43 to 28 million) was the key to his overall victory. Indeed, Obama's margin in just the five largest areas, Chicago, Los Angeles, New York, San Francisco, and Washington-Baltimore, alone provided a margin of ten million votes. The Democrats' total metropolitan margin grew from eleven million votes in 2004 (not enough to win) to eighteen million in 2008 (more than enough).

Delving below the surface, all these two hundred counties hardly behave alike. The largest number of these counties actually increased in their Democratic share, including many in Megalopolis, in Miami-Fort Lauderdale, in Chicago (Cook), Minneapolis, Detroit, Seattle, Portland, and San Francisco. Only a few counties had a lower Democratic share than in 2004 (suburban Boston and Baton Rouge, Louisiana). More significantly, several important counties shifted from Republican to Democrat, sometimes a surprise, for example, Birmingham, Alabama; San Bernardino, Riverside, San Diego, and Stockton, California; suburban Denver, Colorado; Tampa-St. Petersburg, Florida; suburban Chicago, Illinois; Grand Rapids, Michigan; Jackson, Mississippi; Omaha, Nebraska; Reno, Nevada; Raleigh, North Carolina; suburban Portland, Oregon; Charleston, South Carolina; and Dallas, Houston, and San Antonio, Texas.

Many counties remained Republican, but with declining shares; these included Phoenix, Arizona; Salt Lake City, Utah; Mobile, Alabama; Jacksonville, Florida; Boise, Idaho; Oklahoma City and Tulsa, Oklahoma; Greenville, South Carolina; and Knoxville, Tennessee. Only a very few counties actually had increases in the Republican share, mainly suburban New Orleans, Louisiana.

Republicans fare far better with respect to counties experiencing high population gains and losses than they do as to simple population size. The two hundred counties losing population the "fastest" were about evenly balanced between Obama and McCain in 2008, but their aggregate population was not large (only 1,650,000 in aggregate population voting 300,000 Democrat and 304,000 Republican). They are overwhelmingly situated in the Great Plains, a region of long-term population decline, associated with out-migration of the young, and often experiencing natural decrease. While these are historically Republican-leaning areas, their small size reduces their significance. The other areas of loss are Louisiana counties associated with hurricane Katrina, including New Orleans, and heavily black counties of the Delta in Louisiana, Mississippi, and Arkansas. These counties constitute a net loss to the Democrats.

Rapidly growing counties are of all sizes, but generally much larger than the losing counties, with an aggregate population of over 30 million, voting 7.1 million Democrat to 8.7 million Republican. While the Republican domination was less in 2008 than it had been in 2004 (the Republican margin fell from 24 percent to 12 percent), it was still substantial in absolute numbers.

There are three main kinds of rapidly growing counties. Most frequent are suburban counties and satellite metropolitan areas, as around Phoenix, Los Angeles, Sacramento, Denver, Atlanta, Chicago, Indianapolis, Louisville, Washington, D.C. (in Maryland and Virginia), Minneapolis, St. Louis, Reno and Las Vegas, Raleigh, Memphis and Nashville, Dallas, Houston, San Antonio, and Austin, and Salt Lake City. These are strongly Republican in the South but balanced across the North, with several shifting to the Democrats in 2008. The second-most common type are amenity-retirement counties, as in Florida, South Carolina, and North Carolina, but even more in the interior West (Arizona, Colorado, Idaho, Montana, Oregon, and Wyoming). These tend to remain Republican, but with lower shares in 2008; some counties did, however, shift to the Democratic column.

The third type includes fast-growing smaller metropolitan areas; they are entirely in the South and West. These, too, are mainly Republican (with some exceptions), but with lower margins in 2008 than in 2004. Some examples are Yavapai (Prescott) and Pinal (Casa Grande), Arizona; Benton-Washington (Fayetteville), Arkansas; Weld (Greeley), Colorado; several in Florida; Ada (Boise), Idaho; Beaufort, South Carolina; Webb (Laredo) and Brazoria, Texas; and Utah (Provo).

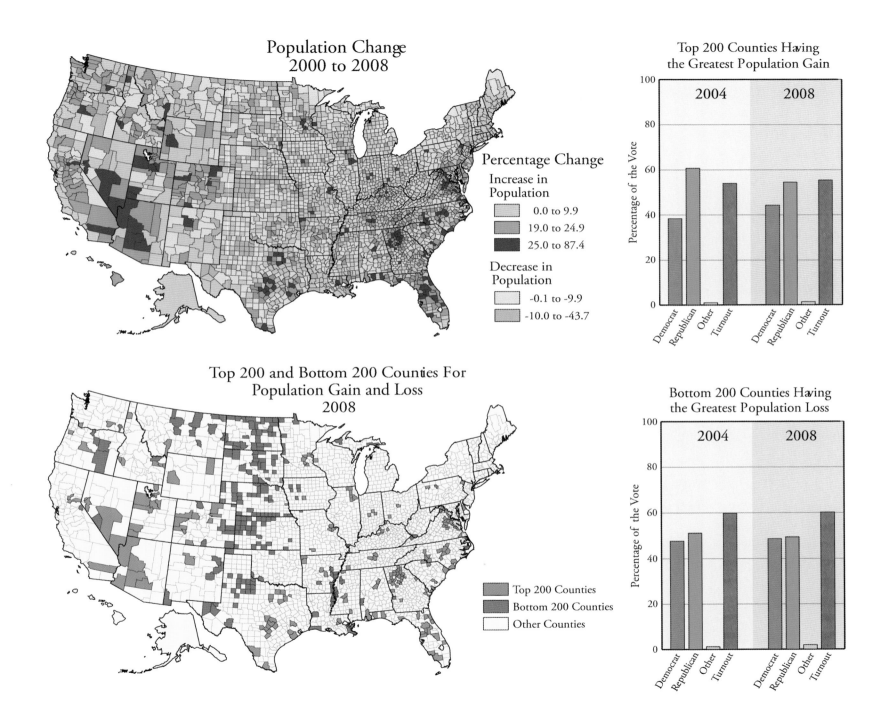

Population Change
2000 to 2008

Top 200 Counties Having
the Greatest Population Gain

MAP 6.8

Percentage Change

Increase in
Population

0.0 to 9.9
19.0 to 24.9
25.0 to 87.4

Decrease in
Population

-0.1 to -9.9
-10.0 to -43.7

Top 200 and Bottom 200 Counties For
Population Gain and Loss
2008

Top 200 Counties
Bottom 200 Counties
Other Counties

Bottom 200 Counties Having
the Greatest Population Loss

■ POPULATION BY AGE

RICHARD L. MORRILL

POPULATION UNDER EIGHTEEN

These counties in 2004 provided a very large margin for the Republican ticket, mainly because the Hispanic Republican vote in Texas and Arizona and the Mormon Republican vote in Utah and Idaho offset the Democratic votes from black- and American Indian–dominated counties. Their aggregate population is a moderate 17 million, which voted 5.0 million Democratic to 5.4 million Republican). The margin changed (decreased) markedly in 2008 because of substantial Hispanic shift to Obama and because of high turnout in these and in black and American Indian areas. The Mormon realm remained Republican, but again with reduced margins.

The extreme counties are of six kinds. By far the most important in aggregate population are counties high in Hispanic populations in Texas, extending into Oklahoma and Kansas, Arizona, California, and Washington. Hispanic areas along the Rio Grande became more Democratic or shifted Democratic, but those in the Panhandle remained Republican or became even redder. A few Hispanic counties in California either shifted to Democratic or experienced reduced Republican shares.

The second case of high shares of the young is the Mormon culture area, centered on Utah, but strong in Idaho and increasing in Arizona and Washington. Third, many counties, but mostly those with small populations, are dominantly American Indian (South Dakota, North Dakota, Montana, Arizona, and New Mexico). These increased in the Democratic share or even shifted Democratic. However, in South Dakota, several counties outside areas with reservations increased their Republican share. Fourth, several counties, mainly along the Mississippi Delta (Mississippi, Arkansas) are majority black. These had a high Democratic share and turnout. Fifth are rapidly growing suburban counties, as around Atlanta, Chicago, Minneapolis, and Denver. These are almost all Republican, but again with lower shares in 2008 than in 2004. Sixth are a few counties with major military bases.

POPULATION OVER SIXTY-FIVE

These results mirror exit polls, which found that the elderly tend to lean Republican, but less in 2008 than in 2004 (the Republican margin fell from 19 to 15 percent). There are two main kinds of counties with high elderly shares, with only a fairly small aggregate population of about five million, voting 1.2 million Democratic to 1.45 million Republican. The most frequent by far are small counties in the Great Plains with a long history of out-migration of the young, aging in place of those remaining, with subsequent natural decrease. Related are a few counties in Michigan's Upper Peninsula and northern Wisconsin.

These are relatively Republican, although most had declining Republican shares. The second kind of county, with a large aggregate population, consists of amenity retirement areas. Florida is the archetype, with by far the most population, but there are also several more rural areas in the west (Arizona, New Mexico, Nevada, California, Oregon, and Washington), as well as in the Ozarks (Arkansas). Most of these counties in Florida and the Great Plains tend to be experiencing moderate Republican declines, while those in Washington are far more Democratic (with a radical logging history), and those in Arkansas and Arizona had increased their Republican shares.

Percentage of Population Age Under 18
2008

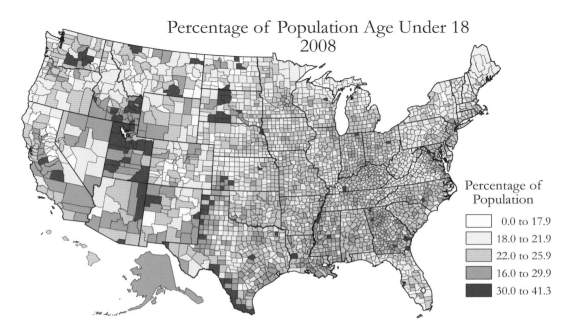

Percentage of
Population

	0.0 to 17.9
	18.0 to 21.9
	22.0 to 25.9
	16.0 to 29.9
	30.0 to 41.3

Total U.S. Popular Vote and
Turnout Percentage

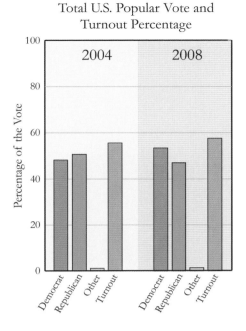

MAP 6.9

Top 200 Counties Having the Highest
Percentage of Population Under 18 Years
2008

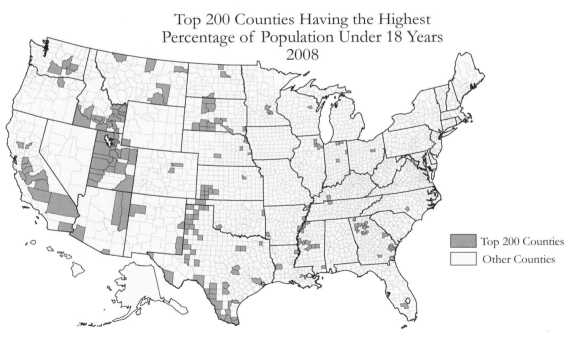

	Top 200 Counties
	Other Counties

Vote and Turnout in the Top 200
Counties Having the Highest Percentage
of Population Under 18 Years

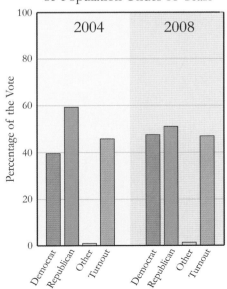

MAP 6.10

Percentage of Population Age 25 to 44
2008

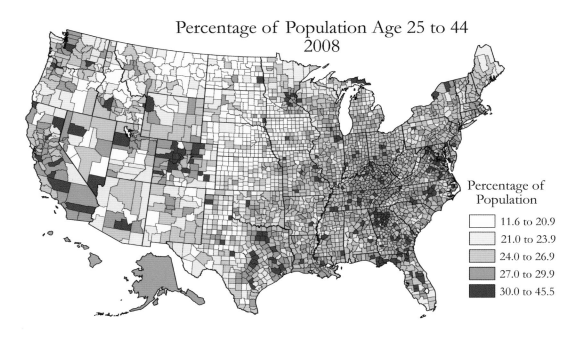

Percentage of
Population

- 11.6 to 20.9
- 21.0 to 23.9
- 24.0 to 26.9
- 27.0 to 29.9
- 30.0 to 45.5

Total U.S. Popular Vote and Turnout Percentage

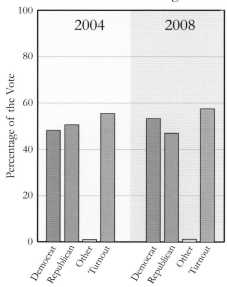

Top 200 Counties Having the Highest Percentage of Population Age 25 to 44
2008

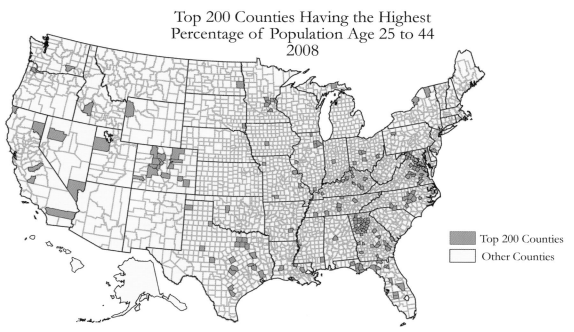

- Top 200 Counties
- Other Counties

Vote and Turnout in the Top 200 Counties Having the Highest Percentage of Population Age 25 to 44

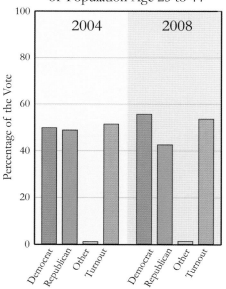

Percentage of Population Age 65 and Older
2008

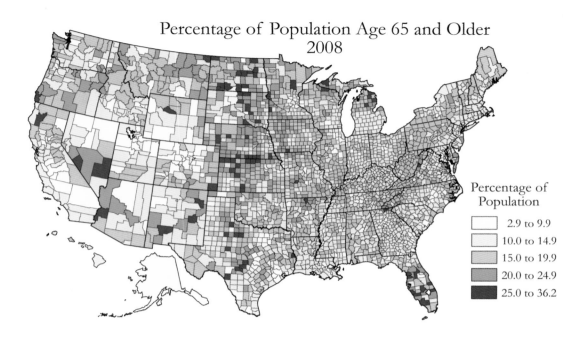

Percentage of
Population

2.9 to 9.9
10.0 to 14.9
15.0 to 19.9
20.0 to 24.9
25.0 to 36.2

Total U.S. Popular Vote and Turnout Percentage

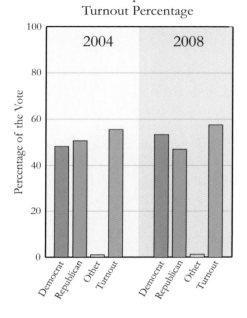

MAP 6.11

Top 200 Counties Having the Highest
Percentage of Population 65 Years and Older
2008

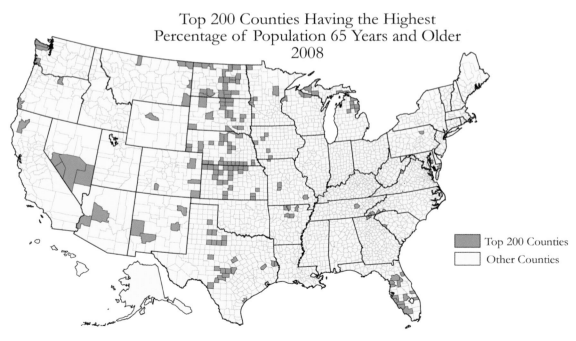

Top 200 Counties
Other Counties

Vote and Turnout in the Top 200
Counties Having the Highest Percentage
of Population 65 Years and Older

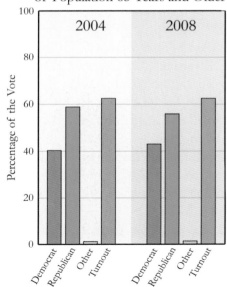

LEADING IN- AND OUT-MIGRATION COUNTIES

RICHARD L. MORRILL

The maps of net migration and of counties with the highest rates of net in-migration (including both internal migration and immigration) and with the highest net out-migration broadly parallel patterns of overall population growth and decline and would appear to be of comfort to Republican aspirations, since the fast in-migration counties voted strongly Republican, even if less so in 2008 than in 2004. The extreme out-migration counties, on the other hand, voted Democratic.

The geography of the fast in-migration counties is threefold. About half are large metropolitan suburbs, especially in the South, with a few in the Midwest and West. A second set are exurban, resort, and retirement counties, especially in the West (and, obviously, Florida). A third set are several small metropolitan counties, mainly in the South.

Republican voting was strong in the Mountain West (Arizona, Utah, Idaho, Colorado, and Wyoming), while Democrats prevailed in only a few Far Western counties, notably Riverside, California, and Clark, Nevada (Las Vegas). In the North, the few high in-migration counties split in Minneapolis suburbs, favored Democrats in Illinois, and favored Republicans in New Jersey. In the South, Republicans dominated in suburban and small metropolitan areas in Texas, Arkansas, Tennessee, and Georgia but split with Democrats in suburban and small metropolitan areas in Virginia and North Carolina.

Change in patterns for high in-migration counties was complex. Of the two hundred high in-migration counties, the dominant pattern of change was for Republican declines, 139 counties. But the next most common was Republican gains (thirty-three counties). This pattern is evident in counties across the South, from Arizona to Delaware. One county in Kentucky had a Democratic decline, and five experienced a Democratic gain: Clark, Nevada (Las Vegas); St. Lucie (Fort Pierce), Florida; and three counties in North Carolina (Mecklenburg [Charlotte], Hoke [part of Ft. Bragg], and Chatham [exurban Chapel Hill]). A significant twenty-two counties switched from Republican to Democratic, giving Democrats some solace. Six were scattered across the West, including Riverside, California; suburban-exurban Sandoval, New Mexico; Clark, Washington; and several environmental counties, including Ouray, Colorado; Teton, Idaho; and Gallatin, Montana. Exurban Monroe in Pennsylvania switched, as did Jefferson in West Virginia, now in exurban Washington, D.C. The three switches in Illinois were suburban and exurban to Chicago. The eleven remaining in the South include Kent, Delaware; Osceola and Flagler in Florida; Douglas and Newton, Georgia (west and east suburbs of Atlanta); Wake (Raleigh) and Franklin (east of Raleigh) in North Carolina; and four in Virginia: Prince William and Loudoun (suburban to Washington, D.C.), Caroline (between Richmond, Virginia, and D.C.), and Suffolk (suburban Norfolk).

Republican gains, thirty-three counties, included a suburb of Birmingham, Alabama; fast-growing Yavapai and Mojave counties, northwest from Phoenix; two suburban counties of Little Rock, Arkansas; four Florida counties between Tampa and Tallahassee; and nine counties in Georgia, one a southern exurb of Atlanta, but eight northeast of Atlanta, toward the border with Tennessee and North Carolina. Two were in southeastern Mississippi, including Lamar (Hattiesburg), two in North Carolina, one in Appalachia, one south of Norfolk, one in Oklahoma, east of Tulsa, five in Tennessee, including suburbs or exurbs of Knoxville, Nashville, and Memphis, only three in Texas, exurban to Dallas and Fort Worth, and two in Louisiana, suburban-exurban between New Orleans and Baton Rouge.

The high out-migration counties are mostly an expected, well-known set: black majority counties mainly in the Mississippi Delta, but also overwhelmingly small, sparsely populated counties in the Great Plains. The black majority counties voted strongly Democratic, while the much larger number of Great Plains counties voted Republican. How, then, can the bar chart show a very high Democratic margin? This is simply an artifact of the domination of the statistics by strongly Democratic Orleans County. Since the entire set of counties' voting age population was only three million, they are not politically very consequential.

The most common patterns of change between 2004 and 2008 were Republican declines in the majority of Great Plains counties (except for Democratic gains in a few American Indian reservation counties) and Republican gains, especially in western Kansas and Texas. Only a couple of counties switched from Republican to Democratic; they were in Montana and North Dakota. Among the majority black counties, most experienced Democratic gains, while the two high out-migration counties in Appalachia were a Democratic decline and a switch from Democratic to Republican.

Net Migration 2000 to 2009

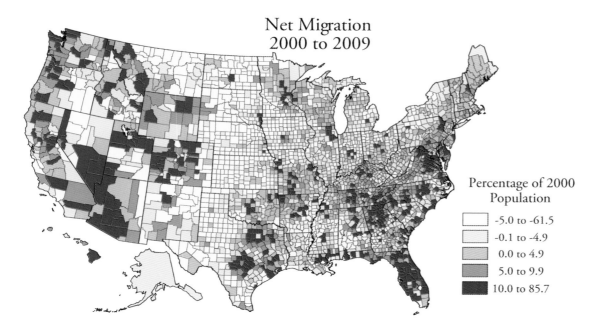

Percentage of 2000 Population

- -5.0 to -61.5
- -0.1 to -4.9
- 0.0 to 4.9
- 5.0 to 9.9
- 10.0 to 85.7

Top 200 Net In-Migration Counties and Bottom 201 Net Out-Migration Counties 2000 to 2009

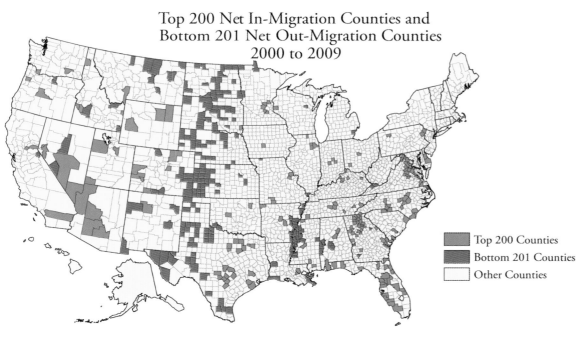

- Top 200 Counties
- Bottom 201 Counties
- Other Counties

MAP 6.12

Top 200 Counties Having Net In-Migration

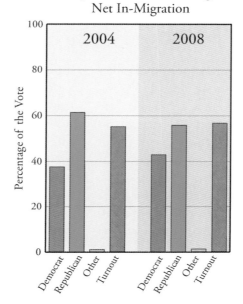

Bottom 201 Counties Having Net Out-Migration

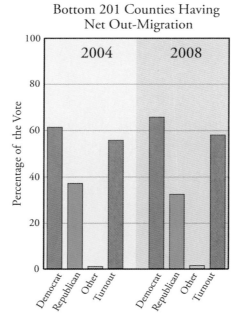

■ MEDIAN HOUSEHOLD INCOME

RICHARD L. MORRILL

Historically, conventional wisdom held that areas with lower incomes would vote Democratic, while high-income areas would vote Republican. Yet in 2008 the simple correlation of median household income and the percentage for Obama was $r = .18$, quite low but positive. Such has been the effect of the profound restructuring of the political parties, with increased shares of the more affluent shifting Democratic, often because of environmental or social liberal concerns, and increasing shares of the less well off shifting Republican because of economic restructuring, including a much weakened role in the Democratic party, and because of a more traditional value set, in turn related to less education and a stronger role of religion. It does remain true (from exit polls) that the majority of the poor really did vote Democratic, but they are largely the metropolitan poor and masked by the use of county averages.

The richest two hundred counties are dominantly metropolitan, with an aggregate population at a substantial 53.3 million people of voting age, voting 18.4 million Democratic to 13.4 million Republican. Most prominent is Megalopolis, but also Chicago, Minneapolis, Denver, satellites of Los Angeles, San Francisco, Portland, and Seattle. The others are mainly environmental amenity counties, often attracting affluent and educated retirees from the metropolitan hubs, as to Colorado, Utah, Idaho, and Wyoming.

The dominant pattern of change from 2004 to 2008 was a decline in the Republican share (ninety-four counties), largely suburban, a substantial number (thirty-eight) shifting from Republican to Democratic, including both suburban counties, as around Atlanta, Denver, Chicago, Minneapolis, Omaha, Portland, Philadelphia, and Washington, D.C. Many long-term Republican areas also shifted, including San Diego and Ventura, California, Nashua-Manchester, New Hampshire, and Raleigh, North Carolina.

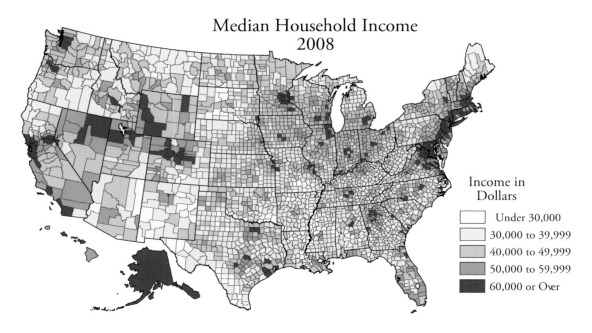

Median Household Income
2008

Income in
Dollars

☐ Under 30,000
☐ 30,000 to 39,999
☐ 40,000 to 49,999
☐ 50,000 to 59,999
☐ 60,000 or Over

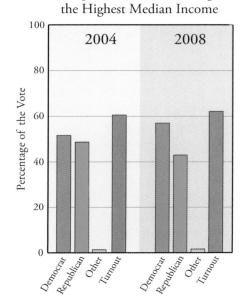

Top 200 Counties Having
the Highest Median Income

2004   2008

Percentage of the Vote

Democrat Republican Other Turnout   Democrat Republican Other Turnout

MAP 6.13

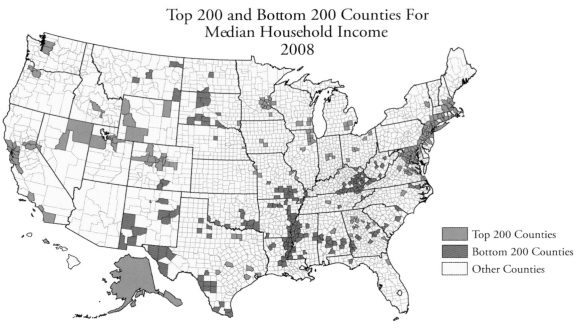

Top 200 and Bottom 200 Counties For
Median Household Income
2008

☐ Top 200 Counties
☐ Bottom 200 Counties
☐ Other Counties

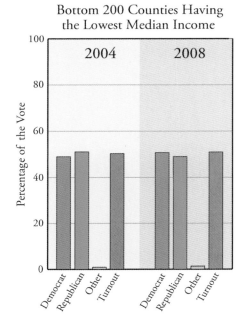

Bottom 200 Counties Having
the Lowest Median Income

2004   2008

Percentage of the Vote

Democrat Republican Other Turnout   Democrat Republican Other Turnout

■ HUSBAND-WIFE HOUSEHOLDS

RICHARD L. MORRILL

The single variable that most distinguishes areas voting Democratic versus Republican is the share of husband-wife families, another key component of a "modern" versus a more "traditional" lifestyle. Exit polls showed that married persons voted 47 percent for Obama, but those not married voted 65 percent.

The counties with the highest shares of families housed a smallish 6.3 million people of voting age; they voted 2.5 million Republican to 1.4 million Democratic and are most obviously the Mormon-dominated areas of the West (Utah and Idaho), the western Great Plains, some Hispanic areas, and many suburban and exurban counties, primarily across the East, including many small-town and rural areas, as in Ohio, Indiana, Iowa, and Nebraska. These counties are overwhelmingly Republican (154 of these 200 counties), although many areas experienced Republican declines.

Areas with the lowest shares of families contained far more people, a moderate 37 million people of voting age; they voted 14.6 million Democrat to 6.3 million Republican. Included are three distinctive kinds of counties. Covering the most territory are areas dominated by black households, from Louisiana to Virginia, and some American Indian areas, where single-parent families are common. Second are quite a few small counties dominated by universities; third are a few large metropolitan counties, including the cities of Denver, Atlanta, Chicago, Washington, D.C., Indianapolis, Louisville, New Orleans, Baltimore, Detroit, Minneapolis, New York, Cleveland and Columbus, Portland, Providence, Nashville, Austin, and Milwaukee. These counties overwhelmingly experienced increased Democratic shares, and many (twenty-three) shifted from Republican to Democratic, especially in North and South Carolina.

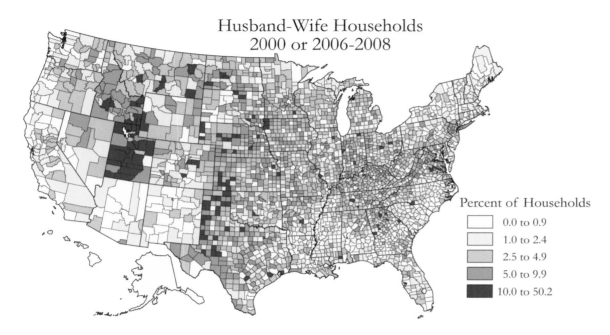

Husband-Wife Households
2000 or 2006-2008

Percent of Households

- 0.0 to 0.9
- 1.0 to 2.4
- 2.5 to 4.9
- 5.0 to 9.9
- 10.0 to 50.2

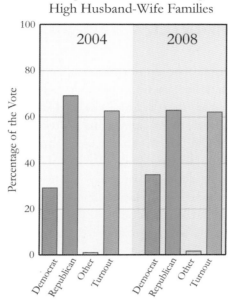

Top 246 Counties Having
High Husband-Wife Families

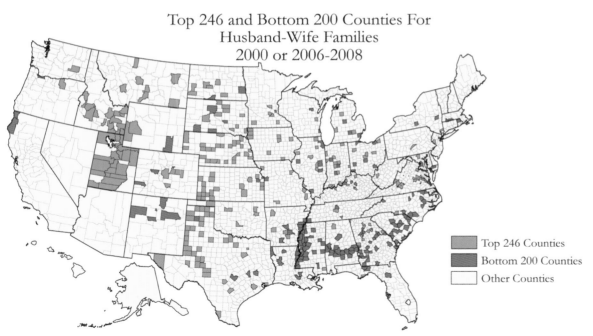

Top 246 and Bottom 200 Counties For
Husband-Wife Families
2000 or 2006-2008

- Top 246 Counties
- Bottom 200 Counties
- Other Counties

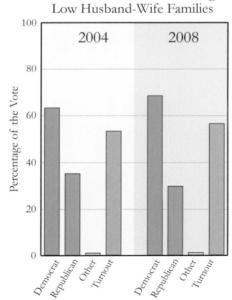

Bottom 200 Counties Having
Low Husband-Wife Families

MAP 6.14

■ POVERTY COUNTIES

RICHARD L. MORRILL

The poorest counties on the map do not house most of the poor, but rather are often small rural counties, somewhat "left behind" by the modern economy and culture, as in Appalachia (white), the Black Belt across the South, American Indian reservations, and heavily Hispanic areas. The only metropolitan high-poverty counties are heavily Hispanic areas along the border with Mexico (El Paso, Laredo, Brownsville, and McAllen, Texas).

The aggregate population of the two hundred poorest counties is only 2.5 million persons of voting age; they voted 1.53 million Democratic and 970,000 Republican. These counties are rather evenly split between Republican and Democratic. Dominantly white areas in Appalachia (mainly Kentucky) and in the Ozarks voted Republican, while most other minority areas voted Democratic (dozens of small black-majority counties across the South, from Arkansas and Louisiana to North Carolina, and American Indian areas in North Dakota, South Dakota, Montana, Arizona, Utah, New Mexico, and Oklahoma).

A few isolated white-majority counties with high shares of poverty are actually university dominated, as Whitman in Washington (Washington State University) or Monroe (Indiana University) in Indiana.

The pattern of change from 2004 to 2008 is also mixed. Those with an increased Democratic share were mainly the black majority counties but included some Hispanic counties. However, a substantial number of mainly white counties increased their Republican share, mainly in Appalachia. Several counties shifted from Republican to Democrat, for example, black-majority counties in Mississippi and Georgia and Hispanic counties in New Mexico and Texas.

Poverty
2008

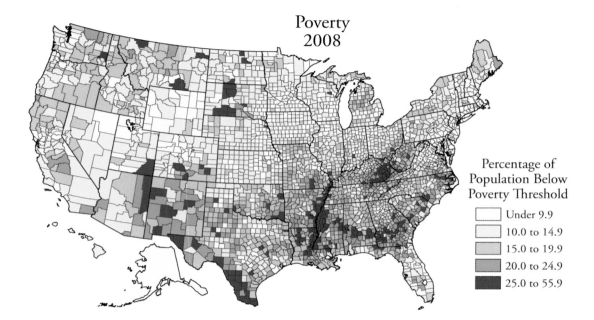

Percentage of
Population Below
Poverty Threshold

	Under 9.9
	10.0 to 14.9
	15.0 to 19.9
	20.0 to 24.9
	25.0 to 55.9

Total U.S. Popular Vote and
Turnout Percentage

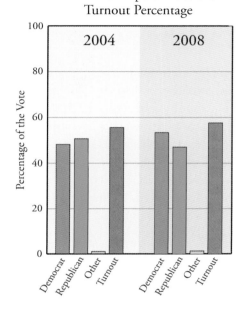

MAP 6.15

Top 200 Counties Below
the Poverty Threshold
2008

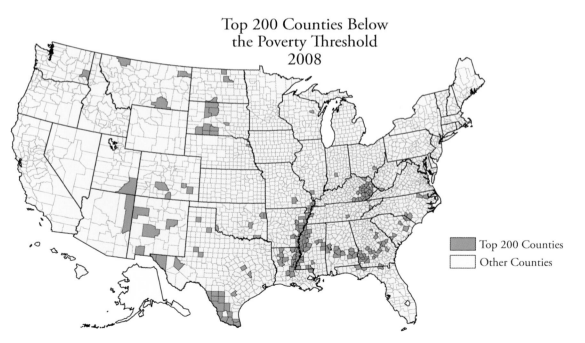

	Top 200 Counties
	Other Counties

Vote and Turnout in the Top 200
Counties Below the
Poverty Threshold Level

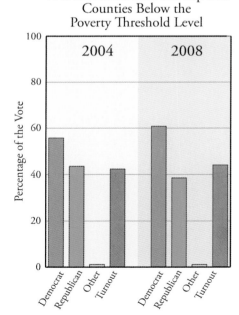

■ PERSONS WITH A B.A. OR HIGHER DEGREE

RICHARD L. MORRILL

Level of education is a major definer of the "culture wars," modern versus traditional dimension of American thought and politics. The restructuring of American politics since the 1980s has led to a shift of many educated and affluent moderate Republicans to the Democratic party, while many less-educated voters, even if not affluent, defected to the Republican side. In 2008 the most highly educated counties voted 60 percent for Obama, while the least educated counties voted only 38 percent Democratic. The most educated counties tend to be in the large metropolitan areas; they contain 55 million people (voting 20.2 million Democratic to 13.8 million Republican). The least educated counties tend to be rural and small town and in aggregate house only three million people; they voted 560,000 Democratic to 880,000 Republican.

The more educated counties are scattered in all parts of the country but are especially prominent in the northern Rocky Mountain states and in the coastal Northeast, from Virginia to Maine. There are three main kinds of counties with high shares of the most educated. Most obvious are university-dominated counties in all regions. These voted strongly Democratic. A second set of counties, containing far more population, are major metropolitan and suburban counties, as in and around San Francisco, Denver, Atlanta, Washington-Baltimore, Boston, Detroit, Minneapolis, New York, Raleigh, Portland, Philadelphia, Nashville, Dallas, Austin, and Seattle. Third are environmental areas, as in Idaho and Colorado. Over half of these counties increased in Democratic share, while a quarter experienced Republican declines, and the remaining quarter switched from Republican to Democratic.

The counties with the lowest numbers of college degrees are almost absent from the West, and there are very few in the North. However, they are fairly common across the rural South and most prevalent in the "left behind" border state area, from Missouri and Arkansas through Kentucky and Tennessee into West Virginia. These counties have become highly Republican, and over half the counties increased their Republican share or shifted from the Democratic to the Republican column. It is interesting that these least educated counties are not ethnic minority counties, either black, American Indian, or even Hispanic.

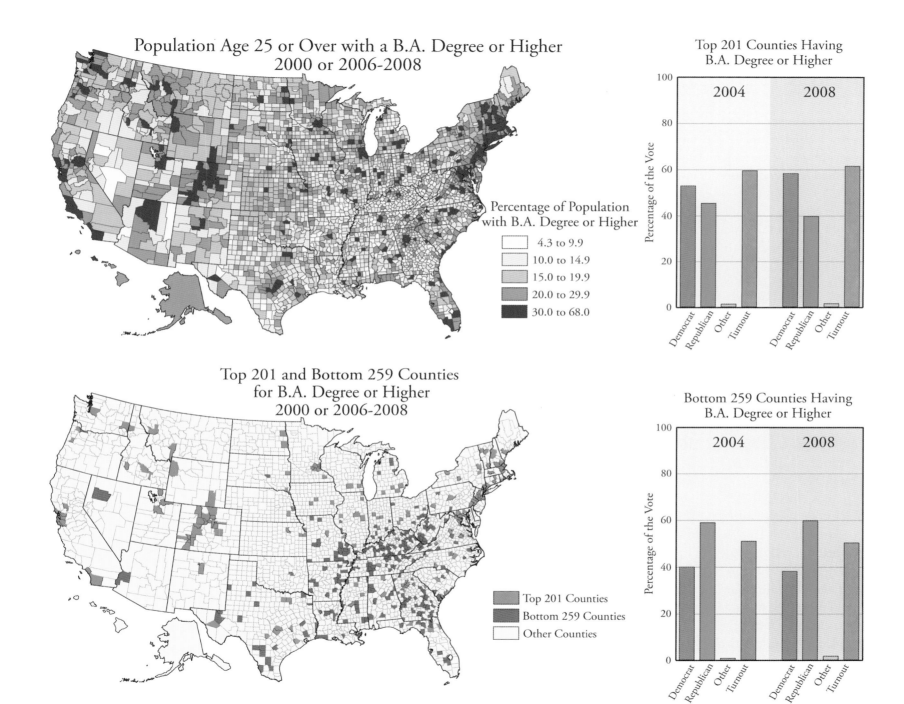

Population Age 25 or Over with a B.A. Degree or Higher
2000 or 2006-2008

Top 201 Counties Having
B.A. Degree or Higher

MAP 6.16

Percentage of Population
with B.A. Degree or Higher

4.3 to 9.9
10.0 to 14.9
15.0 to 19.9
20.0 to 29.9
30.0 to 68.0

Top 201 and Bottom 259 Counties
for B.A. Degree or Higher
2000 or 2006-2008

Bottom 259 Counties Having
B.A. Degree or Higher

Top 201 Counties
Bottom 259 Counties
Other Counties

■ UNIVERSITY AND COLLEGE COUNTIES

RICHARD L. MORRILL

The 175 counties with the largest university and college enrollments played a decisive role in the Democratic victory, yielding a Democratic margin of eleven million votes. The Democratic vote increased over four million (from 23.1 million to 27.3 million), while the Republican vote fell from 17.4 million to 16.2 million. The appeal of Obama to the well educated and to the young is clear. College-rich counties were overall far more Democratic (135 of the 175), far more likely to have switched from Republican to Democratic (thirty-nine counties), and far more likely to be metropolitan (also 135 of the 175) than U.S. counties as a whole. Among the metropolitan counties with major universities, Democrats were overwhelmingly dominant (110 to 25), and even among the forty university-rich nonmetropolitan counties, Democrats won the majority (twenty-five).

There are thus three kinds of counties Democrats did especially well in. First are the large, core metropolitan counties, whose universities are important and influential but hardly the main economic sectors, for example, Cook (Chicago) or Los Angeles (USC, UCLA, etc.). Second are small metropolitan counties, where the universities or colleges are a major component of the economy and the population, and third are nonmetropolitan counties almost defined by their universities or liberal arts colleges. Counties with major universities, but nevertheless Republican, are not surprising, mainly in the South, but including a few in the West and North, representing historically conservative or Republican regions, for example, Lubbock, Texas (Texas Tech), or Utah (Brigham Young). Yet most of these did decline in Republican support.

Large Democratic metropolitan counties became even more Democratic in 2008. The more university dominated include Pima (Tucson), Bernalillo (Albuquerque), Travis (Austin), and Franklin (Columbus). Three of the four are also state capitals, which also tend to vote more Democratic than their states (even in Republican states). Another forty-eight large counties constitute the leading population and economic capitals across the North and West. Large metropolitan counties switching from Republican to Democratic include Wake (Raleigh), North Carolina, and Ingham (Lansing), Michigan, which are also state capitals; as well as Fresno and San Diego, California; Hillsborough (Tampa) Florida; Hamilton (Cincinnati), a major surprise, and Wood (Toledo), Ohio; Harris (Houston) and Bexar (San Antonio), Texas; and Chesapeake, Virginia.

A significant twenty-nine small metropolitan Democratic counties became even more Democratic in 2008. They were in twenty states, including three counties in Iowa and three in Michigan. An impressive twenty counties switched to the Democratic column, including San Luis Obispo and Butte (Chico), California; Larimer (Ft. Collins), Colorado; McLean (Bloomington), Illinois; Delaware (Muncie), St. Joseph (South Bend), and Tippecanoe (Lafayette), Indiana; Fayette (Lexington), Kentucky; Baton Rouge, Louisiana; Boone (Columbia), Missouri; Lancaster (Lincoln), Nebraska; Washoe (Reno), Nevada; Saratoga, New York; Cass (Fargo) and Grand Forks, North Dakota; Centre (State College), Pennsylvania; Charleston, South Carolina; Cameron (Brownsville), Texas; and Winnebago (Oshkosh), Wisconsin.

Fifteen nonmetropolitan Democratic counties became even more Democratic in 2008 and were joined by ten nonmetropolitan Republican counties switching to Democratic, including Latah (Moscow), Idaho; DeKalb, Illinois; Oktibbeha (Starkville), Mississippi (Mississippi State); Gallatin (Bozeman), Montana; Boone, North Carolina; Brookings, South Dakota; Montgomery (Blacksburg), Virginia; Harrisonburg, Virginia; Whitman (Pullman), Washington; Monongalia (Morgantown), West Virginia; and Albany (Laramie), Wyoming. These Democratic islands were often in highly Republican states or regions. It is little wonder that conservatives rail against universities' insidious influence on their youth. As a result of the switches, only forty of the 175 counties voted Republican, and all but four of these experienced declines in the Republican share—the exceptions are small metropolitan Washington (Fayetteville) and Craighead (Jonesboro) in Arkansas, Lafayette, Louisiana, and Oconee (Clemson), South Carolina.

Overall, Democratic (Obama) shares were higher for university counties than for all counties, which is no surprise, rising from a high 56 percent in 2004 to a really high 62 percent in 2008. The highest marginal changes were for university counties that switched from Republican to Democratic, as in Wake, North Carolina (17 percent); Larimer, Colorado (15 percent); McLean, Illinois (17 percent); Delaware, Indiana (29 percent); Tippecanoe, Indiana (31 percent); and Lancaster, Nebraska (18 percent); but Republican support margin declines were also quite high for their large metropolitan counties (losing nine, e.g., Fresno, San Diego, Bexar, and Chesapeake, Virginia, all down 16 percent, and retaining nine, e.g., Orange, California, –17 percent, Ottawa, Michigan, –20, and Tarrant, Texas, –14 percent).

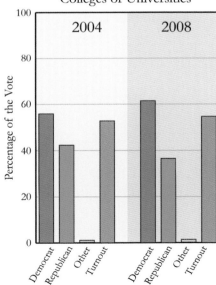

Total U.S. Popular Vote and
Turnout Percentage

Vote and Turnout in the Top 175
Counties With Major
Colleges or Universities

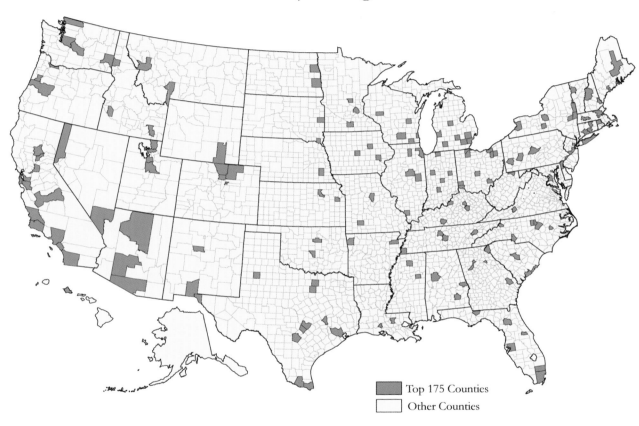

Counties with Major Colleges or Universities

Top 175 Counties
Other Counties

MAP 6.17

■ MILITARY COUNTIES

RICHARD L. MORRILL

The seventy-six counties with the highest absolute numbers or shares in the armed forces were examined in part to find whether they were more Republican than all U.S. counties. While the large majority of these counties (forty-eight) voted Republican, the simple average Democratic share was thus only 47 percent, but in absolute numbers the Democratic share rose significantly from 44 percent of the total vote to 52 percent from 2004 to 2008. Overall, Republicans tended to carry the small metropolitan and nonmetropolitan counties, and Democrats the large metropolitan counties, a generalization that was true for all counties.

Counties that were Democratic in 2004 all became more Democratic in 2008; also, ten counties shifted from the Republican to the Democratic column (eight metropolitan and two nonmetropolitan—see the list below). All Republican counties in large metropolitan areas (six) became less Republican in 2008 (Duval-Jacksonville, Florida; Leavenworth, Kansas; Anne Arundel, Maryland; Sarpy, Nebraska; Greene, Ohio; and Stafford, Virginia), and of nineteen Republican small metropolitan counties, eighteen experienced declines in Republican margins. Of twenty-four Republican nonmetropolitan counties, twenty-two had declines in Republican support. The military counties were certainly not a holdout category for the Republican cause.

In other words, military-dominated counties' experiences were not very different from that of all counties. The military counties were not more or less Democratic and did not shift from Republican to Democratic more or less frequently. Rather, they seemed part of the overall shift in the U.S. electorate in 2008. Overall, there seems to have been a slightly larger shift from Republican to Democratic than for the nation as a whole.

Some of the more interesting shifts from Republican to Democratic, probably for a bundle of reasons, include Chattahoochee, Georgia (Ft. Benning); Kent, Delaware (Dover Air Force Base); Cumberland, North Carolina (Ft. Bragg); Grand Forks, North Dakota (Grand Forks Air Force Base); Charleston, South Carolina (Charleston Air Force Base); Bexar, Texas (San Antonio and Brooks Air Force Base); Cascade, Montana (Malmstrom Air Force Base); Oak Harbor, Washington (Naval Air Station Whidbey Island); Chesapeake, Virginia (Oceana Naval Air Station); and Prince William, Virginia (Ft. Belvoir). These shifts occurred across the spectrum from large metropolitan (Bexar) to nonmetropolitan (Island, Washington). The only Republican increases were in Louisiana (Bossier Parish and Barksdale Air Force Base, and Vernon Parish and Ft. Polk) and Arizona (Cochise County and Fort Huachuca).

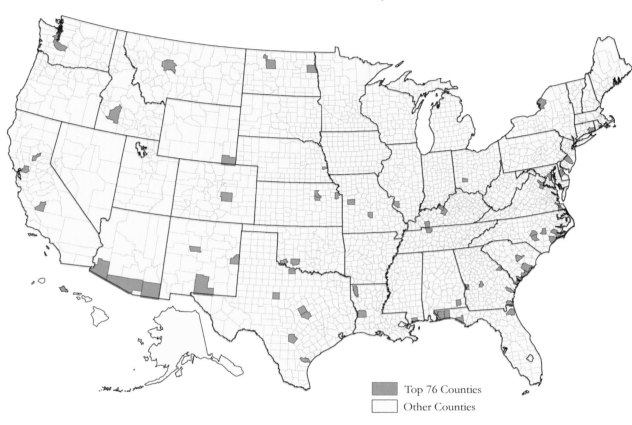

Counties with Military Bases

Top 76 Counties
Other Counties

MAP 6.18

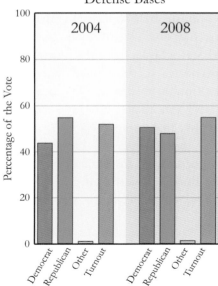

Total U.S. Popular Vote and
Turnout Percentage

2004   2008

Vote and Turnout in the Top 76
Counties With Major
Defense Bases

2004   2008

■ OBAMA, RACE, AND THE 2008 ELECTIONS: DISSIMILARITY INDEX

RYAN D. ENOS

Questions of how Obama's race affected the 2008 election will likely remain long after Obama has left office. When Obama gained the Democratic nomination, many observers thought 2008 would serve as a test of how much the United States has escaped its troubled racial past. To a certain extent, this question was answered decisively: the United States elected an African American president—an outcome that was once unimaginable. This outcome suggests that the racial attitudes of the American electorate have changed dramatically over a period of several decades. But looking more deeply, we can ask how much the political landscape has really changed. Obama's national victory is only one outcome in 2008—there are fifty states and over three thousand counties in the United States—each with different racial histories and circumstances. What about the outcome in each state or in each county? What do these outcomes reveal about how thoroughly the United States broke from the past in 2008? Should we expect areas of the United States with scars of deep racial trouble to support Obama in the same way as areas with a more placid racial past?

We can begin to answer this question by looking at the geography of the election outcome. How different was the support for Obama in different parts of the country? Where does it appear that a legacy of troubled race relations still affected the election outcome?

An obvious starting place is to examine the South in relation to the non-South. While the exceptionalism of the South's racial attitudes is debatable, there is little doubt about the prominent place that race relations played in structuring Southern politics, even until recent times (Key 1949; Carmines and Stimson 1989). Looking at the 2008 election, it appears that the legacy of race relations in the South may have persistent political effects: in counties in the South, Obama received, on average, about nine percentage points less of the vote share than he did in non-Southern counties. Nine percentage points is a tremendous amount considering that in the typical county, nationwide, Obama and McCain were separated by only about 8.5 percentage points.

Obama's poor performance in the South might be due to many factors, but some facts about the 2008 election suggest that the tendency of Southern counties to turn against Obama may reflect the South's legacy of troubled race relations. First, the nearly universal support for Obama among African American voters means that if we account for the number of African Americans in a county, the difference in support for Obama between counties in the South and non-South is almost entirely due to the nonblacks. The nine percentage point disadvantage for Obama in the South takes account of the number of African Americans living in the county, so it was nonblacks who voted nine percentage points less for Obama in the South. Second, we might also note that the South seems like solidly Republican territory, so maybe Obama's poor showing there was something any Democratic candidate should expect. However, this nine percentage point figure accounts for the previous performance of Democrats in the county, so

Obama did even worse in the South than the average Democrat. Moreover, looking at other recent Democratic candidates for president—Bill Clinton, Al Gore, and John Kerry—while all did relatively poorly in Southern counties, none did as poorly as Obama. In fact, Obama typically did twice as poorly in Southern counties, relative to non-Southern counties, as other recent Democratic candidates. Obama is obviously different in many ways from these previous Democratic nominees, but the most glaring difference is his race—so race is a logical, although not conclusive, reason to account for the unusually poor showing for Obama in the South.

So it seems that that even when accounting for their typical anti-Democratic vote, Southern white voters reacted more negatively to Obama than did whites in the rest of the United States—and that they reacted differently than with previous Democratic nominees. This suggests that the legacy of the South's racialized past may still affect political behavior.

But is the story of race and the 2008 election only a story of the South? If it is, then the United States has, indeed, come very far from its troubled racial past. After all, the intertwining of racism and politics was not limited to the South. For example, the openly segregationist George Wallace of Alabama captured states outside the South when seeking the Democratic nomination in 1964. And some scholars have argued that the entire history of American politics is centered on questions of race (Edsall and Edsall 1992). So if race is now a political issue only in the South, then this would be a sign that a good portion of the country has moved away from the troubled race relations of the past.

However, if the influence of race in the 2008 election was not confined to the South, where else might race have mattered? To answer this, we can again look at the places where race seems to have mattered the most in the past: that is, the places in which race drove people to reshape entire cities. Residential racial segregation—that is, racial groups living separately—is a legacy of racial attitudes and institutionally racist policies (Massey and Denton 1993). While the reasons for segregation are too complex to explore here, in some parts of the United States whites and African Americans live in close proximity, while in other parts of the country, whites and African Americans are highly segregated into different areas. Cities in the United States have not always been this way. The bulk of segregation first occurred in the 1950s and 1960s as whites left central cities. This period of residential movement shaped the urban landscape of the United States that is familiar today: largely white suburbs and racial minority central cities (Massey and Denton 1993). Of course, racial segregation occurs for many reasons, but it is probably safe to assume that segregation is, at least, somewhat a reflection of the racial history of a place. The most highly segregated cities, places like Detroit and Chicago, have certainly had periods of significant racial strife (e.g., Sugrue [1996]).

In 2008, for counties in both the South and non-South, racial segregation is closely tied to Obama's performance in the county: the more segregated a county between whites and African Americans, the less well Obama did (segregation is measured by the Dissimilarity Index, which is a commonly used measure that, essentially, asks how separated into different neighborhoods are blacks and whites within a city, county, or other larger unit; see Massey and Denton [1988]). Obama's poor performance in highly segregated counties is found even when we take account of the proportion of blacks in the county, the proportion of Hispanics, the proportion of the county that is urban rather than rural, the median income in the county, and the previous performance of Democratic candidates in the county. The relationship between segregation and less Obama vote is highly statistically significant. So this relationship appears to mean that whites in the areas with the most poignant racial pasts were also the most opposed to Obama. Moreover, the relationship between segregation and support is only found with Obama as the candidate: no such relationship existed when Kerry, Gore, and Clinton were running for president.

Underscoring that the connection between a history of racial tension and support for Obama was not just a Southern phenomenon is the fact that the relationship between segregation and voting for Obama is strongest in the non-South. The effect of segregation on Obama support in a county is more than twice as large in the non-South as it is in the South.

One possible explanation we can offer for this relationship between segregation and Obama vote is persistent racial attitudes: a large number of whites, across the entire United States, that once moved their residences because of negative attitudes about African Americans still have strong enough racial attitudes that they will not vote for a black man for president.

This explanation paints a fairly grim picture of the legacy of racism in the United States: despite Obama's victory, the same attitudes that caused massive residential segregation a half-century ago are still affecting politics today. However, there is another explanation that might be considered more optimistic. Social psychologists have long theorized and tested what is known as the contact hypothesis, which argues that the more contact individuals have with members of another race, the more favorably they tend to view that racial group as a whole (Allport 1954). This view would expect that whites in the most segregated cities should have the most negative view of blacks, not necessarily because of a legacy of racism, but simply because they do not come into contact with many blacks. In more integrated cities, where white voters might be more likely to have African American neighbors or come across African Americans in everyday life, perhaps racist beliefs were mitigated and, therefore, whites were more likely to vote for Obama.

This contact explanation sees American racial attitudes as much less dependent on the past and much more determined by what takes place in the future, and this theory may hold reason to be optimistic about the future of race relations. After all, the exposure of an African American president to the white public is unlike any that has ever before been seen. If contact with African Americans affects white racial attitudes, then the almost daily "contact" on television, in newspapers, and on the Internet with an African American president may have a profound effect on American racial attitudes.

MAP 6.19

Dissimilarity Index Values
2000

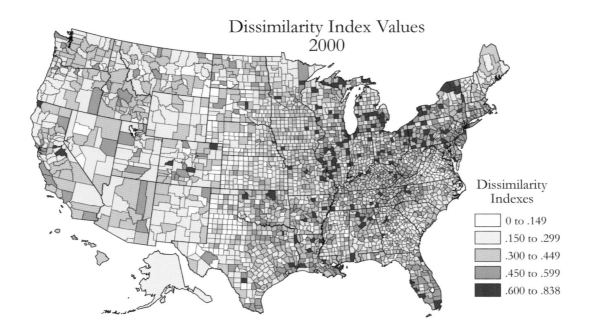

Dissimilarity
Indexes

- 0 to .149
- .150 to .299
- .300 to .449
- .450 to .599
- .600 to .838

Top 200 Counties Having the Highest Dissimilarity Indexes

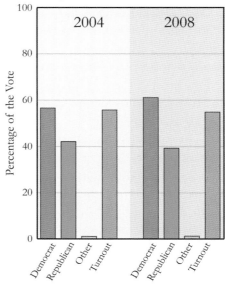

Top 200 and Bottom 200 Counties For
Dissimilarity Index Values
2000

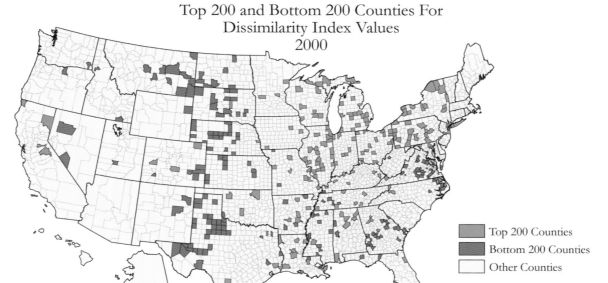

- Top 200 Counties
- Bottom 200 Counties
- Other Counties

Bottom 200 Counties Having the Lowest Dissimilarity Indexes

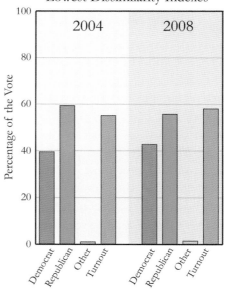

■ ENVIRONMENTALISTS

RICHARD L. MORRILL

Exit polls and widespread commentary on the election results suggested that areas known for their environmental amenities and/or with high membership in environmental organizations, which are generally metropolitan areas with high shares of educated professionals, were more likely to support Democrat Obama for president in 2008. I am grateful to Thomas Wikle, geography professor at Oklahoma State University, for providing an excellent data set of members in three major organizations, the World Wildlife Fund, Nature Conservancy, and the Natural Resources Defense Council. He collected and analyzed the membership data for these three environmental organizations in 1998.

Although the county data used in this analysis are from 1995, they are very useful in our correlating environmental membership patterns with voting results in November 2008. Map 6.20 shows the location quotients for U.S. counties. The quotient is defined as: county numbers/1,000 divided by national members/1,000. Not unexpectedly, there are many more small values (the national mean is .58), because environmentalists are biased to large metropolitan areas. High values are concentrated in counties along the Pacific Coast, the Rocky Mountains, the metropolitan northeast from Virginia to Maine, and peninsular Florida. Moderate values are found in the Great Lakes region. The bias is metropolitan except for widespread rural areas of the scenic West and New England. Low values dominate the South, especially the border South and the Great Plains,

regardless of ethnicity. These low values are similar to the distribution of the county Republican vote in 2008. Exceptions in the South are the prized amenity and university cities, including Austin, Dallas, Houston, Atlanta, and both far western North Carolina and the Raleigh-Durham area.

From the accompanying table, we observe that counties with location quotients below .5 voted 14.5 to 10 million for McCain, that is, almost 60 percent for the Arizona senator. Counties close to the mean (.58), with quotients from .5 to .75, split evenly between the two major parties; and counties with quotients above .75 voted almost 60 percent for Obama. Many of the largest metropolitan areas, including greater Megalopolis, the entire West Coast, Chicago, and much of Florida, voted for Obama.

MAP 6.20

Environmental Group Membership Location Quotient 2008

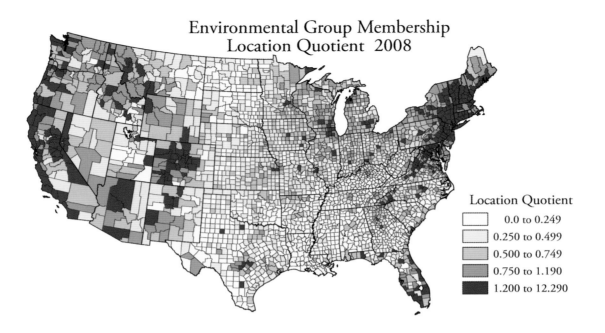

Location Quotient

- 0.0 to 0.249
- 0.250 to 0.499
- 0.500 to 0.749
- 0.750 to 1.190
- 1.200 to 12.290

Top 198 Counties Having High Environmental Group Membership

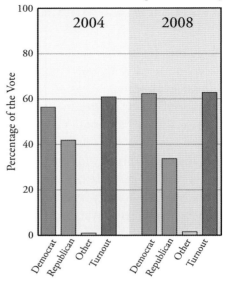

Top 198 and Bottom 200 Counties For Environmental Group Membership 2008

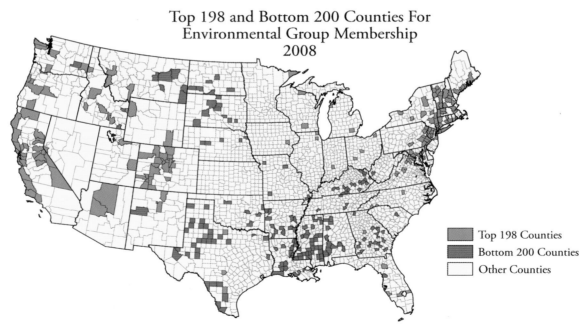

- Top 198 Counties
- Bottom 200 Counties
- Other Counties

Bottom 200 Counties Having Low Environmental Group Membership

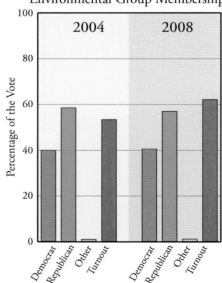

■ FEDERAL EXPENDITURES VERSUS RECEIPTS BY STATE

RICHARD L. MORRILL

No one will be surprised that federal tax revenues from states are not likely to match federal expenditures in those states very closely. Indeed, among the states the ratio of expenditures to receipts varies from a high of 2.02 and 2.03 for Mississippi and New Mexico to a low of .61 and .65 for Nevada and New Jersey. The accompanying map shows these ratios and also illustrates the voter share for Obama. Those states friendly to Obama are rarely rewarded.

There is a moderate inverse correlation showing that Republican states are often the ones receiving the greatest federal benefits, while the Democratic states are often losers in the battle for federal dollars. The correlation is a moderate −.44, since some Democratic states, such as Hawaii, New Mexico, Virginia, and Maryland have many government operations; Republican Texas also receives fewer dollars than it sends (.94). States with high receipts, yet solidly Republican, are Alabama, Alaska, Arkansas, Kentucky, Louisiana, Mississippi, North and South Dakota, Oklahoma, and West Virginia, while the Democratic states of California, Connecticut, Illinois, Massachusetts, Michigan, Minnesota, New Hampshire, New York, Oregon, Washington, and Wisconsin are net payers, mainly because they are among the wealthier states.

MAP 6.21

Federal Expenditures per Dollars Received

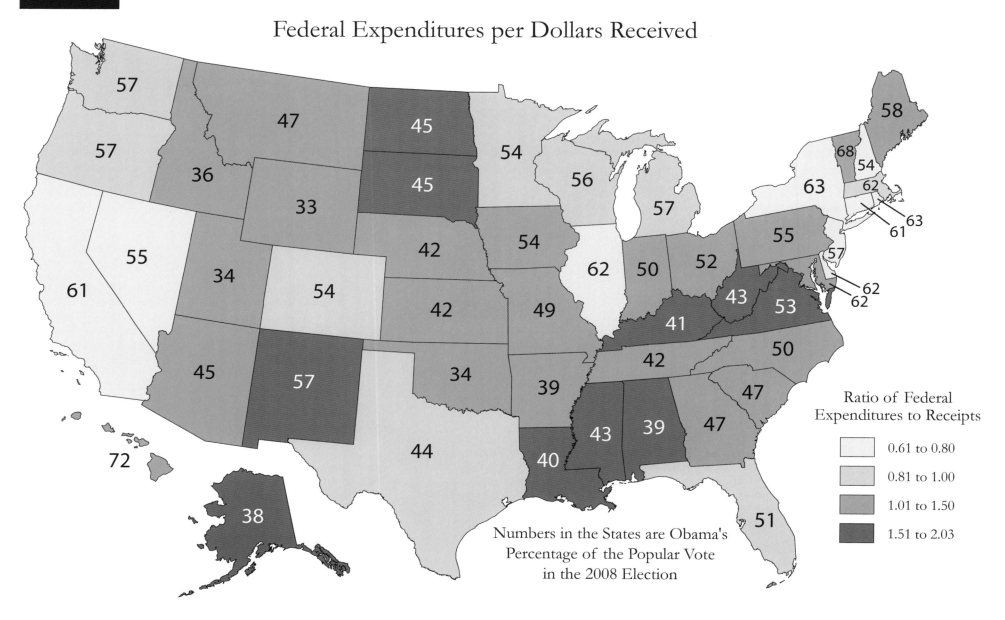

Numbers in the States are Obama's
Percentage of the Popular Vote
in the 2008 Election

Ratio of Federal
Expenditures to Receipts

	0.61 to 0.80
	0.81 to 1.00
	1.01 to 1.50
	1.51 to 2.03

■ MAJOR RACIAL/ETHNIC GROUPS

MARK E. REISINGER AND JOHN W. FRAZIER

INTRODUCTION

Demography in many ways is a good measure of political destiny in the United States. In general, congressional and state representation and electoral votes in presidential elections are apportioned on the basis of population. As a result, demography along with geography significantly determines the allocation of political power in the United States. The projected growth of ethnic populations, especially Hispanics, has profound geopolitical implications for the nation's political life.

In this section we analyze the spatial population distribution of five ethnic groups: Asians, Hispanics, blacks, American Indians, and non-Hispanic whites. In addition, we analyze the voting patterns in the top two hundred counties (percentage) of each group. As might be expected, the spatial population patterns and voting patterns of each group are varied. However, there are some interesting similarities as well. We begin by looking at the Asian population.

ASIAN POPULATION

The Asian population has a long history but has grown rapidly since the 1965 Immigration and Naturalization Act. Historically, the West Coast has been the hearth of Asian settlement. In the last half-century Megalopolis, especially the New York-New Jersey metropolitan region, has become a second major settlement area for ethnic Asians. Finally, the Asian population has dispersed in substantial numbers in recent decades, settling in the American South and interior regions of the country. These patterns are discernable from the accompanying maps.

In map 6.22, the map of the total Asian population by county in 2008 illustrates the dominance of Hawaii and California as Asian population settlement areas. Honolulu County had 384,000 Asians, but Los Angeles has the largest Asian population (nearly 1.3 million) of any U.S. county. Santa Clara County (540,000), Orange County (486,000), and Alameda (360,000) also have large Asian populations. This pattern of relatively large Asian populations continues southward to the U.S.-Mexican border and also spills into Clark County (Las Vegas), Nevada. Smaller but significant clusters of Asian populations occur in the Seattle metropolitan regions, including in King and Snohomish counties, and also Washington County (Portland), Oregon.

Map scale makes counties in the eastern United States more difficult to discern. However, the New York-New Jersey metropolitan region is a significant Asian population center. Queens (494,000) is the anchor, but Kings (236,000), New York (Manhattan) (174,000), Nassau (95,000), and Suffolk (52,000) contribute to this cluster, as do the New Jersey counties of Bergen (128,000), Hudson (68,000), Somerset (41,000), and Morris (41,000).

In northern Megalopolis, the Boston metropolitan area contains three notable counties with Asian populations larger than 50,000: Middlesex (126,827), Suffolk (55,102), and Norfolk (52,000). In southern Megalopolis, counties in the Baltimore and Washington, D.C., metropolitan regions are among the top fifty U.S. counties with the largest Asian populations. These include Fairfax, Virginia (160,000), Montgomery County, Maryland (126,000), Loudoun County, Virginia (36,000), Howard County, Maryland (32,000), and Arlington, Virginia (20,000).

Regarding other U.S. regions with significant Asian populations, two metropolitan regions are distinct. In the Chicago region, Cook (301,000), DuPage (92,000), and Lake (42,000) counties represent a significant cluster of Asians. In the Detroit region, the numbers are smaller, but the combined total of a three-county area (Oakland, Washtenaw, and Macomb) in 2008 was 118,000.

In the South, several counties in Texas and Georgia emerge as having relatively large Asian populations. In the Houston metropolitan region, Harris (221,000) and Fort Bend (80,000) counties are important. In the Dallas-Ft. Worth region, Dallas (109,000), Collin (76,000), Tarrant (73,000), and Denton (36,000) have relatively large Asian populations. There also are relatively large Asian populations in the Austin area, which is located in Travis County, Texas. Finally, the Atlanta region also emerges as a significant and growing cluster of Asian populations, including Gwinnett (75,000), Fulton (44,000), DeKalb (30, 000), and Cobb (29,000) counties.

The second map in map 6.22 illustrates the locations of the Asian population as a percentage of the total county population. In addition to Alaska and Hawaii, the patterns generally reinforce those presented in the previous section: dominance of West Coast counties, especially those in California that spill into Nevada, as well as the metropolitan regions of Oregon and Washington. California counties account for five of the top ten counties (San Francisco, Santa Clara, Alameda, San Mateo, and Orange). The importance of Megalopolis also is apparent from this map. Queens, New York, and Middlesex, Bergen, and Somerset, New Jersey, counties are among the top twenty-five counties for Asians as a percentage of the total population and range between 21.5 percent and 12.8 percent of the county population. In addition to counties previously mentioned in Megalopolis, counties in the Philadelphia metropolitan region, such as Philadelphia, Montgomery, and the Delaware counties are among the top one hundred counties based on their percentages. There also are a few counties outside Megalopolis, such as Broome and Tompkins counties in New York and Centre County, Pennsylvania. All three have major universities (Binghamton, Cornell, and Penn State). The metropolitan regions of Houston, Dallas-Ft. Worth, and Austin, Texas, and Atlanta, Georgia, have the highest percentages among the Southern counties. However, when the Asian percentage of the total population is mapped, other Southern counties also emerge, such as the counties in the Raleigh-Durham-Chapel Hill, North Carolina, region, the Charlotte metropolitan region, and Duval (Jacksonville) and Orange (Orlando) counties in Florida.

Similarly, counties of the Chicago and Detroit regions, urban and suburban, have important Asian populations, as do some additional Midwestern counties where Asian populations may not be as large as those on the two coasts but are a relatively large percentage of the total population. Some of these counties are among the top two hundred Asian county populations in terms of percentage and are noteworthy due to their recent Asian population growth. These include counties in the Columbus, Ohio, Madison, Wisconsin, Minneapolis-St. Paul, Minnesota, Bloomington, Indiana, and Champaign, Illinois, metropolitan regions. All have universities and diversified economies.

Finally, a few counties in the central region of the United States, while not having large numbers of Asians, emerge in the top two hundred map based on their Asian percentage of the total population. These include state capitals and university-based counties, including counties containing Oklahoma City, Oklahoma, and Lincoln and Omaha, Nebraska.

Thus, different portrayals of the Asian population data reveal some interesting patterns. In addition to their bicoastal distribution, these patterns reflect the general dispersal of Asians in the United States, including all regions, but with an apparent attraction to traditional and emerging gateway cities as well as to university-based communities and state capitals, which tend to have stable and diversified economies.

Voter Turnout and Voting in the Top Two Hundred Asian Counties

The voter turnout for the entire nation appears with the maps of the Asian population. The graph indicates that about 58 percent of the registered voters turned out in 2004, while a slightly higher proportion, 59 percent, turned out to vote in 2008.

The overall voter turnout by political party indicates a shift between 2004 and 2008. In 2004, 48 percent of the total voters were registered Democrats while 50 percent were Republicans. In 2000, the Republican turnout amounted to only 44 percent of the total turnout, while the Democrats' share increased to about 55 percent.

In 2004, the total voter turnout for the top two hundred Asian counties was about 56 percent. This increased to 58 percent in 2008. In 2004, 58 percent of the vote went to the Democrats in these two hundred counties. By 2008, that share increase to about 61 percent. Thus, Republican votes slipped as a percentage of the total turnout, from 41 percent to 38 percent. Geographically, these two hundred counties represent the turnout and vote of counties earlier described as indicative of a bicoastal distribution but also representing an Asian population that was dispersing throughout the nation by 2008. Thus, these patterns also indicate the political behaviors of Asians scattered in select Southern urban areas, such as those in Atlanta, Orlando, Houston, Austin, Dallas-Ft. Worth, and an increasing number of Midwestern and Northeastern urban-suburban communities anchored by universities and diversified economies.

THE HISPANIC POPULATION

The maps for the Hispanic population provide distributions of their percentage of the total population and of the two hundred counties with the highest percentage of Hispanics in the total county population. Both maps indicate the importance of the U.S.-Mexican legacy and, in particular, California-Texas and the other borderlands along the southern U.S. border with Mexico. Of the six counties with the largest Hispanic populations over one million, two are in California (Los Angeles and Orange counties), while one each is in Texas (Harris), Arizona (Maricopa), and Florida (Miami-Dade). Only Cook County (Chicago) has more than one million Hispanics in the Midwest. It is noteworthy that all six counties are located in what can be considered as gateway states.

Texas counties (Bexar, Dallas, El Paso, and Hidalgo counties) each have Hispanic populations between one-half and one million persons. Tarrant County (Ft. Worth) has nearly a half-million Hispanics (455,000). California counties in the same Hispanic population range (greater than five hundred thousand and less than one million) include San Bernardino, Riverside, and San Diego counties. In addition, Santa Clara County has nearly a half-million Hispanics (458,000). It becomes clear that the largest number of Hispanics reside in California and the borderlands. These include many Hispanics residing in rural counties, but the largest populations live in metropolitan counties.

Similar patterns occur in less dramatic form in the eastern United States. Clearly, Florida and New York-New Jersey contain the counties with the largest Hispanic populations. Miami-Dade has the fifth-largest Hispanic population among all U.S. counties. Adjacent Florida counties, although having substantially fewer Hispanics, add significantly to the perception of south Florida as a Hispanic region. These include Broward (Ft. Lauderdale) and Palm Beach counties, which together account for 646,000 Hispanics. Orange County (Orlando)

had 267,000 Hispanics in 2008. Finally, the map of the top two hundred counties also reveals the results of what has been termed the Latinization of the South, particularly in counties in the Carolinas and Georgia, such as Mecklenburg, North Carolina (Charlotte) and Gwinnett, Georgia (suburban Atlanta).

Proceeding north along the Atlantic Coast to Megalopolis, three boroughs of New York City contain a combined total of more than 1.5 million Hispanics, including Bronx (720,000), Queens (613,000), Kings (504,000), and New York (401,000) counties. In adjacent New Jersey, Hudson (242,000) and Passaic (174,000) counties contain a combined total of nearly a half-million Hispanics. It is clear that particular gateway states and gateway counties in or near large metropolitan areas contain very large Hispanic populations.

Regarding the Hispanic percentage as a percentage of the total population in each county, the map of the top two hundred counties reinforces the patterns just discussed. California and the borderland states contain counties with the highest percentages of Hispanics. The top ten counties are located in borderland states, and four of these are in Texas (Hidalgo, 89 percent; El Paso, 82 percent; Nueces, 60 percent; and Bexar, 58 percent) and two are in California (Imperial, 77 percent, and Tulare, 58 percent). Only Miami (Dade County, 62 percent) is in a nonborderland state. Overall, Florida has the most counties in the top two hundred of any eastern state.

Outside of the borderland states, the counties with the highest percentages of Hispanics include the historical crop-growing areas of Colorado (Adams,

Arapahoe, and Weld), Idaho (Canyon), and Washington (Yakima), as well as counties in the Midwest and central regions of the nation.

Voter Turnout and Voting in the Top Two Hundred Hispanic Counties

The overall voter turnout for the two hundred counties with the highest percentages of Hispanics appears in the charts accompanying the Hispanic maps. In 2004, about 42 percent of the population voted, whereas 45 percent did so in 2008. A significant shift in votes for the two political parties occurred between the 2004 and 2008 elections in these two hundred "Hispanic" counties. Approximately 42 percent of each party received votes in these counties in 2004. However, a major shift occurred in the 2008 election, when 58 percent of the vote went to Democrats, an increase of 16 percent from 2004. On the other hand, Republicans received only 41 percent in these two hundred "Hispanic" counties. This represents only a 1 percent decline in Republican turnout compared with 2004, but the Democratic Party realized a dramatic increase in the same counties during the period. Geographically, the Hispanic voting pattern disproportionately represents the American West, especially the borderland states and counties, as well as rural areas of northern New Mexico and Texas and rural Colorado, Washington, and Idaho. It also represents rural and urban California and southern and central Florida, as well as the Bronx, New York. This level of voter turnout and resulting voting pattern by Democrats, of course, helped propel Barack Obama into the presidency.

THE BLACK POPULATION

The maps for the U.S. black population and the top two hundred counties with the highest percentage of blacks portray some meaningful facts concerning the black population distribution across the nation. In addition, the accompanying histograms of black voter turnout for the 2004 and 2008 elections provide some further insight into party affiliations of voters for those two elections.

Both maps reflect the black experiences of the nineteenth- and twentieth-century United States. They also represent the results of continuing internal black migration and immigration. Before interpreting the concentrations of blacks by county based on their percentage of the total population and the top two hundred counties where black percentages are highest, it is worthwhile to discuss briefly the processes that contribute to these patterns.

The American South was the long-established location of blacks due to the legacy of slavery. The Chesapeake Bay region of Virginia and Maryland and, secondly, the Carolinas served as the initial focus of black slavery and population concentration. By the mid-1800s a shift to the Deep South, particularly the Southern states within the Mississippi River Delta region, had occurred. These two geographic patterns have long persisted as focal points of African American settlement. Both patterns are apparent in the two maps of black population in 2008. In fact, counties stretching from the Chesapeake Bay region to eastern Texas shape a distinct crescent of black settlement in the United States.

The map of the top two hundred black counties illustrates the core of this distribution. The leading twelve counties in terms of rank based on the highest percentages of blacks are in the Washington, D.C.-Baltimore region (Prince George's County, 66 percent black; Baltimore City, 63 percent; Washington, D.C., 52 percent) and farther south, in the Norfolk-Virginia Beach area (Portsmouth County, 52 percent). Others among the top dozen are in the Deep South, including two counties in the Atlanta metro area (Clayton County, 61 percent; DeKalb County, 53 percent) and one that borders the South Carolina-Georgia metropolitan area of Augusta-Aiken (Richard County, 51 percent). Hinds County (Jackson), Mississippi, had the highest black percentage of any U.S. county—66.4 percent in 2008. All twelve of these largest of the top two hundred black counties had black population percentages exceeding 50 percent in 2008. The remaining of these counties are New Orleans, Louisiana (New Orleans, 61 percent), Jefferson, Arkansas (Little Rock, 53 percent), and Shelby, Tennessee (Memphis, 50.7 percent).

Extending this perspective to the next thirteen counties (or top twenty-five overall) with the highest percentages of blacks in 2008 largely reinforces the American South pattern and includes some counties with relatively large black populations, notably St. Louis, Missouri; Richland (Columbia), South Carolina; East Baton Rouge, Louisiana; and Fulton County (Atlanta), Georgia.

This discussion would also be incomplete without the mention of the urbanization, especially since 1940, and the relatively recent suburbanization of blacks. The Great Migration, which occurred between 1910 and 1970, greatly influenced the population of various counties in the northern and western United States. Some counties appear on the map of the population, 2008. Many have both large black populations and, due to the legacy of black/white segregation, large percentages of blacks. Another factor influencing some of these "black" counties is the rapid growth of black immigrants from Africa and the Caribbean. In many cases, black immigrants have strong financial and/or social capital, which permits direct settlement in the suburbs of major metropolitan regions. Combined with the positive outcomes of the civil rights movements of the 1960s, black suburbanization exploded in recent decades, particularly within major metropolitan areas that already contained large black populations. As a direct result, one-third of all blacks resided in suburbia by 2000.

Among the northern counties with relatively large black populations are the locations of historically early black populations, including the New York City boroughs, Chicago (Cook County), Boston, and Philadelphia. In the case of New York City, four boroughs contained about 1.9 million blacks in 2008. These are Kings (Brooklyn, 844,000 and 33 percent), Bronx (46,000 and 31 percent), Queens (414,000 and 18 percent), and New York (219,000 and 13 percent) counties. Until recently, Cook County (Chicago) claimed the highest black population in the United States at 1.3 million. Blacks accounted for almost 25 percent of the total. Philadelphia was one of the earliest northern cities with black settlement. By 2008 it had 615,000, or 42 percent, of the total population. New Castle County, Delaware, and Delaware County, Pennsylvania, parts of the same metropolitan region, had 118,000 and 100,000, respectively, in 2008; these amounted to 22 percent and 18 percent of those counties' populations. In the case of the Boston area, Suffolk County's black population was 138,000, or 19 percent of its total. Although Suffolk's black population is much smaller than those previously mentioned northern cities and counties, its black percentage of the total population is substantially higher than the national average.

The later stages of the Great Migration swelled the black populations and black percentage of other cities and counties in the North, South, and West. In the North, Wayne County (Detroit) became a growing black center (785,000 in 2008 and 40 percent of its total population). Other areas included Essex County (Newark), New Jersey (305,000 and 40 percent), Cuyahoga County (Cleveland), Ohio (368,000 and 29 percent), Marion County (Indianapolis), Indiana (219,000 and 25 percent), and Milwaukee County (Milwaukee), Wisconsin (233,188 and 24 percent).

In the South, Atlanta was an early focus of black settlement; it became the largest U.S. black community in the region by 2008, due in part to the "Black Reverse (or Return) Migration" that began in 1965 and continues to the present. The Atlanta region included these leading black counties: Fulton (430,000 and 42 percent), Rockdale (33,000 and 40 percent), Newton (35,000 and 36 percent), Douglas (45,000 and 35 percent), Henry (62,000 and 32 percent), Cobb (160,000 and 23 percent), and Gwinnett (163,000 and 21 percent).

Texas and Florida counties and cities also are a part of the growing Southern black population increases. The Houston region contains Harris County (714,000 and 18 percent), Fort Bend County (107,000 and 20 percent), and Jefferson County (83,000 and 34 percent), among other counties displayed on the map of black population percentages in 2008. The Dallas-Ft. Worth (477,000 and 20 percent) region includes Tarrant County (Ft. Worth) (237,000 and 13.5 percent), and Smith County (36,000 and 18 percent).

Several Florida counties have significant long-term African American neighborhoods and also have benefited from the recent African and Afro-Caribbean immigrant populations. Although south Florida is typically viewed as a center of Hispanic settlement, a large black population is also present. Three south Florida counties have both traditional black settlements and black immigrants; together they have more than one million blacks: Dade County (Miami, 424,000 and 17 percent), Broward County (Ft. Lauderdale, 419,000 and 24 percent), and Palm Beach County (194,000 and 15 percent). All three exceed the national county average black population. Other significant black settlements occur in the Jacksonville-Orlando, Tampa, and Tallahassee metropolitan areas of northern and central Florida.

There are few counties in the Great Plains and the western United States with large numbers and percentages of black population. Due to the latter phase of the Great Migration, blacks migrated to cities and counties on the California coast and, to a lesser degree, the Seattle region of Washington. Blacks are present in significant percentages in counties in the San Francisco-Oakland, Los Angeles, and San Diego metropolitan areas.

Voter Turnout and Voting in the Top Two Hundred Black Counties

The bar graphs depict the black voter turnout and voting patterns by political parties in the two hundred U.S. counties with the highest percentage of blacks in 2008. These patterns are similar to the Hispanics, but their two hundred counties represent more different geographical patterns than the Hispanics. The black patterns are largely concentrated in a crescent shape from Virginia westward into the Deep South and Mississippi Delta region. The turnout and voting pattern indicate the traditional strength of the Democratic Party in these areas of black dominance. Overall voter turnout in these two hundred counties increased from 53 percent to 59 percent between the 2004 and 2008 elections. Republican votes represented only 37 percent of the votes there in 2004 and decreased to 29 percent in 2008. The Democratic vote in the same counties constituted 62 percent of the 2004 total votes and 70 percent in the 2008 election. These patterns of high voter turnout of blacks and other Democrats and the black and other minority votes for Democrats helped propel Barack Obama into the White House in 2008.

AMERICAN INDIANS

The inhabitants of the Americas prior to the arrival of Europeans in the late fifteenth century are the ancestors of today's American Indians; they are the original Americans. In the nearly five hundred years that have followed the initial European contact, they have been reduced in rank to one of the smallest of the American minorities. They occupied lands that now form the contiguous United States and Alaska. Most of their descendants are now either intermingled with non-American Indians in urbanized landscapes or reside on reservations. Their concentrations are not uniformly distributed within the nation. The modern distribution of American Indian peoples reflects historical patterns of the national growth of the United States and federal government policies that were developed to deal with them.

American Indians are, in a modern sense, a minority among minorities. Although once the dominant population of the Western Hemisphere, disease, war, famine, and interracial mixing have reduced their numbers and diluted the purity of bloodlines. It may be concluded, then, that despite the relatively high birthrate among American Indians, drastic population reductions between the time of initial European contact to the present have resulted in a populace that is about the same size now as it was five hundred years ago. American Indian populations now appear to be growing at a relatively rapid rate. When compared to other racial and ethnic minorities, however, the American Indian ranks a distant fourth after Hispanics, blacks, and Asians.

Five states, all in the Southwest, contain 46 percent of the total Indian population. In rank order, these states are Oklahoma, California, Arizona, New Mexico, and Texas. Our maps support this pattern as they show that the counties with a high proportion are concentrated in the West and Southwest. Texas is the exception, as it has a relatively large American Indian population, but it does not make up a large proportion in any single county. A northern fragmented tier of states contain 15 percent of the total American Indian population. These states include, in rank order, Washington, New York, Michigan, South Dakota, and Minnesota. Again, the maps of American Indian population illustrate this, with each of these states mentioned having counties where American Indians are a significant proportion of the total population. Alaska, with its large Eskimo (Inuit) and Aleut population, has a little over 4 percent. The remaining American Indian population is spread throughout the United States.

From a historical perspective, American Indian populations have changed quantitatively and spatially.

As previously noted, disease and warfare initially reduced their numbers, and later, relocation policies and practices gradually shifted the Indians to the western portions of the country. Even though Indian populations have grown through natural increase in the past several decades, they remain concentrated in the western half of the country.

Voter Turnout and Voting in the Top Two Hundred American Indian Counties

The overall voter turnout in these counties remained about the same, at about 58 percent, in both 2004 and 2008. Republican votes represented about 58 percent of the votes in 2004 and decreased only slightly to about 57 percent in 2008. The Democratic vote in these same counties constituted 41 percent of the 2004 total votes and 42 percent in 2008. Several of the states that contain a large proportion of American Indians are considered to be traditional red states, that is, states that typically form a base for the Republican Party. Again, these two hundred counties are strongly regional and illustrate patterns that disproportionately represent the American West.

NON-HISPANIC WHITE POPULATION

The counties with the highest proportion of non-Hispanic whites are concentrated above a line about 37

degrees north. The concentration of these counties is particularly evident in the Upper Midwest, the East (especially west of the cities that comprise Megalopolis), and the Great Plains. The northern section of the South, especially West Virginia and Kentucky, also contain a significant number of counties that have a high proportion of non-Hispanic whites. This ethnic group is most certainly an urban/suburban population. However, the counties with very high proportions of non-Hispanic whites appear to be rural in nature. For example, counties such as Tuscarawas, Ohio, Blair and Butler, Pennsylvania, Oswego, New York, Harrison, West Virginia, Grand Traverse, Michigan, and Gallatin, Montana were all above 95 percent white in 2008.

It is worth noting the lack of ethnic diversity in these top two hundred counties. All are greater than 87 percent non-Hispanic white. The top fifty counties are greater than 93 percent white and include counties in Ohio, Pennsylvania, Maine, Missouri, New Hampshire, Wisconsin, and New York for the most part. The second fifty counties fall between 91 and 93 percent non-Hispanic white. The same states appear in this group with the addition of counties in Michigan, Rhode Island, Massachusetts, Vermont, Idaho, Iowa, Tennessee, Kentucky, and West Virginia. Many of the counties in Tennessee, Kentucky, West Virginia, and Pennsylvania are the traditional coal mining areas. The next one hundred counties ranged between 87 and 91 percent non-Hispanic white. These counties are concentrated in states such as Iowa, Nebraska, North and South Dakota, and eastern Montana.

Voter Turnout and Voting in the Top Two Hundred Non-Hispanic White Counties

These counties had an overall voter turnout of approximately 61 percent in 2004, a percentage that decreased slightly to about 59 percent for the 2008 election. One feature that stands out in these counties is that they were fairly consistent in their voting patterns. In 2004 Republicans received about 59 percent of the votes and Democrats 40 percent. In 2008 there was little change as the Republicans took 58 percent of the vote and Democrats 41 percent. In both years "other" received 1 percent of the vote. The top two hundred counties are in Republican stronghold states, including West Virginia, Kentucky, Iowa, Nebraska, Montana, and the Dakotas; all are traditionally more conservative and tend to vote for Republican candidates. However, several of these states are relatively small in population and have few votes in the Electoral College; thus collectively, they do not have a substantial impact on election outcomes.

SUMMARY

The ethnic makeup of the United States is changing dramatically, both quantitatively and spatially. Through the processes of migration, immigration, and variations in natural increase, new ethnic concentrations are being formed and old ones are being dismantled. Increasingly, these new quantitative and spatial patterns will be reflected in the voting patterns that emerge. The most recent presidential election in 2008 illustrates a bifurcation in the voting patterns of the various ethnic groups in the United States. Democrats increased their share of the vote among Asians, blacks, and possibly more significantly, Hispanics during the 2008 election. Republicans, on the other hand, continue to receive the majority of non-Hispanic white and American Indian votes.

The Asian and Hispanic population continues to grow in the United States, and these two groups constitute an increasing percentage of the population. The black population percentage remains fairly stable. If these trends continue, this may favor the Democrats in future elections. This is especially true as the non-Hispanic white and American Indian proportion of the population, the Republican "base," continues to decline. Of course, the Republicans may change their politics in an effort to attract voters from the growing ethnic groups. The spatial distribution of the various ethnic populations is important as well. Non-Hispanic whites maintain a proportional advantage in several large states in the Midwest and North that gives them an advantage in the Electoral College. As the spatial patterns of Asian, Hispanic, and black populations change through migration and immigration, the non-Hispanic white distribution in the key Electoral College states may be diluted. These trends are difficult to project, but there is little doubt but that the political outcomes of the future in the United States will be influenced by the quantitative and spatial population patterns of these ethnic groups.

Asian Population
2008

Percentage of
Total Population

	0.0 to 3.9
	4.0 to 7.9
	8.0 to 15.9
	16.0 to 31.9
	32.0 to 58.2

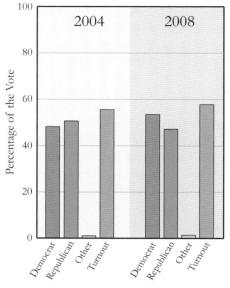

Total U.S. Popular Vote and
Turnout Percentage

Top 200 Counties Having the Greatest Asian Population
2008

	Top 200 Counties
	Other Counties

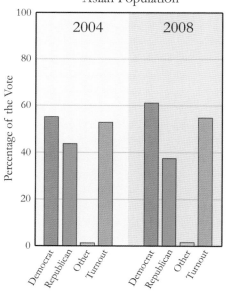

Vote and Turnout in the Top 200
Counties Having the Greatest
Asian Population

Hispanic Population
2008

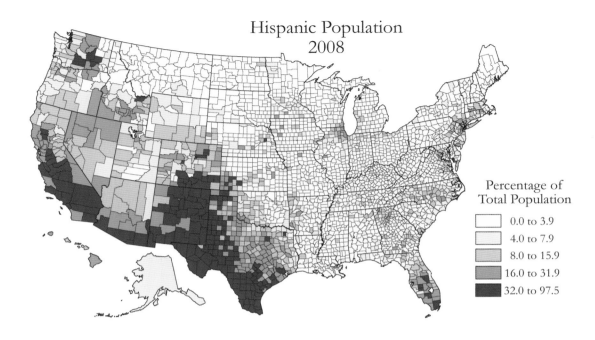

Percentage of
Total Population

- 0.0 to 3.9
- 4.0 to 7.9
- 8.0 to 15.9
- 16.0 to 31.9
- 32.0 to 97.5

Total U.S. Popular Vote and Turnout Percentage

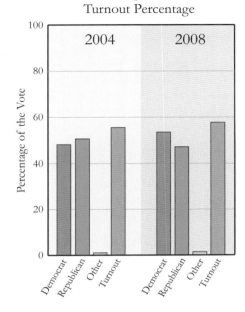

2004   2008

Percentage of the Vote

Democrat Republican Other Turnout   Democrat Republican Other Turnout

MAP 6.23

Top 200 Counties Having the Greatest Hispanic Population 2008

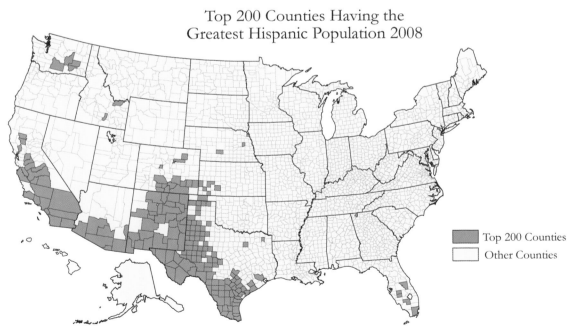

- Top 200 Counties
- Other Counties

Vote and Turnout in the Top 200 Counties Having the Greatest Hispanic Population

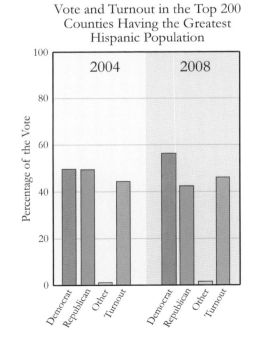

2004   2008

Percentage of the Vote

Democrat Republican Other Turnout   Democrat Republican Other Turnout

MAP 6.24

Black Population 2008

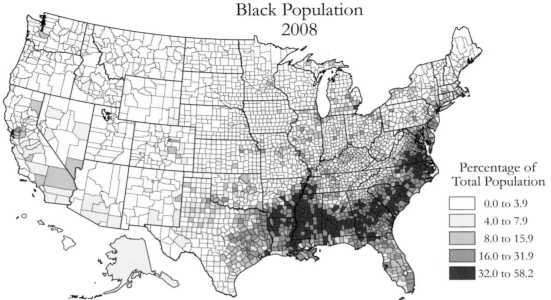
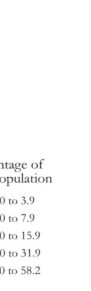

Percentage of
Total Population

	0.0 to 3.9
	4.0 to 7.9
	8.0 to 15.9
	16.0 to 31.9
	32.0 to 58.2

Total U.S. Popular Vote and Turnout Percentage

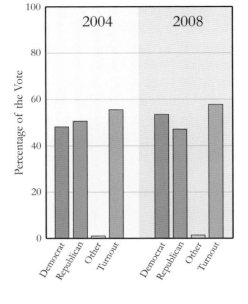

Top 200 Counties Having the Greatest Black Population 2008

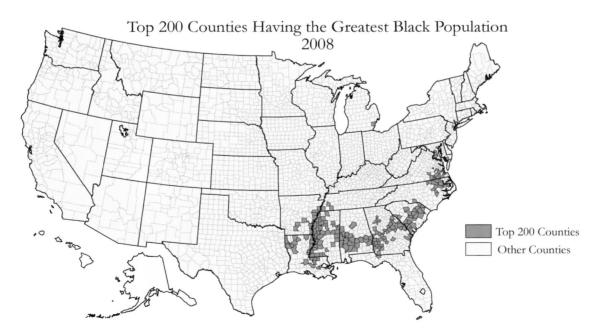

	Top 200 Counties
	Other Counties

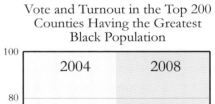

Vote and Turnout in the Top 200 Counties Having the Greatest Black Population

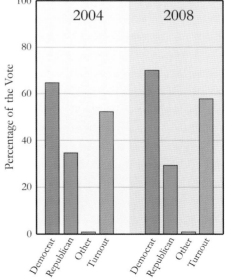

MAP 6.25

American Indian Population 2008

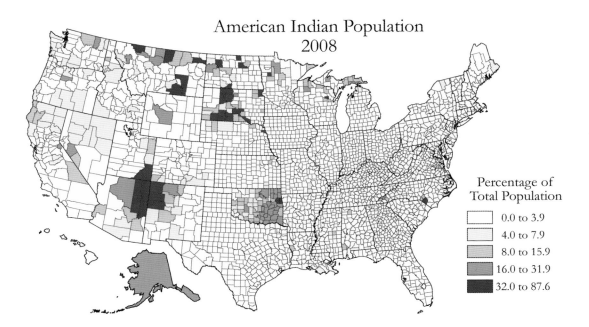

Percentage of
Total Population

☐ 0.0 to 3.9
☐ 4.0 to 7.9
☐ 8.0 to 15.9
☐ 16.0 to 31.9
☐ 32.0 to 87.6

Total U.S. Popular Vote and Turnout Percentage

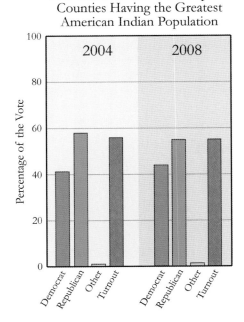

Top 200 Counties Having the Greatest American Indian Population 2008

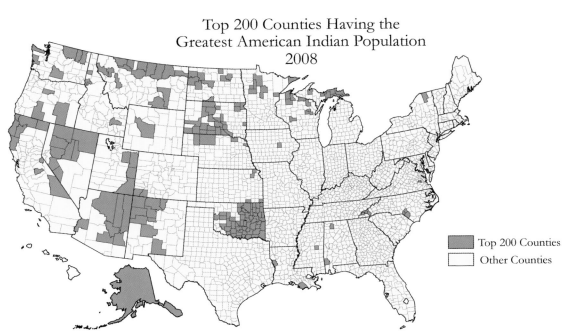

☐ Top 200 Counties
☐ Other Counties

Vote and Turnout in the Top 200 Counties Having the Greatest American Indian Population

MAP 6.26

Non-Hispanic White Population 2008

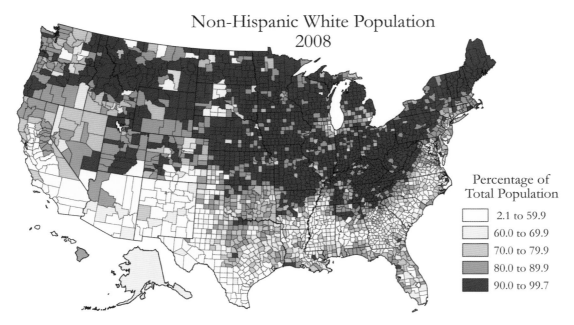

Percentage of Total Population

- 2.1 to 59.9
- 60.0 to 69.9
- 70.0 to 79.9
- 80.0 to 89.9
- 90.0 to 99.7

Top 200 Counties Having the Greatest Non-Hispanic White Population 2008

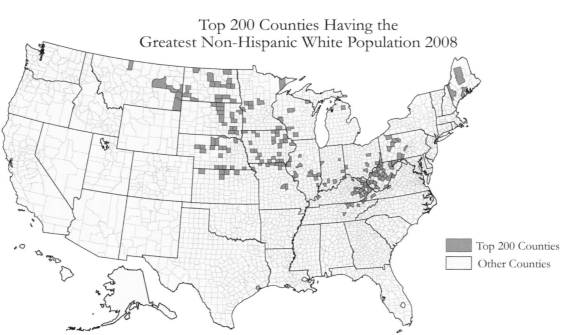

- Top 200 Counties
- Other Counties

Total U.S. Popular Vote and Turnout Percentage

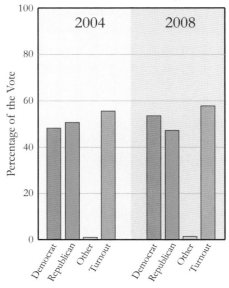

Vote and Turnout in the Top 200 Counties Having the Greatest Non-Hispanic White Population

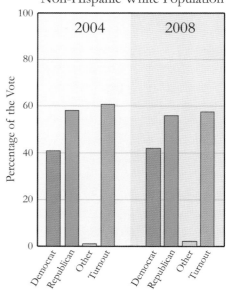

■ LATINO VOTERS IN THE 2008 ELECTIONS

MELISSA R. MICHELSON

For half a century, observers have noted the potential political power of the growing Latino population in the United States. Because both major political parties see Latino partisan loyalty as relatively undecided, in recent election cycles Latinos increasingly have been the target of campaign outreach. Yet Latinos have repeatedly fallen short of their potential. Latino voter turnout is low, and most Latinos do not live in swing states. In 2008, Latino turnout increased significantly, in part due to increased mobilization efforts and also in part due to the historic nature of the campaign; yet while Latinos played some role in the primary contests, their votes were not crucial to Barack Obama's general election victory.

In the early 1960s, commentators began to refer to the Latino population in the Southwest as a "sleeping giant" that could soon become a potent economic and political force (García 2003: 18). Subsequent decades saw continued "sleeping giant" references, but despite increasing Latino turnout and increasing numbers of Latino elected officials, Latinos were repeatedly unable to transform this potential into true political power in the national arena, even in the very close election of 2000 (Garcia and Sanchez 2007). Both the 2000 and 2004 presidential elections were decided by relatively small margins in states with growing Latino populations, making Latinos potential kingmakers in the 2008 general election. This was enhanced by the increasingly widespread perception—somewhat exaggerated at the time—that Latinos were fairly open to voting Republican and not necessarily committed to the Democratic Party, as

evidenced by results from the 2000 election, when 40 percent of Latinos voted for Republican George W. Bush (Leal et al. 2005). Latinos were also expected to be a factor in many primary battles for both parties. Thus, in 2008 both during the primary campaign and during the general election, more resources than ever were spent in pursuit of Latino support.

Increasing population size and a shifting electoral context brought Latinos into play in 2008 as never before. From 2000 to 2008, the size of the Latino population grew from 35.2 million to 46.8 million, growing from 12.5 percent of the population to 15.4 percent. The black population, meanwhile, grew from 12.0 percent to 12.1 percent, while the white non-Latino population shrank from 69.1 percent to 65.4 percent (Pew Hispanic Center 2010). Latinos are the fastest-growing racial/ethnic group in the country and are predicted by the U.S. Census to make up a third of the U.S. population by 2050 (U.S. Census Bureau 2008). Most states with significant Latino populations are generally considered safely Republican (e.g., Texas) or Democratic (e.g., California), and thus they are not the focus of significant efforts by presidential election campaigns. The one exception to this is Florida, where both 2004 campaigns expended considerable resources reaching out to Latino voters (de la Garza 2008). In 2008, however, several Latino-heavy states were considered battlegrounds, including not only Florida but also Colorado, Nevada, and New Mexico.

Both campaigns were more visibly seeking Latino support than in prior elections, as evidenced by their speeches to major Hispanic organizations,

Spanish-language websites, and major advertisement buys on Spanish-language television stations. Within the same fifteen-day period in the summer of 2008, Barack Obama and John McCain spoke at national meetings of the National Council of La Raza (NCLR), the League of United Latin American Citizens (LULAC), and the National Association of Latino Elected and Appointed Officials (NALEO). The Internet also saw major outreach to the Latino community (Dannheisser 2008).

In addition to candidate- and party-driven efforts, community organizations spent significant resources during the 2008 election cycle to register and mobilize Latino voters. Organized under the umbrella campaign *Ya Es Hora, ¡Ve y Vota!* (It's Time, Go Vote!), community groups walked precincts, conducted phone banks, held forums, and distributed Spanish-language voter guides. The nonpartisan effort was seen as the culmination of the effort that began in the spring of 2006, when groups marched for immigrant rights in protest of proposed new federal legislation under signs proclaiming, "Ahora marchamos, mañana votamos (Now we march, tomorrow we vote)." This was followed by community organization efforts to naturalize Latino and Asian immigrants; the third phase was to get those new citizens registered and to the polls. Spanish-language media worked to increase Latino turnout independently of ad buys by the candidates and political parties. Spanish-language newspapers included voter registration cards in their weekend editions, while radio and television stations ran public service announcements urging participation (Gorman 2008).

Latino turnout surged in both the primary and general election cycles, reflecting both the competitiveness of the race and increased mobilization efforts by campaigns and community organizations. According to a postelection survey by the Pew Hispanic Center, 74 percent of Latinos were more interested in the 2008 election than in the 2004 election, and 38 percent said they were contacted and encouraged to register to vote or to get out to vote by a partisan and/or a nonpartisan campaign (Lopez and Livingston 2009). Further, among those reporting that they were contacted, 59 percent said they were contacted by the Obama campaign, while 43 percent said they were contacted by the McCain campaign. While the Obama campaign may thus have contacted more Latino voters, that such a strong proportion of Latino respondents indicated that they were contacted by the Republican candidate emphasizes the conventional wisdom that Latinos were persuadable and not committed to the Democratic Party.

Two-thirds (67 percent) of Latino voters supported Democrat Barack Obama in his successful presidential bid in November 2008 (Lopez 2008). While the Democratic leanings of Latinos in 2008 did not nearly approach the 95 percent rate of support for Obama among black voters, it is still a stronger Democratic tendency than for white voters, who were split 43 percent to 55 percent in favor of McCain (Lopez 2008; Preston 2008). While Latinos may not have been crucial to the outcome of the general election, given Obama's sweeping victory, they were a major player in the Democratic Party primary season. Hillary Clinton would not have won the primaries in California, Texas, or New Mexico if Latinos had not voted in such large numbers and had not supported her by such large margins (Minushkin and Lopez 2008). In Texas, 32 percent of those who went to the polls were Latino, as were 30 percent of those voting in California, up from 24 percent and 16 percent, respectively, in 2004. Latinos also made up 35 percent of New Mexico primary voters. In all three states, Latinos preferred Clinton over Obama by two to one. This support stemmed from name recognition for the former first lady and also from a history of outreach to the Latino community by both Clintons reaching back as far as 1968, when Hillary Clinton helped organize Latino voters in San Antonio. Strong Latino support for Clinton kept the nomination in play through the final contests on June 3.

Latinos also were a major factor in the Republican nominating contests. In 2007, Rudy Giuliani was the front-runner, with double-digit leads in the polls, but in January 2008 Mike Huckabee surged ahead in the Iowa caucuses, McCain won in New Hampshire and South Carolina, and Mitt Romney came out on top in Michigan and Nevada. The race then moved to Florida, with McCain as the tentative new leader. McCain entered the race with a strong record of promoting immigration reform and of support among Latinos in his home state of Arizona, winning 74 percent of the Latino vote in his most recent Senate race (CNN 2004). César Martínez, president of MAS Consulting Group and a member of the McCain campaign team, credits Florida with giving McCain the crucial win in the state and thus cementing his new position (which he then finalized on Super Tuesday a week later). "It was that Latino vote that made John McCain win the primary vote in Florida, and the rest is history."[3]

Despite their influence on the election outcomes, Latinos have historically failed to exert their full potential political power. The 2008 election was no exception. Rates of Latino voting lag far behind those of non-Latino whites and African Americans. This long-standing pattern of low voter turnout is generally due to a variety of factors: lower levels of citizenship, lower levels of English-language proficiency, and low median levels of age, income, and education, all of which are strong predictors of turnout. Even among Latinos eligible to vote, participation lags behind that of whites and blacks. In November 2008, 65.2 percent of blacks and 66.1 percent of whites voted, compared with only 49.9 percent of Latino citizens and only 31.6 percent of the Latino voting-age population (U.S. Census Bureau 2009; File 2008; Holder 2006). Despite representing 15.4 percent of the population, Latinos constituted only 7 percent of the electorate in November 2008; blacks were 12 percent; and whites, 76 percent (Hess and Herman 2009).

It is unclear the degree to which candidate, party, and independent organization-led efforts are responsible for the unprecedented level of Latino participation seen in the 2008 primaries and general election. As with non-Latinos, excitement for this election cycle was high. Latinos were likely to vote because of the closeness of the Democratic Party nomination contest, the presence of a Republican candidate in the primaries who was friendly on immigration reform, and the historic nature of the Obama candidacy. Regardless of what spurred increased Latino turnout in 2008, their influence was felt in the primary races, and Latinos are sure to be a visible and highly courted community in future election contests.

■ FOREIGN-BORN POPULATION

RICHARD L. MORRILL

Areas with higher shares of the foreign born strongly supported Obama. The two hundred counties with the highest shares voted 61 percent Democratic, while the two hundred counties with the lowest foreign-born share voted only 41 percent for Obama. The high share of counties contained 60 million people; they voted 27.5 million Democratic to 16.4 million Republican, compared to only 2 million total population in the low-foreign-born share counties; they voted 470,000 Democratic to 652,000 Republican.

While the largest area of high shares of the foreign born are clearly Hispanic areas along the border with Mexico, in Texas, Arizona, and New Mexico and extending into Oklahoma and southwestern Kansas, they also concentrate in eastern Washington (the Columbia Basin irrigation project) and Florida (from Cuba and Latin America, generally). Large absolute numbers are of a broader immigrant origin, including from Europe and Asia, and are concentrated in the economic capitals of New York, Boston, Washington-Baltimore, Chicago, Denver, Atlanta, and Seattle. The dominant pattern of change from 2004 to 2008 for these counties was their increased Democratic shares, reduced Republican shares, and switches from Republican to Democratic, including several major cities in California, Florida, and Texas.

Areas with the lowest foreign-born shares also form a distinctive pattern, amazingly coincident with the Mississippi, Ohio, and Missouri river basins of the American heartland, in Appalachia, the east South central region (Louisiana, Mississippi, Arkansas, and Alabama) and into Missouri, Nebraska, and the Dakotas; these are often areas of economic stagnation. In contrast to the pattern of change for the counties with high foreign-born shares, the low-share counties are overwhelmingly Republican. While almost half the counties had declining Republican shares, several had increased Republican shares, mainly in Kentucky and Arkansas.

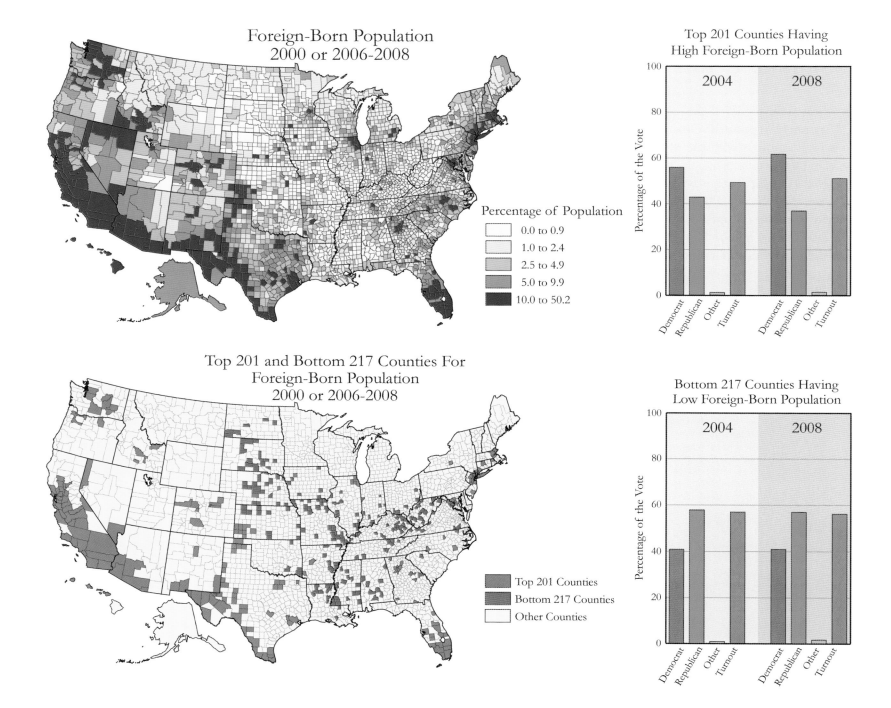

MAP 6.27

Foreign-Born Population
2000 or 2006-2008

Top 201 Counties Having
High Foreign-Born Population

Percentage of Population
0.0 to 0.9
1.0 to 2.4
2.5 to 4.9
5.0 to 9.9
10.0 to 50.2

Top 201 and Bottom 217 Counties For
Foreign-Born Population
2000 or 2006-2008

Bottom 217 Counties Having
Low Foreign-Born Population

Top 201 Counties
Bottom 217 Counties
Other Counties

■ RELIGION

BARNEY WARF

The American religious landscape reflects a long history of different faiths in the country, which exhibit enormous and growing diversity. As a magnet for waves of immigrants from around the world, the United States is one of the most religiously diverse societies in the world. Christians of different denominations still comprise 84 percent of the total population, but that proportion has gradually declined in the face of growing non-Christian immigration, particularly in larger cities. Religion has played an important role in American politics since the country's founding. The recent rise of politically conservative Protestants is perhaps the most visible recent face of this phenomenon.

Catholics represent the largest single faith in the United States and form substantial shares of the electorate in New England, New York, Wisconsin, and much of the Southwest. The Catholic population is diverse culturally and politically and includes Irish, Polish, Italian, Portuguese, and Latin American constituencies. As a whole, Catholics tended to vote more heavily Democratic in 2008 than they did in 2004.

Protestant denominations tend to be politically and culturally conservative and support Republican presidential candidates. Baptists, the largest Protestant denomination, are mostly concentrated in the South. Major segments include the Southern Baptist Convention, which is largely white, and the African American Baptist tradition. Traditionally conservative and Republican, Baptists voted overwhelmingly for McCain. Methodists tend to be clustered in Appalachia and in parts of the Great Plains. Such areas tended to vote overwhelmingly Republican. The Mormons, or Church of Jesus Christ of Latter-day Saints, are a uniquely American denomination highly concentrated in Utah, southern Idaho, and a few other Western states. Pentecostals, clustered largely in the Pacific Northwest and with a few pockets throughout the Midwest, also tended to vote Republican.

Two small religious groups in the United States tended to vote Democratic in 2008, however. Muslims, who are found mostly in the Detroit region, New York, and Southern California, cast their votes decisively for Barack Obama. Similarly, Jews, who are found in three clusters in the Northeast, southern Florida, and the Southwest, also voted heavily for the Democratic candidate.

Religious diversity is a complex phenomenon that can be measured in many ways. The Shannon Index, a widely used measure of diversity, indicates that the most religiously diverse counties of the country tend to be found in the Pacific Northwest and in a belt running horizontally across Illinois to Washington, D.C. In part, this pattern reflects the geography of ethnic diversity. Generally speaking, the more religiously diverse counties were in 2008, the more likely they were to vote Democratic; in contrast, counties with little religious diversity—typically rural and white—voted heavily Republican. In short, religious diversity both reflects and contributes to the complicated quilt of voters that forms the American electoral landscape.

MAP 6.28

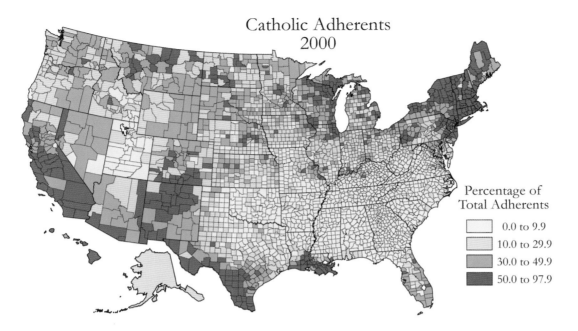

Catholic Adherents
2000

Percentage of
Total Adherents

0.0 to 9.9
10.0 to 29.9
30.0 to 49.9
50.0 to 97.9

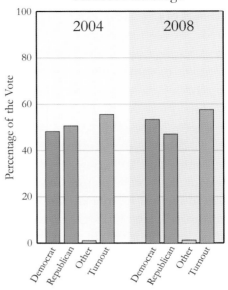

Total U.S. Popular Vote and
Turnout Percentage

Percentage of the Vote

2004   2008

Democrat Republican Other Turnout   Democrat Republican Other Turnout

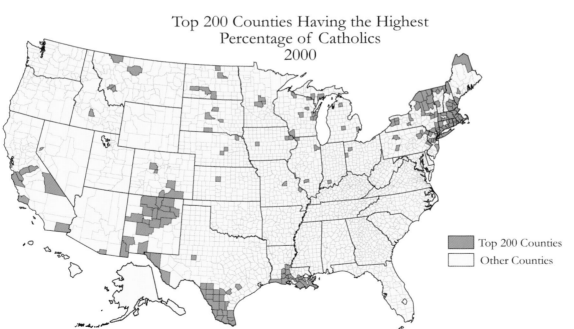

Top 200 Counties Having the Highest
Percentage of Catholics
2000

Top 200 Counties
Other Counties

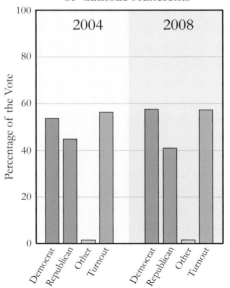

Vote and Turnout in the Top 200
Counties Having the Highest Percentage
of Catholic Adherents

Percentage of the Vote

2004   2008

Democrat Republican Other Turnout   Democrat Republican Other Turnout

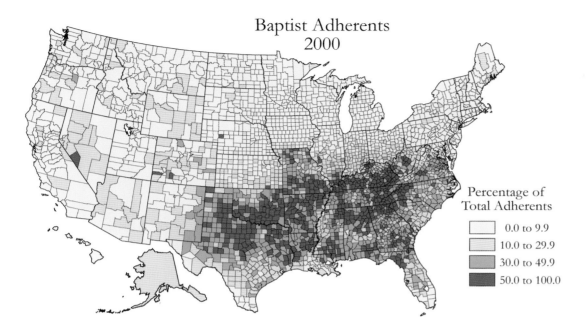

Baptist Adherents
2000

Percentage of
Total Adherents

0.0 to 9.9
10.0 to 29.9
30.0 to 49.9
50.0 to 100.0

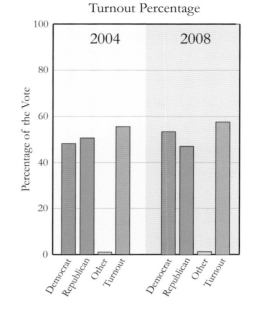

Total U.S. Popular Vote and
Turnout Percentage

2004   2008

Percentage of the Vote

Democrat Republican Other Turnout   Democrat Republican Other Turnout

MAP 6.29

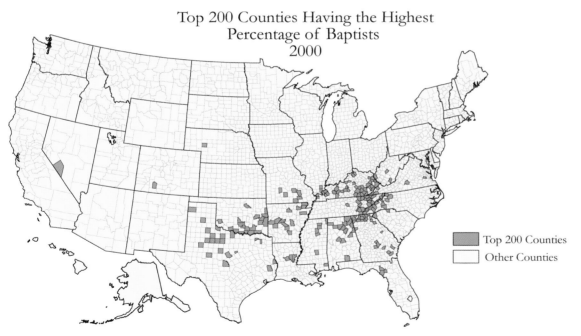

Top 200 Counties Having the Highest
Percentage of Baptists
2000

Top 200 Counties
Other Counties

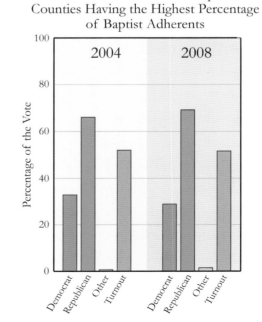

Vote and Turnout in the Top 200
Counties Having the Highest Percentage
of Baptist Adherents

2004   2008

Percentage of the Vote

Democrat Republican Other Turnout   Democrat Republican Other Turnout

MAP 6.30

Jewish Adherents 2000

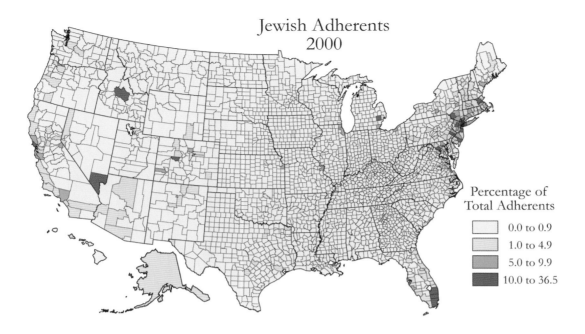

Percentage of
Total Adherents

- 0.0 to 0.9
- 1.0 to 4.9
- 5.0 to 9.9
- 10.0 to 36.5

Top 200 Counties Having the Highest Percentage of Jews 2000

- Top 200 Counties
- Other Counties

Total U.S. Popular Vote and Turnout Percentage

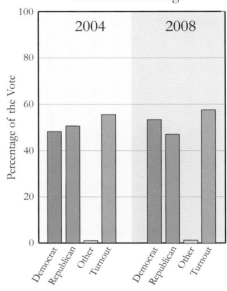

Vote and Turnout in the Top 200 Counties Having the Highest Percentage of Jewish Adherents

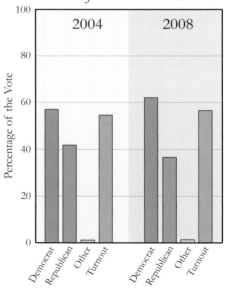

Methodist Adherents
2000

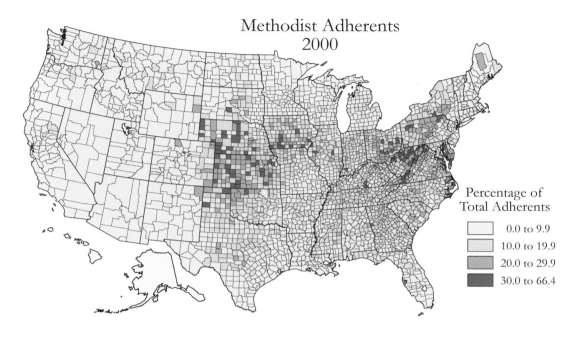

Percentage of
Total Adherents

- 0.0 to 9.9
- 10.0 to 19.9
- 20.0 to 29.9
- 30.0 to 66.4

Top 200 Counties Having the Highest
Percentage of Methodists
2000

- Top 200 Counties
- Other Counties

Total U.S. Popular Vote and
Turnout Percentage

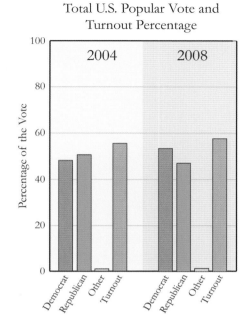

Vote and Turnout in the Top 200
Counties Having the Highest Percentage
of Methodist Adherents

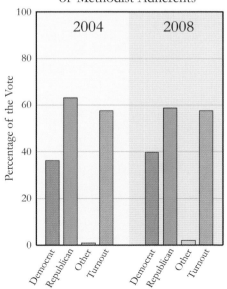

MAP 6.31

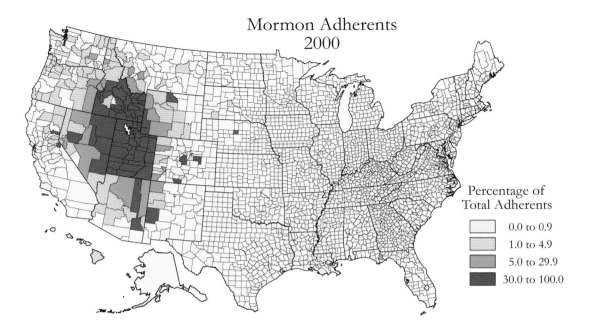

Mormon Adherents
2000

Percentage of
Total Adherents

0.0 to 0.9
1.0 to 4.9
5.0 to 29.9
30.0 to 100.0

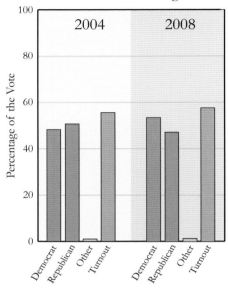

Total U.S. Popular Vote and
Turnout Percentage

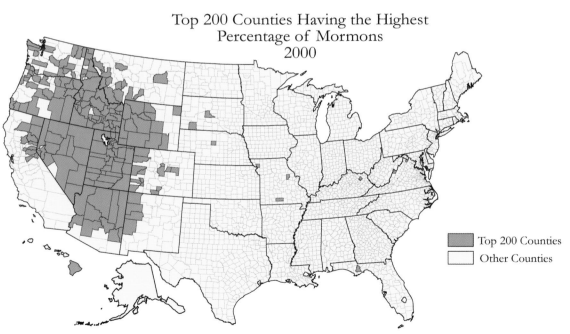

Top 200 Counties Having the Highest
Percentage of Mormons
2000

Top 200 Counties
Other Counties

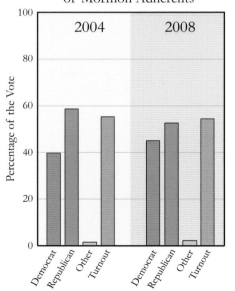

Vote and Turnout in the Top 200
Counties Having the Highest Percentage
of Mormon Adherents

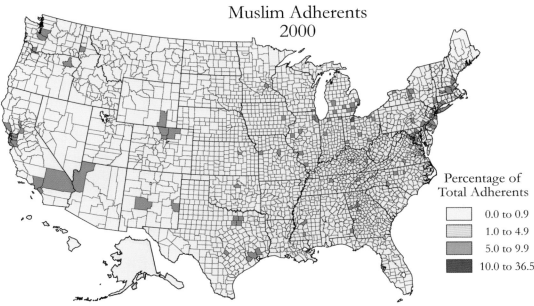

Muslim Adherents
2000

Percentage of
Total Adherents

- 0.0 to 0.9
- 1.0 to 4.9
- 5.0 to 9.9
- 10.0 to 36.5

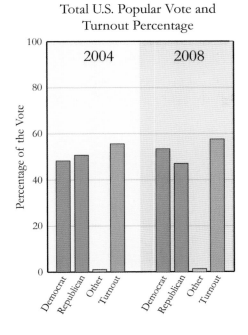

Total U.S. Popular Vote and
Turnout Percentage

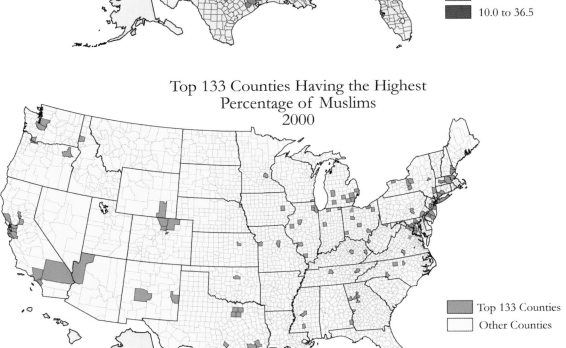

Top 133 Counties Having the Highest
Percentage of Muslims
2000

Top 133 Counties

Other Counties

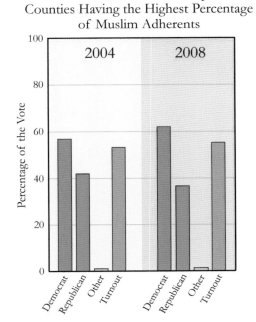

Vote and Turnout in the Top 133
Counties Having the Highest Percentage
of Muslim Adherents

MAP 6.33

MAP 6.34

Pentecostal Adherents
2000

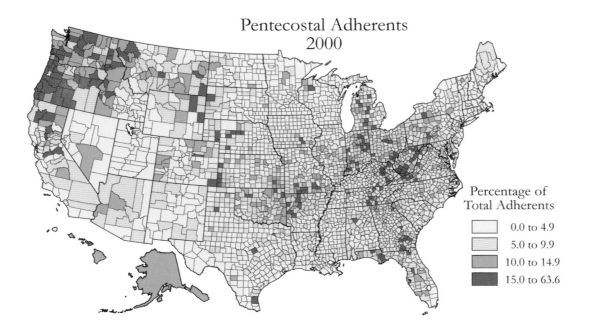

Percentage of
Total Adherents

0.0 to 4.9
5.0 to 9.9
10.0 to 14.9
15.0 to 63.6

Total U.S. Popular Vote and
Turnout Percentage

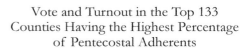
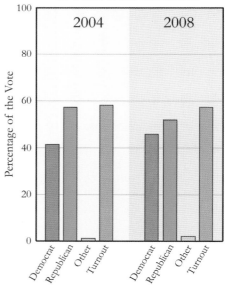

Top 133 Counties Having the Highest
Percentage of Pentecostalists
2000

Top 133 Counties
Other Counties

Vote and Turnout in the Top 133
Counties Having the Highest Percentage
of Pentecostal Adherents

■ BIBLE BELT

GERALD R. WEBSTER

The term *Bible Belt* was coined by journalist H. L. Mencken following his coverage of the Scopes "monkey" trial in Dayton, Tennessee in 1925. The term has been regularly used since then to refer to a religiously conservative region in the southeastern quarter of the United States. In spite of repeated allusions to the region, its specific location has been ill defined.

In 1978, Charles Heatwole defined the geographic extent of the Bible Belt based on the distribution of twenty-four Protestant denominations that believe in the literal interpretation of the Bible. Here we replicate Heatwole's map, using 2000 data from the Glenmary Research Center. In total there were more than 29 million members of Bible Belt denominations in 2000, with nearly 20 million being members of the Southern Baptist Convention. The other large denominations included the Lutheran Church-Missouri Synod (2.5 million), Christian Churches and Churches of Christ (1.4 million), Seventh-day Adventists (923,000), and Church of the Nazarene (907,000). While counties with high proportions of members of Bible Belt denominations are located in western North Carolina to northern Florida and west to the Texas panhandle, the Bible Belt's core would today appear centered on the Oklahoma-Texas borderlands.

How do residents of the Bible Belt vote? During the past few decades, the Republican Party has highlighted its positions on so-called social issues, including abortion, same-sex marriage, and school prayer, among others, to attract religious conservatives. It is therefore not surprising that in 2008, voting in the two hundred counties with the highest proportions of members of Bible Belt denominations was overwhelmingly for Republican presidential nominee John McCain. In spite of the fact that Democrat Barack Obama won the election with 53 percent of the vote nationally, in the aggregate, the top two hundred Bible Belt counties supported John McCain with nearly 68 percent of their votes to 31 percent for Obama. Notably, though there was a national shift to the Democratic Party in 2008 as compared with 2004, the top two hundred Bible Belt counties increased their support for the Republican nominee by a full percentage point between the two elections.

Many of the top Bible Belt counties are sparsely populated, with small total populations. For example, the average U.S. county or county equivalent has approximately one hundred thousand residents, but the top two hundred Bible Belt counties have an average population of just over 25,000 people. Also, while the mean population density in the United States as a whole is over eighty people per square mile, the population density of the top two hundred Bible Belt counties is forty people per square mile. The populations of Bible Belt counties also tend to have fewer members of minority groups. Sixty-six percent of the U.S. population is non-Hispanic white, but non-Hispanic whites constitute over 80 percent of the population in the top two hundred Bible Belt counties. Finally, education levels lag in the top two hundred Bible Belt counties, with less than 15 percent of the adult population having an undergraduate degree, compared with more than 24 percent nationally. Thus, these religiously conservative counties tend to be sparsely populated, largely composed of white residents, and strongly supportive of the Republican Party.

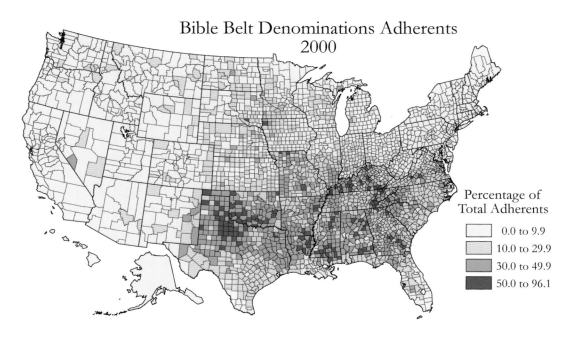

Bible Belt Denominations Adherents
2000

Percentage of
Total Adherents

- 0.0 to 9.9
- 10.0 to 29.9
- 30.0 to 49.9
- 50.0 to 96.1

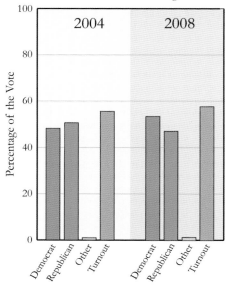

Total U.S. Popular Vote and
Turnout Percentage

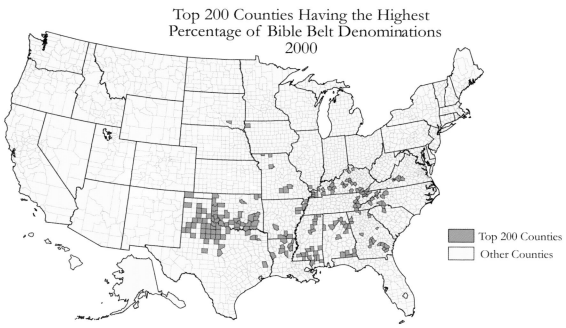

Top 200 Counties Having the Highest
Percentage of Bible Belt Denominations
2000

- Top 200 Counties
- Other Counties

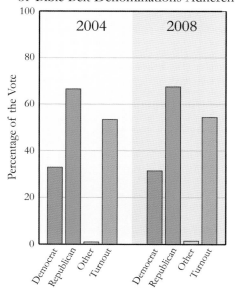

Vote and Turnout in the Top 200
Counties Having the Highest Percentage
of Bible Belt Denominations Adherents

MAP 6.35

NOTES

1. Florida is currently Professor of Business and Creativity at the Rotman School of Management, University of Toronto.
2. Since states are the key geographical units of the Electoral College, correlations are at the state level. For a more thorough discussion of these results, see Richard Florida's analysis of socioeconomic class and the 2008 election at www.creativeclass .com/creative_class/2009/03/24/class-personality- and-the-2008-election/.
3. Personal communication, June 2, 2009.

REFERENCES

Allport, Gordon W. 1954. *The Nature of Prejudice*. Cambridge, Mass.: Addison-Wesley.

Carmines, Edward G., and James A. Stimson. 1989. *Issue Evolution: Race and the Transformation of American Politics*. Princeton, N.J.: Princeton University Press.

CNN. 2004. "Election Results—America Votes 2004." http://www.cnn.com/ELECTION/2004/pages/results/ states/AZ/S/01/epolls.0.html, accessed August 17, 2009.

Dannheisser, Ralph. 2008. "Obama, McCain Compete in Wooing Hispanic Voters." *America.gov*, August 19, 2008. http://www.america.gov/st/elections 08-english/2008/August/20080819181648rressiehn nad0.1129267.html?CP.rss=true, accessed March 24, 2009.

de la Garza, Rodolfo O. 2008. "The Latino Vote in 2008." *New Labor Forum* 17 (3): 38–44.

Edsall, Thomas Byrne, and Mary D. Edsall. 1992. *Chain Reaction: The Impact of Race, Rights, and Taxes on American Politics*. New York: Norton.

File, Thom. 2008. "Voting and Registration in the Election of November 2006: Population Characteristics." U.S. Census Bureau report P20-557. http://www .census.gov/prod/2008pubs/p20-557.pdf, accessed February 3, 2010.

Florida, Richard. 2005. *Cities and the Creative Class*. New York: Routledge.

———. 2002. "The Economic Geography of Talent." *Annals of the Association of American Geographers* 92 (4): 743–55.

———. 2002. *The Rise of the Creative Class . . . And How It's Transforming Work, Leisure, Community and Everyday Life*. Cambridge, Mass.: Basic.

Frazier, J. W. 2003. "Asians in America: Some Historical and Contemporary Patterns." In *Multicultural Geographies of the United States*, edited by J. W. Frazier and F. M. Margai. Binghamton: SUNY Press.

Frazier, J. W., J. T. Darden, and N. F. Henry (eds.). 2009. *The African Diaspora in the United States and Canada at the Dawn of the 21st Century*. Binghamton: SUNY Press.

Frazier, J. W., F. M. Margai, and E. L. Tettey-Fio. 2003. *Race and Place: Equity Issues in Urban America*. Boulder: Westview.

Frazier, J. W., and E. L. Tettey-Fio (eds.). 2006. *Race, Ethnicity, and Place in a Changing America*. Binghamton: SUNY Press.

Garcia, F. Chris, and Gabriel Sanchez. 2007. *Hispanics and the U.S. Political System: Moving into the Mainstream*. Upper Saddle River, N.J.: Prentice Hall.

García, John A. 2003. *Latino Politics in America: Community, Culture, and Interests*. Lanham, Md.: Rowman & Littlefield.

Gorman, Anna. "Learning to Exercise a Vital Right; Nonpartisan Groups Work to Teach New Citizens, Primarily Latinos and Asians, the Logistics of Voting." *Los Angeles Times*, October 21, 2008, B3.

Heatwole, Charles. 1978. "The Bible Belt: A Problem in Regional Definition." *Journal of Geography* 77 (2): 50–55.

Hess, Douglas R., and Jody Herman. 2009. "Representational Bias in the 2009 Electorate." Project Vote report. http://projectvote.org/reports-on-the-electorate-/ 440.html, accessed November 18, 2009.

Hess, Gary R. 1998. "The Forgotten Asian Americans: The East Indian Community in the United States." In *The History and Immigration of Asian Americans*, edited by Franklin Ng. New York: Garland, 106–126.

Holder, Kelly. 2006. "Voting and Registration in the Election of November 2004: Population Characteristics." U.S. Census Bureau Report P20-556. http://www. census.gov/prod/2006pubs/p20-556.pdf, accessed February 3, 2010.

Jones, D. E., S. Doty, C. Grammich, J. E. Horsch, R. Houseal, M. Lynn, J. P. Marcum, K. M. Sanchagrin, and R. H. Taylor. 2002. *Religious Congregations and Memberships in the United States 2000*. Nashville: Glenmary Research Center.

Key, V. O. 1949. *Southern Politics in State and Nation*. New York: Knopf.

Lai, E., and D. Arguelles (eds.). 2003. *The New Face of Asian Pacific America*. Los Angeles: Asian Week.

Leal, David L., Matt A. Barreto, Jungho Lee, and Rodolfo O. de la Garza. 2005. "The Latino Vote in the 2004 Election." *PS: Political Science and Politics* 37 (1): 41–49.

Lopez, Mark Hugo. 2008. "The Hispanic Vote in the 2008 Election." Washington, D.C.: Pew Hispanic Center. http://pewhispanic.org/files/reports/98.pdf, accessed March 26, 2009.

Lopez, Mark Hugo, and Gretchen Livingston. 2009. "Hispanics and the New Administration: Immigration Slips as a Priority." Washington, D.C.: Pew Hispanic Center. http://pewhispanic.org/files/reports/101.pdf, accessed August 17, 2009.

Massey, D. S. (ed.). 2008. *New Faces in New Places: The Changing Geography of American Immigration*. New York: Russell Sage Foundation.

Massey, Douglas S., and Nancy A. Denton. 1993. *American Apartheid: Segregation and the Making of the Underclass*. Cambridge, Mass.: Harvard University Press.

Massey, Douglas S., and Nancy A. Denton. 1988. "The Dimensions of Residential Segregation." *Social Forces* 67 (2): 281–315.

Min. P. G. (ed.). 2006. *Asian Americans: Contemporary Trends and Issues*. Thousand Oaks: Sage Publications.

Minushkin, Susan, and Mark Hugo Lopez. 2008. "The Hispanic Vote in the 2008 Democratic Presidential Primaries." Washington, D.C.: Pew Hispanic Center, June 4, 2008.

Pew Hispanic Center. 2010. "Statistical Portrait of Hispanics in the United States, 2008." http://pewhispanic .org/factsheets/factsheet.php?FactsheetID=58, accessed 02/08/10.

Preston, Julia. "In Big Shift, Latino Vote Was Heavily for Obama." *New York Times*, November 7, 2008, A24.

Price, M., and L. Benton-Short (eds.). 2008. *Migrants to the Metropolis: The Rise of Immigrant Gateway Cities*. Syracuse, N.Y.: Syracuse University Press.

Reisinger, M. E. 2006. "Latinos in America: Historical and Contemporary Settlement Patterns." In *Race, Ethnicity, and Place in a Changing America*, edited by J. W. Frazier and E. L. Tettey-Fio. Binghamton: SUNY Press, 181–198.

Singer, A., S. W. Hardwick, and C. B. Brettell. 2008. *Twenty-First Century Gateways: Immigrant Incorporation in Suburban America*. Washington, D.C.: Brookings.

Singer, A., D. Vitiello, M. Katz, and D. Park. 2008. *Recent Immigration to Philadelphia: Regional Change in a Re-Emerging Gateway*. Washington, D.C.: Brookings.

Smith, H., and O. J. Furuseth (eds.). 2008. *The New South: Latinos and the Transformation of Space*. Burlington, Vt.: Ashgate.

Sugrue, Thomas J. 1996. *The Origins of the Urban Crisis: Race and Inequality in Postwar Detroit*. Princeton, N.J.: Princeton University Press.

Tweedie, Stephen W. 1978. "Viewing the Bible Belt." *Journal of Popular Culture* 11 (4): 865–876.

U.S. Census Bureau. 2008. "An Older and More Diverse Nation by Midcentury." U.S. Census Bureau News Release CB08-123, Aug. 14, 2008. http://www .census.gov/Press-Release/www/releases/archives/ population/012496.html, accessed August 14, 2008.

U.S. Census Bureau. 2009. "Voter Turnout Increases by 5 Million in 2008 Presidential Election." U.S. Census Bureau News Release CB09-110, July 20, 2009. http:// www.census.gov/Press-Release/www/releases/archives/ voting/013995.html, accessed February 3, 2010.

Warf, Barney, and Morton Winsberg. 2008. "The Geography of Religious Diversity in the United States." *Professional Geographer* 60 (3): 413–424.

Xenos, P., H. Barringer, and M. J. Levin. 1989. *Asian Indians in the United States: A 1980 Census Profile*. Honolulu: East-West Center.

CHAPTER SEVEN

OTHER KEY 2008 ELECTIONS

■ 2008 NORTH CAROLINA GUBERNATORIAL RACE

TOBY MOORE

Despite the headwinds Republicans faced nationally in 2008, party leaders had to feel good about their chances of ending their rivals' four-term grip on the North Carolina governor's mansion. Democratic incumbent Mike Easley, term-limited from running for reelection, had anyway seen his popularity plummet in the face of multiple corruption scandals, and the Democratic nominee could hardly escape association with Easley and corruption in Raleigh. She was the incumbent lieutenant governor, Beverly Perdue, who had served previously in both houses of the legislature.

On top of Democratic troubles, Republicans had an attractive candidate in Pat McCrory, who had won seven elections as mayor of Charlotte, the state's largest city. McCrory was seen as a business-friendly moderate conservative in the tradition of the state's most recent Republican governors. McCrory picked up endorsements from most of the state's largest newspapers, which historically backed Democrats, and emerged on top in many preelection polls.

Yet despite what might have looked like a favorable environment—a veteran campaigner running in a state that had not backed a Democrat for president since 1976—McCrory was still running against history. Only two Republicans had won races for governor in the previous hundred years, and Barack Obama brought to the state his formidable field staff and backed it with personal appearances and campaign cash. Democrats planned to take advantage of new election rules and a sizable African American electorate to boost turnout and straight-party voting.

Even McCrory's base in Charlotte was a mixed blessing. No Charlotte mayor had ever won election to the state's highest office, and the last to try, McCrory's predecessor and fellow Republican Richard Vinroot, lost in 2000 and 2004. Despite its size and central location, Charlotte has never been the center of the state's political gravity, and Charlotte politicians have found it a challenge to get their names known in the old cotton mill and tobacco towns where North Carolina elections are often decided. If Charlotte was midway between the traditional North Carolina geographic poles of mountainous Murphy and coastal Manteo, it was also a long way from each.

Perdue herself was no pushover. Unlike McCrory, she had run and won statewide races in the past and had access to the traditional levers of Democratic power in the state, particularly those interested in public education. Throughout the campaign, Perdue took steps to protect her right flank, attacking McCrory as soft on illegal immigration, for example.

Polls were close in the weeks leading to the election, but in the end the 22.6 percent surge in turnout from the 2004 general election helped Perdue win by more than 3 percentage points, narrowly outperforming Obama himself. Like the rest of the top of the ticket, she won by piling up votes in the Piedmont cities along Interstate 85; across the ninety-five least populous of the state's one hundred counties, she lost by close to seven thousand votes. Tellingly, she even beat McCrory on his home turf, narrowly winning Mecklenburg County. Perdue became the first female elected governor of North Carolina, and one of the first elected in the South without first being the wife of an incumbent governor.

■ 2008 WASHINGTON GUBERNATORIAL ELECTION: GREGOIRE VERSUS ROSSI REPRISE

RICHARD L. MORRILL

The 2008 contest was a rematch between Democrat Christine Gregoire and Republican Dino Rossi. The 2004 election ended in a disputed virtual tie, decided ultimately by the courts in favor of Gregoire by 176 votes. She did far better in 2008, winning 53 percent of the vote, although this was well below the margin for Barack Obama (57 percent). But the Gregoire results are indeed a fair description of the underlying partisan balance in the state. However, the simultaneous election of Rob McKenna, Republican, as attorney general, shows that, like Massachusetts in 2010, Democrats can be beaten in statewide offices. Neither Gregoire nor Rossi would be deemed as extremely liberal or conservative.

The state's electoral map would suggest that the state was more Republican than Democratic, but as in many states, it is because Republicans dominate the open spaces of eastern Washington, while the Democratic vote is concentrated in the Seattle metropolitan area. In eastern Washington, Gregoire carried several distinct areas, environmental retirement communities (only two small areas), American Indian reservations, Pullman, the seat of Washington State University, and a few inner-city tracts in the cities of Spokane, Yakima, and the Tri-Cities (Richland). Otherwise, eastern Washington was overwhelmingly Republican, including the Columbia Basin and Yakima Valley irrigation districts, the dryland wheat areas of far eastern Washington, and the ranching and timber areas of northeastern Washington. The Spokane metropolitan area was Republican, but only moderately so.

Western Washington is more a complex mosaic at the state level. The highest rural small-town areas for Gregoire were American Indian reservations in the northwest and environmental amenity retirement areas closely tied to Seattle. Strong Republican areas included the amazingly and consistently conservative Lewis County, dominated by a declining forest products industry, the Lynden area by the Canadian border, home of the very conservative Christian Reformed Church, and a few military-dominated areas, such as the Whidbey Island Naval Air Station. Areas of greater balance, 45–55 percent, occupied much of the exurban areas beyond the "Pugetopolis" core.

The inset map of the greater Seattle region shows the extreme degree of concentration of the Democratic vote. The highest support for Gregoire virtually coincides with the corporate limits of the city of Seattle, extending to the southeast following the displacement of black households, and its two affluent commuter islands to the west, an environmental retirement county to the northwest, and some downtown tracts in the cities of Tacoma and Olympia (by universities or colleges). Moderate Democratic margins blanket the inner suburbs around Olympia and Tacoma, but especially Seattle, while the exurban and rural areas voted Republican. The Republican votes were strongest in military areas and in areas with craft and laboring occupations and lower levels of education.

Support for Christine Gregoire 2008 Washington Gubernatorial Election

MAP 7.1

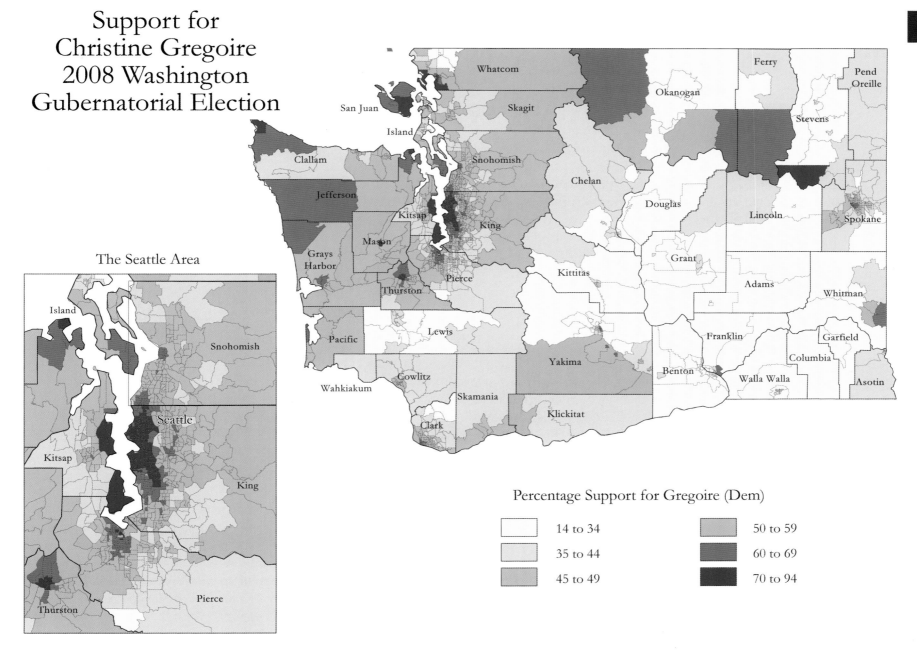

The Seattle Area

Percentage Support for Gregoire (Dem)

14 to 34		50 to 59
35 to 44		60 to 69
45 to 49		70 to 94

2008 MINNESOTA SENATORIAL ELECTION

LARRY KNOPP

The 2008 U.S. Senate race between incumbent Republican Norm Coleman and Democratic challenger Al Franken was the closest in the country. It was ultimately decided in Franken's favor, after a contested recount that took over six months to complete, by 225 votes. The result hinged on a series of judicially adjudicated decisions regarding the disposition of hundreds of individual ballots, including absentee ballots.

The closeness of the election, in what was otherwise a good year for Democrats in Minnesota (known locally as Democratic-Farm-Laborites, or "DFL-ers") and across the country, underscores the competitiveness of high-profile elections in Minnesota despite the state's perceived status by many as reliably blue. In fact, statewide elections in Minnesota, including presidential races, have been competitive since the 1970s.

At least three factors help explain this competitiveness: a substantial shift in population toward suburbs and exurbs and away from the cities of Minneapolis, St. Paul, and the DFL-dominated northeastern portion of the state; the increased influence of religious conservatives in state politics; and a substantial increase in independent and third-party activity in the state. At the peak of the DFL's influence in the mid-twentieth century, its dominance was due largely to the fact that the working-class, unionized counties of the northeast, along with St. Paul's similarly working-class Ramsey County and a smattering of smaller counties with DFL traditions, routinely outvoted Minneapolis's more white-collar and Republican Hennepin County and the remainder of suburban, small-town, and rural Minnesota. But as northeastern Minnesota's heavily unionized, industrial, and mining-based population declined beginning in the 1970s, and while the Twin Cities suburbs and exurbs boomed, the center of gravity in Minnesota population and politics shifted to the latter, particularly the I-94 corridor from the Twin Cities through the St. Cloud, Minnesota, area and beyond, toward Fargo, North Dakota. As cultural politics further divided Minnesota and the country (in Minnesota, particularly around the issue of abortion), the suburbs, exurbs, and some formerly DFL-leaning smaller counties became solidly Republican. Meanwhile, Minneapolis's Hennepin County, and even the affluent and once solidly Republican Olmsted County (home of Rochester and the Mayo Clinic), became more competitive, such that Hennepin County now leans DFL and Olmsted tends to favor moderates (including independent and third-party candidates) regardless of party affiliation. Since the mid- to late 1980s, Republican victories have therefore hinged on large margins in the I-94 corridor and other reliably Republican parts of the state, while Democrats have won mostly by piling up huge margins in the culturally liberal central cities of Minneapolis, St. Paul, the much-less-populated but still heavily DFL-dominated northeast, and a few remaining other DFL strongholds. Complicating matters for both parties have been very strong independent and third-party candidacies. In Minnesota these campaigns have tended to take votes at least as much from DFL-ers as from Republicans, despite the independent and third-party candidates' somewhat conservative (or at least libertarian) leanings. The most famous of these, of course, is Jesse Ventura, who won election as governor in 1998 by doing exceptionally well in the greater Twin Cities metropolitan area. He carried even Hennepin and Ramsey counties (albeit by very slim pluralities).

This complex and volatile political dynamic can be seen quite clearly in the 2008 Senate race voting pattern and even in recent presidential voting patterns. Franken's narrow victory was due almost entirely to large margins in Ramsey County and northeastern Minnesota and a plurality showing in other DFL-leaning counties. Former interim U.S. senator and Jesse Ventura campaign chair Dean Barkley, meanwhile, earned a respectable 15 percent of the vote statewide, running on the Independence Party ticket. He pulled votes roughly equally from both Franken and Coleman and held both major candidates to less than 50 percent of the vote in all but a handful of counties. Coleman was strongest in the western suburbs of the Twin Cities and in a few traditionally Republican rural counties. He did, however, earn a plurality of the vote in the vast majority of Minnesota counties.

These results are similar to those in several other recent statewide races, including the gubernatorial races of 1998, 2002, and 2006 (none of which was won by a DFL-er). Even the 2004 and 2008 presidential results mirror, in broad terms, the pattern described here. While Obama ran significantly ahead of Franken virtually everywhere (carrying several of the more closely contested counties that Franken lost), Franken's and Coleman's areas of greatest strength and weakness were also those of Obama and McCain, respectively. Kerry in 2004 did less well than Obama, but still better than Franken in 2008. The biggest surprise in the 2004 and 2008 presidential results may, in fact, have been that Kerry and Obama did not do better in Minnesota. Kerry won the state by a relatively narrow 51–48 percent margin, and Obama improved only modestly on this compared with other states (54–44 percent, a margin that is only slightly higher than he won nationally). By contrast, neighboring Wisconsin, a state generally seen as *more* competitive than Minnesota, swung much more heavily toward Obama (including in traditionally Republican areas).

Considering that Minnesota is the state with the longest unbroken string of wins for Democratic presidential candidates in the country, these results should be seen as a particular warning for the DFL. A 225-vote victory in a high-profile Senate race and comparatively unremarkable results in recent presidential races (including 2008, which was otherwise a good year for Democrats and DFL-ers overall) is hardly impressive. On the other hand, Republicans are clearly not dominant either. Neither party, then, can take anything for granted in this closely divided swing state.

MAP 7.2

2008 Minnesota Senatorial Election

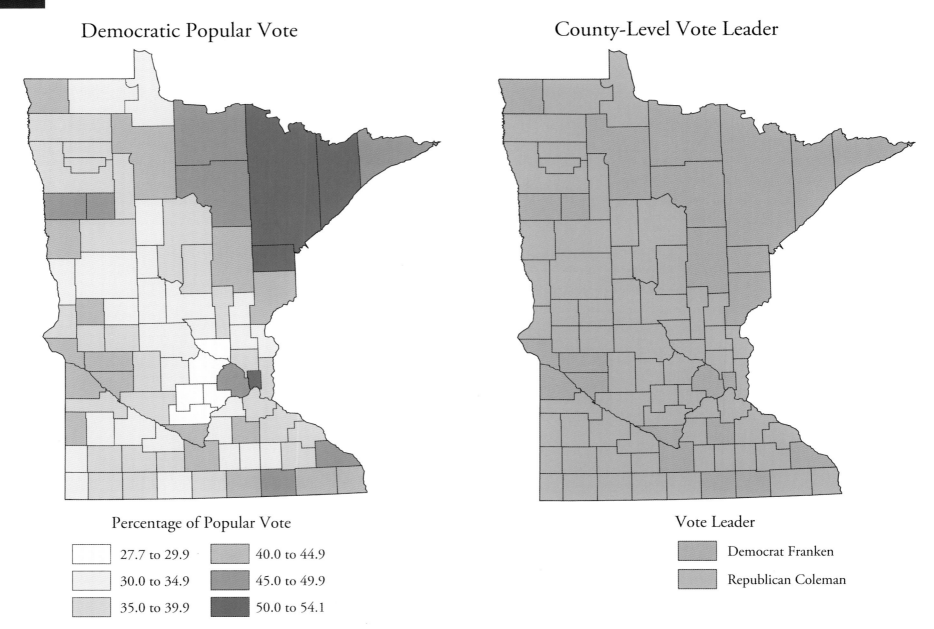

Democratic Popular Vote

County-Level Vote Leader

Percentage of Popular Vote

	27.7 to 29.9		40.0 to 44.9
	30.0 to 34.9		45.0 to 49.9
	35.0 to 39.9		50.0 to 54.1

Vote Leader

	Democrat Franken
	Republican Coleman

■ 2008 NORTH CAROLINA SENATORIAL ELECTION

TOBY MOORE

When the tide started turning the Democrats' way across the country in the run-up to the 2008 general election, an early candidate for getting swamped was the first-term junior senator, Republican Elizabeth Dole. Dole's long service in Washington cast into doubt her ties to the state: she had not lived in the state regularly since 1959 and only became eligible in 2001 when she shifted her legal residency from a Watergate condominium to her mother's house in Salisbury. Her popularity in the state was considered wide but shallow, sufficient in a good year but dangerous in a bad one. In any case, North Carolinians regularly turn out their incumbent senators, defeating reelection bids four times in the 1980s and 1990s.

Dole's easy win in 2002 dampened some of those doubts, and her incumbency was one factor in discouraging several prominent Democrats, including Governor Mike Easley and former governor. Jim Hunt, from jumping into the race. The nomination fell to little-known state senator Kay Hagan of Greensboro.

As the election year started to look better nationally for the Democrats, Dole became a target of national Democrats; the party's Senate Campaign Committee spent more money on behalf of Hagan than for any other candidate in the country. Obama visited the state twelve times during the campaign, and his staff and volunteers pushed Democratic voters to take advantage of the state's new "one-stop" voting period, during which unregistered citizens could register and vote on the same day.

As polls started to shift toward Hagan, Dole blundered with an October television advertisement alleging that the leader of the Godless Americans PAC had held a secret fund-raiser for Hagan. The ad ended with a picture of Hagan over the voice of a woman saying, "There is no God." The backlash was immediate and loud; whatever the merits or accuracy of the ad, it was not the message voters expected from the soft-edged Dole.

Hagan's subsequent win, an upset but not a shock by Election Day, was perhaps the most vivid reminder of the shifting electoral geography in the state. Hagan, who outpolled Obama, won 62 percent of the vote in the state's five most populous counties, where close to one-third of North Carolina voters live. She also held her own elsewhere and was alone among the top of the Democratic ticket in winning (albeit narrowly) the rest of the state. She even extended Obama's success in the eastern part of the state and won a series of small traditionally Republican counties in the mountains along the Tennessee border. Statewide, Hagan won by nine percentage points, the widest margin in a North Carolina Senate race in thirty years, as North Carolina became the first state to have elected female senators from more than one party. According to OpenSecrets.org, Dole spent $19.6 million (including $2.5 million of her own money) compared with $8.5 million by Hagan.

2008 OREGON SENATORIAL ELECTION

ALEX GINSBURG AND MATT LANDERS

As one of the eight Democratic pickups in the 2008 Senate election, Jeff Merkley's victory was especially significant because of Democrats' few opportunities to gain Senate seats in the West. Along with Ted Stevens in Alaska, Oregon's Gordon Smith was one of only two incumbent Republican senators who lost reelection west of Minnesota.

Merkley's victory reflects urban Democratic power in a state with relatively low population and a significant urban-rural division. Receiving 49 percent of the vote to Smith's 46 percent, Merkley carried only seven of Oregon's thirty-six counties.[1] His most significant support came in the largely urbanized Multnomah and Lane counties. In these areas, representing Oregon's largest metropolitan areas of Portland and Eugene, Merkley out-tallied Smith 2.5 to 1 and 1.5 to 1, respectively.

All seven counties that Merkley won are located in western Oregon. Of these, four counties are in the Willamette Valley, including Multnomah and Lane counties. Approximately 70 percent of Oregon's 3.8 million residents live in this corridor along the Willamette River.[2] Portland and Eugene are located in the valley, and residents of both consistently vote Democratic. The Democratic Party's control of these cities is clear in the political affiliations of statewide officeholders. At the time of the 2008 election, Smith was the only Republican to hold statewide office, and so his defeat has resulted in effective single-party control of statewide elected office. In Oregon's sparsely populated eastern and southern counties, Republicans dominate the polls, and Smith easily won all of these counties. While voting margins were closer along the Oregon coast, Smith also won four of seven counties in this region.

The political division of the Willamette Valley from the rest of the state is largely tied to a strong urban-rural divide. Oregon's liberal reputation is largely a function of its major metropolitan areas. Portland is recognized as a leader in progressive planning, environmentalism, and leftist politics. The university towns of Eugene and Corvallis are similarly progressive-leaning. Meanwhile, Oregon's rural communities have been severely affected by declining basic industries and have limited opportunities for economic development. Voters in these areas have trended Republican and have been mobilized by ballot measures on such divisive issues as property rights, taxes, and gay rights. In addition, southwest Oregon has long been isolated from the rest of the state and developed a unique political identity, which includes a pseudosecessionist movement around the potential "State of Jefferson." This region of Oregon has consistently voted Republican.[3]

While Democratic dominance in urban areas is clear, the party's control of the state's politics is not as overwhelming as it appears on the surface. The significant power of the Republican minority is evidenced by the fact that moderate Republicans held Merkley's Senate seat from 1967 to 2008. Moreover, Merkley's margin of victory in the Senate race (3.4 percent) was much lower than Barack Obama's margin of victory over John McCain in the presidential election (16.4 percent).[4] Obama outperformed Merkley in every county, by 9 or 10 percent, with an overall difference of 8.1 percent. These percentages translated into an Obama victory in an additional four counties, including Jackson County in southern Oregon and Wasco County in eastern Oregon. Such a disparity suggests that Oregon voting patterns shift significantly in relation to individual candidates.

2008 Oregon Senatorial Election

MAP 7.3

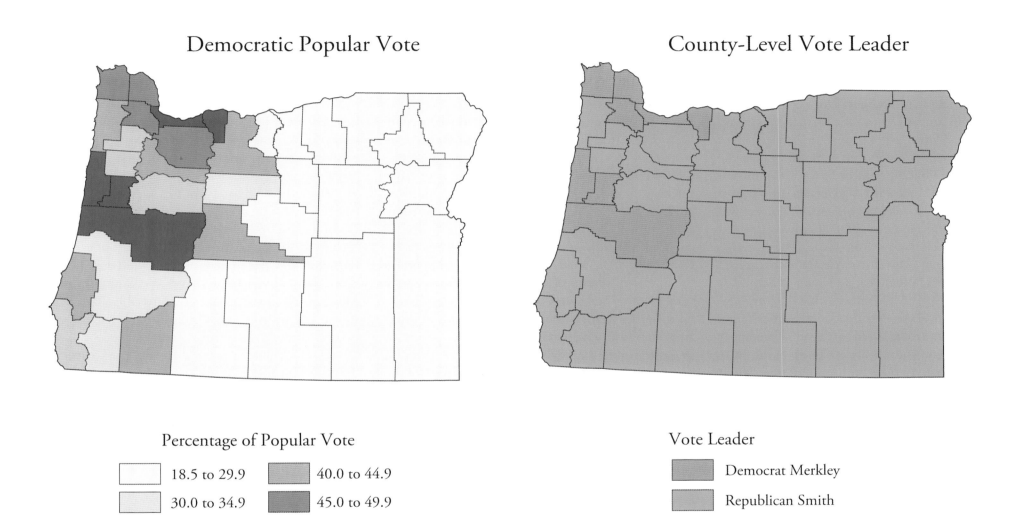

Democratic Popular Vote

County-Level Vote Leader

Percentage of Popular Vote

	18.5 to 29.9		40.0 to 44.9
	30.0 to 34.9		45.0 to 49.9
	35.0 to 39.9		50.0 to 68.9

Vote Leader

Democrat Merkley

Republican Smith

2008 GEORGIA SENATORIAL ELECTION

TAYLOR JOHNSON AND TOM VANDERHORST

In the wake of the 2008 general election, the race for a Senate seat from Georgia, the results of which could provide the Democrats with a filibuster-proof majority in the Senate, became a focus of the national spotlight. On the tide of large national gains for the Democratic Party in the general election, Jim Martin, the Democratic challenger for the Georgia Senate seat, forced a runoff against the incumbent Republican, Senator Saxby Chambliss, a notable accomplishment in a generally conservative state. Chambliss, a resident of south Georgia, was first elected to the Senate in 2002 after having served as the U.S. Representative from Georgia's eighth district for eight years. Martin, an Atlanta native, served for eighteen years in the Georgia House of Representatives (1983–2001) while representing the forty-seventh district. He also held subsequent political posts and made an unsuccessful bid for Georgia lieutenant governor in 2006. After their close finish in the 2008 senatorial general election, both candidates received increased attention and financial support from their respective national parties to campaign for the runoff election.

In the November 4 general election, Saxby Chambliss received 49.8 percent and Jim Martin received 47.8 percent of the popular vote, with third-party candidates receiving the remainder. Neither candidate won a simple majority in five counties, and tied in Mitchell County of southwest Georgia. A comparison between the presidential and senatorial election results in Georgia shows that the Democratic candidates, Obama and Martin, fared similarly in both races, with each getting approximately 47 percent of the total vote. The results for the Republican candidates, of which Chambliss received fewer votes than McCain, were split by the margin of votes received by senatorial Libertarian candidate Allen Buckley. In both races, the Democratic candidates tended to fare best in more urban counties and counties with greater minority populations; they won all counties with at least a 50 percent black population. Regionally, Chambliss garnered strong support in the northern suburbs of metropolitan Atlanta and in rural areas of north and southeast Georgia. Martin, on the other hand, had his strongest results in urban areas located around major Georgia cities, specifically in central and southeast metropolitan Atlanta, as well as a belt of support extending from the Columbus area, in southwest Georgia, to Augusta, on the eastern edge of Georgia. Voter turnout for this election was generally highest in the center of the state between Macon and Athens and in the northern suburbs of Atlanta. The expected increase in Democratic voters, a result of increased voter registration and an expected increase in minority voter turnout, appears to have helped the Democratic candidate, but the question of whether these same voters would return lingered for the month leading up to the December 2 runoff election.

In the December 2 runoff election, Chambliss received a more commanding 57.4 percent of the popular vote. Both candidates were strong in the same areas as the general election, with Chambliss gaining a stronger hold in north Georgia, including more suburban counties surrounding Atlanta, and in the southeast coastal plain of Georgia. Overall, Martin's strength decreased across the state, yet he maintained support from the same geographic areas, including urban counties, fall line counties, and the southwest region of Georgia. One exception to this decreased support was in Early County, where Martin took the majority after Chambliss had won in the general election. On average, voter turnout decreased across the state by about 30 percent, from 72 percent down to around 41 percent. Turnout decreased the most along the border between Georgia and Florida, the central Georgia coast, and the northern border between Georgia and South Carolina. The shift in voter turnout provides support for the idea that Martin's success in the general election had been greatly influenced by the high voter turnout among Democratic Party supporters; however, in the end, the Republican Party maintained its ability to filibuster in the U.S. Senate.

2008 Georgia Senatorial Election

MAP 7.4

General Election Vote Leader

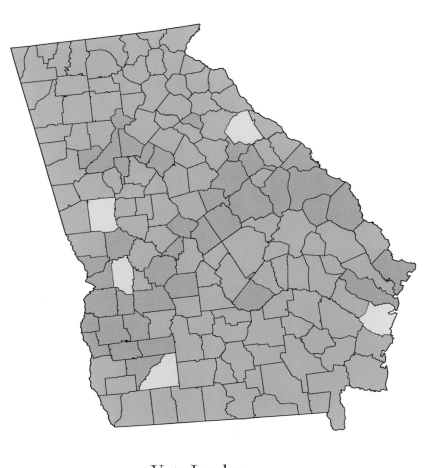

Vote Leader

Democrat Martin   Republican Chambliss

No majority leader

Run-Off Election Vote Leader

Vote Leader

Democrat Martin   Republican Chambliss

NOTES

1. Oregon Secretary of State, "Official Results—November 4, 2008 General Election," www.oregonvotes.org/nov42008/g08results.html (accessed June 24, 2010).
2. William G. Loy et al., *The Atlas of Oregon* (Eugene: University of Oregon Press, 2001).
3. Loy et al., *The Atlas of Oregon*.
4. Oregon Secretary of State, "Official Results—November 4, 2008 General Election," www.oregonvotes.org/nov42008/g08results.html (accessed June 24, 2010).

REFERENCES

"Total Raised and Spent: 2008 Race, North Carolina Senate," http://www.opensecrets.org/races/summary.php?cycle=2008&id=NCS1.

NONPARTISAN REFERENDA

■ BALLOT MEASURES IN THE 2008 ELECTION

JOSHUA R. MEDDAUGH, MEGAN A. GALL, AND JOSHUA J. DYCK

Direct democracy was initially a Progressive Era mechanism used to put a direct check on state legislatures by allowing citizens to act as primary actors in the policy process by proposing and voting on laws, rather than by electing representatives to make policy decisions (Cronin 1989). Through the institutions of the initiative, which allows (1) citizens to propose, qualify, and vote on measures without the input from the legislative branch, the referendum, (2) legislators to defer important policy questions to a popular vote, and the recall, (3) citizens to remove corrupt politicians from office before their terms expire, thus citizens have taken a greater role in the governance of their states. All in all, twenty-four states have some form of the ballot initiative, the most powerful of these tools. Originally designed more as checks, these institutions (and particularly the citizen initiative) have evolved into the standard

way in which salient and controversial policies are ultimately arbitrated in the states that allow this process, something that was highlighted in 2008.

The 2008 general election witnessed not only a high-profile presidential contest, but in many places, a slate of ballot measures that would shape or change that state's policies for years to come. Of the 153 ballot propositions voted on, 59 percent were approved while 41 percent of the fifty-nine proposed initiatives passed, equaling the historical approval average of 40 percent. Of the fifty-nine initiatives, the most controversial measures dealt with social issues such as gay marriage and abortion. Social conservatives won big with the passage of Proposition 8 in California as well as Proposition 12 in Arizona and Proposition 2 in Florida, which defined marriage as a union between one man and one woman. At the same time, conservative evangelical groups also witnessed defeat as

Amendment 48 in Colorado, an endeavor to limit abortion by defining a "person" as existing at any moment of fertilization and therefore guaranteeing due process of law, and Initiated Measure 11 in South Dakota, which was an effort to reinstate a ban on abortion; both failed.

Besides social issues, 2008 witnessed multiple measures that dealt with the taxing and spending policies of the states. In a rebuff of the Bush-era tax polices, all three major tax-cutting ballot measures (Question 1 in Massachusetts, Statutory Measure 2 in North Dakota, and Measure 59 in Oregon) overwhelmingly failed, with each garnering less than 36 percent of the votes cast. Even though these voters rejected cutting taxes, the country as a whole was just as reluctant to vote to raise revenue by increasing taxes. Voters in Colorado rejected three proposed tax increases, while Florida voted down one. Although both Minnesota and Montana passed measures increasing taxes, neither was surprising, especially in Montana, where voters every ten years continually increase funding for the state's public universities.

Colorado had the distinction in the 2008 election of having the longest ballot, with fourteen measures. Ten of the fourteen measures were citizen-sponsored initiatives, accounting for approximately 17 percent of all initiatives proposed nationwide. The fourteen measures are the second-highest total in the state's electoral history, second to the 1912 presidential election, when thirty-two measures, twenty of which were initiatives, made the ballot. Still, this past general election measure total could have been slightly higher, with a total of eighteen, if a deal brokered under the wire between backers of four union-sponsored initiatives and the state of Colorado's business community failed to occur. The final deal led to the removal of the union initiatives believed to be detrimental to the state's business environment, thereby dropping the overall total to fourteen. In return, the business community provided the human resources and three million dollars in funds to fight three anti-union measures that remained on the ballot: both Amendments 47 and 49, both of which dealt with union membership and dues, and Amendment 54, which dealt with campaign contributions and government contacts. Number 47 attempted to make Colorado a "right-to-work" state, one in which unionism is not forced, while 49 was a "paycheck protection" measure. Amendment 54, a "pay to play" measure, prohibited all organizations that donated over $100,000 to campaigns from winning government contracts, therefore affecting unionized employees. The last-minute deal paid off for both sides, as both Amendments 47 and 49 failed in November, while Amendment 54 was ruled unconstitutional by the Colorado Supreme Court the following February.

One of the most interesting Colorado measures in 2008 dealt with the initiative process itself. Referendum O, a legislatively referred constitutional amendment, was an attempt to make the process of proposing initiated constitutional amendments more difficult by increasing the signature requirement. However, ultimately the process for an initiated state statute was made easier by decreasing the number of signatures required. Also, the amendment called for a geographic component to be added to the process, making it necessary for at least 8 percent of petition signatures to be collected from each congressional district. Regardless of the fact that Governor Bill Ritter and former governor Bill Owens both supported Referendum O, the measure failed.

Overall, the 2008 election continued to mirror the trends of increased direct democracy usage decade by decade. Already the current decade is on par with the 1990s and will outpace that era after 2010. Also, the current decade is the second busiest in terms of direct democracy usage. The western states of Oregon and California continue to drive proposal numbers, with Colorado, North Dakota, and Arizona rounding out the top five. Regardless, the historical passage rate of 40 percent has remained static, suggesting that having a large number of initiatives in an election does not necessarily increase the probability that the proposals will be passed. In the end, 2008 witnessed a variety of measures in multiple states but will be most remembered for the repeal of gay marriage in California due to Proposition 8.[1]

TABLE 8.1. Ballot Measure Description and Vote Percentage

State	Issue Number	Measure Description	Pass/Fail	Percent Vote
Alabama	Proposition 102	Marriage defined as one man and one woman	Pass	56.2%
Arkansas	Proposed Initiative Act 1	No one outside of a valid marriage, man and woman, may adopt or be a foster parent to a minor	Pass	57.0%
California	Proposition 2	Starting January 1, 2015, no farm can confine pregnant pigs, egg-laying hens, or calves raised for veal in an area where they cannot turn around freely or stretch their limbs	Pass	63.5%
California	Proposition 8	Eliminates the rights of same-sex couples to marry	Pass	52.3%
Colorado	Amendment 48	Defines a "person" to be any human from the moment of fertilization, giving that person due process of the law	Fail	26.7%
Florida	Amendment 2	Marriage defined as one man and one woman; no other legal union recognized	Pass	61.9%
Massachusetts	Question 3	Prohibits any dog race where gambling occurs	Pass	56.2%
Michigan	Proposal 08-1	Permits the use and cultivation of marijuana for specified medical conditions	Pass	62.7%
Ohio	Issue 6	Amend the Ohio Constitution to allow a casino in southwest Ohio	Fail	37.2%
Oregon	Measure 58	Prohibits teaching public school students in a language other than English for more than two years	Fail	43.6%
South Dakota	Initiated Measure 11	Reinstate prohibition of abortion	Fail	44.8%
Washington	Initiative 1000	Allowing certain terminally ill competent adults to obtain lethal prescriptions	Pass	57.8%

Source: Data provided by the National Conference of State Legislatures.

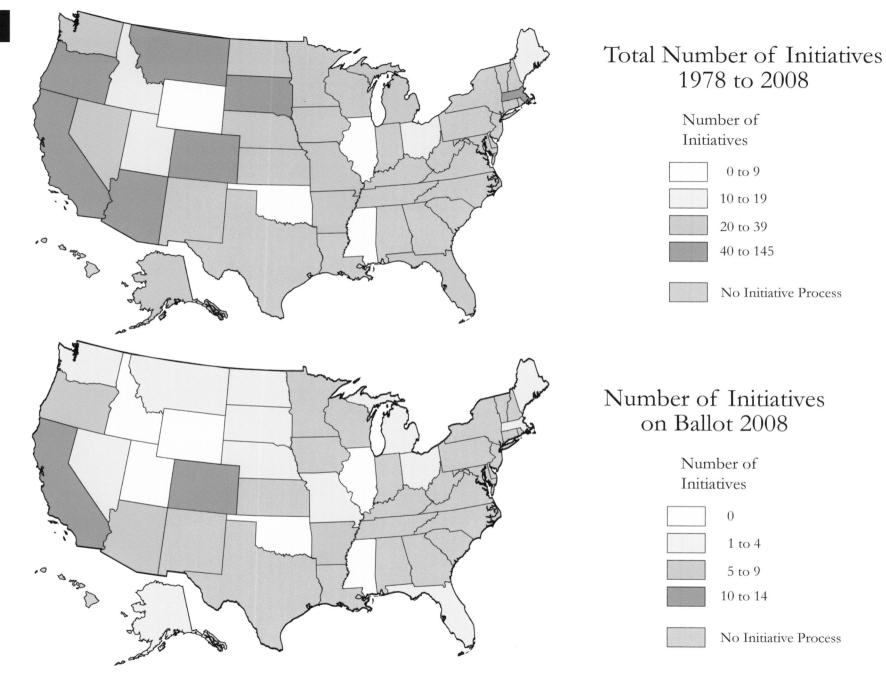

MAP 8.1

Total Number of Initiatives
1978 to 2008

Number of
Initiatives

	0 to 9
	10 to 19
	20 to 39
	40 to 145

No Initiative Process

Number of Initiatives
on Ballot 2008

Number of
Initiatives

	0
	1 to 4
	5 to 9
	10 to 14

No Initiative Process

■ ARIZONA: SAME-SEX MARRIAGE REFERENDUM

THOMAS E. CHAPMAN

In what was one of the longest and most acrimonious debates in Arizona legislative history, state legislators narrowly approved a voter referendum in early 2008 that would amend that state's constitution to ban the legalization of same-sex marriage. Known as Proposition 102, the ballot proposal was subsequently approved by voters in the 2008 general election by a vote of 56 percent to 44 percent. The initiative won every county in the state except Pima, where the city of Tucson is located (Arizona's second-largest city). It is worth noting that exit polls in Arizona showed that slightly over half of 18- to 24-year-old voters rejected Proposition 102, while those over 65 supported the measure by an overwhelming majority of 3 to 1[2].

Same-sex marriage in Arizona was previously prohibited by a state law passed in 1996, and in succeeding years the statute was upheld by the state's courts. Interestingly, Arizona voters also rejected a similar ballot measure in 2006 (Proposition 107), becoming the only state to reject such a proposal by voter referenda. Much of the reason for this is attributed to the 2006 ballot language that would have also banned legal domestic partnerships and civil unions for all unmarried partners (including heterosexuals), jeopardizing the legal partnership status that many Tucson residents enjoyed under local law (Tucson is the state's second-largest city). Many of Arizona's libertarian conservatives also saw the measure as an unnecessary government intrusion and voted against the measure. As a result, the 2008 ballot language was narrowed to address only the definition of marriage as a "union between one man and one woman," making the proposal more palatable to those who voted against the proposal in 2006.

Earlier in 2008, state courts in Connecticut and the neighboring state of California struck down their respective state laws banning same-sex marriage (voters in California ultimately reversed the court's decision by voter referendum in the same election). The measure's proponents made effective use of these court decisions, arguing that a constitutional amendment was necessary in order to provide a stronger legal remedy that could withstand future judicial scrutiny in Arizona. In order to bolster their argument, supporters also pointed out other earlier court decisions in other states where these laws were declared unconstitutional, particularly in Massachusetts, where same-sex marriage became legal in 2004.

Opponents of Proposition 102 urged a "no" vote primarily based on the argument that legislators should respect the will of the voters, who had previously rejected such a proposal in 2006. Invoking Arizona's affinity for libertarianism, they also argued that these amendments do not protect the sanctity of marriage but amount to government involvement in people's private lives.

■ FLORIDA'S MARRIAGE AMENDMENT

THOMAS E. CHAPMAN

The Florida Marriage Amendment, also known as Proposition 2, appeared on the 2008 ballot as a voter-initiated referendum that would amend that state's constitution to prohibit same-sex marriage. Out of a total 7,478,654 votes cast, the amendment passed with 62.1 percent of the vote (Florida requires a 60 percent majority for passage of voter-initiated referenda). With its passage, Florida became the twenty-seventh state to ratify a statewide constitutional ban on same-sex marriage.

Supporters of the amendment argued that although same-sex marriage was already illegal in Florida,[3] writing the ban into the state's constitution would prevent state judges from overturning the law on constitutional grounds, as was done by the Massachusetts State Supreme Court in 2003. Conservative evangelical religious groups were strongly in favor of the amendment based on moral grounds, arguing that its passage would result in the indoctrination of schoolchildren into a "gay lifestyle," as well as take away parents' rights to determine school policy concerning the teaching of homosexuality as an "acceptable lifestyle."

Opposition to the measure focused in large part on various arguments that would restrict social and economic rights. For example, the amendment's passage would run counter to Article I of Florida's constitution (known as the Declaration of Human Rights), which sets a precedent for establishing civil rights rather than limiting them. Another argument against passage was that health care and pension benefits that legally cover unmarried couples would adversely affect them, particularly the large number of unmarried senior-citizen couples in Florida who enjoy the financial benefits of such arrangements. Another argument against passage was that the amendment's scope and purpose was much larger than banning same-sex marriage. Indeed, the amendment ballot language was written in such a way that its passage restricts civil and economic rights of heterosexual relationships that are not defined as a legal marriage under this statute.

The spatial distribution of the vote shows that the amendment went down to defeat in areas with large urban populations, particularly the south Florida megalopolis of Palm Beach-Ft. Lauderdale-Miami, as well as the Tampa-St. Petersburg metropolitan area. In addition, voters residing in the two counties where the state's largest university communities are located also defeated the amendment, Leon County (Florida State University) and Alachua County (University of Florida). The highest concentrations of the vote in favor of passage were in central Florida and the panhandle counties, where large concentrations of fundamentalist Christian evangelicals reside. These areas are also the most politically and ideologically conservative in the state.

MAP 8.2

MAP 8.3

Arizona Proposition 2
Ban Same-Sex Marriage
2008

Florida Proposition 2
Ban Same-Sex Marriage
2008

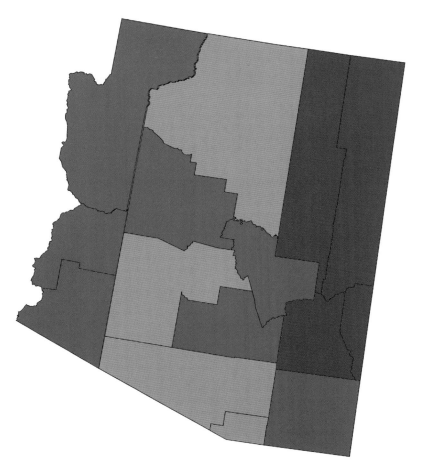

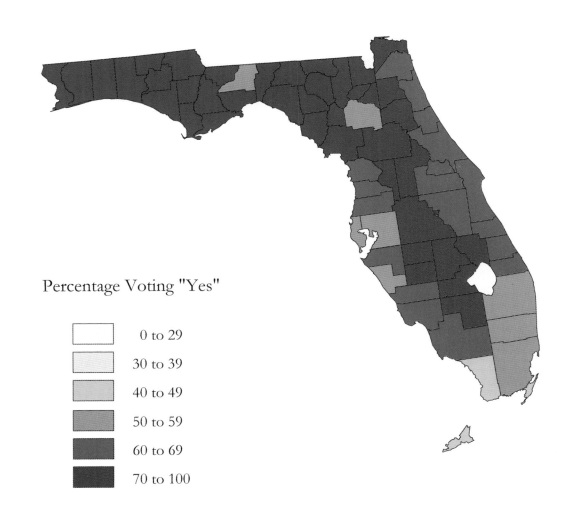

Percentage Voting "Yes"

	0 to 29
	30 to 39
	40 to 49
	50 to 59
	60 to 69
	70 to 100

CALIFORNIA PROPOSITIONS 7 AND 10: ALTERNATIVE ENERGY PROPOSALS

WESLEY J. REISSER

Although Proposition 4 on abortion and Proposition 8 on same-sex marriage garnered most of the headlines in 2008, two environmental proposals were also tabled on the statewide ballot. California, long known as a leading state on environmental regulation, would see both ballot measures go down by large margins, with even major environmental organizations opposing the measures.

Proposition 7 focused on the generation of electricity from alternative fuels. According to the Department of Energy's Energy Information Administration (EIA), California already had the second-largest renewable energy portfolio in the United States behind Washington, home to the largest hydroelectric projects in the country. The EIA also ranks California as the largest producer of renewable power from non-hydroelectric sources. Despite these numbers, prior to the 2008 election, only 22 percent of its electric needs were met by renewable sources. Proposition 7 would have mandated utilities in the state to procure 50 percent of their energy from renewable resources by 2025. Penalties would have been imposed if these stringent standards were not met. A large network of groups came out against Proposition 7, including many leading environmental organizations. Opponents included major utilities, both state political

parties, and the Sierra Club, one of the state's most influential environmental groups. This large array of opponents led to an unusual distribution of votes for a California ballot proposition. Only 35.4 percent of voters approved Proposition 7, with only one county, Imperial County, in the state's far southeastern corner, voting in favor of the proposition. Rarely in California politics does an environmental proposition go down with such strong opposition in the state's most liberal area, around San Francisco Bay. Throughout the Bay Area, voters went against Proposition 7 with over 60 percent opposition. It is likely that the little support that was garnered for Proposition 7 was in inland areas, where wind or solar projects likely would have blossomed to meet the stringent requirements for implementing the proposition.

Proposition 10 was instead focused on alternative fuels for transportation. Proposition 10 included both incentives to purchase fuel-efficient and alternative-fuel vehicles and grant money to fund research on alternative fuels for transportation, all funded through a five billion dollar bond issued by the state. T. Boone Pickens, a Texas oilman turned advocate for energy independence, was one of the leading supporters of Proposition 10. However, Proposition 10 also failed to gain the support of major environmental groups

during the campaign. Proposition 10 gained broader support than Proposition 7, winning 40.4 percent of the vote, but failed to gain a majority in any California county. Unlike Proposition 7, the vote on Proposition 10 split quite differently, with Proposition 10 coming much closer to passing in Southern California, with strongest opposition in the far northern parts of the state. Unlike most environmental propositions, Proposition 10 gained better support in Los Angeles and San Diego than it did in the Bay Area. Southern California, as a region where the car is king, was clearly more enthused about tax breaks for purchasing cleaner, more efficient cars than other parts of the state were. However, just as with Proposition 7, the vote divide does not match the liberal/conservative divide of the state.

Both Propositions 7 and 10 provide an interesting case where the normal electoral geography of California failed to appear in election results. Normally, the liberal coastal areas are set out from more conservative inland regions and the San Diego metropolitan area in the far south. In this case, the more conservative areas were, especially in the case of Proposition 10, more likely to offer some support than the most liberal portions of the state near San Francisco, where both alternative-energy propositions went down by large margins.

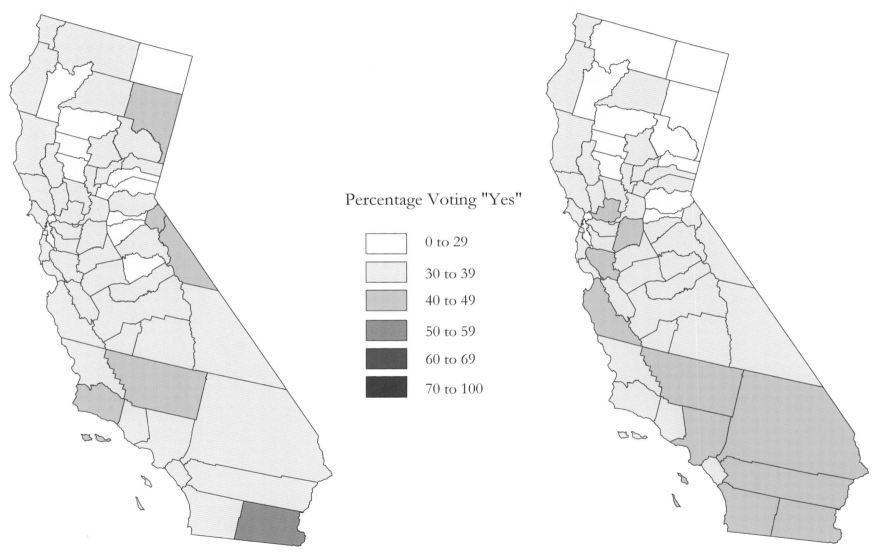

Proposition 7
Renewable Energy Generation
2008 Referendum

Proposition 10
Alternative Fuel Vehicles
and Renewable Energy Bonds
2008 Referendum

MAP 8.4

Percentage Voting "Yes"

- 0 to 29
- 30 to 39
- 40 to 49
- 50 to 59
- 60 to 69
- 70 to 100

CALIFORNIA PROPOSITION 2: PREVENTION OF FARM ANIMAL CRUELTY ACT

MARK DRAYSE AND JONATHAN TAYLOR

Proposition 2 was placed on the November 4, 2008, ballot in California. It passed by a wide margin, with 63.4 percent voter approval. It was sponsored by Californians for Humane Farms, a coalition including the Humane Society and Farm Sanctuary. The purpose of Proposition 2 is "to prohibit the cruel confinement of farm animals in a manner that does not allow them to turn around freely, lie down, stand up, and fully extend their limbs." While limited in scope, Proposition 2 is part of a growing movement in the United States against the negative animal welfare, health, and environmental impacts of industrial agriculture. The main target of the proposition is the use of battery cages to confine egg-laying hens—typically, four hens are in a cage sixteen inches wide (Farm Sanctuary 2010). Other confinement systems addressed by the proposition include veal crates and gestation crates for pregnant pigs. Laws banning or limiting some of these practices have already been passed in Arizona, Florida, and Oregon, and in the EU.

Proposition 2 was opposed by the California and national egg and poultry industry, represented by groups such as the American Egg Board, which presented economic and health arguments. The industry argued that shifting to larger cages would increase production costs and result in a decline in egg production in California. They also argued that changing current confinement practices would increase the incidence of avian influenza, salmonella, and other diseases.

The geography of the vote on Proposition 2 reflects the growing east-west divide in California politics between the coastal and interior counties (Douzet and Miller, 2008). The coastal counties, anchored in the metropolitan regions of Los Angeles and San Francisco Bay, are more urbanized, politically liberal, and ethnically diverse than the interior counties in the Central Valley, Sierra Nevada, and desert regions. The California livestock and poultry industry is concentrated in the Central Valley, where a majority of voters in several counties opposed Proposition 2. For example, only 42 percent of the voters supported Proposition 2 in Merced County, where industrial farms housed more than 3.6 million layers in 2007, or 17 percent of the state's total (USDA 2010). Voters in nearby Stanislaus County, another major egg producer, also opposed Proposition 2.

The vote on Proposition 2 closely reflected the results in the presidential race between Obama and McCain. By large margins, Obama won all sixteen counties whose voters supported Proposition 2 with at least 63.4 percent of the vote. On the other hand, McCain won eight of the eleven counties where a majority of voters opposed Proposition 2.

California Proposition 2
Prevention of Farm Animal Cruelty
2008 Referendum

MAP 8.5

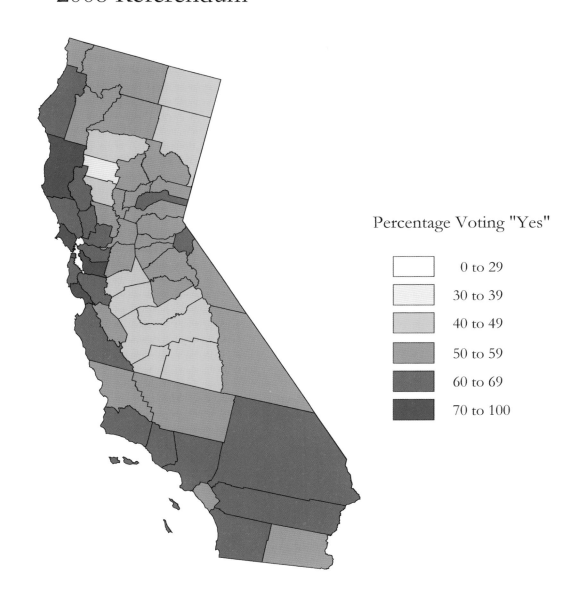

Percentage Voting "Yes"

	0 to 29
	30 to 39
	40 to 49
	50 to 59
	60 to 69
	70 to 100

■ CALIFORNIA'S SAME-SEX MARRIAGE REFERENDUM: PROPOSITION 8

THOMAS E. CHAPMAN

California's Proposition 8 appeared on the 2008 ballot as a constitutional amendment that would eliminate the right of same-sex couples to marry. Voters approved the amendment 52 percent to 48 percent, making California the only state where the legality of same-sex marriage was revoked after it had been previously established as a constitutionally protected right, affirmed by the state Supreme Court earlier that year. As a result, somewhere between 15,000 and 20,000 same-sex marriages took place before the constitutional ban was passed by voters.[4] California's culture war over the issue of same-sex marriage has a long and tumultuous history, beginning in 1977, when the state was the first in the nation to pass a law that explicitly defined marriage as a "civil contract between a man and a woman." Subsequent battles over this issue were often high-profile events, culminating in a 2004 showdown, when San Francisco mayor Gavin Newsom performed same-sex marriages in open defiance of state law. The event gained national media attention and would ultimately lead to the decision by California's highest court to strike down state laws prohibiting same-sex marriage.

The campaign over Proposition 8 was perhaps the most fiercely contested of the five state marriage initiatives that would appear across the country that year. The aftermath of the vote saw nationwide protests and numerous litigations challenging various aspects of the initiative process. One of these lawsuits would end up in federal court, paving the way for a possible decision by the U.S. Supreme Court to hear the case in the near future.

Many national religious organizations backed the passage of Proposition 8, most notably the Church of Jesus Christ of Latter-day Saints (Mormons). Through fund-raising appeals to church members, millions of dollars were raised to finance the "Yes on 8" campaign, causing a backlash that culminated in large protest rallies in front of LDS churches nationwide shortly after the election. Nationally known evangelical minister Rick Warren was also a high-profile supporter of the amendment, urging his thirty thousand church members to support its passage.

The same-sex marriage issue split voters in the usual ways of political party ideology, religion, and age. In California, this split also is represented by a regional divide between those highly urban counties along the central and southern coast and those rural counties in the Central Valley and northern interior. Margins of victory in these counties were the highest, as they represent the state's most socially conservative regions. Voters in the San Francisco Bay Area counties rejected the ban by large margins, ranging from 66 percent voting "no" in Sonoma County to 75 percent in San Francisco and Marin counties. In the Los Angeles basin the amendment was rejected, but by very narrow margins, most notably Los Angeles County, where voters rejected the amendment by a mere 0.5 percent margin. Voters in Orange County approved the amendment by an 8 percent margin, while in San Diego County, voters approved the amendment by a 4 percent margin.

California Proposition 8
Eliminate Same-Sex Marriage
2008 Referendum

MAP 8.6

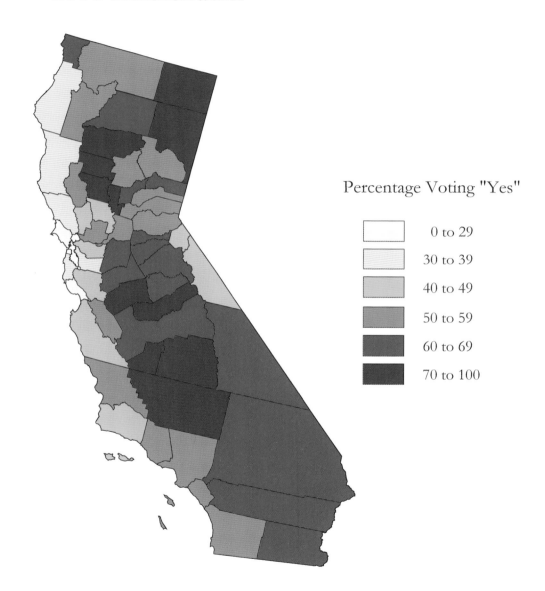

Percentage Voting "Yes"

	0 to 29
	30 to 39
	40 to 49
	50 to 59
	60 to 69
	70 to 100

CALIFORNIA'S PROPOSITION 8 (SAME-SEX MARRIAGE) AND THE RACE QUESTION

MEGAN A. GALL, JOSHUA R. MEDDAUGH, AND JOSHUA J. DYCK

California Proposition 22, an initiative to restrict California's definition of marriage as being between a man and a woman, was passed in the 2000 primary election with over 60 percent of the vote. Despite this statute and what seemed to be overwhelming partisan support, the mayor of San Francisco ignored the measure and began marrying same-sex couples in 2004. Those marriages, even though eventually annulled, helped move the issue of same-sex marriage to the front of the docket of the California Supreme Court. In a 4–3 ruling in 2008, the court ruled Proposition 22 unconstitutional on grounds that the measure violated the equal protection clause of the California Constitution. In direct response to the overturn, ProtectMarriage.com, as well as proponents of Proposition 22 and others, joined together and used the initiative process to get a new marriage proposal on the 2008 ballot. Unlike Proposition 22, a citizen-initiated state statute that can be constitutionally checked by the courts, Proposition 8 was written as a citizen-initiated constitutional amendment, a measure that cannot be ruled on by the state Supreme Court. This change in measure type was purposely done in order to thwart efforts to overturn the law if the measure passed.

The overarching goal of Proposition 8 was to specify that rights of marriage are confined to unions between opposite-sex couples. This in turn would end future same-sex marriages in California but would fail to annul the approximately 20,000 same-sex marriages that took place between 2004 and 2008 because laws are rarely retroactive (*Los Angeles Times* 2008). In the short period of time that it took backers to reach the signature requirement to put Proposition 8 on the ballot, a nationwide debate erupted over the measure with high-profile backers taking a stand on either side of the issue. By Election Day 2008, over $60 million was raised by both sides of the issue, making Proposition 8 the most expensive initiative battle to date (Oresick 2008).

The result of the vote on Proposition 8 was cast as a great irony in the 2008 elections. California voters simultaneously helped elect the nation's first black president and denied gays and lesbians the right to marry. Many pundits put this paradox squarely on the shoulders of the African American community, who turned out in droves to support Obama but who were also more likely than whites to support Proposition 8.

The 2008 presidential election was a surge election for the Democratic Party as partisans and informed peripheral voters turned out in droves to vote for the popular Obama/Biden ticket. Combining the fact that African Americans predominantly vote Democratic with the addition of the first viable African American presidential candidate, the 2008 election also witnessed a surge of African American voters at the polls. Due to this, the political talking heads began telling the story that the increased participation of racial and ethnic minorities, who tend to vote conservatively on social matters, were largely responsible for passing the measure. Citing numbers from exit polls from the likes of CNN and others, which tallied African American support for the proposition at 70 percent, with African American women polling at 75 percent, the pundits were able to weave a web of passage deception. Latinos were more divided, with 53 percent supporting the proposition. Within the Latino community, the divisions were by age. Approximately 58 percent of Latinos over the age of thirty voted yes. Conversely, exit polls showed 49 percent of whites voting for the measure (CNN 2008). Self-described Christians and voters with spouses and/or children were also cited as supporters (Grad 2008). Summing up the common wisdom, in an often-quoted *Los Angeles Times* article, African Americans "played a crucial role in the outcome" of Proposition 8 (Morain and Garrison 2008).

Does the conventional wisdom hold up? Did African Americans drive the 2008 elections in California? Bivariate correlations provide mixed results. First, African Americans and voting "yes" on Proposition 8 are related to a statistically significant level; however, with a correlation of $r = .0213$, the relationship is quite weak. To uncover whether any evidence is found in regard to the media's much-hyped explanation, we estimated a regression model. Negating the pundits' conclusions, we found that once education and religiosity are controlled for, the effect of the percentage of African Americans voting "yes" on Proposition 8 is actually negative. This finding was also statistically significant. Stated otherwise, when we examine the voting behavior of African American voters and white voters with similar sociodemographics (income, education, religion, etc.), African Americans were less likely than their white counterparts to support Proposition 8. However, the African American community has lower levels of income and

education and higher levels of religiosity than whites in California—all indicators that predict support for Proposition 8.

The 2008 presidential election was a historic one. Proposition 8, like most ballot measures aimed at limiting marriage to a man and a woman, passed. Through a national lens, passage was not surprising,

but a constitutional ban on gay marriage in California caught the country off guard. Initial results from exit polls gave pundits and political spectators nationwide an easy explanation to a puzzling result that had a salacious twist: African Americans passed Proposition 8. This great irony of the 2008 elections is not born out in a more detailed look at the data.

■ MICHIGAN PROPOSITION 1: A LEGISLATIVE INITIATIVE TO PERMIT THE USE AND CULTIVATION OF MARIJUANA FOR SPECIFIED MEDICAL CONDITIONS

LISA M. DECHANO-COOK AND MARK A. MOODY

Using marijuana for medicinal purposes has been an issue in recent years with studies over its potential medical benefits. In 2008 Michigan became the fourteenth state to pass such a law with 63 percent of voters approving of the measure. The law allows for a registered, qualified patient to possess up to 2.5 ounces of marijuana and a qualified caregiver to have up to twelve plants that are kept in an enclosed, locked facility (Michigan Department of State 2008). Marijuana may be used to treat the following debilitating conditions: cancer, glaucoma, HIV/AIDS, hepatitis C, amyotrophic lateral sclerosis, Crohn's disease, Alzheimer's disease, and nail patella, among others (Michigan Department of State 2008). Of the other thirteen states that have passed a similar referendum, their medical marijuana laws passed by either the voters or state lawmakers with absolute majorities. At

least one state, South Dakota, failed to pass such a measure within recent years (Hakala 2008). Similar to other states' initiatives, Michigan did have its support and opposition groups. The largest support group, Michigan Coalition for Compassionate Care, believed from the start that this initiative would pass (Hakala 2008). An opposition group called Citizens Protecting Michigan's Kids had law enforcement and medical community members supporting them, who waged a campaign that warned of "a dystopia of strip-mall pot shops, teens with easy access to a so-called gateway drug, and crimes unpunished because of a medical marijuana defense" (Satyanarayana 2008: 1).

With 63 percent of voters approving of the measure, there was no overall clear county pattern compared to the presidential vote. However, there were some exceptions. The highest percentage of

those approving of medical marijuana and voting for Obama occurred in and around the Detroit-Ann Arbor metropolitan areas (Wayne, Oakland, Washtenaw counties). These counties also exhibit the highest median family income in Michigan. Ingham (Lansing), Marquette, and Muskegon counties also had high approval ratings for medical marijuana use and Obama. While the Detroit and Lansing votes correspond with major metropolitan areas in the Lower Peninsula, Marquette is the major metropolitan area in the Upper Peninsula and the home of Northern Michigan University. Muskegon County is home to a large artist population, which may explain its higher majority approval of medical marijuana use.

The Interstate 94 counties of Van Buren, Kalamazoo, Calhoun, Jackson, Washtenaw, and Wayne had a large majority of people vote for Obama and medical marijuana use. It should be noted that

Washtenaw and Kalamazoo Counties are homes to the University of Michigan and Western Michigan University, respectively. Three other counties that house state universities, namely, Ingham (Michigan State University), Isabella (Central Michigan University), and Marquette (Northern Michigan University) also exhibited this same pattern. Popular belief is that college towns and larger cities are more progressive and accepting of changes within society.

When age is examined in relation to the county voting patterns seen for this issue, distinct patterns existed for the youngest and oldest age groups; those 18–29 and over 65, respectively. A higher percentage of residents in the counties along the I-94 corridor belong to one of these two age groups; these counties had the highest percentages of support for medical marijuana. A similar pattern exists for Muskegon County. When comparing these data with religious preferences, surprisingly, no clear pattern emerges with any one denomination. However, many of the counties along the I-94 corridor as well as Ingham and Muskegon exhibit both a high amount of religious diversity and a high percentage of "yes" votes for this ballot issue. Five of these same counties are also among of the top two hundred counties having the highest religious diversity in the country. This result suggests that while one specific religious affiliation was not dominant, the collection of all religions in a county may have had some influence on the voting results.

Since the medical marijuana use referendum passed, other issues related to its passage have arisen. One is whether or not to include or amend county zoning codes for medical marijuana plant growth. State senators have introduced legislation that would no longer permit authorized patients to grow their own supply. The legislation seeks to have "licensed marijuana growing facilities" instead, with no more than ten licensed facilities per year (Associated Press 2010). If passed, this legislation would mean that medical marijuana could be dispensed only by a pharmacist.

Overall there are some positive correlations between the county pattern of the medical marijuana vote and variables such as the 2008 presidential election, median family income, cites of universities, and age. Regardless of what the driving forces were behind the voter results, there remain lingering issues at both the state and county levels that need to be addressed and will continue to fuel debates in the coming months and years.

Medical Use of Marijuana
Michigan 2008 Referendum

MAP 8.7

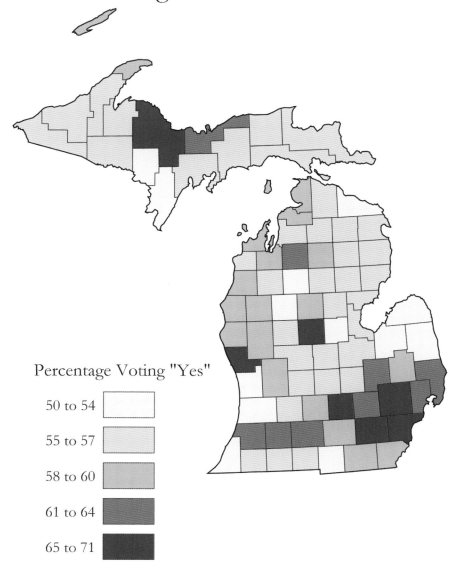

Percentage Voting "Yes"

50 to 54

55 to 57

58 to 60

61 to 64

65 to 71

MICHIGAN PROPOSITION 2: A PROPOSAL TO AMEND THE STATE CONSTITUTION TO ADDRESS HUMAN EMBRYO AND HUMAN EMBRYONIC STEM CELL RESEARCH IN MICHIGAN

LISA M. DECHANO-COOK

Proposition 2 was the second major state issue on the ballot in 2008 and the more controversial of the two (the other being medical marijuana use). This proposal amended the state constitution to expand embryonic stem cell research with certain restrictions in place. Some of these restrictions include that embryos cannot be taken more than fourteen days after cell division begins (unless the embryo was frozen); embryos must have been created for the purpose of fertility treatment; and only embryos that would have otherwise been discarded because they were unsuitable for implantation or are more than are clinically needed are allowed for use (Michigan Department of Community Health 2001–2010). Both supporters and resisters of this amendment fought hard and were well funded in their endeavors. Led by the nonpartisan group Cure Michigan, proponents advocated that these embryos may hold the key to medical advancements, including the potential for curing diseases. Opponents cited religious grounds as an objection to the destruction of embryos and tax increases to cover the costs associated with this research as an additional factor. They also felt that the proposal would limit the state government's ability to regulate stem cell research (Satyanarayana 2008).

An examination of the geographic variations in the Proposition 2 vote provides some insight into the categories of those who ratified this change. Many of the counties whose population voted for this proposition also voted for President Obama. This was also shown in exit polls, where 69 percent of the voting Democrats voted for expanded stem cell research. These counties also had the largest populations in the state; there were a few minor exceptions, such as Alcona County on the shore of Lake Huron. While backed financially through the Michigan Catholic Conference (Satyanarayana 2008), counties with the highest percentages of adherence to Catholicism were not necessarily the counties with the lowest percentage of "yes" votes. Some counties such as those adjacent to or near the Detroit metropolitan area have a strong Catholic adherence but also gave large majority votes for this proposal. Those voters with a college degree and those who have completed postgraduate work were the largest group supporting this issue (*Grand Rapids Press* 2008). In general, these voters correspond with the counties that exhibited the greatest percentage of "yes" votes. The counties north of Saginaw Bay on the Lake Huron shores were the exception to this generalization. These counties voted for the proposal but have a higher percentage of residents who have either no college or some college education. Voter "yes" percentages also correspond with median age categories. Voters ages 18–24 and 25–29 constituted the cohorts most strongly supporting this issue (CNN 2008). Where these age populations tended to be higher in the counties, they also exhibited the greatest amount of support.

While Proposition 2 was a controversial issue, those voters who constituted the greatest cohorts of support were younger adults and those who had a college education and/or some postsecondary education. Where these cohorts were concentrated, so was the strongest support for this referendum on stem cell research.

Since the referendum passed, the University of Michigan has been awarded over $6.8 million in grants toward stem cell research (Karoub 2009). These awards suggest that stem cell research is important in biomedical research; however, debates are still lingering. One such argument is its economic impact. Michigan's pro-life group sees no noticeable impact for the state with few new private sector jobs having been created. The University of Michigan is to invest five billion dollars for the establishment of a new research institute consortium, which would hire new faculty members, but the economic impacts and medical advancements of this would most likely not be seen for several decades (Bomey 2010). The passing of this referendum is also being looked at as a reason why Michigan may not be able to keep and attract recent college graduates in this area. The state Senate passed a bill that would tighten regulations on stem cell research. Critics believe that if this bill becomes law, it could lead these young, bright scientists to go to other places (Haglund 2010).

Stem Cell Research
Michigan 2008 Referendum

MAP 8.8

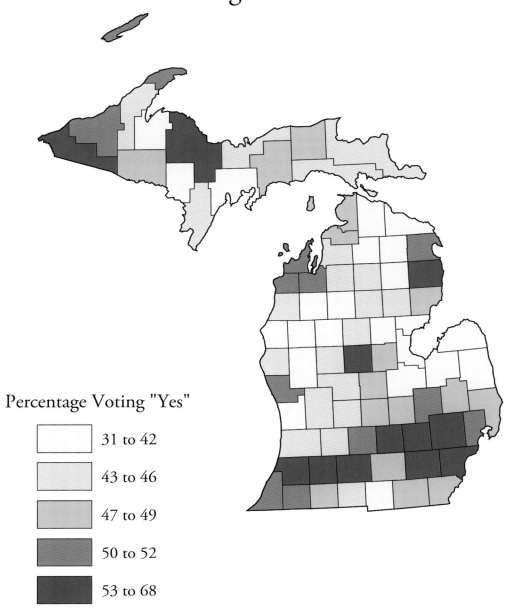

Percentage Voting "Yes"

31 to 42

43 to 46

47 to 49

50 to 52

53 to 68

■ ASSISTED SUICIDE REFERENDA IN WASHINGTON

KATHLEEN O'REILLY AND RICHARD L. MORRILL

In 2008, Washington voters successfully passed Initiative 1000 (58 percent to 42 percent), which gave permission to terminally ill, mentally competent, adult Washington residents predicted to die within six months the ability to request and self-administer lethal drugs prescribed by a physician. The statewide victory was surprisingly strong, considering its earlier loss in 1991.

While there is a strong correlation between religious affiliation and opinions on assisted suicide, this connection does not dominate Washington's referenda due to the large number of residents who declare no religious affiliation. Nevertheless, organized religion did attempt to exercise its influence. The Roman Catholic Church, the largest denomination in the state (716,000 members), heavily funded the Coalition Against Assisted Suicide's bid to defeat Initiative 1000. Yakima, Benton, Franklin, Grant, Douglas, Adams, and Lincoln counties, with rather high shares of Mormon or Catholic populations, and a high Hispanic Catholic ethnicity, defeated the initiative. Areas of highest opposition were the Columbia Basin and Yakima Valley irrigation districts, with high Hispanic Catholic and Mormon populations. The main area of high opposition at the border with Canada is the city of Lynden, home of the very conservative Christian Reformed Church.

Lack of religious affiliation suggests that examining referenda results by religion is unlikely to offer a robust explanation for the outcomes of assisted suicide voting statewide. However, American religious populations are more Republican than the rest of the voting public (Ladd 1995), and substantially more Republican than Americans who declare no religious affiliation. Such evidence offers political party affiliation as a useful indicator of voting on assisted suicide. At the county level, the Republican presidential vote in 2008 was of strong explanatory value when explaining opposition to Initiative 1000 ($r^2 = 0.710$). The 2008 Washington election showed no Democratic counties voting against assisted suicide legislation. However, there were eight counties in the eastern part of the state that voted in favor of a Republican president but also in favor of Initiative 1000—Kittitas, Chelan, Okanogan, Ferry, Pend Oreille, Walla Walla, Columbia, and Asotin counties. A single county, Lewis, located west of the Cascade Mountains, voted Republican in the presidential race but also favored passage of assisted suicide legislation.

In addition, a connection between social conservatism, Republicanism, and rural western counties suggests a geographic dimension according to the outcomes of assisted suicide referenda. Socially conservative voters tend to vote Republican, and Republican voting in the western United States is most associated with rural and sparsely populated areas. Washington's voting in the presidential election of 2008 had nearly all urban, western counties voting Democratic. On the other hand, eastern rural counties voted Republican, with the exceptions of Klickitat, Spokane (home to the city of Spokane), and Whitman (city of Pullman) counties.

An urban-rural split was not dominant in Washington over Initiative 1000. All counties with cities in the top ten largest cities in the state, with the exception of Yakima County, passed the initiative. However, although nine rural, sparsely populated Washington counties opposed Initiative 1000, another nine counties that were also rural and sparsely populated supported the initiative. Garfield, Adams, and Lincoln counties, among the top four opponents, have some of the lowest population densities in the state (first, eighth, and third, respectively) and no major urban areas. But other counties with similarly low population densities voted in favor of the measure, for example, Skamania, Ferry, and Columbia counties (fifth, second, and fourth, respectively).

While Republican voting explains 71 percent of oppositional votes, counties with high shares of the elderly, counties like Lincoln, Garfield, Columbia, and Okanogan, were opposed or only slightly supportive, signifying eastern Washington as conservative overall on controversial social issues. At the detailed census tract level, high support for 1000 was limited to a few affluent retirement areas and to Pullman, home of Washington State University, with a young population. Additionally, small-city rural counties supporting the initiative in the Olympic peninsula and southwestern Washington have high shares of the elderly and retired, especially those counties dominated by Seattle-area educated retirees, Jefferson and San Juan counties.

Numerically, King County provided the dominant margin for 1000, 260,000 of 460,000 statewide; but King was not enough. Seattle's support for 1000, while quite high, was markedly less than for Obama, while far suburban, exurban, and rural area support was much stronger. This is perhaps explained by its older residual rural population, but there could also be a hint of a rural independent or libertarian streak. In the city of Seattle, while areas with high concentrations of the elderly were highly supportive of 1000, the highest levels of support were in the area of highly educated, often younger nonfamily populations in Capitol Hill, Wallingford, and Fremont, all near the University of Washington. The only area with a majority against 1000 was the poorer area of southeast Seattle, with higher levels of recent immigrants and ethnic and racial minorities (also the case in Bellevue). Overall weaker support for 1000 in Pierce County than in Snohomish or King probably reflects a younger, less affluent, and more military-dependent population.

Washington voting patterns favoring assisted suicide legislation can be explained partially by voters' geographic locations in the state and their county's population density. Affiliation with a church that opposes assisted suicide played a role in only a few counties with high religious membership. All counties that opposed assisted suicide lie east of the Cascade Range and off the I-5 corridor, but not all eastern counties opposed the initiative. However, the vote for 1000 differed from that for partisan races by the greater support of the elderly and weaker support of minority populations.

MAP 8.9

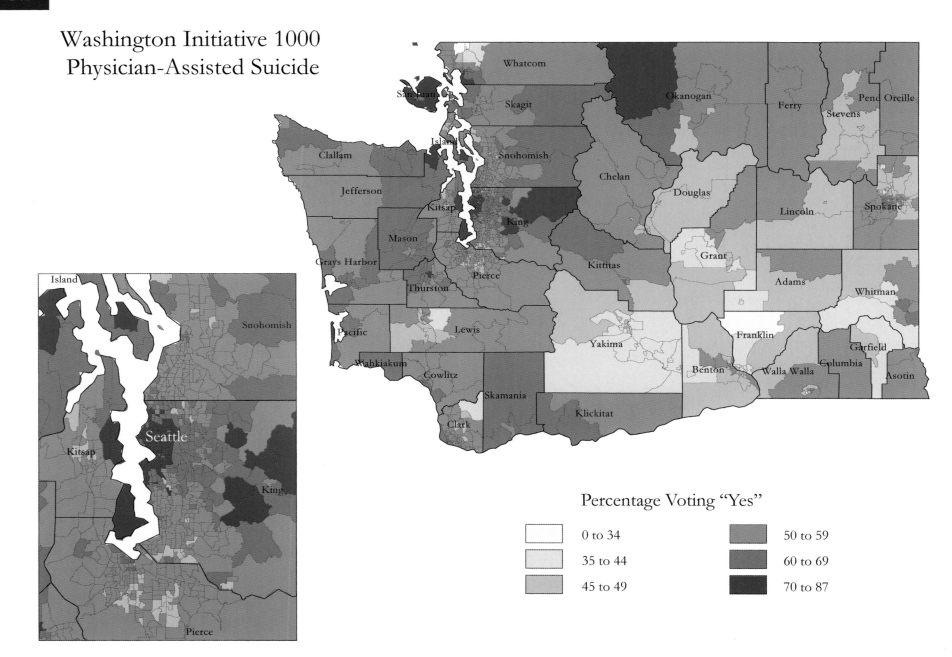

Washington Initiative 1000
Physician-Assisted Suicide

Percentage Voting "Yes"

▢ 0 to 34		▨ 50 to 59	
▢ 35 to 44		▨ 60 to 69	
▨ 45 to 49		▨ 70 to 87	

NOTES

1. Data provided by the Initiative and Referendum Institute and the National Conference of State Legislatures.
2. CNN exit polling data at www.cnn.com/ELECTION/2008/results/polls/#AZI01p1.
3. In 1997, Florida legislators passed a Defense of Marriage Act (DOMA) (Florida Statute 741.212).
4. In 2009, the state Supreme Court ultimately upheld the validity of these marriages.

REFERENCES

Associated Press. 2010. "Lawmakers Consider Changes to Michigan Medical Marijuana Law." WZZM 13. Retrieved from http://www.wzzm13.com/news/news_story.aspx?storyid=117633 on June 12, 2010.

Ballotpedia. "Arizona Proposition 102." http://ballotpedia.org/wiki/index.php/Arizona_Proposition_102_%282008%29 (last accessed 5/23/2010).

Ballotpedia. "Florida Marriage Amendment, Amendment 2 (2008)." http://ballotpedia.org/wiki/index.php/Florida_Marriage_Amendment,_Amendment_2_%282008%29 (last accessed April 10, 2010).

Barabak, Mark Z. "New Poll Confirms Who Liked—and Opposed—Prop 8 on Same-Sex Marriage." *Los Angeles Times*, December 3, 2008. http://latimesblogs.latimes.com/washington/2008/12/the-public-poli.html (last accessed June 1, 2010).

Bomey, Nathan. "Stem Cell Jobs in Michigan: Inevitable or Unlikely?" *AnnArbor.com*, May 3, 2010. Retrieved from http://www.annarbor.com/business-review/stem-cell-jobs-in-michigan-inevitable-or-unlikely/ on June 12, 2010.

Bowser, J. 2008. "Four Labor Initiatives Withdrawn in Colorado." National Conference of State Legislatures. http://www.ncsl.org/Default.aspx?TabId=16477.

CNN ElectionCenter. 2008. Exit Polls; Ballot Measures; California Proposition 8: Ban on Gay Marriage. Retrieved from http://www.cnn.com/ELECTION/2008/results/polls/#val=CAI01p1 on February 9, 2011.

CNN ElectionCenter. 2008. Exit Polls; Ballot Measures; Michigan Proposition 2: Allow Stem Cell Research. Retrieved from http://www.cnn.com/ELECTION/2008/results/polls/#val=MII02p3 on June 8, 2010.

Cronin, T. E. 1989. *Direct Democracy: The Politics of Initiative, Referendum, and Recall*. Cambridge, Mass.: Harvard Univerisity Press.

Douzet, F., and K. Miller. 2008. "California's East-West Divide." In *The New Political Geography of California*, edited by F. Douzet, T. Kousser, and K. Miller, 9–43. Berkeley: Institute of Governmental Studies.

Farm Sanctuary. 2010. "Factory Egg Production." Accessed June 8, 2010, from http://www.farmsanctuary.org.

Follow the Money. "I-1000: Assisted Suicide." http://www.followthemoney.org/database/StateGlance/ballot.phtml?m=443.

Grad, Shelby. "70% of African Americans Backed Prop. 8, Exit Poll Finds." *Los Angeles Times*, November 5, 2008.

Grand Rapids Press. 2008. "Michigan Voters Approve Stem Cell Research Measure." *Grand Rapids Press*. Retrieved from http://www.mlive.com/politics/index.ssf/2008/11/michigan_voters_approve_stem_c.html on June 8, 2010.

Haglund, Rick. 2010. "Anti-Immigration Measures, Stem Cell Research Restrictions Hurt Michigan's Hopes of Attracting Young Talent." Retrieved from http://www.mlive.com/business/index.ssf/2010/05/anti-immigration_measures_stem.html on June 12, 2010.

Hakala, Josh. 2008. "Michigan Voters Approve Medical Marijuana Measure." Retrieved from http://www.mlive.com/politics/index.ssf/2008/11/michigan_voters_approve_medica.html on June 2, 2010.

Herreras, Mari. "After Making History in 2006, Arizona Voters Again Have to Decide on the Definition of Marriage." *Tucson Weekly*, September 25, 2008. http://www.tucsonweekly.com/tucson/familiar-feeling/Content?oid=1092525 (last accessed May 13, 2010).

Holden, J. 1993. "Demographics, Attitudes, and Afterlife Beliefs of Right-to-Life and Right-to-Die Organization Members." *Journal of Social Psychology* 133 (4): 521–527.

Kam, Dara. 2008. "If Amendment 2 Fails, Backers Say Kids Will Be Led into 'Gay Lifestyle.'" *Palm Beach Post*, October 22, 2008. http://www.palmbeachpost.com/politics/content/state/epaper/2008/10/22/1022gaymarriage.html?cxntlid=inform_artr (last accessed April 10, 2010).

Karoub, Jeff. 2009. "University of Michigan Awarded 13 Fed Stimulus Grants Totaling $6.8M for Stem Cell Research." *Stem Cell Research News*. Retrieved from http://blog.taragana.com/health/stemcell/2009/10/22/university-of-michigan-awarded-13-fed-stimulus-grants-totaling-68m-for-stem-cell-research-3968/ on June 12, 2010.

Ladd, E. 1995. "The 1994 Congressional Election: The Postindustrial realignment continues." *Political Science Quarterly* 110 (1): 1–23.

Los Angeles Times. "How Will Prop. 8 Affect Married Same-Sex Couples?" October 28, 2008.

Matsusaka, J. 2008. "Election 2008: Mixed Results." *Initiative and Referendum Institute Ballotwatch*. http://www.iandrinstitute.org/BW%202008-3%20Results%20v4.pdf.

Mauraskas, G., C. Archer, and F. Shelley. 1988. "Metropolitan, Nonmetropolitan, and Sectional Variations in Voting Behavior in Recent Presidential Elections. *Western Political Quarterly* 41 (1): 63–84.

McKinley, Jesse. "Same-Sex Marriage on the Ballot in Arizona, a Second Time." *New York Times*, October 29, 2008. http://www.nytimes.com/2008/10/30/us/politics/30marriage.html (last accessed May 14, 2010).

McKinley, Jesse, and Laurie Goodstein. "Bans in 3 States on Gay Marriage." *New York Times*, November 5, 2008.

http://www.nytimes.com/2008/11/06/us/politics/06marriage.html (last accessed April 8, 2010).

Michigan Department of Community Health. 2001–2010. "Information on Proposal 08-2—Stem Cell Research." Retrieved from: http://www.michigan.gov/mdch/0,1607,7-132--206361--,00.html on June 8, 2010.

Michigan Department of State. 2008. "Notice: State Proposals—November 4, 2008." Retrieved from http://medicalmarijuana.procon.org/sourcefiles/MichiganProp1.pdf on June 2, 2010.

Morain, Dan, and Jessica Garrison. "Focused beyond Marriage: Prop. 8 Supporters Shrewdly Warned of Implications for Schools, Churches and Children, Analysts Say." *Los Angeles Times*, November 6, 2008.

O'Reilly, K., and G. Webster. 1997. "The Electoral Geography of Oregon's Ballot Measure 16: The Death with Dignity Act." *Geographical Bulletin* 39: 70–80.

Oresick, Jake. "California Battle Sets Fundraising Records." *Jurist: Legal News and Research*. University of Pittsburgh School of Law, October 27, 2008.

Satyanarayana, Megha. 2008. "Heated Battle over Stem-Cells Ends as Prop 2 Passes." *Detroit Free Press*. Retrieved from http://www.freep.com/article/20081105/NEWS15/811050448/Heated-battle-over-stem-cells-ends-as-Prop-2-passes on June 8, 2010.

Satyanarayana, Megha. "Is Marijuana Good Medicine?" *Detroit Free Press*, October 25, 2008. Retrieved from http://www.freep.com/article/20081025/NEWS15/810250341/Is-marijuana-good-medicine on June 2, 2010.

Scott, Anna. "Amendment Banning Same-Sex Marriages Closing in on Ballot Spot in November 2008. *Herald Tribune*, November 5, 2007. http://www.herald-tribune.com/article/20071105/NEWS/711050540# (last accessed 4/10/2010).

Sullivan, Andrew. "Prop 8 Exit Polls." *Atlantic*. November 5, 2008.

United States Department of Agriculture (USDA). 2010. "Census of Agriculture. California. 2007." Accessed June 8, 2010, from http://www.agcensus.usda.gov.

Vance, Kevin. "The Marriage Juggernaut: Why Arizona Flipped on Gay Nuptials." *Weekly Standard*, Vol. 13, no. 12, December 2, 2008.

Webster, G. 1987. "Size of Place and Voting in Presidential Elections in the Interior West." *Geographical Perspectives* 59: 78–92.

CHAPTER NINE

POST-2008: CONGRESSIONAL VOTES

OVERVIEW

As this chapter illustrates, electoral geographers are interested in more than presidential races. The first maps show the results of the 2008 election at the congressional district level (maps 9.1 and 9.2). These results are important because they show us the support Democrats and Republicans had in the 111th Congress or the first two years of the Obama administration. During these two years there were many resolutions and bills introduced about the economy, health care, education, transportation, energy, the environment, and defense. We include maps and analyses of four crucial votes, votes that were not simply divided on strict party lines. These maps show the results of how members of Congress vote. Thus, readers can look at their congressional districts and find out how their member in the House of Representatives voted on these four resolutions:

Fuel-efficient cars
Health care overhaul with a ban on abortion
Health care overhaul passage
Greenhouse gas emissions

Members of Congress vote on many issues, and their votes are closely monitored by many public interest and lobby groups. Many of these groups tabulate the congressional votes at the end of a session and publish a "rating" for each member of the House or Senate. Each organization that calculates a rating has a specific policy agenda that it hopes members of Congress will support. The votes by Congress are matters for the public record, and so are the ratings of these groups. The ratings can run from a high of 100 percent, which means that a member of Congress was in complete agreement with all the issues a group or organization decided to include in its rating. The number of issues used to calculate a rating may be ten or twenty or more. A rating of 50 percent would mean

that member of Congress supported only half of the group's favored legislation.

We consider the congressional ratings of six groups; each has a specific objective and focus when it comes to votes in the House of Representatives. While there are many ratings for Congress, the half-dozen we chose run the gamut of issues that are voted on in the House in a given Congress. The organizations we selected are the ADA (Americans for Democratic Action, a liberal-oriented group), ACU (American Conservative Union, a conservative group), AFL-CIO (a labor organization concerned with unions' interests in health care, worker protection, etc.), Environment America (a pro-environment group), Gun Owners of America (supportive of Americans' right to bear arms), and *National Journal*'s Foreign Policy rating (which rates votes on a range of foreign policy issues). These maps can be compared with how a given congressional district voted in the 2008 election (for Obama or McCain), how counties voted in previous presidential elections, or how they voted in nonpartisan elections (see chapter 8).

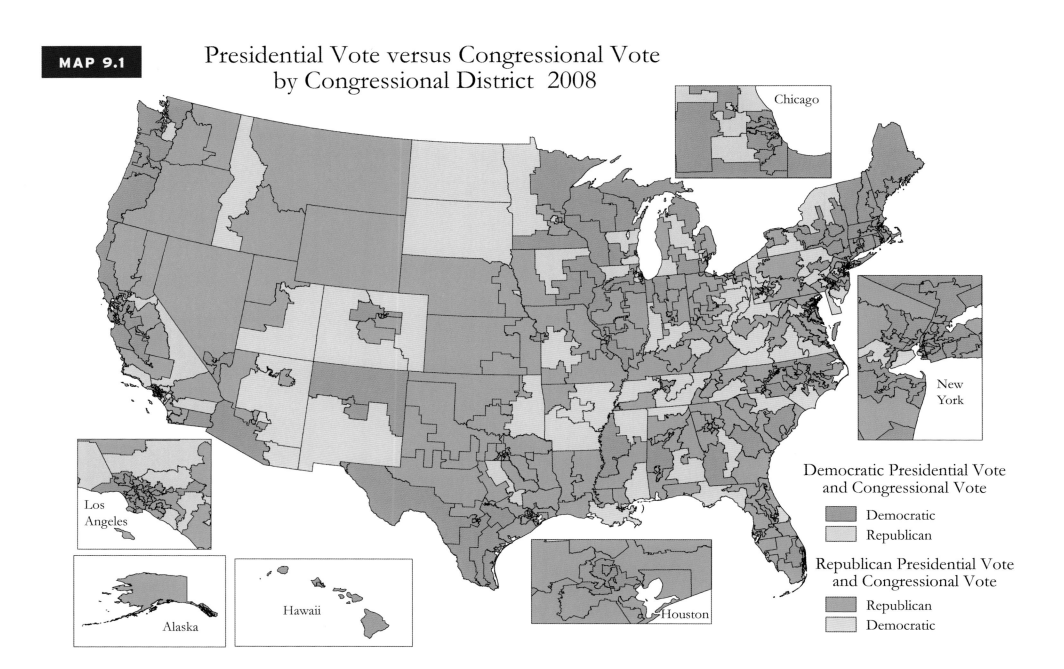

MAP 9.1

Presidential Vote versus Congressional Vote
by Congressional District 2008

Chicago

New
York

Los
Angeles

Alaska

Hawaii

Houston

Democratic Presidential Vote
and Congressional Vote

Democratic

Republican

Republican Presidential Vote
and Congressional Vote

Republican

Democratic

Democratic Presidential Vote by Legislative District
111th House 2008

MAP 9.2

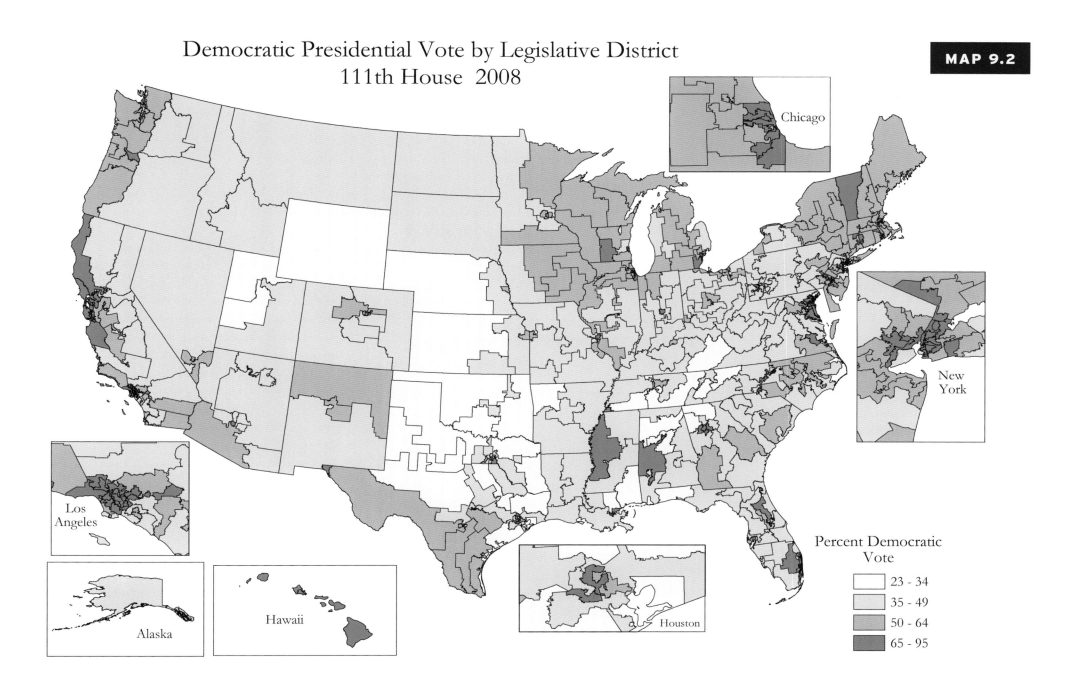

Chicago

New York

Los Angeles

Alaska

Hawaii

Houston

Percent Democratic Vote

23 - 34
35 - 49
50 - 64
65 - 95

■ CONGRESSIONAL VOTE: CAR VOUCHER PROGRAM, JUNE 2009

KENNETH C. MARTIS

H.R. 2751

Legal Title: Consumer Assistance to Recycle and Save Act

Common Reference: Fuel Efficient Car Voucher Program or "Cash for Clunkers"

Primary Sponsor: Representative Betty Sutton (Ohio 13th District)

Roll Call Date: June 9, 2009

Roll Call Vote: 298 Yea (D 239, R 59), 119 Nay (D 9, R 110), 15 Not Voting, 2 Present, 1 Vacant

BILL SUMMARY

The Consumer Assistance to Recycle and Save Act established a program that provided vouchers of $3,500 to $4,500 to offset the purchase or lease of a new passenger car or truck if a qualifying vehicle was traded in. The qualifying trade-ins were older, larger, heavier, and with very low mileage ratings. The media and the public used the phrase "cash for clunkers" in describing the legislation. Local automobile dealerships were responsible for certifying the eligibility of the trade-in vehicles and were required to transfer title to the United States. The dealers had the additional responsibility to certify that the trade-in "has not been, and will not be, sold, leased, exchanged, or otherwise disposed of for use as an automobile in the United States or in any other country . . . " and will eventually be "crushed or shredded. . . ." The goals of the legislation were several, including (1) stimulating automobile production in the United States during a period of recession, and (2) improving the mileage of the U.S. automobile fleet, thereby reducing the demand for gasoline with accompanying environmental benefits.

ILLUSTRATIVE DEBATE FROM THE CONGRESSIONAL RECORD

Representative Betty Sutton of Ohio (D) speaking in favor:

> Mr. Speaker, I rise today on behalf of over 2,000 men and women who work in the Ohio assembly plant in my district and approximately 50,000 Ohioans whose jobs are associated with that plant. I rise for the 159,000 Ohioans with auto-related jobs and the 3 to 5 million Americans who rely on the auto industry to provide for their families. I rise today on behalf of the environment, as we turn the corner to reduce greenhouse gas emissions, improve fuel economy, and to help reduce our reliance on foreign oil. I rise today on behalf of the consumers throughout our great country who continue to struggle during this global recession.

Representative Jeff Flake of Arizona (R) speaking against:

> Madam Speaker, this bill is a bad idea. . . . The first bad idea was to bail out the auto industry in the first place. The second bad idea was for the government to essentially take over the auto industries. We all know that government is not very good at manufacturing anything, so it has to manufacture demand. And that's what this bill is about. It is defying the laws of economics and saying we can manufacture enough demand to keep the auto industries afloat without other measures that they need to take to stay afloat. We can't simply manufacture demand any more than we can defy any of the other laws of economics.

ROLL CALL VOTE MAP ANALYSIS

The legislation had strong support from American and foreign automobile manufacturers, related unions, and dealerships. Automobile manufacturing (including related parts production) in the United States is concentrated in, but not exclusive to, the

Midwest. According to the Bureau of Labor Statistics, in 2009 the top five auto states by employment were Michigan, Ohio, Indiana, Kentucky, and Alabama. Other states with significant auto assembly and parts employment were Texas, New York, California, and Wisconsin. The general conservative view is that government intervention in the market economy is misplaced. The liberal point of view is that government intervention in the economy is sometimes required, especially in times of economic peril. The majority of the Democrats supported the bill (239) with only a few dissenters (9), most from the South and West. The majority of the Republicans voted against the bill (110); however, a sizable minority (59), one-third, supported the voucher program. As the roll call vote map and the 2008 party election map indicate, most of the provoucher Republicans came from the Midwest, Northeast, and several Southern districts with high auto-related manufacturing. Especially significant is that all of the Michigan Republicans voted for the bill, as did a sizable number from Ohio, Indiana, and Illinois. In the end, the geography of the roll call vote for passage correlated highly with Democratic districts nationwide, Midwestern Republican districts with a heavy auto presence, and politically moderate northern and/or suburban Republican districts.

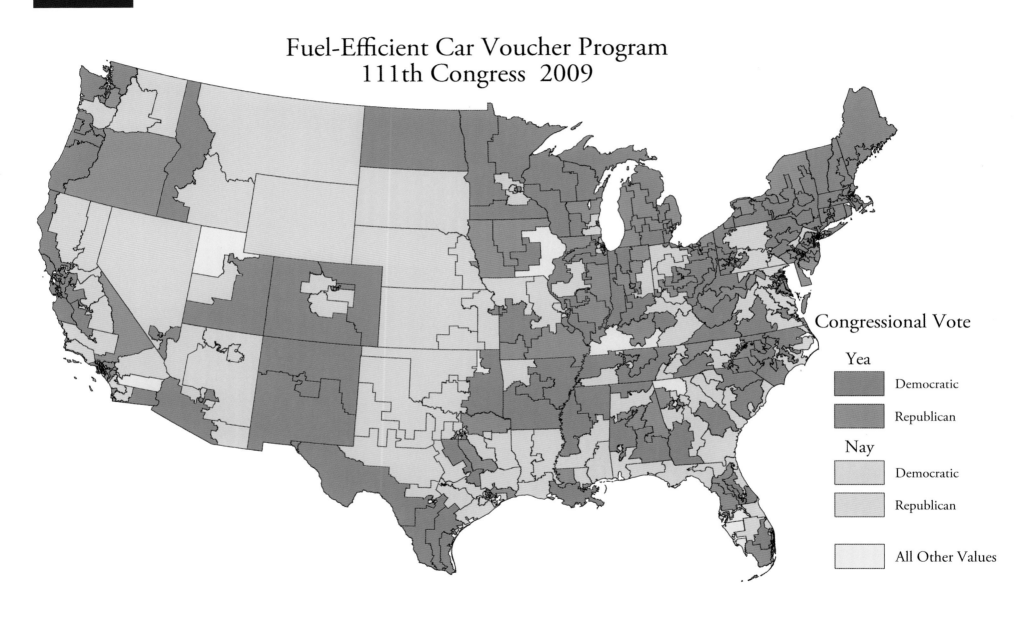

MAP 9.3

Fuel-Efficient Car Voucher Program
111th Congress 2009

Congressional Vote

Yea

Democratic

Republican

Nay

Democratic

Republican

All Other Values

CONGRESSIONAL VOTE: LIMITATION ON ABORTION FUNDING, NOVEMBER 2009

KENNETH C. MARTIS

HOUSE AMENDMENT 509 TO H.R. 3962

Legal Title: Affordable Health Care for America Act—Amendment

Common Title: Abortion Funding Ban

Sponsor: Representative Bart Stupak (Michigan 1st District)

Roll Call Date: November 7, 2009—10:20 p.m.

Roll Call Vote: 240 Yea (D 64, R 176), 194 Nay (D 195, R 0), 1 Present

BILL SUMMARY

This bill was an amendment to the Affordable Health Care for America Act to ban the use of federal funds to perform abortions. This ban included both funds from the "public option" portion of the bill and funds that subsidized coverage from private plans. The amendment proposed to insert the following language into the health care reform bill:

> LIMITATION ON ABORTION FUNDING.
> In General—No funds authorized or appropriated by this Act (or an amendment made by this Act) may be used to pay for any abortion or to cover any part of the costs of any health plan that includes coverage of abortion, except in the case where a woman suffers from a physical disorder, physical injury, or physical illness that would, as certified by a physician, place the woman in danger of death unless an abortion is performed, including a life-endangering physical condition caused by or arising from the pregnancy itself, or unless the pregnancy is the result of an act of rape or incest.

ILLUSTRATIVE DEBATE FROM THE CONGRESSIONAL RECORD

Representative Sam Farr of California (D) speaking against:

> Mr. Speaker, I rise to express my strong opposition to the Stupak . . . amendment. This amendment ignores the constitutionally protected right for women to choose their reproductive health care. It makes women, and only women, have to purchase an additional policy with their own money to cover women's reproductive health care. That we are considering outlawing a medical procedure—one chosen by patients and their doctors—in existing law. This amendment makes it impossible for women to purchase health care insurance to cover a health care procedure that can only be needed at a time of crisis. It would require women to plan for an unplanned pregnancy. That is plain wrong.

When will we stop treating women like second class citizens?

Representative Brad Ellsworth of Indiana (D) speaking in favor:

> Mr. Speaker, I rise today to urge the passage of this vital amendment. Since this debate started, my goal has been to ensure Federal taxpayer dollars are not used to pay for abortions and to provide Americans with pro-life options on this exchange. I have been proud to work with Mr. Stupak and all my colleagues and the Catholic Bishops to make the goal a reality. Getting to this point has not been very easy, but today we're on the brink of passing health care reform that honors and respects life at every stage, including the unborn. If this amendment passes today, I will support this bill. It is time to fix what's broken in our health care system and begin to fulfill the promises we've made to Americans that we represent.

ROLL CALL VOTE MAP ANALYSIS

The historic Affordable Health Care for America Act passed the House at 11:15 p.m. on November 7, 2009. Prior to its passage, a major roll call vote was taken with respect to federally funded abortions.

At 10:20 p.m., the Stupak Amendment to the act, upholding and expanding the ban of federal funds for abortion, passed 240 to 194. Conservatives view life as beginning at conception, and, therefore, abortion is a serious moral question. In addition, many religious denominations believe abortion is morally wrong, including the Catholic Church and the Southern Baptist Convention. Liberals view abortion as a women's rights issue under the time restrictions of the current laws and as upheld by the Supreme Court in the *Roe v. Wade* ruling. The geography of the roll call vote shows strong support for the amendment from all regions of the nation except liberal Democratic centers in the Northeast, Pacific Coast, and major urban concentrations. The map shows support from all Republican areas and Democrats from moderate/conservative swing districts from all sections of the nation. Adding to the pattern are a number of fervent Catholic Democratic representatives or representatives with a heavy Catholic or Southern Baptist population, who support health care reform but could not politically or personally vote for a bill allowing for the possibility of federally funded abortions. For example, three of the four Texas representatives from the relatively poor and heavily Hispanic districts bordering Mexico voted with the Republicans to ban abortion funding but voted for the final health care bill. The Amendment sponsor, Congressman Bart Stupak, a pro-life Catholic Democrat, is a perfect example of this tendency. This pattern replicated itself in districts as varied as normally liberal, but heavily Catholic, suburban Massachusetts and Rhode Island, western Pennsylvania, eastern Ohio, and the Upper Midwest. In the end, sixty-four Democrats, one-fourth of all Democrats in the House, voted for the anti-abortion amendment. However, within less than an hour, twenty-five of these Democrats could, in good conscience, vote in favor of the final health care reform bill, which passed by only four votes.

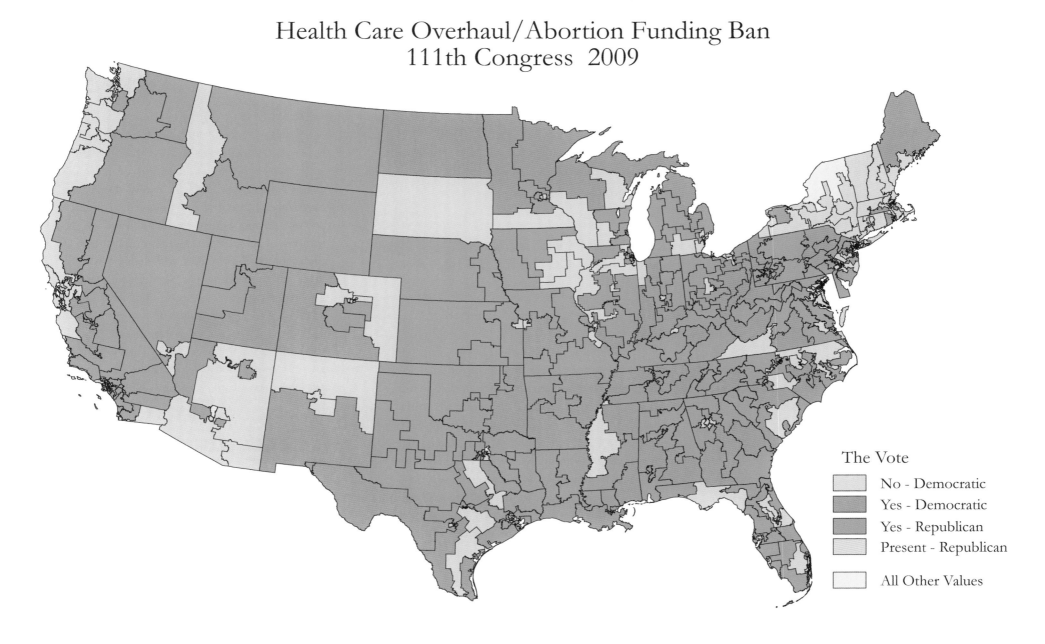

Health Care Overhaul/Abortion Funding Ban
111th Congress 2009

The Vote

No - Democratic

Yes - Democratic

Yes - Republican

Present - Republican

All Other Values

MAP 9.4

CONGRESSIONAL VOTE: HEALTH CARE OVERHAUL PASSAGE, NOVEMBER 2009

KENNETH C. MARTIS

H.R. 3962

Legal Title: Affordable Health Care for America Act
Common Title: Health Care Reform or Universal Health Care Coverage
Primary Sponsor: Representative John D. Dingell (Michigan 15th District)
Roll Call Date: November 7, 2009—11:15 p.m.
Roll Call Vote: 220 Yea (D 219, R 1), 215 Nay (D 39, R 176)

BILL SUMMARY

The Affordable Health Care for America Act, or health care reform, as it was dubbed by the media and public, is one of the major changes in the United States health care system since the 1965 Medicare and Medicaid legislation. Health care reform not only provided for coverage for virtually all non-elderly adult Americans but also changed insurance industry practices, such as the consumer's ability to purchase health care insurance with preexisting conditions. To ensure the widest coverage, the act mandated such items as employers over a certain size to provide health care coverage and, while encouraging private marketplace alternatives, offered a government-run "public option." Various taxes and projections of savings were included in the act to make it theoretically revenue neutral. Prior to its 11:15

p.m. passage, two major roll call votes were taken. First, at 10:20 p.m., the Stupak Amendment to the Act, upholding and expanding the ban of federal funds for abortion, passed. Second, at 10:27 p.m., the Boehner Amendment, or so-called Republican health care alternative, was defeated by a wide 258 to 176 margin.

ILLUSTRATIVE DEBATE FROM THE CONGRESSIONAL RECORD

Representative Steve Cohen of Tennessee (D) speaking in favor:

> Mr. Speaker, today is indeed an historic day. As the plaque over the Speaker's rostrum says, In our time and our generation, we should do something worthy to be remembered. We should have been here 50 or 60 years ago. It is wrong that our country has an infant mortality rate equal to third-world nations. This bill will set out a newborn program that will try to rectify that. It will see that private practice doctors go into the inner cities, with general practitioners having an incentive to go there. With community health centers in the inner cities and wellness and prevention programs not having a deductible, it will bring America into the 21st century.

Representative John Fleming of Louisiana (R) speaking against:

> Mr. Speaker, indeed, this is an historic day. We have a choice today between two bills; one which will have a government takeover of one-sixth of our economy, which will involve the Federal Government into the day-to-day lives of each and every American, or the Republican alternative, which actually goes to the central theme of the problems that we deal with today. Not only that, senior citizens will be the most hurt by this government takeover of health care; $500 billion taken out of Medicare, and with not one scintilla of evidence as to where it's going to come from. It will come from access to care, of course. I would say, in closing, God help us as the government takes over your day-to-day life.

ROLL CALL VOTE MAP ANALYSIS

At 11:15 p.m. on November 7, 2009, the Affordable Health Care for America Act passed the House by only a slim five-vote margin because thirty-nine Democrats bolted the administration. The negotiations, disputes, and vote trading between liberal, moderate, and conservative Democrats were some of the most intense in recent decades. In the end, nearly

15 percent of House Democrats could not support the bill owing to fiscal concerns, philosophical differences, and intense constituency pressure. The majority of the bolting Democrats came from primarily rural and small-town Southern and border state districts. The remainder of the bolters came from all sections of the country, including conservative or swing districts in Northern rural and suburban areas, and rural districts in the Great Plains and interior West.

The conservative point of view was that the act solidified a movement toward big government and was simply too expensive in the age of huge federal deficits. The Republican alternative (Boehner Amendment) incorporated market-based insurance pools, aid to the states for insurance coverage, and reforms such as limitation on medical malpractice awards. The liberal viewpoint was that every other major industrial democratic society in the world has some form of universal health care coverage. The majority of Democrats believed that health care was a right and a moral duty, especially for those citizens least likely to afford coverage. The roll call vote map shows support for health care reform strongest in Democratic strongholds in central city and large urban areas, the Northeast, many Midwestern areas, the Pacific Coast, and districts in the Southwest with heavy Hispanic voter presence.

MAP 9.5

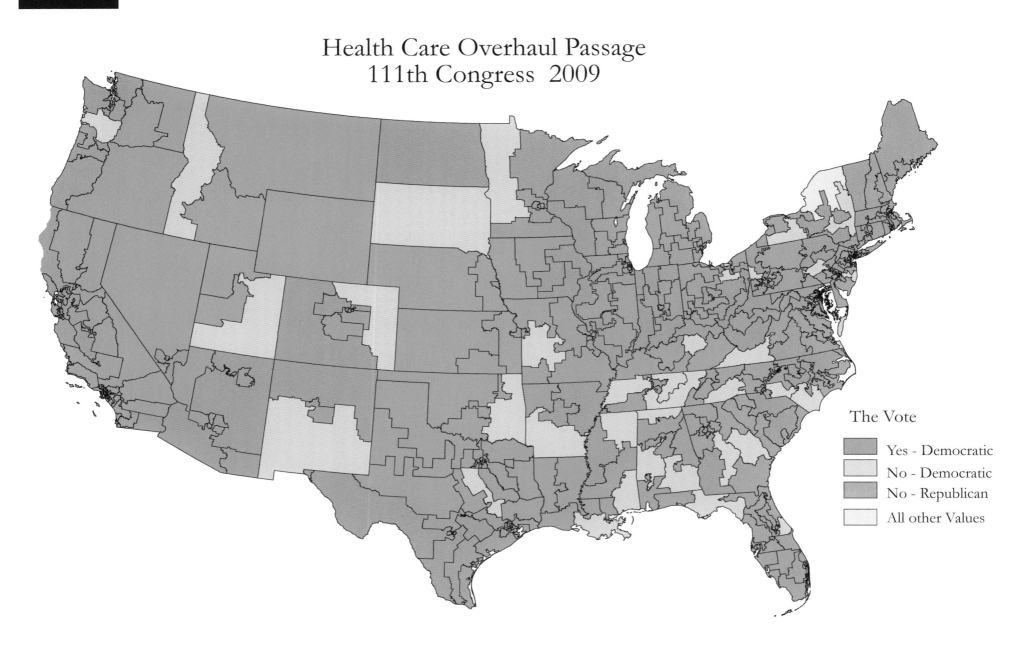

Health Care Overhaul Passage
111th Congress 2009

The Vote

Yes - Democratic

No - Democratic

No - Republican

All other Values

CONGRESSIONAL VOTE: GREENHOUSE GAS EMISSIONS, JUNE 2009

KENNETH C. MARTIS

H.R. 2454

Legal Title: American Clean Energy and Security Act of 2009

Common Reference: Greenhouse Gas Emissions Legislation or "Cap and Trade"

Primary Sponsor: Representative Henry A. Waxman (California 30th District)

Roll Call Date: June 26, 2009

Roll Call Vote: 219 Yea (D 211, R 8), 212 Nay (D 44, R 168), 3 Not Voting, 1 Vacant

BILL SUMMARY

The primary goal of the American Clean Energy and Security Act is to reduce United States global warming carbon-based greenhouse gas emissions with programs such as the promotion of energy efficiencies and development of renewable fuels. The focus of the legislation is setting emissions quotas for the largest greenhouse gas emitters, with those staying below their quota being allowed to trade their savings to those in excess of their quota. Hence, the common term in the media and public to describe this legislation was "cap and trade." Total CO_2 emissions would be reduced over time. In addition, the act was a comprehensive, multifaceted energy bill with numerous provisions, including carbon capture and sequestration, clean transportation, smart electric grid advancement, green jobs and worker transition, and public health and climate change.

ILLUSTRATIVE DEBATE FROM THE CONGRESSIONAL RECORD

Representative Dennis Kucinich of Ohio (D) speaking in favor:

> Millions of Americans have been and are under the threat of violent weather changes, floods, droughts, scorching heat, extraordinary cold, and food insecurity. We are running out of time to craft practicable, workable solutions to moderate the effects of global climate change brought on by global greenhouse gasses. We are past the tipping point, and instead of talking about saving ourselves, we are talking about saving the coal industry. The American people are waiting to be inspired with a vision and a reality of a green future.

Representative Adrian Smith of Nebraska (R) speaking against:

> I rise in opposition to the cap-and-trade bill. . . . Agriculture is one of the Nation's most energy-intensive industries and will be negatively impacted by this legislation. Even a small increase in operating costs could devastate rural farmers and ranchers, and this bill could prove to be a huge burden on our agricultural producers. U.S. farmers would also be at a severe disadvantage compared to farmers in nations which do not have cap-and-trade systems with the correspondingly high input costs.

Representative Mark Souder of Indiana (R) speaking against:

> My congressional district in northeast Indiana is the number one manufacturing district in the United States. In my district, we have 30,000 jobs related to the recreational vehicle area. We have 40,000 jobs related to auto and truck. We have axle factories and windshield factories. We are the manufacturing center, along with Joe Donnelly's district in the South Bend area and Pete Visclosky's in northwest Indiana. We have the most efficient steel factories in America . . . yet we are looking at energy costs that could go up 80 to 100 percent because, you know what, you can't power a steel plant in Indiana with solar panels.

ROLL CALL VOTE MAP ANALYSIS

The greenhouse emissions/cap and trade bill passed the House with a slim seven-vote margin (219–212). Conservatives were generally skeptical about either the existence of global warming, or its severity, or its human component. In addition, they felt the costs of the legislation would increase energy expenses to the detriment of the consumer and international competiveness of the American economy. Liberals contended the science of global warming is compelling and it is a severe threat to the national and international environment. In addition, they felt the new green domestic sources of energy would eventually give America energy independence, especially from unstable foreign sources of petroleum. The legislation vote was close because forty-four Democrats bolted the administration. The Democratic bolters had a strong regional component and had three general characteristics. First, Democrats from Appalachian and Midwestern coal-mining and steel-producing districts strongly opposed the legislation. For example, the two West Virginia Democrats, usually stalwart party loyalists, voted against. Second, a number of moderate Southern Democrats did not support the administration, including several from the oil- and gas-producing states of Texas and Louisiana. The third group of Democrats came from the Great Plains and the West, many of which had both mining and agricultural interests. Ironically, the greenhouse gas legislation passed because of eight moderate Republican bolters. Most of these were from the Northeast; however, one was from Southern California (a desert district with great wind, solar, and geothermal energy potential) and two from suburban districts near Seattle and Chicago. The geography of the roll call vote correlated highly with Democratic districts nationwide, with especially strong support from the Megalopolis Corridor and the Northeast and progressive areas in the Upper Midwest and Pacific Coast.

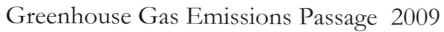

Greenhouse Gas Emissions Passage 2009

MAP 9.6

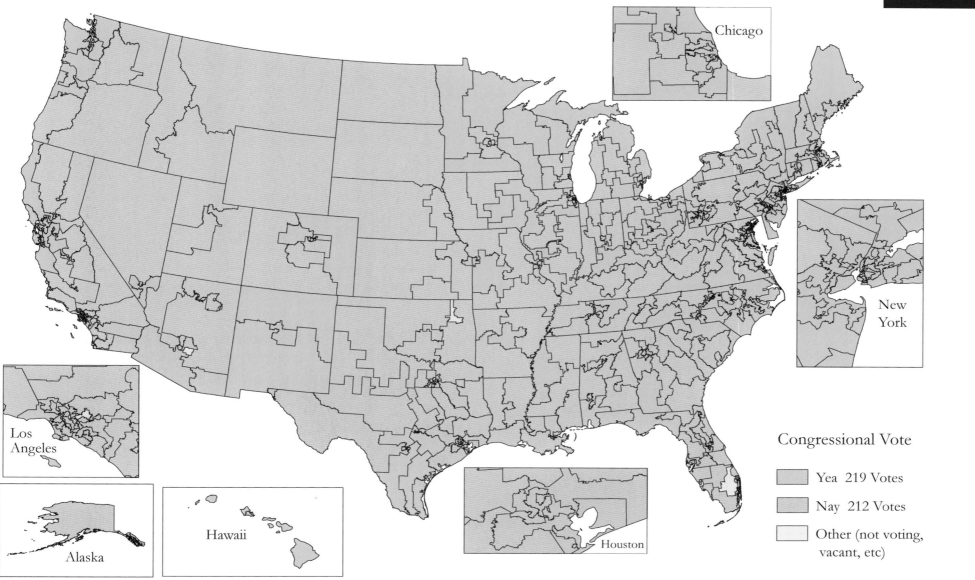

Chicago

New York

Los Angeles

Alaska

Hawaii

Houston

Congressional Vote

Yea 219 Votes

Nay 212 Votes

Other (not voting, vacant, etc)

■ CONGRESSIONAL RATINGS: 111TH CONGRESS (2009-2010)

GERALD R. WEBSTER

INTRODUCTION

At the end of the 110th Congress (2007–2008), the Democrats held 235 seats in the House of Representatives and the Republicans 199 seats, with one seat vacant. In the 2008 congressional elections, the Democrats expanded their majority by twenty-two seats to 257, while Republican seats fell to 178. Thus, as the first session of the 111th Congress (2009) began, the Democrats occupied 79 more seats in the House of Representatives than the Republicans.

Many interest groups rate members of Congress based upon whether a member voted in support or in opposition to the group's legislative priorities. Here we map five such ratings for members of the House of Representatives based upon their roll call votes. The groups selected are diverse in their ideological orientation and include Americans for Democratic Action, the American Conservative Union, the AFL-CIO, Environment America, Gun Owners of America, and *National Journal*'s Foreign Policy rating. With the exception of the Gun Owners of America and *National Journal* ratings, explained further below, the ratings examined here range from 0 percent to 100 percent, with 100 percent indicating the member of Congress voted in complete agreement with the interest group's position, and 0 percent in complete opposition.

AMERICANS FOR DEMOCRATIC ACTION

Americans for Democratic Action (ADA) is a liberal activist interest group. The ADA's 2009 rating is based on twenty roll call votes in the House of Representatives. Among these are support for the economic stimulus package, an expansion of the federal hate crimes law to include sexual orientation, gender, and disability, a bill to reduce greenhouse emissions ("cap and trade"), "cash for clunkers," a bill to overhaul federal regulation of the financial services industry, and opposition to the ban on abortion funding as it pertained to the legislation overhauling the country's health care system.

The mean ADA score for Democrats in the House was 90 percent and 8 percent for Republicans. Not surprisingly, the correlation between ADA ratings for House members and percentage of each district's support for Barack Obama in the November 2008 general election was 0.73. The ADA description of its 2009 ratings also confirms there was greater polarization in 2009 when compared with 2008. While fifty-nine House members scored 100 percent in 2008, ninety-five members, all Democrats, scored 100 percent in 2009. Only sixteen House members scored 0 percent in 2008, but seventy-five did so in 2009, with all being Republicans. The ADA defines a "moderate" score as 40–60 percent. In 2008 there were forty members of the House with scores in this range, but in 2009 only twenty members had moderate scores.

Geographically, those House members with high ADA scores represented districts in New England, along the Pacific Coast, in the Hispanic borderlands of Arizona and Texas, in the northern Midwest states of Wisconsin, Minnesota, and northern Michigan, in the country's larger metropolitan areas such as Los Angeles and New York, and in the majority African American districts in the South in otherwise conservative states such as Mississippi, Alabama, Georgia, South Carolina, and North Carolina. Members with low or conservative ADA scores were concentrated in the country's interior from eastern California to eastern Kentucky, and from central Texas north to Nebraska. Many of the House members with 0 percent scores were elected from rural districts with low population densities.

The map aids in dispelling assumptions of uniformity in different parts of the country, particularly in the Deep South, where the ADA scores are highly variable from district to district. For example, South Carolina's six-member delegation included four scores of 0 percent, but one at 95 percent and another at 100 percent. Mississippi's four House members had scores ranging from 0 percent to 95 percent.

Clearly there are distinct partisan contrasts in ADA scores, with Republicans generally having low conservative scores and Democrats having high liberal scores. Notably, the only Republican to have a "liberal" rating above 50 percent in the House was comparatively liberal Delaware's representative Castle, at 55 percent. The most conservative Democrats are from the comparatively conservative South, including Representative Bright (20 percent) from Alabama and Representative Taylor (35 percent) from Mississippi.

AMERICAN CONSERVATIVE UNION

The American Conservative Union (ACU) was "founded in 1964 to promote the principles of liberty and the strength of the Constitution," and the organization's website states that it is the "largest and strongest grassroots conservative organization. . . ." Like the ADA, the ACU rates the voting records of members of Congress annually.

The ACU ratings are based on twenty-five different votes in 2009, five more than used by the ADA. The votes selected for analysis by the ACU overlap significantly with those used by the ADA, though their position on the votes is opposite. Hence, the ACU opposed the economic stimulus bill, the hate crimes expansion bill, the "cash for clunkers" legislation, and the emission limits bill ("cap and trade"), and supported the prohibition against abortion funding related to the health care bill. The ACU's rating system was also based on some legislation not included in the ADA's analysis. Among these were a bill earmarking funds for an airport in Johnstown, Pennsylvania, named after Representative John Murtha, an amendment that would have eliminated funding for Planned Parenthood, and two bills pertaining to the status of the estate tax.

In 2008, thirty-one members of the House, all Republicans, scored 100 percent on the ACU rating. In 2009, the number jumped to fifty-six Republican members. In 2009, 143 House members, all Democrats, had 0 percent scores on the ACU's ratings, an increase of fifty-eight members over 2008. The ACU defines a conservative as a House member with a score of 80 percent or above, and a liberal as a member with a score of 20 percent or below. Using this standard, there were 154 conservatives and 236 liberals in the House of Representatives.

Given the overlap in votes considered between the ADA and ACU, there is a similar though reversed pattern in the geography of the ACU's ratings. Low scores are found in New England, along the Pacific Coast, in the country's larger cities such as Los Angeles and New York, along the U.S.-Mexico border in Arizona and Texas, in the majority African American districts in the South, and in the Upper Midwest states of Wisconsin, Minnesota, and northern Michigan. The most conservative scores are found in the interior Southwest, Mountain states, Plains states, and the southeastern United States, though the voting records of House members from the South are highly diverse. Though reversed in terms of numeric values, these regional patterns mirror those of the ADA's ratings. Notably, the correlation between the two measures is an extremely high –0.99, and the correlation between ACU House member scores and each district's percentage of support for Barack Obama in the November 2008 general election was -0.72.

AMERICAN FEDERATION OF LABOR AND CONGRESS OF INDUSTRIAL ORGANIZATIONS (AFL-CIO)

The American Federation of Labor and Congress of Industrial Organizations (AFL-CIO) is a labor union focused on working family issues, strengthening Social Security and Medicare, improving workplace safety, and guarding the right to join a union. Unlike the broader ideological interests of the ADA and ACU, the AFL-CIO's rating of members of Congress specifically focuses on labor issues.

The AFL-CIO's rating of House members in 2009 was based on twenty-one different votes. Among these were bills pertaining to wage equity between men and women doing the same work, the economic stimulus package, home foreclosure relief, the credit cardholder's bill of rights, expansion of the federal hate crimes statute to include sexual orientation, gender, or disability, and health care reform. The AFL-CIO supported passage of all of the bills noted above.

For the 2009 votes selected by the AFL-CIO there was a distinct partisan contrast in ratings scores, with the mean score for House Democrats being 94 percent and the mean for Republicans being substantially less at 16 percent. Only thirteen members received 0 percent scores, and all were Republican. An additional forty-two Republicans scored 5 percent, meaning over 30 percent of House Republicans had AFL-CIO rating scores of 5 percent or less. A total of 167 Democrats scored 100 percent, with another nineteen scoring 95 percent, meaning over

72 percent of House Democrats scored from 95 to 100 percent on the rating.

Not surprisingly, the AFL-CIO generally supports the liberal position with respect to pending legislation. As a result, the geographic pattern of ratings largely reflects the partisan orientation of congressional districts, states, and regions. The correlation between the AFL-CIO's ratings and the proportion of support for Barack Obama in the November 2008 general election is a significant 0.72. High ratings are found along the Pacific Coast, in New England, in the Upper Midwest states of Minnesota, Wisconsin, and Northern Michigan, in the Dakotas, in the country's larger cities, in the U.S.-Mexico borderlands with large Hispanic populations, and in the majority African American districts in the South. Low scores were found in the interior West, Mountain states, Plains states from Texas to Nebraska, and in most of the majority white congressional districts in the South.

ENVIRONMENT AMERICA

Environment America is an advocacy group comprising twenty-eight state-level environmental organizations that lobbies government at the local, state, and federal level to pass environmentally friendly legislation. Unlike the other organizations discussed here, the votes used by Environment America in its 2009 ratings are not exclusively drawn from the first session of the 111th Congress, but rather from May 2007 through September 2009. Due to turnover in the House, there are no scores for six House members that took office near or after the end of the time period.

The votes used to construct Environment America's rating included bills to limit offshore drilling for oil, bills for wilderness preservation, tax incentives for the development of wind and solar energy, support for public transit, environmental education programs, and clean water. There was a significant partisan division on this rating, with the mean Democratic score being 93 percent as compared with 24 percent for House Republicans. Seventeen Republican members of the House had 0 percent scores, most representing districts in conservative states in the West including Utah, Wyoming, Kansas, and Texas, as well as the Southern states of Mississippi, Louisiana, Tennessee, and Georgia. Environment America notes that there has been a substantial reduction in the number of House members receiving 0 percent scores from 114 in 2006 to only seventeen in 2009.

As noted above, Democrats generally had higher scores on this indicator than Republicans—the mean score for Democrats was 93 percent while for Republicans it was 24 percent. In total, 146 Democrats received 100 percent ratings supporting Environment America's position on all fifteen roll call votes. The correlation between Environment America's rating and support for Barack Obama in the 2008 general election was 0.68. Hence, not surprisingly, House members receiving high scores were concentrated in New England, the Pacific Coast, the Southwest including Colorado, New Mexico, and the U.S.-Mexico borderlands, the Dakotas, the Upper Midwest states of Wisconsin and Minnesota, and the majority African American districts in the South. It is also notable that there are few environmental moderates with scores from 40 to 60 in the West. House

members with moderate scores are overwhelmingly found east of the Mississippi River.

GUN OWNERS OF AMERICA

The Gun Owners of America (GOA) was formed in 1975 to "preserve and defend the Second Amendment rights of gun owners." With a membership of 300,000, the GOA is frequently critical of the National Rifle Association (NRA), arguing that the latter is too willing to compromise on gun rights issues. It has also been critical of the NRA's ratings of members of Congress, suggesting the organization's ratings are inflated for some members, including 2008 Republican presidential nominee Senator John McCain.

The GOA used six votes on which to rank members of the House of Representatives in the first session of the 111th Congress. If a member voted in opposition to the GOA's position on all six votes, he or she received a 0 rating. Alternatively, if a member voted in support of the GOA's position on all six votes, he or she received a rating of 6. Four of the votes used to rate members of the House pertained to gun bans in the National Parks. The remaining two pertained to health care reform and the stimulus package. The GOA argued that the health care bill will likely result in "gun-related health care data being dumped into a government database" that could be used to prevent citizens from owning guns. The GOA's objection to the stimulus package is similar in that it argues the bill will require physicians to computerize medical records, including psychiatric information that could be used by the government to "impose gun bans on people who have sought treatment."

The scores awarded by the GOA were polarized, with 78 percent of House members receiving either a 0 or a 6. Notably, 215 members, all Democrats, received a 0 score, having voted in opposition to the GOA's position on all six votes. Scores of 6 were awarded to 126 members, all Republicans. As a result, the geography of the ratings largely reflects the geography of party affiliation. Low scores were found in New England, the Upper Midwest including the Dakotas, Minnesota, and Wisconsin, along the West Coast, in the U.S.-Mexico borderlands, and in the majority African American districts in the South. High scores were found in much of the West, from eastern Washington and eastern California to Missouri, and in the majority white districts in the South.

NATIONAL JOURNAL'S FOREIGN POLICY RATING

National Journal (NJ) is a weekly founded in 1969 devoted to politics and policy issues. It has published ideological ratings based on roll call votes for members of Congress since 1981. NJ's ratings focus on social policy, economic policy, and foreign policy.

While the rating systems discussed above consider the proportion of the time that a member of Congress voted in line with the organization's position, NJ's scale is based on how conservative or liberal a member is relative to other members. Thus, a conservative value of 75 means a House member is more conservative than 75 percent of his or her colleagues.

NJ used twenty different votes on foreign policy issues to judge the ideological rankings of all member of the House in 2009. Among these votes were bills pertaining to funding the State Department, legislation requiring the president to impose sanctions on companies providing refined oil to Iran, the allocation of military aid to Pakistan, the status of the Guantanamo Bay detention center, and military procurement spending.

As would be expected, the mean conservatism rating for all House Republicans of 71 percent was much higher than for Democrats, who had a mean of 28 percent. Thirty-nine House members received 0 percent ratings, meaning collectively they were the least conservative or most liberal in the chamber. All thirty-nine were Democrats. A large number of House members tied as the most conservative with scores of 75 percent. In total, 108 members, or 25 percent of

the House, received a score of 75 percent, meaning three-quarters of House members were less conservative than this group. All of these House members were Republicans. The correlation between NJ's foreign policy score and district support for Obama in the 2008 general election was –0.71.

The geography of NJ's foreign policy conservatism scores is complex. As noted earlier, 108 members tied with the highest possible conservative score of 75. This group dominates much of the western half of the country, from eastern California to Louisiana, and north to Wyoming and Montana. There are also conservatism concentrations in Florida, Ohio, and the Mid-Atlantic states. Liberal, or at least less conservative, concentrations are found along the Pacific Coast, in the Great Lakes states of Minnesota, Wisconsin, and Michigan, in New England, and in the country's larger urban areas. Notably absent from the patterns of liberalism found on the earlier maps are many of the majority African American districts in the South. Thus, African American House members from the South voted much more similarly to their white colleagues on foreign policy issues than on bills pertaining largely to domestic issues such as labor and the environment.

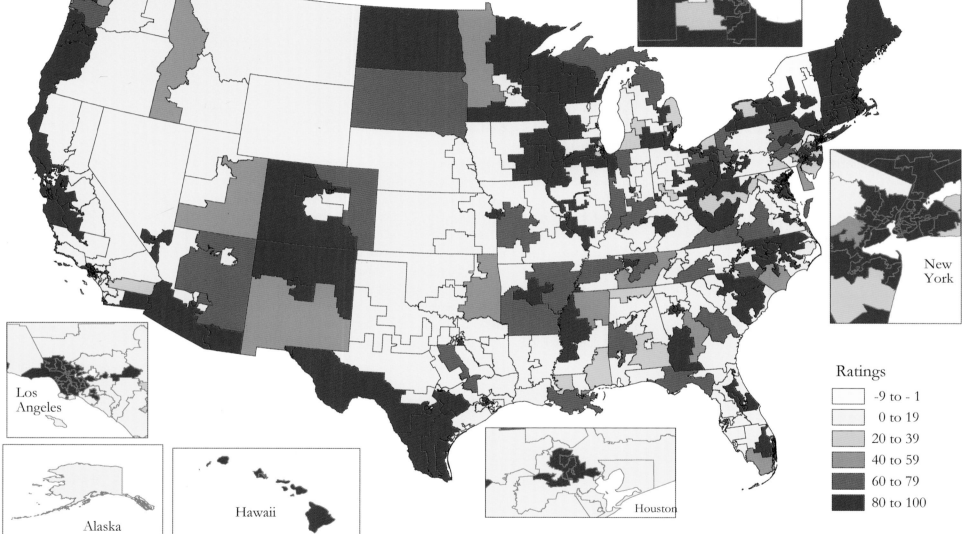

MAP 9.7

ADA RATINGS
111th House 1st Session

Chicago

New York

Los Angeles

Alaska

Hawaii

Houston

Ratings

	-9 to - 1
	0 to 19
	20 to 39
	40 to 59
	60 to 79
	80 to 100

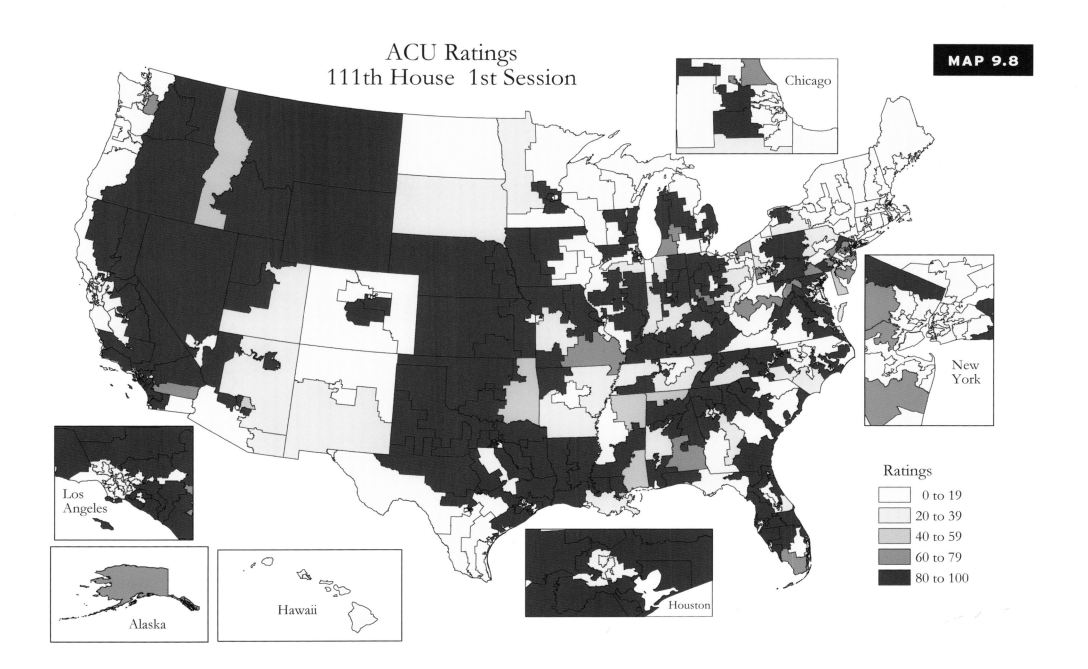

ACU Ratings
111th House 1st Session

MAP 9.8

Chicago

New York

Los Angeles

Alaska

Hawaii

Houston

Ratings

0 to 19
20 to 39
40 to 59
60 to 79
80 to 100

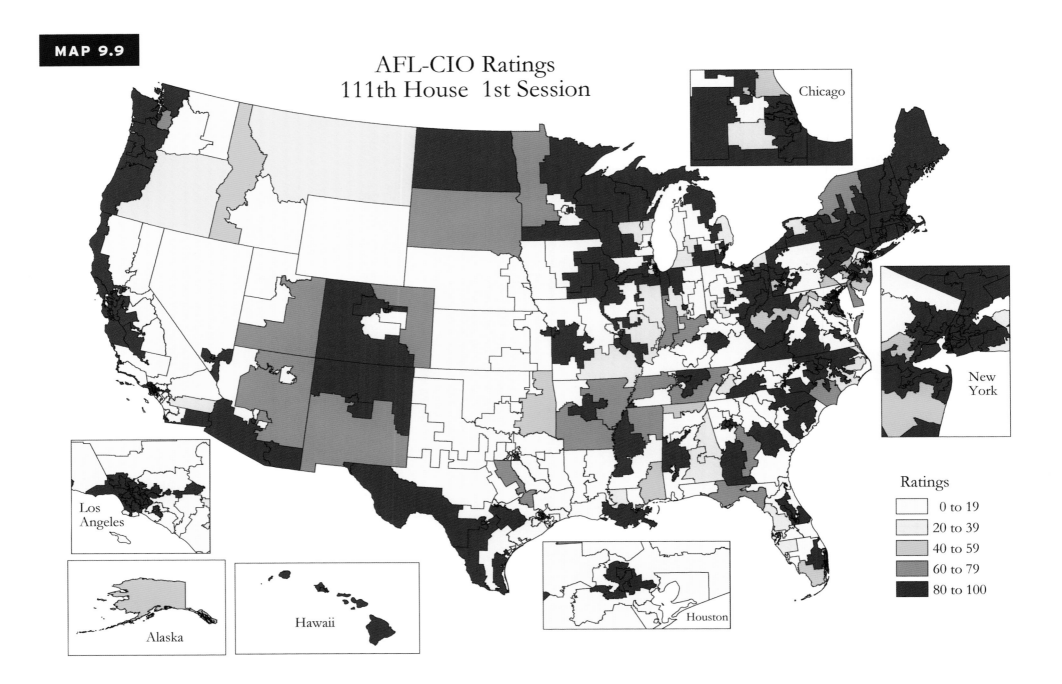

MAP 9.9

AFL-CIO Ratings
111th House 1st Session

Chicago

New
York

Los
Angeles

Alaska

Hawaii

Houston

Ratings

0 to 19

20 to 39

40 to 59

60 to 79

80 to 100

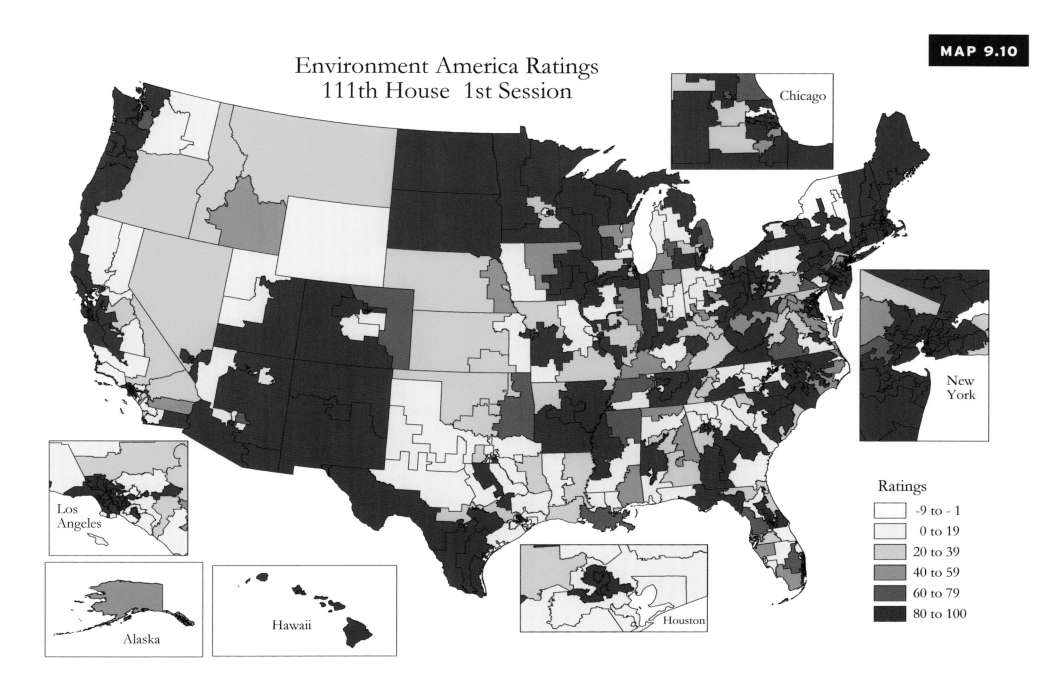

Environment America Ratings
111th House 1st Session

MAP 9.10

Chicago

New York

Los Angeles

Alaska

Hawaii

Houston

Ratings

☐	-9 to -1
☐	0 to 19
▨	20 to 39
▨	40 to 59
▨	60 to 79
▨	80 to 100

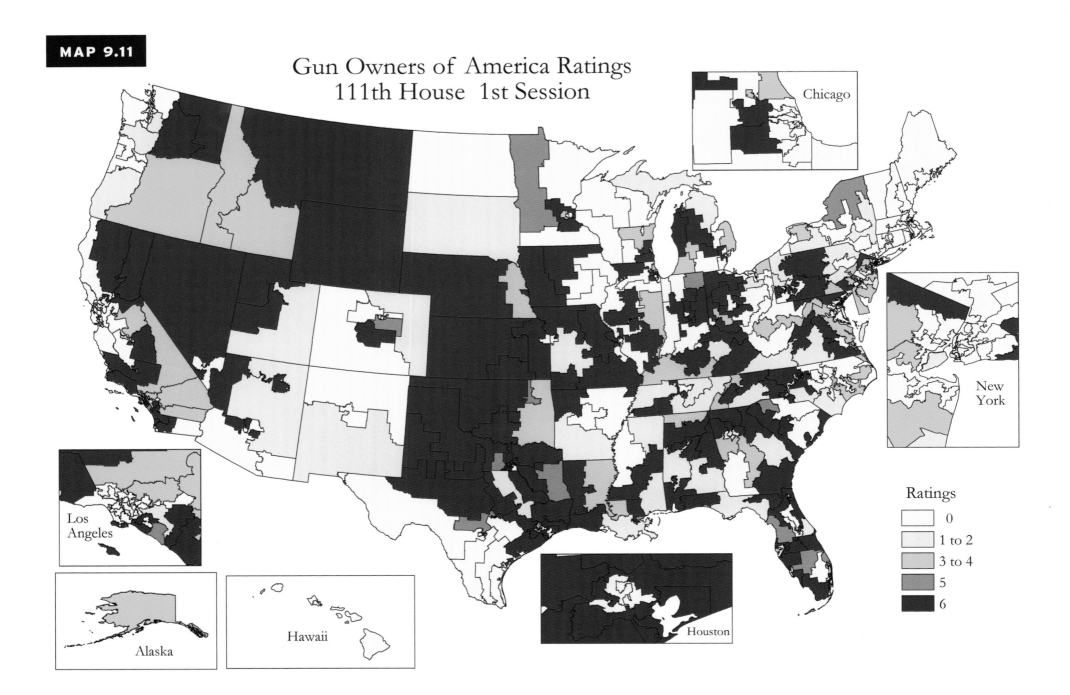

MAP 9.11

Gun Owners of America Ratings
111th House 1st Session

Chicago

New York

Los Angeles

Alaska

Hawaii

Houston

Ratings

0
1 to 2
3 to 4
5
6

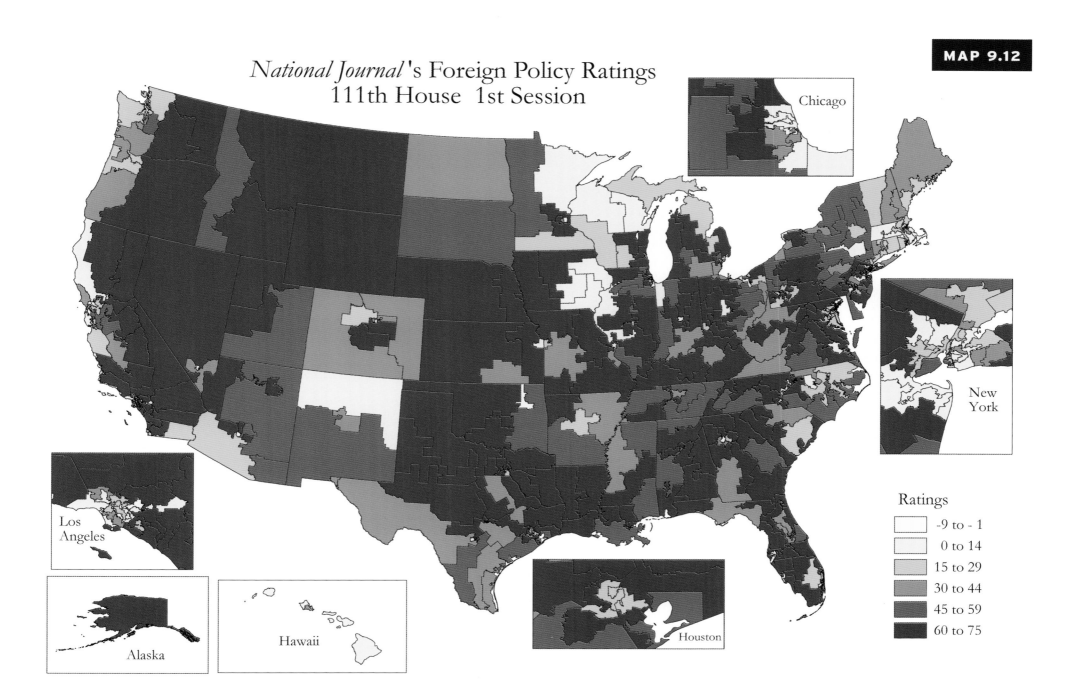

National Journal's Foreign Policy Ratings
111th House 1st Session

MAP 9.12

Chicago

New York

Los Angeles

Alaska

Hawaii

Houston

Ratings

	-9 to -1
	0 to 14
	15 to 29
	30 to 44
	45 to 59
	60 to 75

REFERENCES

American Conservative Union. http://www.conservative
.org/.
American Federation of Labor and Congress of Industrial
Organizations. http://www.aflcio.org/.
Americans for Democratic Action. http://www.adaction
.org/.
Environment America. http://www.environmentamerica
.org/.
Gun Owners of America. http://gunowners.org/.
National Journal. http://www.nationaljournal.com/njonline/.

TOWARD A MORE PERFECT UNION: TEN SCENARIOS

Many initial reports considered the 2008 presidential election to be truly distinctive or "watershed" in nature. While that feature held true as it marked the first time an African American was elected to the nation's highest elected office, it was not truly watershed in nature when the resulting geographic patterns were studied. In fact, a number of political scientists, including many contributing essays to this volume, attest there were striking similarities to several previous elections. These similarities are evident throughout this atlas, whose maps have illustrated clearly that region and party remain distinctive features of the American electoral system. These distinctions were apparent in the 2008 presidential elections and also in elections held during the 1960s, 1970s, 1980s, and 1990s. While there is always some fluidity in the state and county voting patterns, there is also more than a fair degree of continuity.

Although long-term continuity is a trademark feature of the American electoral landscape, significant new features emerge that need to be considered in any in-depth analysis at national and regional scales. Examples of "new and distinctive" features in the past were granting women the vote as a result of the Nineteenth Amendment in 1920, the enfranchisement of more African Americans as a result of the Voting Rights Act of 1964, the migration of many northerners to the Sunbelt from the 1970s onward that contributed to the emergence and strength of the Republican party in the South, the growing elderly populations in Florida and the Southwest, and the increased registration of Hispanics in the South and Southwest. Each of these developments has altered the political landscape and election process, not only in general elections but in the selection of party nominees, their choices of running mates, and national campaign strategies. These trends also influence the decisions regarding which states are competitive or in a "swing" category in determining the voting done by the Electoral College.

What can also be stated with more than some degree of certainty is that the voting processes and the final voting results themselves will continue to experience changes in the coming years. Not only will there be decisions about the eligibility of voters, but also the technologies that can/might be used on election days. One can only dream what instant voting by cell phones or the ability to vote from multiple possible sites might bring to the electoral process, the reporting and predictions of results before voting stations close, and the almost certain-to-be legal challenges by losing candidates and special interest groups. There will also likely be legal challenges to online or voice registration and whether a "vote" by voice or computer at home or office constitutes the same as an electronic ballot in an official precinct.

The 2008 election cycle was significant not only because of its outcome but also because of the intense level of interest that it generated among new voters and the impacts of the Internet and new voting technologies on the results. Given these innovations, it is appropriate to ask: what might happen in the future? We offer the following ten scenarios about the American electoral landscape. Whether any or all of these will eventually actually occur is not our major objective. What is important is that we recognize that in all likelihood there will both be some changes that will occur as a result of grassroots organizations petitioning for reform, lawsuits challenging the existing process, and shifts in the demographics of society and interests of voters. These ten are offered as food for thought; they are not listed in any order of importance.

1. REGIONAL SUPERPRIMARIES

Regional superprimaries could replace the current system in which some states hold caucuses or primaries early in the election year while others hold theirs later. In regional superprimaries, each state within a region would hold its primary election on the same day in the spring of an election year. (It should be noted that this proposal surfaced in the 1980s and 1990s in the Southeast but never resulted in any long-term, coordinated, nationwide effort or support by the two major political parties.) One possibility would be to have all primaries on the same day. Another would be to divide the states into groups at random, with ten states holding their primaries the same day in January, another ten states holding theirs in February, and another ten in March, in April, and in May. An advantage of superprimaries would be that Democratic and Republican voters living in all states in a given region would have an opportunity to vote on all those declaring their candidacy for the presidency, rather than a small number of states having a clear advantage in the final selection process.

2. THIRD AND FOURTH PARTIES

Strong third and fourth parties could emerge and play a major role in the election of the president. Many Americans are dissatisfied with the degree of polarization characterizing the contemporary Democratic and Republican parties. To the extent that the Democratic Party continues to move to the left and the Republican Party continues to move to the right, there may be more opportunity for a centrist party that will emerge and draw support from more conservative Democrats and more liberal Republicans. At present, any third or fourth party has many legal hurdles to overcome in the hope of having its candidates' names appear on the primary or final ballots. Also, those wishing to cross party lines are disenfranchised in many states in voting in the primaries. These third and fourth parties may emerge across the country. However, it is also possible that they would emerge in key regions where a specific issue commanded their attention. These may be parties with key interests in immigration, environmental/green issues, religious issues (abortion, same-sex marriage, etc.) and funding priorities (domestic or international). American politics is provided with examples of groups, including the Populists, the Progressives, labor union and civil rights groups, whose major goals were not to win elections but to influence the dominant political parties, which they did. What were once "fringe" issues often became accepted as "mainstream" over time.

For the past two hundred years, American presidential elections have been dominated by two major political parties. The Republican and Democratic parties have been the major political parties in the United States for the past 160 years. Zachary Taylor, a Whig elected in 1848, was the last elected president who was neither a Democrat nor a Republican. Both parties, past and present, are loose with often uneasy coalitions of various niche populations or subcultures within the United States. These niche populations have included farmers and factory workers, immigrant groups, members of particular religious communities, retirees, and ethnic minorities. Other niche groups have emerged on the basis of political issues, such as specific foreign policies, economic priorities, or environmental protection. Many political movements in the past, including the Populists, the Progressives, labor union movements, and more recently civil rights movements and green/environmental interests, are significant in American history because they introduced ideas into the political arena that are now considered mainstream.

The Republicans in the nineteenth century were a coalition of political progressives, abolitionists, industrialists, and small Northern and Western farmers. The Democratic coalition of the mid-twentieth century included most Southerners, big-city political machines, labor union members, and intellectuals. As these coalitions have evolved, and as old niche populations have declined in importance and new ones become dominant, the geography of presidential support for each party has evolved and continues to evolve. For example, agricultural interests have little influence in American politics today, given that only about 1 percent of the U.S. workforce is now employed in agriculture. On the other hand, rapid increases in the Latino population have made this group an increasingly important niche population within the American political spectrum.

3. REFORMING THE ELECTORAL COLLEGE

Rather than having the Electoral College meet in the month following the election, the candidate who received a plurality of the popular vote would be declared the winner. Alternatively, a special runoff election between the two top finishers could be held if no candidate received a majority of the popular vote, a decision that experienced and novice voters could understand. However, a shift from the Electoral College to the direct election of the president would have profound impacts on campaign strategies. Much less attention would be paid to swing states. Parties would make stronger efforts to turn out their supporters in large numbers, regardless of where these supporters reside. Also, all parties and candidates would pay much more attention to large metropolitan areas with their concentrations of voters than is currently the case. Also, many residents of rural areas would likely oppose moving to a direct popular election of the president because they fear that issues of interest to people in nonmetropolitan areas would be ignored. Eliminating the College would be difficult with the organization of Congress, the media, and state legislatures privileging the two-party system. Also, getting rid of the winner-take-all voting would likely weaken the two major parties and open the likelihood of a centrist party's winning.

It should be mentioned that replacing the Electoral College with a system of direct popular vote would require amending the Constitution, which in turn requires a two-thirds majority of both Houses of Congress and concurrence of the legislatures of three-quarters of the states.

4. PUBLICLY FINANCED ELECTIONS

Rather than large donors, powerful interest groups, and large corporations wielding excessive influence in presidential elections and where politicians seek money from individuals and corporations, national elections would be funded by the public. Such elections would permit all potential candidates to compete, rather than providing an advantage to those with wealth, name recognition, and built-in powerful corporate or party support. In January 2010 the U.S. Supreme Court ruled in *Citizens United v. Federal Election Commission* that corporations are "associations of persons" that therefore have the same right as do individuals to contribute to election campaigns. The impact of this decision on future elections may shed light on the potential value of public financing of elections. Almost certain issues to arise would be the public financing of third or fourth parties or even minor and lunatic-fringe parties of the left and right.

5. AUTOMATIC REGISTRATION FOR VOTING

To streamline the voting process and to encourage greater actual voting, all individuals who are over eighteen would be granted a voting card they could use on Election Day. Some states use a so-called motor-voter procedure in which people are registered to vote automatically when they apply for drivers' licenses or state identification cards. The impact of this change is unknown, which may be one reason why the major political parties are unsure for whom the new voters would vote. However, in some areas Republicans have been more skeptical of automatic registration than Democrats, because turnout among Republican-leaning voters tends to be higher than turnout among Democrats. The possibility of required voting (done in Belgium) is remote in the United States.

6. IMPACTS OF THE INTERNET AND ELECTRONIC SOCIAL NETWORKING

The rapid introduction and diffusion of new information and communications technologies are changing the face of American society and the public arena. It could be argued that they could also weaken local community bonds and strengthen long-distance bonds between people. Voting is no longer considered a community act, especially as the Internet and mail voting are being increasingly used. (Oregon seems to be taking the lead on some innovative measures to increase voter awareness and participation.) Many voters are relying more on the Internet, blogs, listservs, and so on for political information as opposed to "mainstream" print and visual media. These trends further fragment people and could lead to a deepening of existing cultural and regional divides.

7. CHANGING THE ELECTION DAY

The national voting day would be moved to an early fall date, for example, the second Saturday and Sunday in September, rather than early November, when there is often inclement weather in the Northeast, Middle West, and Pacific Northwest. Extending the voting to two days and not on a regular work day may also increase voter turnout, which is now just above 50 percent (nationwide average) in national elections. (The rates are much lower, often embarrassingly low, in most off-year and state and local elections.) Also, individuals would be able to vote by phone or from a computer. More and more people now vote early or absentee; remote voting may become increasingly popular in future elections. (Note that changing the election date would also require a constitutional amendment as both the election and inauguration dates are spelled out in the Twentieth Amendment.)

8. TRANSBOUNDARY CONGRESSIONAL DISTRICTS CROSSING STATE LINES

Currently, all seats in the House of Representatives are awarded to states and in whole numbers. District boundaries do not cross state lines, even though many residents in large metropolitan areas regularly cross multiple state lines to work, shop, recreate, and worship and watch and read local news that is interstate in nature. Decisions regarding political districting and redistricting congressional districts would look initially at large metropolitan areas' populations, not the stated populations of states following the decennial census counts. At present the number of state residents per House member varies from state to state. The U.S. average is 647,000 per House district. North Carolina and New Jersey both elect thirteen members; the average-size district for North Carolina is 615,000, and for New Jersey, 647,000. Iowa and Oklahoma both have five representatives; the district average for Iowa is 580,000 and for Oklahoma, 690,000. The average district size for Nevada is 854,000, for Mississippi, 711,000, for Connecticut, 680,000, for Nebraska, 566,000, and for Washington, 535,000. Changing the redistricting system would also require amending the Constitution, which states specifically that seats in the House are awarded to each state on the basis of population. Another possibility would be to award states with fractions of votes.

9. INCREASING THE SIZE OF THE HOUSE OF REPRESENTATIVES

The size of the U.S. House of Representatives at 435 members has been the same since 1912. In 1789 there were about 30,000 constituents per district; today the number is approaching 700,000 people. Thus there is precedence for increasing the House membership. An enlarged House would result in more districts being carved out of existing states and metropolitan areas but also require more expenses for representatives, their staffs, offices, and so on. On the plus side, there would likely be less diversity in the demographics of many present districts. Many representatives elected today have to balance great differences in their districts' age cohorts, income and education levels, economic livelihoods, ethnic and racial diversities, and religious differences when running for office and voting on legislation. An enlarged House could also likely result in representatives being elected from third or fourth parties, who may have special interests and agendas not shared by the two dominant parties.

10. PROLONGED NATIONAL STALEMATE WITH SHARP REGIONAL DIFFERENCES

Whereas the fifty years 1930–1980 were marked by a convergence toward a national culture of reduced inequality, the decades since, and extending into the future, will be marked by deepening inequality, economic volatility and uncertainty, and, almost certainly, greater cultural division. That is, the "red-blue" divide that exists will continue and deepen. By default the states will gain power and became havens for like-minded people. The roots of the malaise are deindustrialization, deepening economic inequality, and the widespread failure of public education. Some of the more balanced (political) states may be able to resist this pessimistic scenario. Also, the rise of third and fourth parties (regional or national) and powerful extreme interest groups will likely aggravate the collapse of consensus.

ELECTORAL REFORMS: FROM REMOTE TO POSSIBLE

How likely are the changes mentioned above to occur? These changes may come about gradually, that is, working their way through the political systems of Congress and state legislatures. Some may be affected by decisions of the Supreme Court, which has stepped into controversial political decisions in the past, for example, in reapportionment and redistricting cases, in the controversial 2000 election, and recently in the *Citizens United* campaign financing case. On the other hand, they may come from specific positions taken by presidential candidates or from grassroots movements that present challenges to the existing system. Convening a new constitutional convention (which would require a two-thirds vote of both houses of Congress and three-fourths of state legislatures) to address some or any of the issues mentioned above is considered a remote possibility. Should one be convened, constitutional scholars disagree on whether the agenda would be addressing specific issues or open to discussing other issues.

REFERENCE

Leib, J., and G. R. Webster. 1998. "On Enlarging the U.S. House of Representatives." *Political Geography* 17 (3): 319–29.

FIGURE 10.1
Obama and
Biden Bumper
Stickers

FIGURE 10.2
McCain and
Palin Bumper
Stickers

History repeats
itself.
McCain/Palin '08

FIGURE 10.3
Obama Stamps
from Different
Countries:
Inauguration
and Presidency

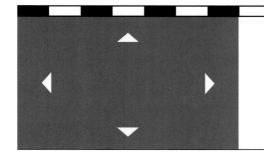

INDEX

Note: Page numbers in *italics* refer to graphs or maps; page numbers followed by "t" in italics refer to tables.

abortion: ballot measures on, 253; congressional vote on funding limits, 283–84, *285*; Northeast and, 124
ACU. *See* American Conservative Union
ADA. *See* Americans for Democratic Action
Adams, John Quincy, 3
advertising: outlays on, 27–28, *29*; television, effects of, 27
Affordable Health Care for America Act, 286–87, *288*; Stupak Amendment, 283–84, *285*
AFL-CIO, 277; ratings of congressional votes, 293–94, *298*
African Americans. *See under* black
age: and exit polls, 68; and medical marijuana, 268; population by, 188, *189–91*; and rural/urban gap, *72t*; and stem cell research, 270; and 2008 vote, *67*; and voter turnout, *102–3*
Agnew, John, 146–47
agriculture: employment in, and election, 178, *179*; in Midwest, 136; in Minnesota, 244; Prevention of Farm Animal Cruelty Act, 262, *263*
air conditioning, 131
Alabama, *128*; ballot measures in, *255t*; ideological identification in, *122t*

Alaska, 147, *148*; American Indian population in, 218, *223*
alternative energy referenda, 260, *261*
American Clean Energy and Security Act, 289–90, *291*
American Conservative Union (ACU), 277; ratings of congressional votes, 293, *297*
American Federation of Labor and Congress of Industrial Organizations (AFL-CIO), 277; ratings of congressional votes, 293–94, *298*
American Indian majority counties, 136, 138; versus farming employment, 178; in Montana, 156; in Mountain West, 143, *145*; in Pacific, 147; partisan margins in, 59; poverty in, 198, *199*; youth population in, 188
American Indian population, 217–18, *223*
Americans for Democratic Action (ADA), 277; ratings of congressional votes, 292–93, *296*
animals, Prevention of Farm Animal Cruelty Act, 262, *263*
Appalachia, 123, 126–27, *128*, 135, 166; females in labor force in, 176; poverty in, 198, *199*
Arizona, 142, *145*; ballot measures in, 253, 257, *259*; campaign stops in, *35*; donors in, 30
Arkansas, *128*; ballot measures in, *255t*; ideological identification in, *122t*
Asian population, 213–14, *220*
assisted suicide, ballot measures on, 272–73, *274*

ballot measures, 253–76, *255t, 256*; on alternative energy, 260, *261*; on animal cruelty prevention, 262, *263*; on assisted suicide, 272–73, *274*; on same-sex marriage, 257–58, *259*, 264, *265*, 266–67
Baptists, 229, *231*, 237
Barkley, Dean, 244
Barr, Bob, popular vote 2008, *55*
bellwether counties, 5
bellwether states: Missouri, 134, 155; Ohio, 75, 134, 161. *See also* swing states
Berentsen, William, 121–24, 162
Bible Belt, 237, *238*
Biden, Joseph, 2, 9, 16–17; bumper stickers for, *307*; campaign stops, 33–34, *35, 37*
Bigot Belt, *118*, 129–30
Billings County, 184
Black Belt, 126; poverty in, 198, *199*
black majority counties: versus construction employment, 180; household composition in, 196; versus manufacturing employment, 182; micropolitan areas in, 109; migration and, 192; partisan margins in, 59; in Tennessee, 165; youth population in, 188
black population, 216–17, *222, 225*; and marriage referenda, 266–67
border states, definition of, 120n3

Boston: Asian population in, 213, *220*; black population in, 216–17; Route 128, 172; suburban, 123

Brown, Scott, 123

Brownback, Sam, 9

Bush, George W., 2–3, 75; in Great Plains, 138, *141*; manufacturing employment and, 182; in Midwest, *137*; in Mountain West, *145*; newspaper endorsements, 40; in Northeast, *125*; in Pacific, *148*; in South, 127, *128*

Byrd, Harry, Jr., 166

California, 146, *148*; Asian population in, 214; ballot measures in, 253, 255*t*, 260, *261*, 262, *263*, 264, *265*, 266–67; and Colorado, 149; donors in, 30; electoral college votes, 104; Hispanic population in, 214–15, *221*; historical context, 76; ideological identification in, 122*t*

campaigns, 27–49; and early voting, 69; stops, 33–34, *35–39*

cap and trade legislation, 289–90, *291*

carpetbaggers, 130–34; term, 131

Carter, Jimmy, 16, 75–76, 133

cartogram: definition of, 105; of electoral vote, *105*

car voucher program, 280–81, *282*

Cash for Clunkers, 280–81, *282*

Catholics, 229, *230*; and assisted suicide, 272; and stem cell research, 270; and Stupak Amendment, 284

caucuses, 9–10, *11*; Iowa, 16–17, *18*

centers of partisan voting, 47, *48*

Chambliss, Saxby, 250, *251*

Chapman, Thomas E., 171–72, 257–58, 264

Cheney, Dick, 2

Chiang, Chun-Fang, 40

Chicago, 107; Asian population in, 213–14, *220*; black population in, 216; donors in, 30; Hispanic population in, 215, *221*; placemark poll, 43, *44*

Christian Reformed Church, 242, 272

Christians, demographics of, 229

Church of Jesus Christ of Latter-Day Saints. *See* Mormon counties

cities. *See* urban areas

Citizens United v. Federal Election Commission, 305

class, and 2008 vote, 65, *66–67*

Clinton, Hillary, 2, 9; Hispanic population and, 226; in Iowa caucus, 16–17, *18*; in New Hampshire primary, 14, *15*; in Pennsylvania primary, 19, *20*; in primaries, 10, *13*, 21–22, *24*

Clinton, William J., 155, 159

closed primaries, 10

Cohen, Steve, 286

Coleman, Norm, 244–45, *246*

college. *See* university/college counties

Colorado, 142, 149, *150*; ballot measures in, 253–54, 255*t*; historical context, 75; voter turnout in, 98, *101*

Comanche County, 75

congressional districts: and electoral vote distribution, 138; transboundary, 306

congressional votes, 277–302; Affordable Health Care for America Act, 286–87, *288*; Consumer Assistance to Recycle and Save Act, 280–81, *282*; on greenhouse gas emissions, 289–90, *291*; versus presidential vote, 278; ratings by interest groups, 292–95, *296–301*; Stupak Amendment, 283–84, *285*

Connecticut, *125*; ideological identification in, 122*t*

conservative identification, 122*t*; in Northeast, 123–24

construction employment, 180, *181*

Consumer Assistance to Recycle and Save Act, 280–81, *282*

contact hypothesis, 207

convenience voting. *See* early voting

conventions, *11*

Cook County, 107

Costilla County, 178

counties: bellwether, 5; creative class, 143, 149, *150*; demographics of, 171–240; with highest/lowest partisan margins, 59, *60–61*; migration and, 192, *193*; population change by, 186, *187*; rapidly growing, types of, 186; swing, 114–15, *116–19*, 152, 155; voter consistency by, 114–15, *116–19*. *See also specific type*

craft occupations, 174, *175*

creative class: in Colorado, 149, *150*; definition of, 171; in Mountain West, 143; occupations, 171–72, *173*

crowdsourcing, Twitter Vote Report, 45, *46*

Crump, Jeffrey R., 178, 180, 182, 184

Dahlman, Carl T., 30

Darmofal, David, 62–63

DeChano-Cook, Lisa M., 267–68, 270

Delaware, 123, *125*; ideological identification in, 122*t*

Democratic-Farm-Laborites (DFL), 244

Democratic Party: American Indian population and, 218, *223*; areas with highest/lowest margins, 59, *60–61*; Asian population and, 214, *220*; black population and, 217, *222*; candidates, donors to, *31*; center of partisan voting, 47, *48*; in Colorado, 149, *150*; construction employment and, 180, *181*; craft occupations and, 174, *175*; education and, 200, *201*; farming employment and, 178, *179*; federal receipts and, 211, *212*; in Florida, 153–54; foreign-born population and, 227, *228*; in Georgia, 250; in Great Plains, 138–39, *141*; gubernatorial races, 241–42, *243*; and health care reform, 286–87, *288*; Hispanic population and, 215, *221*, 225–26; historical context and, 76, *79–86*; household income and, 194, *195*; husband-wife households and, 196, *197*; in Indiana, 153–54; manufacturing employment and, 182, *183*; in Midwest, 135–36, *137*; military counties and, 204, *205*; in Minnesota, 244–45, *246*; in Missouri, 155, *157–58*; in Montana, 156, *157–58*; in Mountain West, 142, *145*; in North Carolina, 159, *160*, 241–42, 247; in Northeast, 123, *125*; in Oregon, 248, *249*; in Pacific, 146–47, *148*; in Pennsylvania, 162, *163–64*; popular vote in 2008, *52*, *57*; population change and, 186, *187*; presidential vote analyses, *278–79*; primaries, *11–13*; and realignments, 62–63, 63*t*–64*t*; rural/urban gap and, 71, *74*, 107; senate races, 244–45, *246*, 247–48, *249*, 250; in South, 126–27, *128*, 129–31; in swing states, 167–68; unemployment and, 184, *185*; university/college counties and, 202, *203*; voter consistency and, 112, *113*, 114–15, *116–17*;

voter turnout and, 97–98, *99–101*; in Washington, 242, *243*; white population and, 219, *224*

Detroit: Asian population in, 213–14, *220*; black population in, 217

Dingell, John D., 286

direct democracy, 253–54

Dissimilarity Index, 207, *208*

District of Columbia, ideological identification in, 122*t*

Dodd, Christopher, 9, 16–17

Dole, Elizabeth, 247

donor-sheds, 30, *31–32*

Drayse, Mark, 262

DuPage County, 107, 135

Dyck, Joshua J., 253–54, 266–67

Eagle County, 180

early voting, 69; date of adoption of, *70*; and exit polls, 68; in North Carolina, 159, *160*; by state, *70*

Easley, Mike, 241, 247

economy: ballot measures on, 253–54; car voucher program, 280–81, *282*; median household income, 194, *195*; poverty counties, 198, *199*; rural/urban gap and, 71; unemployment, 184, *185*

education: B.A. or higher degree, 200, *201*; and rural/urban gap, 72*t*; and stem cell research, 270; and 2008 vote, 65, *67*. *See also* university/college counties

Edwards, John, 9–10, 16–17, *18*

Elazar, Daniel J., 136

elderly: and females in labor force, 176; population over sixty-five, 188, *191*. *See also* age

Election Day, future possibilities for, 305

election of 2000, 75

election of 2004, 75

election of 2008: Democratic vote in, *52*; historical context of, 62–63, 63*t*–64*t*, 75–78, *79*; independent candidate vote in, *56*; Libertarian vote in, *55*; polling conditions, Twitter Vote Report, 45, *46*; popular vote, *52–58*; presidential vote versus congressional vote in, *278*; Republican vote in, *53*; third party vote in, *54*; voter consistency in, 112, *113*, *116*; as watershed, 303

Electoral College, 3, 104; congressional district method and, 138; Florida and, 151; future possibilities for, 304–5; proportional outcome, 2008, *106*

Elliot County, 178

Ellswirth, Brad, 283

endorsements, newspaper, 40, *41–42*

energy, alternative, ballot measures on, 260, *261*

Enos, Ryan D., 206–7

environmental amenity counties: education in, 200, *201*; household income in, 194, *195*; partisan margins in, 59

environmental issues: car voucher program, 280–81, *282*; Environment America ratings of congressional votes, 294, *299*; greenhouse gas emissions legislation, 289–90, *291*

environmentalists, 209, *210*

Environment America, 277; ratings of congressional votes, 294, *299*

Ervin, Daniel, 69

ethnic group: and 2008 vote, *67*. *See also* racial/ethnic majority counties; *specific group*

exit polls: precautions with, 68; uses of, 68–69

farming: employment in, and election, 178, *179*. *See also* agriculture

Farr, Sam, 283

federal government, expenditures versus receipts, by state, 211, *212*

Flake, Jeff, 280

Fleming, John, 286

Florida, 126, *128*, 151, *153–54*; ballot measures in, 253, 255*t*, 258, *259*; black population in, 217; campaign stops in, 33–34, *35*; donors in, 30; Hispanic population in, 215, *221*, 225; historical context, 75; migration and, 131–33, 132*t*; retirement counties in, 188, *191*; voter turnout in, 98, *101*; youth vote in, 68

Florida, Richard, 171

foreign-born population, 227, *228*

fourth parties, future possibilities for, 304

Franken, Al, 244–45, *246*

Frazier, John W., 213–19

fuel efficient car voucher program, 280–81, *282*

fund-raising, 27; individual contributions, 30, *31–32*

Gall, Megan A., 253–54, 266–67

gay marriage, ballot measures on, 253, 257–58, *259*, 264, *265*, 266–67

Gelman, Andrew, 65

gender: and exit polls, 69; women in labor force, 176, *177*

general elections, 51–119

Georgia, *128*; U.S. senate race, 250, *251*

Geoweb, 43, *44*

Gimbel, James G., 71–72

Ginsburg, Alex, 248

Giuliani, Rudolph, 9, 226

Gore, Al, 104

Gorman, Sean P., 45

governors, elections for: North Carolina, 241–42; voter consistency in, 112, *113*; Washington, 242, *243*

Graham, Mark, 43

Great Lakes. *See* Midwest

Great Migration, 216–17

Great Plains, 138–40, *141*; composition of, 120n3, 138; elderly in, 188, *191*; farming in, 178, *179*; micropolitan areas in, 110*t*; unemployment in, 184, *185*

greenhouse gas emissions legislation, 289–90, *291*

Gregoire, Christine, 242, *243*

Gun Owners of America, 277; ratings of congressional votes, 294–95, *300*

HadleyDike, Nathaniel, 69

Hagan, Kay, 247

Hampton Roads region, 133, 166

Harrison, Benjamin, 3

Hawaii, 147, *148*; ideological identification in, 122*t*

health care reform: Affordable Health Care for America Act, 286–87, *288*; Northeast and, 124; Stupak Amendment, 283–84, *285*

Heatwole, Charles, 237
Heppen, John, 134–36, 155, 161
Hispanic majority counties: versus farming employment, 178; in Great Plains, 138–39; micropolitan areas in, 109; in Mountain West, 143; in Pacific, 146; partisan margins in, 59; poverty in, 198, *199*; unemployment in, 184; youth population in, 188
Hispanic population, 214–15, *221*, 225; and marriage referenda, 266; and Stupak Amendment, 284; and 2008 elections, 225–26
historical context of 2008 election, 62–63, 63*t*–64*t*, 75–78
Hollen, Heather, 14, 16–17, 19, 68–69
homosexuality: same-sex marriage, ballot measures on, 257–58, *259*, 264, *265*, 266–67; tolerance of, creative class and, 171
household composition, husband-wife, 196, *197*
household income, 194, *195*
House of Representatives, future possibilities for, 306
Huckabee, Mike, 2, 9; Hispanic population and, 226; in Iowa caucus, 16, *18*; in primaries, 10, *13*, 14, *21*, *24–25*
Hunt, Jim, 247
Hunter, Duncan, 9
husband-wife households, 196, *197*

Idaho, 142–44, *145*; ideological identification in, 122*t*
ideological identification, 122*t*
Illinois, *137*. *See also* Chicago
Imperial County, 184
income, 194, *195*
independent candidates, popular vote 2008, *56*
Indiana, 135, *137*, 152, *153–54*; historical context, 75; voter turnout in, 97, *100*; youth vote in, 68
Individualistic political culture, 78, 136
Initiative 1000 (Washington), 272–73, *274*
initiatives, 253
Internet: future possibilities of, 305; placemark poll, 43, *44*; Twitter Vote Report, 45, *46*
Iowa, 135, *137*; caucuses, 9–10, 16–17, *18*; early voting in, 69; historical context, 75

Iron County, 136
Islam. *See* Muslims

Jews, 229, *232*
Johnson, Lyndon B., 76
Johnson, Taylor, 250

Kaine, Tim, 166
Kansas, *141*
Karnes, Kimberly, 71–72
Kennedy, John F., 161
Kentucky, *128*
Kerry, John, 2, 75; in Great Plains, 138, *141*; in Midwest, *137*; in Mountain West, *145*; newspaper endorsements, 40; in Northeast, *125*; in Pacific, *148*; in South, 127, *128*
Key, V. O., 62
Knight, Brian G., 40
Knopp, Larry, 244–45
Kucinich, Dennis, 9–10, 289

labor unions: AFL-CIO ratings of congressional votes, 293–94, *298*; ballot measures on, 254; craft occupations and, 174, *175*; manufacturing employment and, 182; in Minnesota, 244
Landers, Matt, 248
Latah County, 142
Latinos. *See under* Hispanic
Leib, Jonathan I., 126–27, 166
liberal identification, 122*t*, 123
Libertarian Party, popular vote in 2008, *55*
Limbaugh, Rush, 135
Loudon County, 133
Louisiana, 127; ideological identification in, 122*t*
Lowndes County, 182

Maine, 121, *125*; electoral college votes, 104; ideological identification in, 122*t*
manufacturing employment, 182, *183*
marijuana, medical, 267–68, *269*

marriage, 196, *197*; same-sex, ballot measures on, 253, 257–58, *259*, 264, *265*, 266–67
Martin, Jim, 250, *251*
Martínez, César, 226
Martis, Kenneth C., 280–81, 283–84, 286–87, 289–90
Maryland, 123, *125*; ideological identification in, 122*t*
Massachusetts, *125*; ballot measures in, 253, 255*t*; ideological identification in, 122*t*; and same-sex marriage, 258
McCain, John, 1–2; areas with highest/lowest margins, 59, *60–61*; Bible Belt and, 237, *238*; breakdown of vote, *66–67*; bumper stickers for, *308*; campaign stops, 33–34, *35*, *38*; construction employment and, 180, *181*; craft occupations and, 174, *175*; creative class and, 172, *173*; early voting and, 69; and Electoral College, 104, 104*t*, 105–6; and fundraising, 27; in Great Plains, 138, *141*; Hispanic population and, 226; individual contributions to, 30, *32*; manufacturing employment and, 182, *183*; micropolitan areas and, 109, 110*t*, *111*; in Midwest, *137*; in Montana, 156; in Mountain West, *145*; in New Hampshire, 14, *15*; newspaper endorsements, 40, *42*; in North Carolina, 159, *160*; in Northeast, *125*; in Pacific, 147, *148*; placemark poll, 43, *44*; popular vote, 58, 59, *60–61*; in primaries, 10, *13*, 14, *15*, *21*, *23–25*; rural/urban gap and, 71–72; in South, 126–27, *128*, 129; unemployment and, 184, *185*; in Virginia, 166
McCrory, Pat, 241–42
McDonnell, Bob, 166
McKenna, Rob, 242
McNulty, John, 130–34
Meddaugh, Joshua R., 253–54, 266–67
media: advertising outlays, 27–28, *29*; newspaper endorsements, 40, *41–42*
medical issues, ballot measures on: marijuana, 267–68, *269*; stem cell research, 270, *271*
Megalopolis: Asian population in, 213–14, *220*; definition of, 19; and environmental issues, 209, *210*, 290; Hispanic population in, 215, *221*; household

income in, 194, *195*; population change in, 186; population density in, 47; voter persistence in, 114

Mencken, H. L., 237

Merkley, Jeff, 248, *249*

Methodists, 229, *233*

metropolitan counties. *See* urban areas

Miami-Dade County, 151; Hispanic population in, 215, *221*; migration and, 131–33

Michelson, Melissa R., 225–26

Michigan, 135, *137*; ballot measures in, 255*t*, 267–68, *269*, 270, *271*; primary, *23*; unemployment in, 184, *185*

microcontributions, 30

micropolitan areas, 51; definition of, 109; voting patterns, 109, 110*t*, *111*

mid-Atlantic states, 121–24; definition of, 120n3; political culture of, 77–78. *See also* Northeast

Midwest, 134–36, *137*; definition of, 120n3; manufacturing employment in, 182, *183*; micropolitan areas in, 110*t*

migration: and Asian population, 213; and black population, 216; and Colorado, 149, *150*; leading counties, 192, *193*; partisanship and, 72; and South, 131

military counties, 204, *205*; in Great Plains, 139; historical context, 75; and migration, 133; in Northeast, 123

Minnesota, 134–35, *137*; ballot measures in, 254; U.S. senate race, 244–45, *246*

Mississippi, *128*; donors in, 30; ideological identification in, 122*t*

Missouri, 134–35, *137*, 155, *157–58*; primaries, *21*

moderate identification, 122*t*, 123; in Northeast, 123–24

Montana, 142–43, *145*, 156, *157–58*; ballot measures in, 254

Moody, Mark A., 267–68

Moore, Toby, 159, 241–42, 247

Moralistic political culture, 77–78, 136

Mormon counties, 143–44; husband-wife households and, 196, *197*; partisan margins in, 59; youth population in, 188

Mormons, 229, *234*; and assisted suicide, 272; and marriage referenda, 264

Morrill, Richard L.: on ballot measures, 272–73; on craft occupations, 174; on demographics, 176, 186, 188, 196, 227; on economic issues, 194, 198, 211, *212*; on education, 200, 202; on environmentalists, 209; on migration, 192; on partisan areas, 47, 59; on voter consistency, 112, 114–15; on voter turnout, 97–98; on Washington gubernatorial election, 242

Mountain West, 142–44, *145*; definition of, 120n3; education in, 200, *201*; micropolitan areas in, 110*t*

Muslims, 229, *235*

Nader, Ralph, *56*

National Journal, Foreign Policy Rating, 277, 295, *301*

National Rifle Association (NRA), 294

Native American. *See under* American Indian

Natural Resources Defense Council, 209

Nature Conservancy, 209

Nebraska, 138–39, *141*; electoral college votes, 104

Nevada, 142–43, *145*; historical context, 75; primaries, 9

New Deal realignment, 62

New England, 121–24; definition of, 120n3; micropolitan areas in, 110*t*; and Midwest, 136; political culture of, 77–78. *See also* Northeast

New Hampshire, 121, *125*, 162; ideological identification in, 122*t*; placemark poll, 43, *44*; primaries, 9, 14, *15*

New Jersey, 121–23, *125*, 162; Hispanic population in, 215, *221*; ideological identification in, 122*t*

New Mexico, 142, *145*; historical context, 75; voter turnout in, 97–98, *100*

Newsom, Gavin, 264

newspaper endorsements, 40, *41–42*

New West, 143

New York, 121, *125*; black population in, 216; donors in, 30; Hispanic population in, 215, *221*; ideological identification in, 122*t*

nominations: candidate selection method, *11*; process, 9–10

North Carolina, 126–27, *128*; campaign stops in, 33–34, *35*; early voting in, 69; gubernatorial race, 241–42; historical context, 75; migration and, 131, 132*t*, 133–34; primary, *22*; Research Triangle, 172; senate race, 247; as swing state, 159, *160*; voter turnout in, 97, *99*; youth vote in, 68

North Dakota, 138–39, *141*; ballot measures in, 253; ideological identification in, 122*t*

Northeast, 121–24, *125*; Asian population in, 213, *220*; black population in, 216; education in, 200, *201*; ideological identification in, 122*t*; Jews in, 229, *232*. *See also* mid-Atlantic states; New England

Northern California, donors in, 30

North-South differences: in California, 146; in female labor force participation, 176, *177*; in Midwest, 135

Obama, Barack, 1–2; areas with highest/lowest margins, 59, *60–61*; bumper stickers for, *307*; campaign stops, 33–34, *35–36*; construction employment and, 180, *181*; creative class and, 172, *173*; early voting and, 69; and Electoral College, 104, 104*t*, *105–6*; farming employment and, 178, *179*; foreign-born population and, 227, *228*; and fund-raising, 27; in Great Plains, 138–39, *141*; Hispanic population and, 225–26; individual contributions to, 30, *32*; in Iowa caucus, 16–17, *18*; manufacturing employment and, 182, *183*; micropolitan areas and, 109, 110*t*, *111*; in Midwest, 135–36, *137*; in Missouri, 155; in Mountain West, *145*; in New Hampshire, 14, *15*; newspaper endorsements, 40, *41*; in North Carolina, 159, *160*; in Northeast, *125*; in Pacific, 146, *148*; in Pennsylvania, 19, *20*, 162, *163–64*; placemark poll, 43, *44*; popular vote, 58, 59, *60–61*; postage stamps of, *309*; in primaries, 10, *13*, 14, *15*, 19, *20–22*, 24; rural/urban gap and, 71–72, 107, *108*; in South, 126–27, *128*, 129, 133; unemployment and, 184, *185*; university/college counties and, 202, *203*; in Virginia, 166, *167–68*

occupations: construction, 180, *181*; craft, 174, *175*; creative class, 171–72, *173*; farming, 178, *179*; manufacturing, 182, *183*; women and, 176, *177*

Ohio, 134, *137*, 161, *163–64*; ballot measures in, 255*t*; campaign stops in, 33–34, *35*; historical context, 75; youth vote in, 68

Oklahoma, 139–40, *141*; ideological identification in, 122*t*; primary, *24*

Oliver, J. Eric, 129–30

O'Neill, Tip, 142

one-stop absentee voting, 159, *160*

open primaries, 10

Orange County, 146

Oregon, 146–47, *148*; ballot measures in, 253, 255*t*; early voting in, 69; ideological identification in, 122*t*; U.S. senate race, 248, *249*

O'Reilly, Kathleen, 272–73

Owens, Bill, 254

Ozark region, 155; females in labor force in, 176; historical context, 75

Pacific region, 146–47, *148*; micropolitan areas in, 109, 110*t*. See also West Coast

Palin, Sarah, 2, 147; bumper stickers for, *308*; campaign stops, 33–34, *35*, *39*

Paul, Ron, 9–10, 16, *18*

Pennsylvania, 123, *125*, 162, *163–64*; campaign stops in, 33–34, *35*; ideological identification in, 122*t*; primary, 19, *20*

Pentecostalists, 229, *236*

Perdue, Beverly, 241–42

Philadelphia, black population in, 216

Phillips, Kevin, 136

Phoenix, 107

physician-assisted suicide, ballot measures on, 272–73, *274*

Pickens, T. Boone, 260

placemarks: definition of, 43; as presidential poll, 43, *44*

polarization: in Great Plains, 139; in Pacific, 146; and third party possibilities, 304

political culture: definition of, 77; in Midwest, 136; and voter turnout, 77–78

polling conditions, Twitter Vote Report, 45, *46*

population change, by county, 186, *187*

population density, *73*; in Bible Belt, 237

poverty counties, 198, *199*

presidential candidates, primary leaders, *13*

primaries, 2, 9–25, *11*; future possibilities for, 304; process, 9–10; schedules, *12*

Proposition 1 (Michigan), 267–68, *269*

Proposition 2 (California), 262, *263*

Proposition 2 (Florida), 258, *259*

Proposition 2 (Michigan), 270, *271*

Proposition 7 (California), 260, *261*

Proposition 8 (California), 264, *265*, 266–67

Proposition 10 (California), 260, *261*

Proposition 102 (Arizona), 257, *259*

Protestants, 229

proximity, effects of, 1

public financing, future possibilities for, 305

Quinton, Nick, 151, 165

race, 206–7, *208*; and "Bigot Belt," *118*, 129–30; and exit polls, 68–69; and marriage referenda, 266–67; and rural/urban gap, 72*t*; in South, 126–27; and 2008 vote, 65, *66*

racial/ethnic majority counties: in Great Plains, 138–39; in micropolitan areas, 109; in Mountain West, 143; in North Carolina, 134; partisan margins in, 59; proximity effects of, 129–30; voter inconsistency in, 112, *113*. See also specific group

Reagan, Ronald, 76

realignment, 2008 election as, 62

recall, 253

Reconstruction, 76, 130–31

recreation-destination counties: versus construction employment, 180; in Mountain West, 142–43

referenda, 253–76, 255*t*, *256*; on alternative energy, 260, *261*; on animal cruelty prevention, 262, *263*; on assisted suicide, 272–73, *274*; on same-sex marriage, 257–58, *259*, 264, *265*, 266–67; term, 253

regional analyses, 121–69

Reisinger, Mark E., 213–19

Reisser, Wesley J., 260

religion, 229; diversity of, 229; in Pacific, 146; and rural/urban gap, 72*t*

Republican Party: American Indian population and, 218, *223*; areas with highest/lowest margins, 59, *60–61*; Asian population and, 214, *220*; Bible Belt and, 237, *238*; breakdown of vote, *66–67*; candidates, donors to, *31*; center of partisan voting, 47, *48*; construction employment and, 180, *181*; county strongholds, demographics of, 129–30; craft occupations and, 174, *175*; education and, 200, *201*; elderly and, 188, *191*; farming employment and, 178, *179*; federal expenditures and, 211, *212*; in Georgia, 250; in Great Plains, 138–39, *141*; gubernatorial races, 241–42, *243*; Hispanic population and, 215, *221*, 225–26; historical context and, 76, *87–94*; household income and, 194, *195*; husband-wife households and, 196, *197*; manufacturing employment and, 182, *183*; in Midwest, 134–36, *137*; migration and, 192, *193*; military counties and, 204, *205*; in Minnesota, 244–45, *246*; in Montana, 156; in Mountain West, 142–44, *145*; in North Carolina, *160*, 241–42, 247; in Northeast, 121, 123–24; in Oregon, 248, *249*; in Pacific, 146–47, *148*; popular vote in 2008, *53*, *57*; population change and, 186, *187*; presidential vote versus congressional vote, *278*; primaries, *11–13*; rural/urban gap and, 71, *74*, 107; senate races, 244–45, *246*, 247–48, *249*, 250; in South, 126–27, *128*, 129–31; in swing states, 165; unemployment and, 184, *185*; university/college counties and, 202, *203*; voter consistency and, 112, *113*, 114–15, *116*, *118–19*; voter turnout and, 97–98, *99–101*; in Washington, 242, *243*; white population and, 219, *224*

Research Triangle, 172

residential racial segregation, 207, *208*, 216

resource-dependent counties, partisan margins in, 59

retirement counties, 186, 188, *191*

Rhode Island, ideological identification in, 122*t*

Richardson, Bill, 9, 16–17

Richmond, 133
Ritter, Bill, 254
Robinson, Tony, 142–44, 149
Romney, Mitt, 2, 9; in Iowa caucus, 16, *18*; in primaries, 10, *13*, 14, *15*, *21*, *23*, *25*
Roosevelt, Franklin D., 62, 76–77
Rossi, Dino, 242, *243*
rural counties, 71–72; characteristics of, 71, 72*t*; in Great Plains, 139; historical context, 76–77; partisan margins in, 59
rural/urban gap: emergence of, *73*; and marriage referenda, 264; and medical marijuana, 267; in Midwest, 135–36; in Montana, 156; in Mountain West, 143; in Northeast, 123; in Pacific, 146–47; and 2008 vote, *74*

same-sex marriage, ballot measures on, 253, 257–58, *259*, 264, *265*, 266–67
San Diego, 146
segregation, 207, *208*, 216
semiopen primaries, 10
senators, elections for: Georgia, 250, *251*; Minnesota, 244–45, *246*; North Carolina, 247; Oregon, 248, *249*; voter consistency in, 112, *113*
Shannon Index, 229
Shelley, Fred M.: on exit polls, 68–69; on historical context, 75–78; on metropolitan areas, 107; on Montana, 156; on presidential nominees, 9–10; on primaries, 14, 16–17, 19
Shelton, Taylor, 43
Silicon Valley, 172
Silver, Nate, 65
Smith, Adrian, 289
Smith, Gordon, 248, *249*
social networking, future possibilities of, 305
Souder, Mark, 289
South, 126–27, *128*, 129–34; Asian population in, 213, *220*; black population in, 216–17, *222*; definition of, 120n3; education in, 200, *201*; and Great Plains, 140; Hispanic population in, 215, *221*; historical

context, 76; manufacturing employment in, 182, *183*; micropolitan areas in, 110*t*; and Missouri, 155; partisan margins in, 59; political culture of, 77–78; race and, 206, *208*; and rural/urban gap, 72*t*; voter inconsistency in, 112, *113*, 115
South Carolina, *128*; primaries, 9
South Dakota, 138, *141*; ballot measures in, 253, 255*t*; ideological identification in, 122*t*
Southern Florida, donors in, 30
Southwest, American Indian population in, 218, *223*
Specter, Arlen, 162
stem cell research, ballot measures on, 270, *271*
Stupak, Bart, 283–84
suburban areas, 107; black population and, 216; in Midwest, 135; in South, 126
suicide, assisted, ballot measures on, 272–73, *274*
Super Tuesday, 10
Sutton, Betty, 280
swing counties, 114–15, *116–19*; in Indiana, 152; in Missouri, 155
swing states, 51, 112, *113*; analyses of, 121–69; bellwether states, 75, 134, 155, 161; Colorado, 149, *150*; Florida, 151; Minnesota, 244–45, *246*; Missouri, 155; North Carolina, 159, *160*; Ohio, 161, *163–64*; Tennessee, 165; Virginia, 166
swing voters, characteristics of, 161

talent, and creative class, 171
Tancredo, Tom, 9
taxes, ballot measures on, 253–54
Taylor, Jonathan, 262
Taylor, Zachary, 304
technology, and creative class, 171
Tennessee, *128*, 165, *167–68*; primary, *25*
Teton County, 142
Texas, 138–39, *141*; Asian population in, 213; black population in, 217; Hispanic population in, 214–15, *221*
third parties: future possibilities for, 304; popular vote in 2008, *54–57*

Thompson, Fred, 9
tolerance, and creative class, 171
Traditionalistic political culture, 78
Turner, Andrew J., 45
Twitter Vote Report, 45, *46*

unemployment, 184, *185*
unit rule system, 104
university/college counties, 202, *203*; Asian population in, 214; education in, 200, *201*; females in labor force in, 176; in Great Plains, 138–39; household composition in, 196; and medical marijuana, 267–68; in Midwest, 136; in Montana, 156; in Mountain West, 142–43; in Northeast, 123; partisan margins in, 59; in South, 126
urban areas, 71–72; Asian population in, 213, *220*; black population in, 216; characteristics of, 71, 72*t*; Democratic shift in, causes of, 107; education in, 200, *201*, 202, *203*; in Great Plains, 139; historical context, 76; household composition in, 196; household income in, 194, *195*; in Midwest, 135; in Mountain West, 143; in Northeast, 123; in Oregon, 248, *249*; in Pacific, 146; partisan margins in, 59; poverty in, 198, *199*; race and, 207; in South, 126; in Tennessee, 165; voting conditions in, 45, *46*; voting patterns in, 107, *108*. *See also* rural/urban gap
Utah, 142–44, *145*; ideological identification in, 122*t*

Vanderhorst, Tom, 250
variability of vote, historical context of, *83–86*, *91–94*
Ventura, Jesse, 244
Vermont, *125*; ideological identification in, 122*t*; partisan margins in, 59
Vinroot, Richard, 241
Virginia, 126–27, *128*, 166, *167–68*; campaign stops in, 33–34, *35*; early voting in, 69; historical context, 75; migration and, 131, 132*t*, 133; voter turnout in, 97, *99*
voter consistency: by county, 114–15, *116–19*; in Indiana and Florida, *154*; in North Carolina, *160*; by state, 112, *113*; in swing states, *164, 168*

voter registration, automatic, 305
voter turnout, 51; age and, *102–3*, *189–91*; American
    Indian population and, 218, *223*; Asian population
    and, 214, *220*; black population and, 217, *222*;
    craft occupations and, *175*; creative class and, *173*;
    definition of, 77; future possibilities for, 305; in
    Georgia, 250; Hispanic population and, 215, *221*,
    225–26; historical context, 77–78, *95–96*, *103*;
    in North Carolina, 159; role of, in selected states,
    97–98, *99–103*; unemployment and, 184, *185*; white
    population and, 219, *224*

Warf, Barney, 104, 229
Warner, Mark, 166

Warren, Rick, 264
Washington (state), 146, *148*; ballot measures in, 255*t*,
    272–73, *274*; early voting in, 69; gubernatorial
    election, 242, *243*; ideological identification in,
    122*t*
Washington, DC, ideological identification in, 122*t*
Watrel, Robert, 109, 138–40
Waxman, Henry A., 289
Webb, Jim, 166
Webster, Gerald R., 27–28, 33–34, 40, 292–95
West Coast: Asian population in, 213–14, *220*; definition
    of, 120n3. *See also* Pacific region
white population, 218–19, *224*, 225; in "Bigot Belt,"
    129–30; and construction employment, 180; in

poverty counties, 198; race and, 206–7, *208*; in South,
    127
Wikle, Thomas, 209
winner-take-all system, 104
Wisconsin, *137*
women: gender and exit polls, 69; in labor force, 176, *177*
worker counties, partisan margins in, 59
World Wildlife Fund, 209
Wyoming, 142–44, *145*; ideological identification in,
    122*t*

youth: population under eighteen, 188, *189*. *See also* age

Zook, Matthew, 43

ABOUT THE EDITORS AND CONTRIBUTORS

EDITORS

Stanley D. Brunn is professor in the Department of Geography at the University of Kentucky. His interests include social and political geographies, iconography, time/space mapping, and megaengineering geographies.

Gerald R. Webster is professor in the Department of Geography at the University of Wyoming. His research interests focus on redistricting, electoral geography, and nationalism.

Richard L. Morrill is Emeritus Professor in the Department of Geography at the University of Washington. His interests are political geography, population and settlement, social inequality, and urban planning.

Fred M. Shelley is professor in the Department of Geography at the University of Oklahoma. He is interested in political geography, political economy, and the historical geography of the United States.

Stephen J. Levin was professor in the Department of Geography at the University of Nebraska–Lincoln. His interests included cartography.

J. Clark Archer is professor in the Department of Geography at the University of Nebraska–Lincoln. His interests are political geography and cartography.

CONTRIBUTORS

John Agnew is professor in the Department of Geography at the University of California, Los Angeles.

William Berentsen is professor in the Department of Geography at the University of Connecticut.

Thomas E. Chapman is assistant professor in the Department of Political Science and Geography at Old Dominion University.

Jeffrey R. Crump is associate professor in the Housing Studies Program at the University of Minnesota, Twin Cities.

Carl T. Dahlman is associate professor in the Department of Geography at Miami University.

David Darmofal is assistant professor in the Department of Political Science at the University of South Carolina.

Lisa M. DeChano-Cook is associate professor in the Department of Geography at Western Michigan University.

Mark Drayse is assistant professor in the Department of Geography at California State University, Fullerton.

Joshua J. Dyck is assistant professor in the Department of Political Science at SUNY Buffalo.

Ryan D. Enos is assistant professor in the Department of Government at Harvard University.

Daniel Ervin is a Ph.D. student in the Department of Geography at the University of California, Santa Barbara.

John W. Frazier is professor in the Department of Geography at Binghamton University.

Megan A. Gall is a Ph.D. student in the Department of Political Science at SUNY Buffalo.

Andrew Gelman is professor in the Department of Statistics and Political Science at Columbia University.

James G. Gimpel is professor in the Department of Political Science at the University of Maryland.

Alex Ginsburg is a Ph.D. student in the Department of Geography at the University of Oregon.

Sean P. Gorman is founder and president of FortiusOne in Arlington, Virginia.

Mark Graham is research fellow at the Oxford Internet Institute.

Nathaniel HadleyDike holds an M.A. in Geography, Environment and Natural Resources from the University of Wyoming.

John Heppen is associate professor in the Department of Geography at the University of Wisconsin–River Falls.

Heather Hollen is an undergraduate geography major in the Department of Geography at the University of Oklahoma.

Taylor Johnson is a Ph.D. student in the Department of Geography at the University of Georgia.

Kimberly Karnes is assistant professor in the Department of Political Science and Geography at Old Dominion University.

Larry Knopp is director of Interdisciplinary Arts and Sciences at the University of Washington Tacoma.

Matt Landers is a Ph.D. student in the Department of Geography at the University of Oregon.

Jonathan I. Leib is professor in the Department of Political Science and Geography at Old Dominion University.

Kenneth C. Martis is professor in the Department of Geography and Geology at West Virginia University.

John McNulty is professor in the Department of Political Science at Binghamton University.

Joshua R. Meddaugh is a Ph.D. student in the Department of Political Science at SUNY Buffalo.

Melissa R. Michelson is professor in the Department of Political Science at California East Bay State University.

Mark A. Moody is an M.A. student in the Department of Geography at Western Michigan University.

Toby Moore is project director at RTI International in Research Triangle Park, North Carolina.

J. Eric Oliver is professor in the Department of Political Science at the University of Chicago.

Kathleen O'Reilly is associate professor in the Department of Geography at Texas A&M University.

Nick Quinton is a Ph.D. candidate in the Department of Geography at Florida State University.

Mark E. Reisinger is associate professor in the Department of Geography at Binghamton University.

Wesley J. Reisser is adjunct faculty in the Department of Geography at George Washington University.

Tony Robinson is professor in the Department of Political Science at the University of Colorado Denver.

Taylor Shelton is a Ph.D. student in the Department of Geography at Clark University.

Jonathan Taylor is associate professor in the Department of Geography at California State University, Fullerton.

Andrew J. Turner is research analyst at FortiusOne in Arlington, Virginia.

Tom Vanderhorst is a Ph.D. student at the University of Georgia.

Barney Warf is professor in the Department of Geography at the University of Kansas.

Robert Watrel is associate professor in the Department of Geography at South Dakota State University.

Matthew Zook is associate professor in the Department of Geography at the University of Kentucky.